? Date of founding of
Alan Guttmacher

- churchs w/ married couples
  mentoring newly married

- exp. mothers mentoring
  younger women
- Douala system

Family law act 1969
No fault Divorce LATE 1960's

The Assault on Parenthood

HOW OUR CULTURE UNDERMINES THE FAMILY

DANA MACK

SIMON & SCHUSTER

SIMON & SCHUSTER
Rockefeller Center
1230 Avenue of the Americas
New York, NY 10020

SIMON & SCHUSTER and colophon are registered trademarks
of Simon & Schuster Inc.

Designed by Leslie Phillips
Manufactured in the United States of America

10 9 8 7 6 5 4 3 2 1

Library of Congress Cataloging-in-Publication Data
Mack, Dana.
The assault on parenthood: how our culture undermines
the family/Dana Mack.
p.   cm.
Includes bibliographical references and index.
1. Family—United States.   2. Parenting—United States.
3. Social values—United States.   4. United States—Social conditions—1980–   5. United States—Moral conditions.   I. Title.
HQ536.M233   1997
306.85′0973—dc21   97-3903   CIP
ISBN 0-684-80774-2

Portions of chapters 1 and 5 previously appeared in *Commentary*.

The poem on page 120 is reprinted with the permission of Quest
International from "Skills for Growing." Copyright © 1990 by Quest
International

Acknowledgments

Like every author, I have many people to thank for their creative and critical input into this, my first book. I am grateful for the support of my colleagues at the Institute for American Values, as well as the network of scholars affiliated with the Council on Families in America who have so warmly accepted my presence at their meetings and so readily exchanged ideas with me. Among them: David Blankenhorn, Don S. Browning, Allan Carlson, Jean Bethke Elshtain, Maggie Gallagher, Mary Ann Glendon, Norval Glenn, Sylvia Ann Hewlett, Judith Martin, David Popenoe, Judith Wallerstein, and Barbara Dafoe Whitehead. Also of invaluable help to me in defining and pursuing this project were Hillel G. Fradkin, Heather Higgins, Elizabeth Lurie, and Mabel S. Weil. I owe a huge debt to Jeffrey Bell, Douglas J. Besharov, Greg Erken, Michael Gerpe, Neil Gilbert, Elizabeth Gill, Charlene Haar, Catharine Kempson, Sylvia Simmons Neumann, Verne Oliver, Walter Olson, Denise Roy, Valentina Sarn, Richard Vigilante, Michael Weand, Otto Weiss, and Richard Wexler for sharing their time and various expertise with me.

Writing a book means living several years of what teens today would describe as "bad hair days." I would like to express my appreciation to the staff of the Wilton Library for their invaluable help to me in procuring research materials. I am grateful to my agents, Glen Hartley and Lynn Chu, for their abiding faith in this project and their vote of confidence in my work. I am also fortunate to have had in Becky Saletan an editor who is as kind, encouraging, and open-minded as she is critically perceptive. If there are mistakes, omissions, or inconsistencies in this manuscript, it is probably where I have declined to take a suggestion she has made.

I am also thankful to have a husband who—despite his fervent protests of disinterest in my professional life, and his appeals to me to quit work, sell our house, remove our child from school, and embark on a circumnavigation of the globe—has been a constant source of support and amusement, as well as a valuable sounding board. Perhaps it need not be said that I consider myself the luckiest mom in the world to have been blessed with a child who is growing up an intelligent, thoughtful, compassionate, and loving young lady—and a laugh a minute, to boot. And my acknowledgments would not be complete if I did not express my appreciation to two good friends who have helped keep my life balanced while I wrote this book: my four-hand and duo-piano partners, Suzanne Macahilig Lehrer and Margaret Porter Gregory.

But most of all I must thank the hundreds of parents around the country with whom I have spoken. I can never hope to repay them for their generosity of spirit, their candor, and their patience. It has been an honor to get to know them. I hope they will read this book and find in it some small tribute to their reflections, their hopes, their strength, and their devotion. Meeting them has convinced me more than ever that there is a God, and that—to paraphrase an old Jewish saying—since He couldn't be everywhere at once, He invented parents.

For Nadia,
in loving memory of her
maternal grandparents:

Melville Mack, 1919–1977
Nadia Elman Mack, 1926–1977

Contents

The Assault
on Parenthood

Introduction:
The Family-Hating Culture

W_hen,_ in the spring of 1992, I set out on a research project to investigate the sources of the declining well-being of American children, I had little idea that the subject would soon be catapulted to the center of a national debate. Perhaps I even naively thought the world might stand still for two or three years while I traveled around the country to interview parents about raising children in contemporary America, and came to some conclusions.

No such luck. By 1992 the increasing distress of our children and the troubled state of our teens were so well documented that a national discussion about their causes _had_ to erupt. Measurements of teenage social disaffection especially revealed an urgency that was truly frightening. Between 1987 and 1991 alone, arrests of teenagers for weapons violations increased 62 percent, and arrests for murder went up 85 percent. Homicides among black youths skyrocketed 200 percent between 1985 and 1992; among white youths, the increase was not as dramatic, but it was still alarming, at 50 percent. Each month in the late 1980s, there were around half a million assaults and robberies in American public high schools. By 1990 approximately 135,000 high school kids were

13

bringing guns to school every day, and 20 percent of the high school population reported they bore some sort of weapon at all times.[1]

These statistics, of course, represented only the peak of a slow-growing iceberg of childhood misery in our country. It took three decades to create the crisis of youth we have, thirty years in which—while the teenage population remained for the most part relatively stable—arrests for violent crime among teenagers increased sixfold, from 16,000 to over 96,000. During these same years teen suicide climbed more than 200 percent to become the second leading cause of adolescent deaths. Average SAT scores plummeted 80 points; and the number of high school students achieving a verbal SAT score of 700 or higher fell 60 percent. The number of unmarried teenage mothers tripled, from fifteen per one thousand in 1960 to forty-five per one thousand in 1990.

Most disturbing, serious indications of social pathology were cropping up among children. During the late 1980s, psychologists noted previously unheard-of symptoms of mental psychosis in small children. Preschoolers were committing murders. In 1991, 17,772 offenses could be traced to children under ten, including murder, rape, robbery, car theft, aggravated assault, arson, burglary, and 11,663 thefts.[2]

Taking all this into account, it is hardly surprising that the most hotly debated subject of the 1992 presidential campaign turned out to be sources of moral impoverishment in our youth. Nor is it surprising that a volatile public debate ensued when, in a May 1992 campaign speech, then Vice President Dan Quayle charged that the increasing desperation of inner-city youth had its roots in a crisis of family values encouraged by the glorification of single-parent lifestyles in popular culture. Television shows such as *Murphy Brown*, Quayle claimed, might pretend that children didn't need fathers. But the poorest and most disorderly American neighborhoods were places where fathers had completely disappeared, and boys gleaned models of manhood from gang leaders.

As a campaign gesture, it turned out highly impolitic for Quayle to have picked on Murphy Brown, America's favorite situation comedy character. But as the opening volley in an honest public reappraisal of our most serious social problems, it was a perfect attention-getter. No other icon of popular culture so perfectly reflected the casual attitude toward single parenthood that had dominated the American mind-set for more than a quarter of a century. Indeed, Murphy Brown had been embraced by a cultural elite that saw the rise in single parenthood as a sign of increasing individual liberty, sexual equality, and social tolerance.

If at first Quayle's remarks were greeted with protests and catcalls from the media establishment, the catcalls were soon drowned in a newly open-minded public debate on the problems of single parenthood. Social scientists came forward to support Quayle's allegations about fatherless homes. Marshaling the results of numerous studies on the effects of fatherlessness, they claimed that, indeed, our crisis of youth bore a strong relationship to the rise in out-of-wedlock childbearing. These studies had found that children raised in single-parent, female-headed households were far more likely to suffer emotional problems, to fail in school, and to engage in delinquent behavior than children raised in two-parent families. And this was true almost regardless of their socioeconomic environment.[3]

Many social scientists went even further than Quayle had in castigating single parenthood. In her widely read April 1993 *Atlantic Monthly* article, "Dan Quayle Was Right," family scholar Barbara Dafoe Whitehead charged that illegitimacy was not the only domestic trend that threatened children. Ours, she said, was not only a culture of unwed motherhood, but of rampant divorce. Both of these phenomena, she contended, were by-products of an ideology of expressive individualism that had seized postwar generations and driven them to put self-realization before their children's needs. However noble or valid our ideals of happy adult lives might seem, she warned, they were seriously destabilizing childhood by robbing children of the comforts and security of intact families.

Whitehead's article was perhaps the most influential of a tide of highly visible academic reflections on the effects of single parenthood on children. After its publication, reports in the mainstream media at last began to imply that the two-parent family was not an expendable bourgeois convention, but rather an optimum condition of both a happy childhood and a healthy social order. In June 1992, *Newsweek* had mocked Quayle's remarks, commenting, "The '50s fantasy of mom and dad and 2.2 kids went the way of phonograph records and circle pins." Just a year later, in a cover story entitled "Endangered Family," the magazine fretted, "For blacks, the institution of marriage has been devastated in the last generation. . . . The impact, of course, is not only on black families but on all of society. Fatherless homes boost crime rates, lower educational attainment and add dramatically to the welfare rolls."[4] In retrospect, it appeared that the thoughts Quayle gave voice to were ideas whose time had come, and that his comments signaled a significant change in the attitude of American elites toward family issues.

By now a decided majority of social scientists, political commentators, and journalists admit that both out-of-wedlock childbearing and divorce put kids at risk, and that the crisis of youth has a lot more to do with family structure than we previously thought. A number of local and national organizations have emerged that focus on putting missing fathers back in their children's lives. One of the most prominent has been the Pennsylvania-based National Fatherhood Initiative, a fatherhood advocacy organization that is attempting to provide policy directions that will break the cycle of fathers abandoning children emotionally and financially. The Kansas-based National Center for Fathering, another influential organization, has gathered our nation's largest database of fathering statistics, how-to information, and community resources. The Council on Families in America, a nonpartisan gathering of prominent family scholars, social welfare professionals, and therapists, recently put together a pamphlet entitled "Marriage in America." This "Report to the Nation" is essentially a recipe for strengthening marriage through legal and cultural reforms. In several states, legislation designed to better protect men, women, and children from the ravages of unilateral divorce has been introduced. Manifold legal efforts have been undertaken to penalize "deadbeat dads," and the general tenor of judgment on out-of-wedlock childbearing has become so negative that by 1996 the press rejoiced to report that rates of illegitimate birth were declining.

All of this is encouraging. But in our eagerness to blame single parenthood and divorce for the contemporary crisis of childhood, we are overlooking equally important threats.

For the past few years I have been talking to parents—more than 250 of them in all, from Connecticut to California, Texas to Cape Cod—about the difficulties of raising children in our culture.[5] In focus groups and private interviews, they paint a devastating portrait of what it means to raise children even in the most stable of familial environments. Families are under insurmountable pressures from a culture that undermines child-rearing efforts. Children from broken or bad homes are not the only ones, parents point out, who are vulnerable to delinquency. Drug abuse, pregnancy, sexually transmitted disease, mental illness, and violence can and do strike teenagers from intact homes. These social malaises have transformed childhood from a state of relative happiness, security, and innocence into a cruel test of emotional resilience.

Whatever parents' marital status, they tell me, they have too little power over what becomes of their children. As Rich, a father of four, observes regretfully, "We were the last generation where most of the stimulus came from the parents . . . the home." Many of today's parents apparently feel, as Rich does, that compared with schools, with the media, with the lure of the streets, they are practically helpless to keep their kids on the straight and narrow. "You have less time today to do a harder job; there are so many outside influences that never existed before," laments Steve, a New Jersey father. Estevan, a Texas father, agrees: "When they leave the house, you just pray that the seed you planted in them protects them from the temptations out there. Within the home, within the family structure, you can communicate, you can talk. But the minute they're outside . . . outside of what I call my defensive perimeter . . . you have no control."

Many parents I talked with around the country echo this sentiment. To them, there is a dimension to the crisis of childhood that the public debate on family values has virtually ignored: communal supports for the child-rearing work of even the best families are crumbling. Child development experts as diverse as Jerome Kagan, Robert Coles, Bruno Bettelheim, and William Damon have argued that the wayward adolescent is only a child whom the essential social supports—either in the family or its surrounding institutions—have failed. And in my research, I have found that parents attribute the crisis of youth in large part to the failure of extrafamilial institutions to reinforce their painstaking work.

In fact, parents see the decline of social supports and the breakdown of families as symptoms of a larger phenomenon: the sudden and rapid decay of those stable social values that once fostered a protective culture of childhood.

"There's no respect," they invariably say, when asked how raising children today is different from a generation ago. And by this, they do not only mean that children no longer have enough respect for parents. They mean also that the larger culture no longer supports the family as an inviolate unit engaged in a crucial and worthy task—the task of child-rearing. Says Michael, a father of two girls from the Baltimore area, "Society has to support you [as a parent] . . . and that's not what it's doing." He adds, "What society teaches kids is that you don't have to answer for the problems you create." Says Barbara, a New Jersey mother of a teenage girl, "There's so little respect out there. You do the best you can, but it's the outside that changes everything."

What impediments to their child-rearing work do parents specifically complain about? They say that social and economic pressures on women to work are killing family life by driving the whole family from the home. "Who's home?" asks Ed, a father of three. "Nobody's home anymore!" "I'm not condemning working mothers; I work myself," says Robin, a mother of four. "Nowadays women have to work. But the fact that some of them can't stay home after six weeks . . . that a child has to get taken out of his bed, go out in the early early morning . . . they're put into a situation where there are other children . . . it's hard." Richard comments, "I'd like to see my children once in a while. It's like a revolving door at home."

Parents complain that the media cripples their attempts at moral education by fostering materialism, and by sexualizing even very young children. Comments Mike, from San Francisco, "TV is the biggest villain in family life." "You look at the TV ads," observes Doris, from Baltimore, "the beautiful woman and the car. Now what is being sold, the woman or the car? You have to talk to your kids about that. . . . My daughter always wants a label. . . . [But] how does . . . say, 'Jordache' . . . make you special? I tell my daughter . . . a label cannot make you special . . . it's what is inside that counts."

Parents complain that educators have launched a critique of family life in the classroom and the counseling office that exercises excessive scrutiny of family life, and undercuts their children's faith in them. "Kids are turning their parents in!" exclaims Joe, a New Jersey father, of the provocative health lessons taught in his neighborhood grade school, many of which deal with such sensitive subjects as substance abuse in the home. "All this stuff is drummed into them at school."

Parents complain of unsafe neighborhoods and schools. They complain of negative peer pressure on their children. And curiously, only then, as a final commentary on what they view as a family-hating culture, do parents complain of what all the social scientists are talking about: epidemic family fragmentation.

The attitude of parents toward influences outside the home has probably always been wary. Parents are by nature protective. But today this wariness is accompanied by a sense of disgust, of powerlessness, and of fear. Katherine, an African-American mother of three teenage girls from the Washington, D.C., area, exclaims over the destructive and dangerous influences with which children come face-to-face each day, "I have to look at everything out there, absolutely everything, as a potential threat to my child." Larry, a white father of three from Austin, comments, "As a parent, you always felt vulnerable. But now . . . there are so many more reasons to feel vulnerable."

One of the key reasons parents feel so vulnerable today, they say, is their sense of isolation from a community supportive of the moral virtues, the social discipline, and the sense of family permanence and loyalty they try to instill in their kids at home. "We are little islands out there," laments Jim. "Today," says Rochelle, "you have to know your children's friends. The neighborhood community is lacking. You don't meet on the street anymore."

Studies of inner-city families point quite dramatically to the radical sense of alienation from the larger community that afflicts poor single mothers. A 1993 article in Newsweek describes ghetto women so afraid of neighborhood drug dealers, prostitutes, and gun-toting gangs that they lock their children inside their apartments during school vacations to make sure they are out of danger's grasp.[6] But even affluent, securely married Americans feel isolated in the child-rearing enterprise. Median-income black and Hispanic parents, especially, articulate intense yearnings for a return to a more family-supportive communal life, of which they feel their church affiliation is the only remnant. "I don't mean to discriminate against anybody," says Mel, an African-American father from Baltimore, "but I have my children only associate with children of my religion, because I know that there is a certain structure and a certain discipline . . . the same morals."

Government, child-advocacy groups, and community institutions have invested substantial resources in what they consider to be social supports for families with children—Child Protective Services, counseling and therapy, parenting seminars, support groups, preschools, day care, and after-school activities. But it seems that parents are not impressed by these things. In fact, they complain that many so-called supports for families are more disposed toward harming families than helping them. Working mothers of all income levels tend to stay away from institutional child care for as long as possible, preferring to leave young children at home with relatives. Phyllis, a working mother from Texas, worries, "Someone else is raising my children. Some of the role models, I don't even know." Shirley, an Asian-American mother of two teenage boys, says, "I was lucky, because my parents raised my kids, not day care. So they got all those wonderful traditional values of our family."

Few of the parents I spoke with believe that the increasing drive for parenting-skills programs and therapeutic resources is a boon to family life. Many parents contend that the child-rearing advice given to them in books and parenting support groups is often shallow and fruitless. They complain, moreover, that approaching school counselors or psychologists for help in raising troubled children is at best futile, at worst a booby trap that may bring blame down on them. A startling number of parents I've talked to who have sought private counseling or psychotherapy for troubled children are disappointed and frustrated with the results. "There's a thing at school called counseling," complains Donald. "They [the counselors] can't counsel themselves."

Of the extant "services" families are offered today, those that most confuse and demoralize parents are the child welfare authorities. Parents contend that this powerful government organ stands between them and effective discipline in the home: and that it engages in reckless and destructive interventions in family lives. The impositions of the child welfare system, parents say, start in school, where teachers exhort children to report parents who spank, and send children home with lists of their rights and circulars warning that even verbal criticism is "abusive." "Our hands are tied," laments Albert, a father from San Francisco, of the cultural pressures against any parental discipline at all. Society has forgotten, says Gene, a New Jersey father of two, that "discipline is a form of love." Says John, a Texas father of two, "Everyone knows you're not supposed to ever in your life spank your kid! One swat and you may never see them again!"

The child welfare authorities, however, are only one focus of what appears to be parents' general distrust of a legal culture they say has no regard for family autonomy and integrity. The courts, parents tell me, seem unable to handle divorce, custody, or even adoption disputes in any but the most destructive ways for parents and children.

Parents are no more sanguine about the schools, which they claim only further undermine the mechanisms of family life. Specifically, parents object to the propensity of "life skills" courses to openly challenge the values they teach their kids at home, and to force kids to grow up too fast. Sue reflects, "My kid already knows about condoms—at six! It's so sad." Doug agrees. "Innocence," he says, "is lost on our kids."

Many parents allow that drug education, sex education, and similar school programs may be well-intentioned attempts to stem the tide of high-risk behavior among adolescents. But they note that these programs are failing, and believe this is because they offer kids choices that may actually invite risk-taking behavior rather than delivering the kind of clear behavioral imperatives kids need. Debra, an African-American mother of two, says, "At school, they give them those condoms. And I don't think they should, because that's forcing them to . . . go ahead and have sex!"

Parents regret, moreover, that life skills courses often demoralize children by touching too early on sensitive psychological and emotional issues—issues of sexual orientation, for example. A Cape Cod mother doubts the appropriateness of discussions of homosexuality in the ninth-grade classroom: "Some of these boys, their sexuality is fragile." A Connecticut mother of two comments, apropos of a substance abuse program in her children's grammar school, "Every time I have a glass of wine while fixing dinner, I have to reassure my girls that I'm not an alcoholic."

Perhaps the strongest indication of the wariness with which parents regard the endeavors of educators, community service agencies, child welfare bureaucrats, and even lawyers and judges is the parents' aversion to discussions about what government can do for families. When asked, their suggestions are usually perfunctory and curt. Government should "clean up the streets," they will say, and "throw criminals in jail." Despite an avalanche of propaganda—from parenting magazines to more serious social policy monographs that seek to mold parents into a family policy advocacy group—parents are unenthusiastic family policy lobbyists. Why? The answer is simple. So far, family services and family policies have been directed toward remolding family life to fit an anti-family culture, rather than accommodating the culture to the real needs of parents and children.

To listen, then—and I mean *really* to listen—to parents talk about raising children in America today is to come to the realization that families and social policy thinkers are at loggerheads. Our family policy, it seems, has been based upon a long-standing conviction on the part of educators, psychologists, and social service professionals that parents really should not be too heavily engaged in the child-rearing process, but rather should abandon it to professionals. For almost a century now, child-rearing "experts" have challenged the competence of parents and pushed for ever greater institutionalization of child-rearing. Suspicious of what they considered the backward child-rearing philosophy of parents and the confining loyalties of close family lives, they have done their best to discourage parent-child intimacy and parental influence, encouraging instead ever-earlier integration of children into institutional life and its broader social circles.[7]

Today, in fact, even some of the most compassionate scholarly work on the crisis of childhood as it relates to the deficits of contemporary family life—Sylvia Hewlett's *When the Bough Breaks*, Arlie Hochschild and Anne Machung's *The Second Shift*, or Hillary Rodham Clinton's *It Takes a Village*[8]—betray the fallacious assumption that in the modern world it is up to institutions, and not up to parents, to rear children. These books enjoin government to *relieve* parents of their child-rearing obligations, rather than to support them in these obligations. In advocating more nursery school, more comprehensive schooling, longer school days, broader school services, more organized children's activities, more institutional child care, more therapeutic intervention, and a broader social welfare net, they may be good-hearted attempts to combat serious deficiencies in contemporary family resources. But they reinforce a predilection toward a child-rearing by professionals that parents viscerally resent—because it excludes parents from the kind of influence and participation in children's lives they really want.

Parents are growing impatient with the bureaucratization of children's lives, from the foster care forced on welfare mothers to the proliferation of federal school breakfast programs, from the ubiquity of early-childhood education to ever-younger soccer leagues. They see their relationships with their children impoverished by lack of contact. And they see their children suffering the encumbrances of overdirected lives. Children, they say, have lost "innocence," "spontaneity," "freedom," "independence," even the capability of "imaginative play." But most importantly, they have lost precious time to cultivate emotional intimacy with parents, siblings, and their extended families. Many parents I've talked to contend that the secret to better outcomes is a more authentic and traditional interaction between parents and children, principally one that reaffirms the parent as the child's mentor rather than as a friend or a cheering section. "I see parents overpraising kids a lot," says Terry, noting she thinks the trend is counterproductive. "The time that my parents spent with me growing up," observes Charlie, "was more genuine." Judy remembers, "My father would do the lawn, so to be with him, I'd help him. . . . Whereas now, everything [revolves] around the kids and they are becoming spoiled."

As we will see, parents have a completely different take on how society can help them than do the child-rearing "professionals" who would dictate family policy. Rather than adjust their lives to a heavily bureaucratized culture of childhood, parents long for the means to bring children more firmly into the family fold. When asked how their children's lives could be improved, parents invariably answer: "We need less work . . . and more family time together." Parents' first goal, in fact, would be to unleash themselves from some of the worst pressures of the two-income family culture—the ever-expanding workday for men and women, and the heavy socioeconomic pressures on families to put material gains before the emotional needs of children.

Specifically, they would relieve the pressures on women—even those with school-aged children—to work. Many mothers and fathers I've talked to remember with obvious nostalgia more leisurely and home-oriented family lives. They insist that child outcomes will only improve when women can once again afford to return home to raise their children. Debbie ruminates on the difference between her own home and the one in which she grew up: "My mother didn't work . . . she sewed me clothes and she was always home when I got home. And I think my children miss that, because I was home part of the time with my children, and they notice the difference." Would she stay home if she could afford to? Like the overwhelming majority of women I've talked to, she would.

But parents' agendas go much further than their determination to ease the pressures of the workaday world on family lives. To protect their children from a culture they consider hostile to healthy child development and family relationships, many are retrenching in the home and creating a counterculture of highly privatized family lives. When Estevan from Texas calls his home "my defensive perimeter," he expresses the anxiety and determination of many of his counterparts, who not only are withdrawing from the workforce or slowing down their work lives, but are also exercising careful surveillance and control over their children's schooling, extracurricular activities, and social contacts.

It is no accident that one of the most significant countercultural movements in America today has been the parent-driven expansion of educational alternatives to the public schools—particularly the rise in small public "charter" schools (schools released from mandates and bureaucratic regulations), denominational private schools, and home schooling. The home schooling movement entails a quite radical withdrawal from engagement with the outside culture. According to conservative estimates, the number of children schooled at home in America increased from around ten thousand in 1980 to approximately one million by 1996.

Of course, in their efforts to protect family life and children from the ravages of a hostile environment, home schooling families have not been able to disappear completely from public life. They have been forced by a number of open challenges to their autonomy (the most recent being a provision of Congress's 1994 education bill that would have required teacher certification of any parent who taught his child at home) to wage a fight for their right to educate their children their way.

Other issues, too, have brought parents into the political arena. In the course of the past few years, I have studied a multitude of grassroots parent organizations that have sprung up in response to the government's expanding claims to *parens patriae*. Most of these have been local movements that have spontaneously erupted to protest controversial school policies such as comprehensive sex education and "outcome-based education," or to put school choice on the ballot. Some, however, are well-established parent-run advocacy organizations designed to challenge government incursions on family autonomy, to promote and support at-home mothering, to protest declining entertainment standards, or to take on educational reform. Up to now, these organizations have been only moderately successful in asserting parents' rights over the claims of the educational, social service, and media elites. Parents are busy people, who tend to organize ephemerally around specific issues of the moment and then to disperse, whether the battle has been lost or won. They have only just begun to focus on the central issue behind their many frustrations—the lack of parental empowerment in our society.

But parents across the country are mounting a strong and concerted movement to reclaim the power they've lost. Between 1994 and 1996, five states—Kansas, Michigan, Ohio, Oklahoma, and Utah—passed some sort of parental rights legislation. In Kansas, for example, that legislation not only reaffirmed the rights of parents "to direct the upbringing and education" of their children, but granted them more direct access to legal redress in case those rights are compromised. As of this writing, the proposed Parental Rights and Responsibilities Act, sponsored by Oklahoma's Steve Largent in the House of Representatives and Iowa's Charles Grassley in the Senate, is moving slowly through Congress. Finally, a Parental Rights Amendment, which reads simply, "The right of parents to direct the upbringing and education of their children shall not be infringed," has been introduced in twenty-eight states.

Parental rights legislation represents the most clearly articulated bid for a return to parental engagement in child-rearing to date, and may serve as a banner under which large numbers of parents fighting disparate battles against a family-hostile system can unite in the interests of children's well-being. But it has met heavy resistance from child-rearing professionals, who charge that parents should not be allowed to assert hegemony over the "experts" in determining the future of our children given a growing trend of family disintegration and a decline in parental competence and responsibility. Indeed, in four states where the Parental Rights Amendment has gone to a legislative or popular vote—Kansas, North Dakota, Virginia, and Colorado—it has been defeated under pressure from child welfare advocates, educators, children's rights groups, and health professionals. The National Education Association (NEA), the American Civil Liberties Union (ACLU), the Parent-Teacher Association (PTA), and the American Academy of Pediatrics (AAP) have all declared themselves adversaries of parental rights legislation.

The battle for parental empowerment will be a long and hard one. But the principle behind it is a potent one. Despite the pressures on their time and the rate at which they are breaking down, families are better equipped to set the tone for child-friendly social policies than government and the many extrafamilial institutions that present themselves as "advocates" of families and children. There is no ignoring the fact that there are fewer conscientious parents than there once were. Even parents recognize the failings of many of their contemporaries, who, they say, lack the important parental virtues of "firmness," "consistency," and "commitment." But considering the strains under which family life has been placed, there turn out to be surprisingly few parents who would not rightfully deserve a chance to remake their children's childhood in the image of a richer family life and a more pervasive parental influence.

One of the issues I wish to take up in this book, in fact, is the extent to which our family-hostile, child-hostile culture is driven by a dangerously erroneous idea that parents are bad for children—indeed, that the traditional family is an endemically pathological institution, a child abuse machine. If we examine carefully the bloated statistics on child abuse and neglect produced by the child welfare industry, we find that serious parental transgression is a relatively rare phenomenon, one that is associated less with the failures of traditional family life than with the tragedy of contemporary family breakdown. Yet, the media's obsession with child abuse has distracted attention from the legions of conscientious parents who—in turn—testify that to be a good parent in a family-hating culture is, in itself, an act of heroism.

When Gail, a mother of three, states, "If I were asked to give advice to government . . . I would say, let *me* raise my children. I'll make them happy," she is speaking for millions of parents who believe that the crisis of youth could be solved if government and social institutions got out of the lives of children and trusted families to provide the love, time, protection, and authoritative guidance that kids really need. This book is a petition on their behalf. It is an exposé of the family-hating culture from the top down: from the assault on parental authority and family autonomy waged by government and the legal system to the estranging and destructive world of bureaucratic child-rearing. Finally, it is an exploration of the ways in which parents attempt to cope with and fight the anti-family culture, and what government and the professionals can learn from them. Indeed, parents are on the way to creating a powerful alternative culture—one that, in maximizing the influence of families over children, may carry within it our sole hope of solving the growing crisis of youth. To acknowledge the success of that "counterculture" in producing responsible and productive young men and women is not my only aim. Rather, I hope to show that we might base some ideas for a more fruitful family policy on the methods parents have found work for families. In shaping the family of the future, it seems to me, our government and social institutions should take their primary cues from the thoughts, practices, and values of ordinary mothers and fathers—now, before it's too late to save the next generation of Americans.

Part I

CULTURE AGAINST

THE FAMILY

1

The Parent as Pariah

Not *so* long ago, parents were looked upon as repositories of wisdom and rectitude, and they were the unchallenged custodians of their children's welfare. That is no longer the case. Parents today are relentlessly assailed as abusive, and unworthy of their authority. In the past few years, television has subjected us to countless tales of parental cruelty and lasciviousness—beatings, sexual molestation, even murder. From the testimonials of the Oprah Winfrey production entitled *Scared Silent* to the made-for-TV movie *Child of Rage* to the *PrimeTime Live* segment devoted to "Satanic Child Abuse," TV has spread the disconcerting impression that everywhere sick parents are brutalizing young lives. The published confessions of celebrities and their children—Joan Crawford's daughter, Christina Crawford, and former Miss America Marilyn van Derbur perhaps the best known of these—have fostered a vain and ferocious image of parenthood, convincing the American public that behind even the most glamorous lives lie tawdry tales of family violence and depravity.

Bookstores are flooded with tomes portraying parents as lethal to children and conveying the impression that child mistreatment is a ubiquitous social malaise. A recent visit to the Barnes & Noble "Child-sense" section revealed no fewer than eighty-four titles on the subject of child abuse—many of them best-sellers, and almost all boasting the academic credentials of their authors.

Perhaps the best-known example of this genre is *Toxic Parents,* the 1989 best-seller by Dr. Susan Forward with Craig Buck. Forward, one of the first psychotherapists to charge American parents with widespread child mishandling, has made a veritable science of ferreting out ways in which parents can oppress children. The behavior she assails in her book as "abusive" ranges from incest to occasional moralizing, from life-threatening beatings to the demand that children show up for Christmas dinner.[1] Subtle psychological pressures, she claims, can be just as destructive to children's lives as physical violence. "Many civic authorities," she warns, "have come to recognize the need for new procedures to deal with . . . physical and sexual abuse. But even the most concerned authorities can do nothing for the verbally abused child. He is all alone."[2]

A more recent book, *How to Avoid Your Parents' Mistakes When You Raise Your Children,*[3] indulges in less gruesome imagery, but its definition of parental impropriety is even broader. To judge from educator Claudette Wassil-Grimm's long list of parenting "disorders," children are ruined by the least indication of parental frailty; she considers not only substance abuse, mental illness, divorce, and desertion indications of "dysfunctional" parenting, but overworking, overeating, overspending, moodiness, illness, and even death!

Lest anyone come away from a reading of Wassil-Grimm's book still believing his parenting record clean, there are a number of other books eager to divest him of his smugness. One book bears the provocative title *When Parents Love Too Much.*[4] The thesis: The nicest parents are just rabid wolves in sheep's clothing. Family therapist Mitch Meyerson and educator Laurie Ashner tell horror stories of parents who purchase apartments for their children, help them find jobs, render judgments on the characters of their suitors. Such parents, claim the authors, cleverly deceive themselves and their children into thinking they are generous and conscientious, when in truth they are "controlling" and "manipulative."

Another volume bears the titillating title *The Emotional Incest Syndrome: What to Do When a Parent's Love Rules Your Life.*[5] Here Patricia Love, a doctor of educational psychology, mercilessly prosecutes parents who are not quick enough to detach themselves from their offspring. These parents, the author claims, promote insidious syndromes of "codependency" that recur generation after generation. And who are the culprits? Parents who educate their children at home, spend time with their children in the pursuit of common interests and hobbies, and especially parents who take their children into the parental bed for cuddles. It is all too easy, says the author, to trespass into that danger zone of family life where love becomes "over-involvement." Parents must watch themselves, for they are a source of incalculable emotional anguish to children who, even in adulthood, cannot wrest independence from them.

Television and publishing, of course, did not make the revolution in our cultural image of parenthood. They merely reflect what is in fact the enormous influence of the psychotherapeutic community in metamorphosing our ideas about family life and parental power. "Toxic parenting," "dysfunctional parenting," "incestuous parenting" is the vocabulary much of the psychotherapeutic community uses to describe what it deems the child-persecuting legacy of the baby-boom generation. Baby boomers, they insist, have been devastated by parental abuses on their physical persons, parental violations of their sexual integrity, parental wounds on their self-esteem, parental assaults on their independence, parental obsessions over their welfare, parental displays of affection—in short, by parental depravity *and* parental love.

Are parents really so dangerous? We live in a society in which the family is becoming an increasingly volatile unit. But the overwhelming majority of parents I've talked to insist that they pale as authority figures in comparison to their own parents. "We have, as a generation, a harder time accepting the authoritarian role of parent," a father reflects. One mother observes: "Children today are telling parents what to do, rather than parents children," while another notes, "My kids say things to me I would never have dreamed of saying to my parents." And another dad reminisces:

> I was going to my senior prom and I remember my father yelling out the window, "Are those garbage cans still in front of the house?" And with a tuxedo on, I brought them to the back knowing that that's what I *had* to do. I come home now, it's pouring rain, I've got four kids. . . . There are the garbage pails still on the curb. . . .

Parents today are made of far milder stuff than their own mothers and fathers were. And statistically, they do not seem to be nearly as harmful to children as many in the psychotherapeutic community would make them out to be. True, between 1976 and 1994 reports of child abuse skyrocketed from 669,000 to over 3 million a year. Yet in the past few years child welfare authorities were only able to substantiate a third of all reports. And in about 80 percent of substantiated cases of child maltreatment, says Douglas J. Besharov, founding director of the National Center on Child Abuse and Neglect, no serious danger to a child was posed. Only 3 percent of all substantiated reports involve an injury requiring medical attention. Deaths from child abuse and neglect increased an alarming 54 percent between 1985 and 1991—a phenomenon that some experts have attributed to family breakdown and others to an epidemic of substance abuse in the inner cities. But deaths of children at the hands of their parents are still extremely rare.[6]

The fact is, our cultural definition of child abuse has changed. Even parental foibles that used to be the object of good-natured jibes— chastising too much, demanding too much, worrying too much—are today widely depicted as child-threatening evils. So loose has even the legal definition of harmful parenting become that in my readings on child welfare, I have run across cases where parents have been convicted for child abuse for such "crimes" as restricting their children's television viewing, taking a child out of school for a few days for reasons unacceptable to school authorities, or leaving a ten-year-old home alone afternoons while they worked.[7]

How did we become so hypercritical of parents? It all started at the turn of the century with Sigmund Freud, who disseminated a new and frightening notion: that parents could make monstrous mistakes in raising children. Freud's theories of psychosexual development pointed up the very special intensity of the parent-child bond, as well as its fragility. In exploring infant sexuality, in exposing the sexual etiology of neurosis, and in developing his theories of the Oedipal complex, Freud uncovered the romantic, even erotic dimensions of children's attachment to their parents. By implying that parents' power had a tremendous impact on the future mental health of their children, his theories subverted accepted methods of parenting, and called into question the age-old assumption that austerity and an unequivocal demand for filial obedience were the keys to raising decent human beings.

Freud's child-rearing theories did not have much impact in this country until the Second World War. Until then, the field of child psychology had been dominated by an interest in the impact of evolution and genetics on childhood development, rather than the impact of familial environment and parent-child relations.[8] But, in 1945, the first edition of Dr. Benjamin Spock's Baby and Child Care awakened American parents to a new and more psychologically solicitous role in child-rearing. In his irresistibly folksy way, Spock rehearsed American mothers and fathers as players in the Freudian romance of love, guilt, and repression.

In his discussions of discipline especially, Spock wanted parents to understand children as suffering suitors yearning for Mom and Dad's attentions, rather than as savages in need of civilizing. The key to healthy discipline, Spock implied, was to relinquish the traditional authoritarian approach to parenthood, an approach that he argued tended to oppress children, creating dependent and neurotic adults. Rather, he insisted, parents should become sensitive mentors of their children's evolving psyches.

That childhood naughtiness often derives from psychological anguish, and that this anguish demands compassion and not punitive measures, is, in itself, a sound notion; but Spock drove it home to the point of moral equivocation. In *Baby and Child Care*, for example, he suggested that parents might respond to school-age stealing by "thinking over" whether their child might "need more . . . approval at home," and even a raise in allowance!⁹

For Spock and his disciples the "good" parent was no longer the parent who got his children to behave, but rather the parent who understood why his children might *not* behave. The good parent did not depend upon wielding power. He did not demand; he did not rage; he was careful not to react to provocation with anger. Rather, he empathized with the arduous process of psychic development, and coped with—rather than combated—the passing stages.

Much of the popular child-rearing advice that followed Spock's was in fact an elaboration of this essentially psychoanalytic model of parenthood—a new parenting plan for a brave new, neurosis-free world. In *The Challenge of Parenthood*, a highly influential child-rearing work of 1948, psychoanalyst Rudolf Dreikurs noted:

> The age-old vicious circle of false premises and principles perpetuating themselves must be broken before we can hope to reduce the difficulties of education, lighten the burden of parents, and correct the faults of their children. This is not possible without rehabilitation of the *parents*. If we are to have better children, the parents must become better educators. They must learn to understand children, to know what goes on in their minds and to comprehend the motives for their actions.¹⁰

The most popular authors on child-rearing of the late 1960s and early 1970s, Haim Ginott (*Between Parent and Child* and *Between Parent and Teenager*)¹¹ and Thomas Gordon (*P.E.T. Parent Effectiveness Training*),¹² worked to transform mothers and fathers from wrathful moralizers into poker-faced therapists. These child-rearing experts wrote at a time when the baby-boom generation had grown into rebellious teenagers, and were testing parental tempers to the limit. But Gordon in particular urged parents to try to bridge the generation gap with therapeutic and counseling techniques, suggesting, for example, that parents commit to memory monologues designed to transmit emotionally neutral "behavioral messages."

It is unlikely, of course, that such a studied approach to parenthood penetrated the majority of American homes at the time. The parents I've talked to in the past few years tell me that their own parents had no qualms about imposing authority in their households. Men especially note that corporal punishment was a routine part of their growing up. (Girls seemed to have been disciplined in gentler ways.) One man remembers, "My father brought home the money and beat us. That's what he did." Another recalls, "My father had this board hanging on the wall; he called it the 'board of education.' "

There is no doubt, however, that proponents of the therapeutic parenting model exerted an enormous influence on the best-educated Americans. And their notions about good parenthood came to permeate education, social work, and even the mass media. There was a clear public perception, as early as the 1960s, that the traditional arsenals of parental authority—screaming, chiding, slapping, and threatening—were no longer to be regarded as immutable parental prerogatives for making kids behave. Corporal punishment was disappearing from the schools, and social and public health workers warned against punitive disciplinary measures. Popular television shows portrayed parents as masters of sensitivity and self-control.

Growing up in the 1960s, I remember my own parents breaking into gales of laughter on hearing the aging comedienne Ruth Goldberg quaintly counsel, "Spank your child once a day; if you don't know what he's done to deserve it, he will!" Like many of their peers, they were conscious of being both unfashionably strict and shamefully emotional in their relationships with their children. Yet they refused to adopt the new model of parenting, claiming that the ever-increasing cultural pressures on them to relinquish their authority didn't square with their temperaments, their cultural traditions, or their politics. It seemed clear enough to them that Dr. Spock and his disciples were out to revolutionize not only the relationship between parents and their children but society itself, through the agency of the family.

One of the most striking aspects of the new parenting ideology, in fact, was its pacifism—specifically, its message that the path to world peace must be forged in the home. Spock's repeated warnings in *Baby and Child Care* that the world is "in imminent danger of annihilation," and his pleas for creating a peaceful future for our children, were not made in passing. Spock gave up his professorship in 1967 to devote himself entirely to the Vietnam War protest, and even ran for President in 1972 on the People's Party platform.[13]

Many of Spock's protégés, in fact, adopted political agendas that went well beyond disarmament. Rudolf Dreikurs, in a new preface to the 1958 edition of *The Challenge of Parenthood*, recommended the "family council" as an "essential feature for the democratic family."[14] "The growing rights that society bestows on children, and their awareness of their status as equals," Dreikurs observed, "make it essential that they be accepted as equal partners in the affairs of the family." That the institutions of family life should mimic the institutions of democratic political life was for Dreikurs self-evident, his expectations of the family council being quite specific, right down to the strict "maintenance of parliamentary order." He stressed to his readers that his family council was as much a revolution in family life as the eighteenth-century establishment of self-government in political life. "Tradition," he noted, "does not provide us with guiding lines for living with each other as equals. We have to establish them by trial and error."[15]

The child-rearing prophets of the late 1960s and early 1970s continued this trend, touting a new democracy of the home where children, as well as adults, had inalienable individual rights, and were governed by social contract, not by force. Thomas Gordon chastised parents for being "afraid to give up their power." And he warned against a "distorted perception of the nature of man [that] human beings cannot be trusted and . . . that removing authority will only result in their children becoming savage."[16] He referred to "parent-child battles over hair and other behaviors" as involving "a question of *youth's civil rights* [his italics]."[17] At the beginning of Haim Ginott's *Between Parent and Teenager*, Ginott asked rhetorically, "Can teenagers and parents live together in peace and dignity? Only under certain conditions. What are these conditions? [Establishing] . . . terms of coexistence . . . living in mutual respect."[18]

I remember a close associate of my father's turning his home into a veritable training ground for democracy-in-action à la Gordon's P.E.T.— that is, until it occurred to him that at least one member of the "family council" was repeatedly showing up for meetings stoned out of any legislative frame of mind.

Sometimes the results were more dire. We also knew a number of good-willed parents who, after generously granting their children voting rights and negotiating powers, were forced to rescue them from drug busts, religious cults, and arrests for political subversion.[19] Indeed, as the baby boomers entered adulthood, the shortcomings of permissive parenting became undeniable—in their self-absorption, their greed, their flightiness, and even in their peculiar propensity to violent crime, which between the years 1960 and 1975 alone increased 200 percent.

By the 1980s, faced with incontrovertible statistical evidence of a continuing rise in substance abuse, violence, delinquency, and teen pregnancy, a new generation of experts called for a return to more authority and discipline in child-rearing. Typical of these experts were educational consultants Lee and Marlene Canter, who in their 1985 work, *Assertive Discipline for Parents,* summed up the philosophy and failures of postwar child-rearing:

> Many parents have been told by contemporary child-rearing experts that for the well being of their children, no matter how badly they behave, the parents would avoid "stern" or "authoritarian" approaches and find alternative psychological approaches. These include talking to their children about why they misbehaved (counseling approach), negotiating with their children to change the problem behavior (democratic approach), and/or praising their children only when they behave (behavior modification approach). Each of these approaches has merit; however, none of them provides you with an answer for what to do when you use them and your child still will not behave.[20]

This did not mean that child-rearing experts like the Canters relinquished the therapeutic notion that children who misbehaved were unhappy, not naughty. Nor that they were prepared to relinquish the idea of parenting by social contract, rather than by natural authority. Though they emphasized the necessity of wresting decent behavior from children by authoritative means, they warned against resorting to old-fashioned punitive measures. Demanding obedience, displaying anger, spanking, reproving, or moralizing, they continued to make clear, were ignoble ways of managing children.

How, then, were parents to discipline effectively? By "laying down the law" and offering their children incentives to follow it and penalties for breaching it, said the child-rearing experts. Raising responsible children, they said, did not mean having to terrorize them into good behavior. In fact, it involved nothing more complicated than treating them as they would be treated in the workaday world, expecting them to live up to their "contract" with family and society to behave in an "appropriate" way.

In the real world, contended experts such as educator Dorothy Rich, author of *Megaskills: How Families Can Help Children Succeed in*

School and Beyond, children would eventually be required to cooperate with colleagues, and accept directions from professional superiors, to show responsibility and initiative.[21] And that meant impressing upon them early that self-discipline was a prerequisite to social acceptance and material success. The new child-rearing revisionists warned against what they saw as too much psychological solicitousness on the part of parents. Parents, they said, should not indulge idiosyncratic and incorrect behavior in children. They must be careful not to be too compassionate in regard to bad school marks or antisocial outbursts. Rather, in day-to-day matters of behavior, they must facilitate social adjustment by displaying the same detached resolve and authority that a teacher or an eventual employer might. They must, according to psychotherapist James Windell, "withhold friendliness" or "remove special privileges" when their children acted up.

"Giving rewards has a powerful influence on behavior," Windell advised in *Discipline: A Sourcebook of Fifty Failsafe Techniques for Parents*, his 1991 contribution to the subject of "assertive" discipline.[22] If parents would only implement this elegant principle, he and other child-rearing experts insisted, they would have no trouble raising perfectly civilized children. Good parenting, thus, was conceived along the technocratic lines of the personnel management model.

The "assertive discipline" school of child-rearing still boasts quite a number of adherents today, especially among teachers and behavioral psychologists. It is particularly popular in middle- and upper-middle-class suburbs, where school-sponsored lectures on "positive" parenting techniques attract attentive audiences eager to mete out appropriate "consequences" for "inappropriate" behaviors. But the media, for the most part, has moved on to a newer and radically different theory of child-rearing.

In the early 1980s, the translation of the work of a Swiss psychoanalyst, Alice Miller, took the American psychotherapeutic community by storm. Two of her books, *For Your Own Good: Hidden Cruelty in Child-Rearing and the Roots of Violence* and *Thou Shalt Not Be Aware: Society's Betrayal of the Child*, dealt shattering blows to the optimistic notion that parents, with a few tips, could be remodeled from harsh and punitive autocrats to effective models of sensitivity, justice, and psychological insight.[23]

Parenting, Miller insisted, was not a rational, conscious act dictated by a set of beliefs about how children should be raised. Parenting was not about a philosophy of strictness or permissiveness, nor about child-management techniques. Parenting, asserted Miller, was an unconscious behavioral syndrome—a gut-fed power struggle that invariably ended with parents emerging victorious, and children crushed.

Parents, Miller said, were tyrants, whether they intended to be or not. Hatred, violence, and criminality, she insisted, could be traced to the pathological outbursts of sadism perpetrated every day, and in every home, by parents on their children—regardless of their parenting philosophy. "All advice that pertains to raising children," Miller wrote, "betrays more or less clearly the numerous, variously clothed needs of the adult. Fulfillment of these needs not only discourages the child's development but actually prevents it. This holds true when the adult is honestly convinced of acting in the child's best interests."[24]

Miller urged her readers to "free themselves from clichés about good or bad parents," and from the idea that parents could *choose* to be good or bad.[25] If an adult has been fortunate enough to get back to the sources of the specific injustice he suffered in his childhood and experience it on a conscious level, Miller wrote, "then in time he will realize on his own . . . that in most cases his parents did not torment him or abuse him for their own pleasure . . . but because they could not help it, since they were once victims themselves."[26]

For Miller, childhood "traumata" was an unavoidable condition of family life, stemming from the fact that parents were unwitting slaves to the dark secrets of their own childhoods—to their earliest feelings of disappointment in love. "The individual psychological stages in the lives of most people," Miller wrote, "are . . . to be hurt as a small child . . . to fail to react to the resulting suffering with anger, to show gratitude for what are supposed to be good intentions . . . [and] to discharge the stored-up anger onto others in adulthood."[27]

According to Miller, even parents who never uttered a harsh word, much less raised a hand to their children, visited upon them unbearable psychological pain and cruelty. Repressing the agony of their own childhoods, parents failed to perceive their children's deeper emotional needs. Or, believing that the young must be hardened to the trials of life, they refused to allow their children to express feelings of sadness and anger.

Miller charged that by the mere exercise of their parenting instincts, parents promulgated an ideology of submission to authority and self-denial that amounted to "soul murder." This ideology, which she labeled "poisonous pedagogy," was a legacy of abuse that parents haplessly transmitted to children from generation to generation. So firmly established was this "poisonous pedagogy" as a method of social control that neither parents nor children were aware of its cruelty. Religion, education, even psychoanalysis, she charged, encouraged children to idealize parents for mistreating them. Indeed, the child-rearing conventions of Western culture congratulated parents for committing abuses against their offspring in the name of discipline and civilization.

How to reverse this vicious and allegedly widespread cycle of child abuse? Miller proposed that psychoanalysis concentrate on helping patients release their pent-up "narcissistic rage" against the parents who mistreated them. Patients who by means of psychoanalytic catharsis reexperienced the sources and intensity of their childhood angers and resentments could, she claimed, disengage themselves from the impulse to victimize their children as they themselves had been victimized.

One would have thought that in attempting to support a theory so new and so radical, a theory that posed the existence of a crime inherent to parenting—"soul murder"—Miller would have called upon her clinical records. But, pleading professional discretion, she demurred. One cannot help but wonder if, aside from the problems of protecting her patients' anonymity, she did not consider the lives of her patients too banal to lend her argument the necessary resonance. One thing is certain. The case histories she called to account were almost exclusively those of famous artists and notorious criminals whose lives were inherently fascinating to a broad public. With only the patchiest of historical records and testimony to go by, but a vivid imagination, a passion for theoretical construct, and a gift for fervent rhetoric, Miller simply speculated on the labyrinth of their childhoods. And on the basis of these speculations, she managed to pronounce every one of them, from Sylvia Plath to Franz Kafka, victims of "soul murder."

Miller's main object, of course, was to assign social relevance to her theories by implying that the worst criminal psychotics conformed to her analytical model of childhood victimization. The major subject of *For Your Own Good*, in fact, was Adolf Hitler, whose troubled childhood Miller offered up as a prime example of the results of abusive parenting. In a chapter entitled "From Hidden to Manifest Horror," Miller traced the roots of Hitler's monstrous deeds to childhood thrashings by his father. Basing her account of Hitler's childhood on a passing statement by his sister—that as a boy, Adolf "got his due measure of beatings every day"—Miller charged that it was these cruel punishments that were the original stimulus for Hitler's later crimes.[28]

That a mean-spirited and mercurial parent might tip the balance of a mind inherently disposed to mental illness is a point one would not have ventured to argue with Miller, had she made it. But she did not. Curiously, she saw nothing particularly unusual about Hitler's volatile character, the frequency and harshness of his father's punishments, nor the existence of a schizophrenic maternal aunt who apparently lived with the family. Even Hitler's more extreme symptoms of psychosis—his nighttime hallucinations, for example—Miller treats as the inevitable repercussions of undeserved childhood whippings. She draws a portrait of little Adolf as the normal son of a typically autocratic Austrian father and a typically weak and subservient Austrian mother. Describing Adolf as a "bright and gifted" child terrified of his father's overbearing authority, she compares him lightly to his ethnic German compatriots.[29] "The fact that Hitler had so many enthusiastic followers," she says, "proves that they had a personality structure similar to his . . . and a similar upbringing."[30]

For Miller, then, Hitler's obsessive and murderous anti-Semitism had nothing to do with clinical paranoia but was caused by the real persecutions visited upon him in childhood by his father. In persecuting the Jews, Miller contends, Hitler reenacted the crimes perpetrated against himself: "mistreating the helpless child he once was in the same way his father had mistreated him."[31] Even in his war mongering, Miller contends, Hitler was replaying a childhood drama of household skirmishes on the stage of international politics.

Miller's political motivations for positing Hitler not as a lunatic but as a logical product of a commonplace environment were clear enough; her audience of German psychotherapists—devotees of what was derogated, under the Nazis, as a "Jewish science"—were vitally interested in the deeper reasons for both their professional mortifications and their rotten political legacy. Indeed, by asserting that Hitler appealed to a certain repressed hostility in the German character, Miller set millions of minds to rest on the uncomfortable matter of Hitler's popularity. And she exonerated them as well for their culpability in Nazi war crimes. The question of guilt, she insisted, is a moot one, since "nothing is ever gained by assigning guilt."[32] For Miller, every player in Hitler's drama of revenge—whether Jew, ordinary German, or raving Nazi—was an unwitting victim of German child-rearing conventions.

Of course, by setting up Hitler as a casualty of despotic parenting, and Nazi terror as a reenactment of child-rearing conventions, Miller did not simply offer a clever apology for German political sins. She rendered a portrait of German family life as a veritable seedbed of Nazism. The Germans, she said,

> had been raised to be obedient, had grown up in an atmosphere of duty and Christian virtues; they had to learn at a very early age to repress their hatred and their needs. And now along came a man who did not question the underpinnings of this bourgeois morality . . . someone who . . . put the obedience that had been instilled in them to good use, who never confronted them with searching questions or inner crises, but instead provided them with a universal means for finally being able to live out in a thoroughly ac-

ceptable and legal way the hatred they had been repressing all their lives. Who would not take advantage of such an opportunity? The Jews could now be blamed for everything, and the actual erstwhile persecutors—one's own often truly tyrannical parents—could be honored and idealized.[33]

It would have been a spurious enough indictment of "bourgeois" family life had Miller ended her arguments with the assertion that Hitler's family structure, as that of the majority of his followers, "could well be characterized as the prototype of a totalitarian regime."[34] But Miller reached deeper in her indictment of the family, which she saw not only as a school for fascism, but as a natural adversary of social order—as a profoundly sociopathic institution.

Every crime, Miller said, could be traced to parental tyranny and the "poisonous pedagogy" that demanded childhood submission to that tyranny. And criminals, she contended, did not only emerge, as Hitler did, from homes where they were subjected to consistent physical brutality at the hands of an unloving parent. They were also bred in circumstances where parents interspersed much subtler tortures with expressions of love. It was this insidious interplay of love and hate in parenting, claimed Miller, that was the foundation of most antisocial behavior. The seemingly arbitrary combination of restrictions and indulgences, humiliations and caresses, spankings and kisses that parents dealt out to children confused, demoralized, and terrified them. The most gruesome of criminal acts, Miller insisted, was simply a restaging of the seemingly arbitrary pain and pleasures to which parents all too commonly subjected their children—a reenactment of the at once violent and erotic drama of childhood as distilled in the child's psyche. "Once we have become familiar with the mechanisms that turn child-rearing into a form of persecution," she said, "and we realize the powerful effect these mechanisms have on the individual . . . we see in the life of every 'monster' the logical consequences of childhood."[35]

All acts of violence, including war, according to Miller, had their roots in authoritarian child-rearing practices. "Until the general public becomes aware that countless children are subjected to soul murder every day and that society as a whole must suffer as a result," Miller wrote, "we are groping in a dark labyrinth, in spite of all our well-meaning efforts to bring about disarmament among nations."[36]

The impact of Miller's work on American elites should not be underestimated. The universality of her charges of cruelty as a inexorable condition of parenting—her definition of preanalytic parenting *per se* as a pathological act (for she did believe that, in the end, psychoanalysis could break the cycle of "poisonous pedagogy")—was calculated to attract a wide coalition of political theorists and child-rearing experts.

Certainly Miller's attack on the father as the prototype of reactionary political oppression was bound to catch the attention of feminists. Indeed, in a 1982 trip to the United States, Miller immediately bonded with four feminist authors—Florence Rush, Louise Armstrong, Sandra Butler, and Susan Griffin—whose work on pornography and the sexual abuse of children, she insisted, confirmed her theories about the heavy prevalence of child abuse.[37]

But an enthusiastic American reception to Miller's ideas in the intellectual community had long been prepared. Her depiction of bourgeois family life as an authoritarian political model was a concept already quite familiar to liberal American social thinkers, who had long viewed social pathologies as consequences of authoritarian family structures. The earliest pioneers of social reform at the beginning of the century were convinced that high rates of crime and social disaffection among Southern European immigrants' children had less to do with their poverty than with their ostensibly overheated emotional ties and the hierarchical structure of their families. Dismayed by the slowness with which these groups assimilated into American society, social reformers sought to check the "tyranny of the home" through the introduction of early-childhood education, parent education, and expanded social services for families. These measures, they insisted, would force immigrant parents to recognize the importance of assimilation into mainstream American culture, and inculcate in their children "democratic" habits of mind. Children, they claimed, must be weaned from the retrograde loyalties of their parents. They must learn to identify with the larger goals and values of American society; and this could only be done if professionals took over much of the socialization role that had in more traditional societies devolved to families. As progressive social thinker Charlotte Perkins Gilman wrote in 1903, "There is no more brilliant hope on earth today than . . . the recognition of the 'child,' children as a class, children as citizens with rights to be guaranteed only by the state, instead of our previous attitude toward them of absolute personal ownership [by parents]."[38]

By the late 1930s, the idea that the political dispositions of children were best cultivated by professionals rather than by families had become well accepted in academic circles. Behavioral psychologists were involved in elaborate experiments to test the capability of educators, in particular, to influence the political dispositions of children. In 1939, for example, the German-American psychologist Kurt Lewin headed up an investigation of the effects of autocratic, democratic, and laissez-faire leadership on adolescent boys' behaviors and personalities. Lewin's laboratory experiments, which were closely watched by the academic community, confirmed that in carefully controlled interactions with children, adults might actually shape political dispositions in predetermined ways.[39] This concept had an enormous impact on the future of American social thinking. Postwar scholars in the fields of sociology, psychology, anthropology, and education all stressed the importance to a democratic upbringing of carefully tempered family relationships and as much coolheaded, goal-conscious, professional child-rearing as possible. They also maintained that to be adequately prepared for success in a fast-changing technological society, and to avoid falling prey to the worst pathologies of urban industrial life—crime, neurosis, and economic redundancy—children would have to be educated by the professionals to the kind of flexibility and independence they could never learn in the emotional hothouse of family life.[40]

Along with the educational experiments of behavioral psychologists in the 1930s, there was another important spur to the trend toward viewing the traditional family as a retrograde political institution. The neo-Marxist scholars of the Frankfurt School, resettled in New York at the New School for Social Research during and after the Second World War, spent years pondering whether the seeds of Nazism could be traced to the German patriarchal family structure. The results of their studies, probably the most profound inquiries into the relationship between family structure and political disposition ever produced, were inconclusive at best. That is, the Frankfurt School couldn't decide whether it was the traditional family itself or its impending dissolution under the pressures of modern industrial society that created a special vulnerability to authoritarian political ideology. Nevertheless, the hypothesis that the family and authoritarian politics were somehow related was greeted with serious interest by a number of family scholars, mental health professionals, and sociologists, especially in the aftermath of World War II, when social pathologists pondered the future of the free world with considerable anxiety. Wrote Sidney E. Goldstein, marriage and family counselor and president of the 1946 National Conference on Family Relations, "An autocratic form of family organization can never prepare children for the new democratic social order."[41]

It is not within the scope of this work to elaborate on the many social theories of the 1950s, 1960s, and 1970s that presaged Miller's call for an end to the "tyrannies" of traditional child-rearing. Suffice it to say that from Talcott Parsons, a founder of Harvard's prestigious Department of Social Relations, to Arlene Skolnick, still an influential champion of a revisionist sociology of the family, American academics of the postwar period have sought to remold family life in ways that might produce future generations more adaptable to the vicissitudes of modern industrial life in a democratic society. Looking upon the traditional family as a barrier to individual adjustment as well as to social and industrial progress, some, like Parsons, advocated merely a tempering of the emotional climate of nuclear family life; while others, like Skolnick, have sought nothing less than the complete abolition of the nuclear family and its replacement with more communal forms of child-rearing.[42]

What was to guarantee the success of Miller's ideas among the broader public, however, was not merely their affinity with academic thinking about the alleged sociopathic propensities of traditional family life, but rather the easy solutions Miller proposed to this alleged problem. Previous social theorists of the family had been unable to offer any remedy to its shortcomings except through the lumbering process of social evolution or the cataclysmic process of social revolution. Miller promised immediate, individual help—through the "inner revolution" undertaken on the psychoanalytic couch. Indeed, Miller's philosophy was ready-made for the aging and self-absorbed revolutionaries of the baby-boom generation, who were bound to find appealing the idea that they could effect fundamental societal change by simply exploring themselves. Hardly a wonder, then, that Miller's theories of "poisonous pedagogy" emerged as a public cause célèbre. The big-money, multimedia, confessional credo that "toxic parenthood" is today is testimony to the self-obsession of an American public hungry for easy answers to the hardest questions of life.

Miller's books might have sold well even without the sponsorship of some the biggest stars of the therapeutic world, but New Age therapy guru John Bradshaw deserves much of the credit for the widespread popularity of her theories. Bradshaw brought Miller's ideas forward in the late 1980s and early 1990s in crisp, upbeat formulas that entered the jargon of American pop psychology. Five years after the publication of Miller's *For Your Own Good* in its English translation, Bradshaw produced a ten-week PBS series and book entitled *Bradshaw on: The Family*, in which he asked, after Miller: "How Could Hitler Happen?" And he presented an answer as succinct as anyone could derive from a thorough reading of *For Your Own Good*: "Hitler and Black Nazism are a cruel caricature of what can happen in modern Western society if we do not stop promoting and proliferating family rules that kill the souls of human beings." What rules? Rules of "obedience," he said, and of "submission" to parental authority.[43]

"Soul murder," Bradshaw continued (along Miller's line), is the most "basic" problem in the world. It is not simply Germany's problem.

Americans, he insisted, pointing to Jonestown and My Lai, are also victims of the "poisonous pedagogy" of obedience. Even the most enlightened of modern American parents always fall back on "authoritarian" roles in times of "stress" and "crisis." And it is in these times that they crush the souls of their children. Ninety-six percent of American families, according to Bradshaw, were "dysfunctional." But this diagnosis was not terminal. "Find out what species of flawed relating your family specialized in," Bradshaw advised in his inimitable New Age syntax. "Once you know what happened to you, you can do something about it."[44]

Bradshaw claimed to be able to reverse the process of soul murder and transform the "false self" that emerged from this soul death by means of what he called a "revolutionary method of self-discovery and spiritual renewal." This method, he contended, would return adults to the true childhood self that had been so cruelly crushed. Though he suggested therapy as the best way to get to the bottom of the specific circumstances surrounding the loss of self, he intimated that his "healing" program, based on the twelve-step program of Alcoholics Anonymous that he described in his book and television series, could substitute for a more personalized therapeutic experience.

Bradshaw has provided a model for many other writers, almost all of them therapists, on the subject of family disorders, child abuse, and incest. A myriad of books, with such titles as *Soul Survivors*, *Pockets of Craziness*, and *Twelve Steps to Self-Parenting for Adult Children*, mimic his artless approach to the victimology of childhood, as well as his easy prescriptions for cure. The authors typically begin by assuring readers that abuse is widespread, and all too many parents are poisonous. Just look around you, they say. If parenting were done right, would there be so many unhappy people? Would things in your own life be going so wrong?

Then readers are often presented with a few check list quizzes. Did your parents do things to you that had to be kept secret? As a child, were you afraid of your parents? Did your parents ever employ physical punishment? Did your parents control you with threats or guilt? Did your parents ever ignore your needs, or tell you that you were rude, stupid, or worthless? Did you sometimes feel that no matter what you did, it wasn't good enough for mom and dad? If the reader can answer yes to even a portion of these questions, the authors generally warn, he or she—like countless others—may have been abused.

The reader is then steered through a long index of greater and lesser parenting sins and disorders. Chapter after chapter, the varying pathologies of family life are dissected and diagnosed, described, symptomatized. Should the reader not recognize his own parents among the profiles of child beaters, rapists, criticizers, controllers, substance abusers, and love-smotherers, he is reminded that the self reading this book is (in Bradshaw's words) the "false" or "lost" self—the self that lives to deny parental depravity and childhood suffering, the self that therapists, too, until their recent enlightenment, have suppressed. The real self, the authors tell the reader, has been the victim of soul murder, and is yet too weak to confront the abuse that has been heaped upon it.

The essence of cure, it is emphasized, is in coming to grips with a long-denied reality that something might have been wrong with one's family life, even if it seemed perfectly normal and wholesome, even if one cannot remember anything too horrible about it. The most painful events of childhood, the reader is told, are all too often banished from consciousness, hidden "behind a wall of amnesia" and "denial."[45]

The authors of such volumes are quick to insist that the individuals whose histories they cite are by and large prosperous, successful, and attractive children of prosperous, successful, and attractive parents. But behind their respectably manicured lawns and all-American images lurk cesspools of emotional and physical turpitude. These parents raped, they seduced, they beat their children; they drank and drugged and ate themselves sick; they screamed, they hit, they rebuked, they kvetched. They made and continue to make their children's lives miserable.

It is one of the curious characteristics of the self-help genre that it levels not only all of these alleged parenting crimes, from the sublimely evil to the petty, but also the people who claim to suffer them. When it comes right down to case histories, nothing is left of the richly colored and textured recounting of classical psychoanalytic case histories as we remember them from Freud. There is little ornament of event, not an iota of humor, no reference to the characters or culture of the people whose tales are related—no reference at all to their ideals, their idiosyncrasies, their imaginations, their traditions, or any other aspect of what one might call their individuality. There is simply the dispassionate and distilled recounting of a pointed cultural allegory: the story of an anonymous perpetrator, called "parent," and an innocent victim, called "child," fortuitously thrust into a curious wasteland of family life. The former commits a series of offenses upon the latter on brutal impulse—offenses as removed from real emotions and circumstances as the shoot-outs in a spaghetti Western.

Meet Jesse, for example, whose story John Bradshaw tells:

> Jesse is . . . an alcoholic and a sex addict. . . . He was inappropriately bonded with his mother and was abandoned by his own father. He had two stepfathers. They were both alcoholic. One was

physically abusive. . . . His mother carried the poisonous pedagogy in denying her son his sexual feelings as well as his anger.[46]

Or Richard, a patient of J. Patrick Gannon, who testifies in Gannon's book *Soul Survivors:*

> When my mother could get angry, she would constantly tell me in so many words that I was a loathsome thing. As I got older, it got worse. She would call me a "repulsive, pimply-faced shit." When she was really in full rage, she would kick me and call me a "cunt." . . . Of course, she would also use the classic rant, "You're just like your father. . . . All you ever think of is yourself."[47]

The authors of self-help volumes generally admit that the stories they tell are not drawn straight from actual case histories. They are distilled composites of patient records, altered with the object of protecting patient anonymity and proving "therapeutic" points. But in perusing these wicked, vulgar, and essentially flat stories, one cannot help but have the feeling they are no more than cardboard mock-ups of iniquity. In *Toxic Parents,* for example, a patient of Dr. Susan Forward relates this tragic tale of woe:

> My stepfather was this popular minister with a real big congregation. The people who came to church on Sunday just loved him. I remember sitting in church and listening to him sermonize about mortal sin. I just wanted to scream out that this man is a hypocrite . . . this wonderful man of God is screwing his thirteen-year-old step-daughter![48]

Pop psychology has been enormously successful in turning such confessions into an overriding characterization of family life as pathologically disposed. In the past few years, there has been a rash of accusations of sexual abuse against parents by grown children—accusations that (it is more and more widely recognized) are as likely to be the result of therapeutic suggestion as of actual abuse.[49] The consequence has been embittered and broken families, with no one knows how many innocent, aging parents denounced for crimes they never committed.

The notion of widespread family dysfunction has victimized parents of children who are not yet grown as well. Schools, community associations, and religious organizations have also made parents the targets of unwarranted suspicion and criticism. A National PTA–sponsored pamphlet entitled "Child Abuse and Teen Sexual Assault: What Your PTA Can Do," for example, alleges that child abuse reports "represent the tip of an iceberg of violence within the American family," and that there is a "fine line between" parental "discipline and abuse."[50] In my own community—a small town in Fairfield County, Connecticut—invitations to join parenting "support groups," to attend lectures on parenting "styles" and "stresses," to take advantage of the services of school psychologists and social workers, and particularly to avail oneself of support groups and information on "co-dependency" and "abuse" flood newspapers and mailboxes, and are even included in the literature sent home with children from the public schools. Indeed, public school districts in general are zealous in their attempts to warn parents that they ought not to consider themselves unobserved in the child-rearing process. The African proverb "It takes a whole village to raise a child" seems to serve now as a rallying call for the establishment of a communal authority to set new standards and methods of child-rearing. These standards and methods, it should be said, are—despite the proverb—not inspired by any African model, but rather by the psychotherapeutic model.

Steven J. Wolin, professor of clinical psychiatry at George Washington University and author (with Sybil Wolin) of *The Resilient Self: How Survivors of Troubled Families Rise Above Adversity,* is one of a small but growing group of psychologists and psychotherapists who are beginning to buck the trend of parent-blaming, claiming that it is crippling the ability of families to function properly. Wolin regrets that the word "dysfunctional" has become an overarching label of American family life, and that child abuse is so widely considered a self-perpetuating aspect of traditional family life. "Even in the most . . . destructive [home] situation," he contended in an interview with the *Boston Globe,* "more than half of those people . . . never grow up to become abusers. . . . Somehow, most kids adapt and cope."[51]

Linda Braun, director of Families First, a parent-education organization, observes, "We've narrowed the definition of functional to the point of absurdity." A functional family, she says, is one in which "people feel very good about each other and what's happening between them at least 40 percent of the time." "People," she says, "have a sense that they're supposed to be perfect, and it makes them feel inadequate. . . . Parenting is probably the most challenging task any adult can be called upon to do and . . . all families experience stressful times."[52]

But despite such pleas for a return to reason, the majority of mental health professionals remain intent on convincing Americans of the vulnerability of family life to acute disorders, and of the universal need for therapeutic intervention. Parenting magazines often encourage mothers and fathers to seek help from psychotherapeutic resources as a preventive measure, a psychological "checkup" *before* things start to go wrong. One New York parenting-resource publication I ran across a couple of years ago—a publication that specializes in advertisements for birthday party entertainment and nanny referral services—goaded parents to consider the benefits of family and twelve-step therapy, whether there are problems at home or not. Pointing to the ever increasing suicide rate among teenagers, the article blamed parents who had not availed themselves of the benefits of the psychotherapeutic experience, declaring, in the spirit of John Bradshaw, that "we are more than likely the product of a dysfunctional family system, carrying our pain into our new family."[53]

The credo of family pathology and the panacea of therapeutic intervention is pressed upon children, too. The National Department of Health and Human Services has set aside funds for the establishment of "crisis" centers in communities across the country, appealing to children to bring in their parents for counseling, conflict mediation, and child-rearing intervention. My own community newspaper recently printed a front-page article advertising the services of one such center nearby. Children were invited to call its hotline not only in cases where they have been physically maltreated or are demoralized by family conflict, but also when they are simply "afraid to go home because of a problem at school"—in other words, when they are looking for someone to diffuse the force of parental discipline.[54]

A growing number of day and Sunday schools, moreover, introduce the therapeutic process through school-based "support groups." Geared mostly for those children who have undergone major "separation crises" (divorce, desertion, and death), these groups are made attractive by an exclusive esprit de corps and, as in the case of a New York independent school my child attended, snappy, flippant names like "Banana Splits!" It remains to be researched whether such forums, bringing as they do intensely emotional and private matters before public review, help children to overcome the emotional difficulties of family crises, or whether they actually intensify tendencies to act out the frustrations of home life in a school setting.

A discourse of family pathology and suffering is in any case entering the elementary school classroom, where increasingly children are given the opportunity to publicly air whatever gripes and concerns they may harbor about their home life. Teachers in public and independent schools now commonly set aside daily or weekly time for the purpose of unveiling the specters hanging over each child—from the high tragedy of parental desertion to the low comedy of resented bedtimes. In the public schools, such exercises are usually performed within the context of "comprehensive health" or "life skills" curricula mandated by state governments. These programs instruct children in the delicate subjects of pedophilia, alcoholism, drug addiction, and other dangerous propensities of adults—beginning in many states with sexual abuse prevention programs that start as early as preschool.[55]

The Here's Looking at You, 2000 comprehensive health curriculum, used in part or whole by several thousand schools, provides a good example of the characteristics and pitfalls of such curricula. The kindergarten through third-grade program features a cuddly parrot puppet by the name of Miranda. In the opening lesson for second grade, Miranda implies that when adults scream at children, it usually means they've had one too many bottles of beer. Through songs, stories, films, and "role playing," she encourages kids to check the family cupboards for alcohol, nicotine, and other "poisons," share their "feelings" about the "war" that is their "home life," and confess "problems at home" by "writing secret messages" to the teacher.

How do parents feel about such classroom exercises? Focus group research reveals that they are notably unhappy. Not a few parents complain that confessional "support sessions" violate children's natural discretion, and that sensitive children especially dislike having their private lives and feelings probed. Many children, parents charge, are made to fret that their parents are not living up to the school's standards of family life. Though they joke offhandedly about being "turned in" to school authorities for smoking, drinking, failing to recycle, screaming, or spanking, parents remark with considerably less good humor that the schools are turning their kids into worrywarts. Says a New Jersey dad, "Kids are worrying about everything. . . . I remember there was a guy over at our house, we were having a party, and they were saying, 'You're not supposed to be drinking and driving.' They were panic-stricken about it."

An African-American father from Baltimore reported in a focus group, "The schools sent my daughter home with something saying [to] never use my belt unless to hold my pants up, never do this, never do that. . . . I told her that a good father, Scripture-wise, would discipline his children. . . . I let them [my children] know I would never abuse you, but you act up, I will put that belt on your butt." An African-American mother agreed. "You know, I think I would rather be locked up for trying to keep my child on the straight and narrow than be locked up for not doing it."

I personally know that to have a child in the public schools is to combat anxieties about home life brought home from school. My own child worries that her parents drink wine with dinner, that our marital spats will lead to divorce, and that we haven't the wherewithal to handle an emergency properly. For that eventuality, she has memorized a slew of 800 numbers given to her over the course of the years by her teachers.

■ ■ ■

Is parenthood the repository of brutality, tyranny, and incompetence our culture implies it is? Is family life pathological, and parental authority sadly misplaced? If this were true, the increased influence of educators, health professionals, and the media in postwar child-rearing practices would have already resulted in a psychologically healthier, better socialized youth—in an amelioration rather than an increase of juvenile violence and delinquency. But instead, our youth has become more and more vulnerable to social pathologies as the professionals have moved to restrict parental authority and influence over children.

Parents, of course, appreciate this irony quite fully. To discuss their own child-rearing styles with them is to glean the impression that they feel their children's healthy character development may be impeded by the many social and institutional pressures on them to go lightly on authority. While a large number of parents I've talked to claim to read the child-rearing advice of contemporary psychologists, most are skeptical of the assumption that parents are locked into abusive child-rearing patterns from which they must be freed. Parents especially take issue with theories of pervasive family dysfunction, family violence, and child maltreatment, and with child-rearing advice that labels physical punishment as abuse. Says one mother, "Physical discipline is not the great horrible psychological harm that people have made it out to be. We're not all these terribly wounded people." A father reflects, "My Daddy spanked me; but every time he did, I deserved it! No way was I abused."

It is clear from my talks with parents that today's mothers and fathers are much more restrained in their choice of disciplinary methods than their own parents were—much less disposed to use physical discipline than previous generations. As one man observed, "Today, we are told not to hit our children, and we don't hit them." Yet, these same parents are quick to assess the new "nonviolent" styles of discipline as far from ideal. "Force is abuse now, so you have to go to mind games and manipulation," another man observes. These disciplinary methods, parents note, are hardly kinder than spankings, certainly harder and more time-consuming for parents, and are often less effective. Reflects a mother from Texas, "I think we've been fed all this stuff, how we're supposed to be so understanding of our children and we do want to do that—that is a good goal, but we haven't been given the skills . . . to discipline. Or some of the stuff [suggested by the child-rearing experts] doesn't work."

While most parents I've talked to insist they do not habitually spank as a method of punishment, their reluctance seems to have more to do with fear of social disapproval than any conviction that spanking is wrong or destructive. A San Francisco mother puts it this way: "It's strange. . . . Today they'll take you to jail for slapping a kid's hand. . . . Meanwhile there are thirteen-year-olds out there shooting people." Indeed, surveys of parental attitudes toward spanking show that the majority of parents still think it is appropriate punishment, and most of the parents I talked to have spanked their children at one time or another.[56]

Perhaps the biggest indication of where parents stand on the issue of discipline and authority in child-rearing is that they are far quicker to criticize their peers for being permissive and neglectful than for being tyrannical or oppressive. "Parents today give in too easily. . . . A lot of these kids don't know anything about consequences," one mother notes. A father, however, insists that the problem does not end with lax discipline. "I have a job that takes me out all hours of the day and night," he says. "You'd be surprised. At three or four o'clock in the morning you see these kids all in the street. I am talking about seven-, eight-, nine-year-olds. . . . So where the hell are the parents?"

A San Francisco father observes that many well-meaning parents often forget that their priorities should lie with raising their families and not with achieving a certain economic lifestyle:

> If I have to work forty hours a week and my wife works forty hours a week and there is no time for the kids . . . there just has to be time if you plan on having a family. . . . Don't just *have* the kids and not have time for them and then say, "Well we have to go to work," and then you know, when [your son] is in jail and [your daughter] is pregnant, say, "Well, we had to go to work."

Another dad says, "I think nowadays parenting is really going downhill. Because all you ever see is parents driving up to the baby-sitter, dropping kids off, not spending any time with them."

One of the more trustworthy barometers of rising delinquency, teen pregnancy, and school failure among postwar American youth has been the growing number of parents who neglect their children in striving for economic gain, who leave their children to their own devices, or cede their authority to "professionals," in hopes that they will pick up the parenting slack. Indeed, the postwar "hands-off" child-rearing prescription

for parents has fostered—along with rising delinquency—a veritable ideology of child neglect. This is a problem David Elkind has pointed up in
his book *The Hurried Child*. The underlying impetus of the movement to
"liberate" children from parental control and impositions, Elkind has revealed, has less to do with concern for the welfare of children than with
adults' desire to free themselves from the heavy responsibilities of family
life by leaving schools and communal institutions to raise children, or
worse, leaving children to raise themselves. "Our new family styles (divorce, single parenting, two-parent working families and blended families)," Elkind says, "make it next to impossible for the majority of parents
to provide the kind of child rearing that goes along with the image of
children as in need of parental nurture."[57]

A Baltimore mother believes that baby boomers and those who
came after are having trouble being good parents because they themselves were spoiled by their parents:

> I see . . . the thirty-year-olds, the twenty-some-year-olds . . . they
> are . . . selfish, they are used to having things a lot easier. They
> don't take as much time with their kids as I think they should. It's
> not just because they are selfish, I think that they are caught up in
> the world, both of them working. . . . [But] the new generation . . .
> they got the seventy-, eighty-, ninety-dollar perm. They got the
> money coming in. They aren't doing without . . . but the kids,
> they're doing without . . . without the one-on-one.

In this light, it is telling that while the statistical link between child
abuse and later criminal behavior remains murky at best, the statistical
link between parental abandonment (specifically, fatherlessness) and violent criminality is emerging quite clearly.[58]

In its recent preoccupation with family pathology and child mistreatment, our culture has all too irresponsibly put the institution of parenthood on trial for crimes it only imagines parents are disposed to
commit. This is not to say that children, from time immemorial, have not
suffered the whims of ill-willed, immoral, vindictive, and even vicious
parents, nor to deny that today many, many small cups are filled to the
brim with suffering and oppression. But if parents today display an inherently destructive disposition, it is not so much their tendency to
abuse their offices, but rather their temptation—encouraged by the
child-rearing experts—to abdicate them.

2

Child Welfare,
Family Destruction

It was a spring morning in 1989 when Alicia Wade's parents, James and Denise Wade, admitted the eight-year-old to the San Diego NAVCARE medical facility with acute abdominal pain and vaginal bleeding. Upon examining the child, the doctor on duty was shocked. Alicia's complaints involved no run-of-the-mill illness. In fact, her anus and vagina were so badly torn that surgery was required.

When the doctor confronted the Wades as to the cause of their daughter's physical complaints—namely, sexual assault—they reacted as any loving parents would: they cried. Unfortunately, the doctor did not know how to interpret this response. He thought their weeping might be a sign of guilt, not grief. And he regarded as highly suspicious Alicia's inability to remember or describe the details of her rape. Doctors, like all health professionals, are required by law to report any suspicion of child abuse or neglect, or assume liability for not reporting. So as well as calling the police, Alicia's examining physician called Child Protective Services.[1]

The CPS workers who came to interview Alicia were skeptical of her slowly unfolding story. She claimed that a thin, freckled stranger had entered through her bedroom window in the middle of the night, introduced himself as "Uncle," and carried her out to a waiting green car, where he assaulted her. Separating Alicia's parents for intensive interrogation, they got Denise to admit her husband had a history of alcoholism, and that she herself had experienced "recovered" memories of childhood sexual abuse while attending a "co-dependency" group. These disclosures apparently convinced CPS that Alicia had been raped by her father.

An aggressive interrogation of James followed, in which a policeman hectored him to "just be a man and admit" that he had raped his daughter. Wade broke down. "If you're the experts," he said, "I must be nuts, because I don't remember doing it."[2] That cinched the case for San Diego Child Protective Services. Never mind that a thin man corresponding exactly to Alicia's description was known to stalk the Wades' neighborhood, entering children's bedrooms through windows. Never mind that before and after surgery Alicia consistently proclaimed her father's innocence during cross-examination by police and child welfare workers. Never mind that James Wade, a chief petty officer on the aircraft carrier USS *Independence,* had a spotless naval record, and that Alicia, a straight A student, had never displayed any sign, as far as her teachers could tell, of a malfunctioning family life.

Indeed, Alicia's emotional resilience, attractiveness, intelligence, and obvious trust in the adults around her, which child welfare authorities might have viewed as evidence of the Wades' stable home and competent parenting, were disregarded. Instead she seems to have been regarded as a potential social services success story—an ideal subject for what one prominent child welfare advocate calls a "parentectomy."[3]

And a parentectomy is exactly what child welfare performed on Alicia. Even as she lay in her hospital bed calling for her parents, they were prevented from seeing her. Upon her release from the hospital, Alicia was shipped off to foster care. For the next two years, she was shoved from one secret foster home to another. The repeated petitions of concerned relatives and even her pastor to take over Alicia's care were ignored on the basis of their presumed "allegiance" to her parents. The girl's only consistent contact was her CPS-appointed therapist, Kathleen Goodfriend, whose treatment strategies over a period of eighteen months alternated between badgering Alicia to name her father as the attacker, and teaching her to masturbate.[4]

It cost the Wades their life savings to recover Alicia and to exonerate James from the bogus charges of rape that the County District Attorney's office, in conjunction with Child Protective Services, held against him as late as November 1991. But the material sacrifice was the least of it. During all that time, Alicia never once saw her father, while her mother was kept from visiting for intervals of up to eight months at a time. James Wade himself was coerced into no less than $260,000 worth of spurious CPS-sponsored therapeutic services and sex offender tests— among them, the humiliating "penile plethysmograph," a test that apparently requires the subject to listen to kiddie porn audiotapes while his penis is attached to a mercury gauge.

The Wades, you see, had the misfortune of being tried for child abuse in one of the jurisdictions where child welfare corruption is rife, its psychotherapeutic and foster care networks large and lucrative, and where many family court judges and lawyers, it appears, suspect every family to be a seedbed of child abuse. The Wades' prosecutor, a radical feminist by the name of E. Jane Via, had a particularly strong ideological bent against the family. In another of her well-known cases, Via had sought to arrange the adoption of an infant girl on no more substantial grounds than that her Mormon father's "patriarchal" religious beliefs might someday inspire him to abusive behavior.

Via was determined to terminate the Wades' parental rights, even to the point of obstructing justice. When a much-delayed DNA examination of Alicia's semen-stained underpants revealed that Wade could not have committed the rape (the semen genetically matched that of a known sex offender named Albert Raymond Carder, arrested for the several other child rapes in Alicia's neighborhood), she ordered a DNA retest and pressed ahead for an adoption hearing. A San Diego grand jury gathered to investigate the details of the Wade case described Via's machinations as nothing less than "a race against time to arrange for Alicia's adoption prior to the availability of the results."[5]

Is the Wade story an aberration? No. In the years I've been talking to parents, I have heard many similar stories. A Baltimore man, for example, folds his hands, his steel blue eyes looking straight across the table at me, his voice soft and resolute. "My nephew fell down and hurt his leg, and they took him to the hospital. He was only five. . . . He thought it was funny so he said, 'My father beat me.' The police department was called. . . . The policeman walked in . . . and put his hand on the child's shoulder and put the child under protective custody. . . . My brother-in-law had to go to court to prove he didn't abuse the child." He adds, "They'll take your kid and you can't get him back. They don't care who you are."

Many such byzantine tales of child welfare intervention—and there are thousands each year—end with the children in question lost to the foster care system indefinitely, their parents financially and psychologically destroyed. Indeed, in a review of juvenile court practices prompted by the Wade case, a San Diego County grand jury declared it had found hundreds of similar cases in that county alone. The powers of the child welfare system were out of hand, the jury noted, and it had "isolated" itself from public scrutiny and responsibility "to a degree unprecedented in our system of jurisprudence and ordered liberties."[6] Deputy foreman Carol Lamb Hopkins warned in May 1995 before a Senate subcommittee, "I could share anecdotal stories about the destruction of families, the insensitivity of social workers, the collusion of juvenile court judges which might well cause you to decide that the damage done to children and families in the name of child protection far outweighs the good."[7]

The scandal of child welfare is no secret in government circles. As of February 1996, eleven lawsuits were pending against child welfare administrations around the country. Washington, D.C.'s, child welfare system had been placed in federal receivership, and New York City's Administration for Children's Services was threatened with the same. Judy Meltzer of the Center for Social Policy, which keeps track of child welfare in the District of Columbia, notes her organization has monitored administrations in Alabama, Arkansas, Connecticut, Missouri, Kansas, and Wisconsin. The rise of class-action lawsuits against child welfare agencies, she says, is an indication that a "leadership and a culture change in the bureaucracy" is long past due.[8] But while there is a lot of public fretting over increasing reports of child abuse, little attention has been paid to the manifold and increasing abuses of the child abuse bureaucracy.

Why? For the past twenty years, child advocates have undertaken a relentless public-awareness campaign on the subject of child abuse—a campaign that is heavily ideological in its depiction of the American family as dysfunctional and disposed to child maltreatment. The words of David S. Liederman, executive director of the Child Welfare League of America, typify the campaign's pathos-pandering and parent-bashing propensities:

> Those knowledgeable about the realities of child protection know that the incidence of child abuse has exploded, that overworked child welfare systems are engaged in a system of triage to determine which cases demand investigation, and that if any errors are being made, it is in failing to investigate all situations in which there is the potential of real danger to a child. . . . Hundreds of thousands of children . . . are beaten, whipped, degraded and living in circumstances that no child should be forced to endure. . . . Parents, when confronted with the traumatic effects of their abusive behavior, quite expectedly minimize their responsibility and the impact of their actions on their children.[9]

To a large extent, the press has swallowed such rhetoric hook, line, and sinker. In an October 1992 article entitled "A Time for Healing," for example, *People* magazine glossed over the Wade scandal, which it said pointed up "the extreme difficulty authorities often face getting at the truth when a child is a victim of sexual abuse."[10] Occasional articles or columns have appeared in the *Wall Street Journal, USA Today,* the *National Review,* the *Los Angeles Times, Reader's Digest,* the *Christian Science Monitor,* and *Investor's Business Daily,* warning of the child abuse bureaucracy's routinely abusive practices. But sober calls for a reevaluation and restructuring of the child welfare system tend to be obscured by the attention given to quite exceptional stories of criminal neglect and abuse on the part of parents. Television, newspapers, and magazines accorded, for example, very high profile to the tale of the Schoos, who abandoned their children, ages nine and four, over the 1992–93 Christmas holiday to take a trip to Acapulco, and to Susan Smith, the disturbed young woman who, in the fall of 1994, drowned her two children in a fit of depression.

Thus, when, in the spring and summer of 1995, the Senate set out to reform the federal Child Abuse Prevention and Treatment Act, their efforts got practically no play at all in the press.[11] Rather the next wave of press coverage on the child abuse issue after the Smith children's murder was the sensational case of Elisa Izquierdo, a six-year-old New York girl already known to child welfare services who was brutally tortured and murdered in November 1995 by her drug-addicted mother. The tenor of these reports? That the child welfare system was, if anything, too benign and too respectful of family integrity and parental rights in its day-to-day practices, even that the ultimate blame for CPS's incompetent handling of this tragic case lay with underfunding in the face of an epidemic of murderous child abuse.[12]

It's true, as numerous experts on child abuse and neglect statistics have noted, that as child abuse reports have skyrocketed, the capability of child welfare agencies to adequately attend to serious maltreatment cases has correspondingly diminished. A chronic squeeze on the system's resources and time has enabled many abusive parents like Elisa's mother to beat the system by a combination of calculation and cunning. As long as they show up conscientiously at appointed meetings, attend the prescribed parenting courses, and appear at family court with a "small army" of lawyers and social workers willing to vouch for their compliance, they can go right on abusing their children, and nobody is likely to intervene.[13] But the failure of New York's Child Welfare Administration to heed the many appeals on Elisa's behalf by friends, relatives, and school personnel—as we shall see—was the result not of underfunding but of overreporting. Elisa's caseworkers were so encumbered with the pursuit of *frivolous* child maltreatment investigations that they had no time to pursue with alacrity the many serious complaints made on her behalf.

Unfortunately, overreporting of child maltreatment has become the greatest single problem of the child welfare system. Out of slightly more than 3 million reports of child maltreatment each year in recent years, only about a third can be substantiated after investigation by child welfare investigators. And of these, between 150,000 and 200,000 cases involve serious health-endangering deprivation, physical assault, or sexual exploitation.[14] What could the remaining cases involve?

The great majority involve physical or psychological dangers to children that are negligible at most. Douglas J. Besharov, American Enterprise Institute scholar and the first director of the National Center on Child Abuse and Neglect, says most cases of substantiated maltreatment involve "excessive corporal punishment," "minor . . . physical [or] educational neglect," or "minor emotional maltreatment."[15] Parents have been convicted of child abuse for spanking, for grounding, for home schooling, and even for no reason other than a suspicion on the part of a mandated reporter or social worker that while conditions in the home are at present stable, they may be conducive to neglect or abuse in the future. In fact, parents do not have to commit any offense at all in order to be substantiated for child maltreatment. A 1986 federal study evaluating child welfare caseworkers found that up to two-thirds of substantiated cases of child maltreatment involved no actual wrongdoing on the part of parents.[16] Studies undertaken in the mid-1980s by the American Humane Association on child welfare practices indicated that half of the families child welfare agencies compelled to undergo therapeutic services for child maltreatment never mistreated their children at all, and that many removals to foster care are capricious actions of so-called "preventative intervention"—undertaken on a caseworker's presumption that though a child's home situation poses no immediate dangers or deprivations, it might sometime in the future.[17]

How can it be, you might ask, that the government can remove a child from parents who have done him no harm at all? How, in a democracy, can a government organ violate the integrity of families with total impunity?

The problem started with the original language of the 1974 federal Child Abuse Prevention and Treatment Act, or CAPTA (often referred to as the "Mondale Act," for its sponsor, Walter Mondale). CAPTA cast a large net for child abusers, offering a precariously vague definition of child maltreatment—"the physical or mental injury, sexual abuse or exploitation, negligent treatment, or maltreatment of a child . . . under circumstances which indicate that the child's health or welfare is harmed or threatened thereby"—that became a model for subsequent child welfare legislation in all fifty states.[18] The Mondale Act also linked special federal grants to "mandatory reporting" laws. Such laws—now effective in every state—require teachers, child care workers, and health professionals (and in some states, laymen also) to report *any* suspicion of child maltreatment *on penalty of prosecution.* While requiring child protective agencies to fully investigate each case reported, they grant "mandated" reporters full legal immunity for false reports.

Initially, the rapid increase in reporting that followed passage of the Mondale Act helped significantly to reduce fatalities from child abuse and neglect. In just five years, national estimates of deaths from child maltreatment were reduced by half—from 3,000 to 1,500.[19] But at the same time, far more innocent families began to suffer unwarranted investigations. Indeed the decade following passage of the act saw an explosion of frivolous accusations by mandated reporters fearful of missing a case and eventually being called to account for it. In the year CAPTA was passed, 60 percent of the approximately 600,000 child maltreatment reports could be substantiated after investigation; ten years later, the number of reports had risen to 1.4 million, yet the same percentage were annually dismissed. Indeed, by the late 1980s capricious reports of child maltreatment from mandated reporters had become a serious problem. It seems that teachers were reporting families simply because children showed up at school with insect bites or dirty faces, or because they mentioned they had skipped breakfast.[20]

The vagueness of the Mondale Act's original definitions of child abuse prompted loosely defined revisions of maltreatment laws in all fifty states. The result was that throughout the country the range of parent offenses that child welfare authorities might judge legally worthy of intervention widened significantly. Today, legal definitions of "physical abuse" cover the gamut from life-endangering beatings to, in many jurisdictions, corporal punishment with any object whatsoever.[21] (Parents still have the legal right to spank their children on the bottom with the hand in all American jurisdictions, but I am told that in a few jurisdictions, any spanking that results in reddening of the flesh is considered abusive.) "Emotional abuse" charges can be levied for acts as clearly harsh as "close confinement" (for example, locking a child in a closet for hours) or as vague as "unreasonable verbal castigation."[22] "Sexual abuse" obviously includes rape or soliciting a child to engage in prostitution, but it may also refer to any "intentional touching of the genitals or intimate parts (breasts, groin, inner thigh and buttocks) or the clothing covering them . . . which cannot be reasonably construed to be normal caretaker responsibilities . . . interactions or affection."[23]

Legal definitions of "neglect" are equally plastic, ranging from abandonment or health-threatening "deprivation of necessities" to "lack of supervision" or failure to attend school. In some states neglect definitions are so broad that virtually any parental act or oversight a child welfare worker or judge deems not "proper" care can be prosecuted. In Ohio, for example, the legal definition of neglect covers any "condition or environment . . . such as to warrant the state, in the interests of the child, in assuming his guardianship." In Mississippi, it applies to any situation where a child "is without proper care, custody, supervision or support." In South Dakota, a parent may be charged with neglect when "a child's environment is injurious to his welfare."[24] In some jurisdictions child welfare workers can interpret "lack of supervision" to mean leaving any child under the age of nine home alone for any amount of time. The New York State Department of Social Services guidelines, for example, say that "school aged children (age six to twelve years) may not be ready for the responsibility of being on their own even for short periods of time."[25] In Fairfax County, Virginia, no child under twelve years of age may baby-sit for any amount of time, and no child under fourteen may baby-sit for a child under the age of four. Thus, a Springfield, Virginia, woman was recently found guilty of "level three child neglect" when a social worker found out that she had left her nine-year-old son in charge of her two younger children for a half hour while she and her husband delivered one of their automobiles for repair.[26]

"Educational neglect" is a particularly tricky category. In *Recognizing Child Abuse,* Douglas Besharov's comprehensive guide to child maltreatment laws and child welfare procedures, Besharov warns that parents who let their children stay home from school for any reason other than illness may be subject to neglect laws. "Parents have a legal obligation to encourage and facilitate their child's education by requiring them to attend school. Their failure to do so is educational neglect," he writes, and he continues, "Parents do not have the right to keep their children at home when they disagree with the form or content of instruction."[27]

The supple spirit of maltreatment laws, combined with the broad power given individual caseworkers and judges to substantiate reports and take action, has created a situation in which even the most competent, well-meaning, and loving parent can fall victim to the child protective system. Child abuse charges were pressed against a Colorado stepfather for tickling his nine-year-old stepdaughter on the tummy.[28] A Rochester, New York, couple remains listed in the state's central registry of child abusers for taking their learning-deficient son out of school for a few days in 1984 to complete a news-making cross-country run.[29] A Fairfax County, Virginia, woman lost her children for rapping her son on the knuckles when he misbehaved at a public library.[30] The ten-year-old child of a New York City woman was removed to foster care when she called the New York State Child Maltreatment Hotline to inquire about getting a baby-sitter while she worked.[31]

In interviewing hundreds of parents around the country, and in attending focus groups held by my colleagues at the Institute for American Values, I have been shocked at how commonly parents report that they or close friends and relatives have been visited by child protection authorities—and for acts no more sinister than disciplining a wayward child or seeking medical help for a playground injury.[32] The stories I have heard—frightening tales of long-term investigations, irresponsible therapeutic intervention, even child removals—were not prompted by questions about child abuse, but came up spontaneously in the course of general discussions about how raising kids has changed over the past generation. American parents today take for granted the existence of government agencies that have *carte blanche* to monitor their family lives, censor their child-rearing habits, and even take their children away from them.

A Mississippi man told of the origins of a six-month child abuse investigation: "My nephew bruises real easy, and he got out in the yard one day and had bruises all over his arm where he was wrestling and stuff, all over his leg, and the Health Department came to the house the next day. They were going to take him away from [his parents] . . . for child abuse."

A Connecticut father who grounded his adolescent stepson after the boy assaulted his cancer-ridden mother recounted, "The kid complained at school that he had been punished . . . and suddenly we find someone from the DCYS [Department of Children and Youth Services] at our door." The child was removed to the custody of his birth father, and his mother and stepfather were forced into counseling. "The counselor told us my wife's son shouldn't have to eat dinner with the rest of the family if he didn't want to—that we should serve him dinner in front of the TV in the family room," the man recalled. "I was shocked. I asked her, did she have any children? Of course she didn't. Imagine someone like that giving me advice on how to raise my kids!"

An Austin mother had her own horror story. One afternoon she asked her son to take some vegetable scraps out to the compost pile:

> And he got real stubborn and said, "No, I'm not going to do it, I'm not doing it!" And he ran around [to] the front door and he was

ringing the doorbell and stomped his feet and goes, "No, I'm not going to do it." So I got a belt and I just went out [to] the front door and I said, "If you do this [continue this behavior] I'm going to smack you with the belt . . ." I didn't touch him or anything. . . . But he went and emptied the compost. . . . Do you know that two weeks later, knock, knock, knock, somebody from the Department of Human Services . . . came and said, "You're under investigation for child abuse." Because a lady had walked by my house and seen that incident. You don't know, for six months I was just—. . . I wish someone was here from the Department of Human Services. That threw me off so much. . . . The Department of Human Services made me call up three of my friends; they checked [me out by interviewing them]. . . . They went to my school, you know where I do a lot of volunteer work—and sat down with the school nurse. . . . It was just wild. . . . I think you're never able to be the same with your kids after you go through an investigation. You're afraid. I've become less able to discipline my children because of that!

Even for those 700,000 families each year whose cases—like the Austin mother's—are dismissed, the toll of a child welfare investigation can be high. The investigation process usually lasts about six months. Typically, caseworkers will enter a home for the first time at an odd hour, with no previous announcement, giving no information about the nature of the charge held against the family, nor who has made it. Neighbors and school personnel are questioned about the family, particularly about the reputation, behavior, and habits of the parents. In the course of an investigation, the houses of accused families are always checked—refrigerators opened, for example, and bathrooms inspected. Nor is it unusual in some jurisdictions for child welfare workers to enter homes in the middle of the night, strip children naked, and probe their genitals for evidence of abuse.[33] Finally, they may remove children from their homes, or request they be removed by the police at any time during the course of the investigation—even prior to making a judgment as to whether to substantiate an allegation of maltreatment.

Many critics of the system say that the investigative powers of child welfare workers transcend any notion of constitutionality. Families undergoing child abuse investigations are deprived of their most basic due process rights. Although technically social workers do not have the right to searches without consent or a warrant, it is easy for them to claim the "exigent" or "emergency" circumstances that allow them to enter homes against the will of the inhabitants. This means that for families undergoing child abuse investigations, Fourth Amendment protections against unlawful search and seizure are all too often and all too easily suspended. Many states also suspend the Fifth Amendment's guarantees against self-incrimination and the Sixth Amendment's right to counsel once an investigation is officially underway. Child welfare investigators, further, are not required to read the Miranda warning to accused parents, nor to permit them access to all information and reports kept on them by child welfare agencies.[34]

In an article that appeared in *Reason* in February 1994, Hannah Lapp recounts this among several incredible episodes: In 1989, the Millers, a Phoenix couple, were falsely accused of sexual abuse by an emotionally disturbed child in their neighborhood.

> The Millers were promised that if they brought their three children, ages 7, 10, 12, to county offices to be interviewed, they would not be taken away. The promise was broken as soon as the family arrived at the office. Pelvic examinations, which turned up no evidence of sexual abuse, were immediately performed on the children without the consent or presence of anyone they knew. The three children were separated from each other and their parents for six months, the amount of time it took the family court to recognize that their home was not abusive after all. During this period, the children endured "therapy" sessions that turned into grueling, high-pressure interrogations.

Lapp quotes from a videotaped session in which a CPS-appointed therapist, Tascha Boychuck, interrogated the Millers' seven-year-old son.

> BOYCHUCK: I heard something happened to your butt or your dick.
> RANDY: Pff (hyperventilating, says he is thirsty).
> BOYCHUCK: OK, and I need to understand what that was.
> RANDY: Pff. I don't know.
> BOYCHUCK: Why don't you tell me who it was that did something to one of those two parts?
> RANDY: Michael gave me a bloody nose. (Describes fight with friend.)

"A dozen or more times," Lapp tells us, "Boychuck refers to Randy's private parts, displays anatomically correct dolls, and asks what happened. She continues until Randy starts crying, then continues until he throws his head back and howls, 'I don't want to talk to you anymore!' Still she persists, forcing eye contact: 'I can see you sit there and you're going—

like you're so upset. And I can tell that you're trying to keep things in-side.' She withholds Kleenex and a drink through dozens more ques-tions, until at one point she gets a barely perceptible nod from the child.

"Boychuck: 'OK, and did he put his mouth on your dick?' "[35]

The Millers were lucky. They were not only guiltless, but well re-spected in their community and thus able to draw some media attention to their case. The family emerged from the trauma unscathed. But that hardly diminishes the seriousness of the assault they suffered at the hands of the state.

If the bureaucratic procedures of CPS evince no regard for individ-ual rights and constitutionality, neither do the legal procedures of the courts that try child maltreatment cases. The national organization VOCAL (Victims of Child Abuse Laws) refers people accused of child maltreatment for legal help and has launched a public information cam-paign warning Americans of the pitfalls of family court, where proce-dures are shrouded in secrecy and the standards for bringing evidence and making convictions are far more lax than in the criminal court sys-tem. In family court, a VOCAL pamphlet warns, hearsay evidence is ad-mitted, defense attorneys can be denied access to investigative records, and the standards for conviction is a "fair preponderance of evidence," rather than the criminal court's "beyond a reasonable doubt."[36]

Robert L. Emans, dean of the School of Education at the University of South Dakota, Vermillion, warned in a *Phi Beta Kappan* article of June 1987 that all the procedures of family court conspire to deny fair trials to families falsely accused of child abuse. "Going to court has many risks," Emans writes. "Attorneys and judges assume that the ac-cused is guilty much more frequently in cases involving child abuse than in other kinds of criminal cases, including those involving murder. Since getting a fair trial is very difficult, individuals falsely accused of child abuse are often advised to plead guilty and to accept counseling or other remediation."[37]

Besides its affront to the very notion of democratic due process rights, child welfare intervention also undermines other fundamental democratic freedoms. Neil Gilbert, a social welfare professor at the Uni-versity of California, Berkeley, sees child welfare agencies as a threat to American cultural pluralism. Parents of different religious, ethnic, and racial backgrounds, says Gilbert, raise their children in distinctly differ-ent ways. Yet judges and caseworkers seem not to appreciate these dis-tinctions. In illustration of this, Gilbert and his associate Helen Noh Ahn point to several recent cases in California where Asians have been charged with child abuse and ordered to undergo therapy for fondling the genitals of young male children. In many Asian (as well as Middle

Eastern) cultures, this is not an aberrant sexual act but a common gesture of affection and pride in a male heir.[38]

Gilbert and Ahn's work interviewing parents of different ethnic and racial groups on the subject of "acceptable and unacceptable norms of intimacy" suggests that the child welfare system—in its concern to protect children's "rights" to autonomy and privacy—may be inappropriately imposing uniform standards of family interaction on a population of diverse origins and cultures.[39] They cite CPS's promotion of sexual abuse prevention programs in schools as an area in which zealous "public authorities" should be more careful not to impose their own cultural preconceptions about propriety. Immigrants, they note, tend to conform to most American child-rearing standards after one or two generations. But forcing "prescriptions for family relations . . . [that] contradict values and traditions held by many different cultural groups," they warn, threatens to tip the precarious balance between "the collective obligation to protect children and the wish to respect diversity in family life." [40]

The doubtful practice of prescribing psychotherapy as a means of acculturating immigrants to American child-rearing customs may be widespread. At the Youth Shelter in Greenwich, Connecticut—one facility of many around the country that offer temporary housing and counseling to children and teenagers with conflicts at home—director Shari Shapiro concedes she has prescribed therapy to Haitian and Albanian immigrant parents who, fearful of the temptations of drugs and sex, restrict their teenagers' social lives. She admits however, that the results of her efforts have not been happy. Many immigrant parents her organization counsels, she says, have resented the intrusion. Some, she notes, have sent their kids back to the old country.[41]

■ ■ ■

Critiques of the child welfare bureaucracy have nowhere been more justifiably launched than on its treatment of the more than half a million children each year it keeps in the ostensible "protective" custody of foster care—a system that, more than any other mechanism of Child Protective Services, defies our most basic notions of human rights. What foster care has meant for most children held in the snare of the system is an endless series of hurried, capricious, short-term, and often dangerous placements. Investigations of foster care conditions all over the country have turned up kids tethered to hospital beds, housed in jails, made to carry their belongings in trash bags while living for weeks on end in social workers' offices. Foster care charges have been ensconced with hardened juvenile delinquents in correctional institutions, pumped with psychotropic drugs in mental hospitals, warehoused in drug-infested group shelters. They have been beaten, raped, starved, and even murdered in group care and "family" foster homes.[42] The ACLU Children's Project contends that children removed to foster care are ten times more likely to be maltreated while in the custody of the state than in their own homes.[43] An NYU School of Social Work research project study conducted in Baltimore revealed that 28 percent of the children in the system had been abused while in foster care.[44]

Poor children suffer the impositions of child welfare and foster care most acutely. Families on public assistance are four times more likely than others to be investigated for child maltreatment, and these families are also disproportionately victims of the system's most radical remediative decision: child removals. In his 1991 assessment of foster care entitled "How Child Abuse Programs Hurt Poor Children," Douglas Besharov declares that the child welfare system has become inappropriately involved in the surveillance of families on public assistance, because of the dearth of alternate family services for poor families with household management problems.

Up until two decades ago, Besharov observes, each AFDC (Aid to Families with Dependent Children) recipient family had its own caseworker, who delivered not only cash benefits but whatever social services he or she felt that family needed in the area of practical household and child-rearing help. When AFDC benefits were separated from family services in the mid-1970s, however, these rather benevolent caseworkers disappeared. At the same time, the tide of concern about child abuse and neglect was rising, and the child welfare bureaucracy was expanding. The result was that by the late 1970s and early 1980s many AFDC caseloads suddenly came into the hands of the child protective system. The consequences, says Besharov, were catastrophic for the poor and especially for the homeless, who were suddenly faced with a powerful social service bureaucracy that policed rather than helped them, and that viewed the child, not the family, as its client.[45]

In California, for example, during the 1970s and early 1980s Child Protective Services routinely removed homeless children to foster care when their parents requested emergency shelter. The practice ended only with a 1986 court injunction.[46] A 1988 New Jersey investigation revealed that one out of every four children placed in Newark's foster care system were there only because their families were homeless.[47] Similarly, in a 1989 study of New York "boarder babies" (newborns who were detained in the hospital by Child Protective Services after their mothers were released), homelessness, not crack, was most often the reason for prolonged hospitalization.[48] Critics of the child welfare system have cited evidence that caseworkers in some jurisdictions have not only removed children summarily from parents for lack of housing, but strong-armed impoverished and homeless parents into "voluntarily" signing their children away to temporary foster care by threatening to remove them permanently.[49]

The separation of the child protective and welfare systems, and the expansion of the former at the cost of the latter, has led to an ironic situation in which "foster families who care for . . . children removed from their homes for neglect . . . receive almost twice the amount to care for this child as AFDC allots the parents." The San Diego County grand jury's in-depth investigative report of child protective services, *Families in Crisis*, notes, "In many cases the difference would have enabled the family to provide proper care for the child without incurring the additional societal and monetary costs of the current system."[50]

While child welfare agencies cannot be held responsible for the lack of practical family services for the poor, they have demonstrated a stubborn predilection for confusing symptoms of material want with parental "neglect," and making drastic, destructive decisions on the basis of these faulty judgments. Douglas Besharov comments, "Sometimes consciously, but usually unconsciously the system concludes that . . . [when] parents are unable to maintain the household, they can hardly be expected to meet the child's social needs. This conclusion may or may not be valid."[51]

In April 1988, a child wrongly consigned to foster care because his mother had no housing addressed the House of Representatives Subcommittee on Public Assistance and Unemployment Compensation, eloquently describing the cruelty that results. "It's hard for me to tell you how bad foster care is," said Boyd A. "My mother used to come visit me a lot when I was in care, and when she left, it felt like the whole world was leaving me."[52]

Richard Wexler, author of perhaps the most comprehensive and detailed critique of Child Protective Services to date—*Wounded Innocents: The Real Victims of the War Against Child Abuse*—notes that simple manifestations of poverty (a rat-infested house, an empty refrigerator, an elementary school child left at home without a baby-sitter in the afternoons while her mother works) are all too often confused with child neglect. This is partly because caseworkers are forced to make determinations of maltreatment by consulting agency checklists notorious for measuring child well-being in material rather than emotional terms. A family can still be an emotionally viable unit even when its members are starving, their clothes in tatters, their apartment puny and an offense to the very notion of hygiene. But the child protective agency checklists seem to emphasize possession of material comforts—whether a child has an adequate number of playthings, whether the bathroom faucets leak, whether he or she eats at least one balanced meal a day[53]—over feelings of affection or security that may be impossible to quantify.

James Norman is a good example of the havoc wrought by checklist determinations of child neglect. A Chicago widower, Norman was struck with heart disease at the age of thirty-seven, and couldn't keep up with his bills. In the summer of 1988, a child protection caseworker came to investigate his home. She noted that his children looked happy and healthy, but that the surroundings were untidy, the electricity had been turned off, and food was spoiling in the refrigerator. After dutifully working out the arithmetic on her "at risk" checklist, she resolved to remove James's children immediately to foster care—wrongly, it turned out, not only because James was a conscientious and loving father, but because she had made a mistake in her addition. Norman rode three buses and walked another mile to visit his children in foster care for one year. By the end of that year, he had at least succeeded in finding financial help and in securing a court hearing for the return of his children. But twelve days before that hearing he died of heart failure.[54]

The wrongful use of foster care to solve "what is, in essence, a poverty problem," poses serious dangers to child well-being all the way around.[55] First, it is emotionally devastating for both the children and the parents involved. Second, it deflects the limited resources of the system from an increasing number of children at real risk of danger. Third, it ensnares the poor in a vicious cycle of bureaucratic victimization that undermines rather than fosters the goal of helping them overcome their circumstances. As the National Coalition for Child Protection Reform, a group of lawyers and academics interested in redressing the ills of the child welfare system, puts it, "If a single mother leaves a child alone after school so she can work to stay off welfare, we can continue to take the child saver approach: Throw the child in foster care and send the mother to 'parent education' classes. Or we can provide a space in an after-school program for the child."[56]

We are bound to pay dearly in human misery and social disaffection for the bizarre glitches in the welfare and child protective system that prevent us from providing poor families the simple practical help and services they really need. As Douglas Besharov observes,

> Through some sort of tunnel vision, the system perceives the physical improvement of . . . living conditions while in foster care as proof that the child is better off away from his or her parents. . . . The child's absence from the home is said to provide immediate relief for parents so that . . . they can concentrate on re-ordering their lives. This argument is as therapeutically short-sighted as it

is harmful to children. . . . For the parents, removing the child is . . .
a psychologically jarring experience that often damages their self-
esteem and reduces their bond of affection and dedication to the
child. . . . [For children] this ignores the often devastating effects
of long term foster care limbo on the child's emotional well being.[57]

Several students of the child protection system believe that its thirty
years of ravaging poor urban families have, in fact, created a great deal
of the social desperation that pervades our inner cities. Large numbers
of the homeless, drug-addicted, mad, socially disaffected, and criminally
disposed people who haunt our urban streets, they claim, have been victims at one time or another of the foster care system—ripped from their
homes and subjected over a period of several years to multiple placements that have rendered them emotionally decimated and socially crip-
pled. They charge further that it is no accident that parental competence
and apathy becomes an ever-greater problem among welfare recipients.
This social group is most likely to have suffered disruptions of family life
by child welfare intrusions.[58] Perhaps a quote from a convicted rapist
brought in manacles to family court on behalf of his two sons says it
best: "I don't want them to be shipped from home to home like I was. . . .
They're gonna be put in the same system that ruined my life."[59]

In trying to make sense of the apparent predilection of Child Protective Services to prey on the poor and weak, psychologist Seth Farber,
author of a critique of child welfare practices published in the National
Review, characterizes the child protection system as a "monstrous social
parasite," that seeks to "perpetuate its own existence by continually expanding its clientele beyond its capacity to service them." Its major aim,
he says, is to build little empires of caseworker, counselor and foster care
networks, in order "to capture vulnerable individuals, transform them
into . . . clients, foist . . . 'services' upon them, undermine their autonomy and ultimately incorporate them into its own parasitic body."[60]

Among several examples Farber draws on is the Kafkaesque experience of New Yorker Mary Jackson, a forty-year-old black school-crossing
guard. Jackson had custody of her daughter's three children until she
checked one of them into the hospital for treatment of pneumonia. The
Child Welfare Administration was called, and all three of the children
were taken away on grounds of medical neglect. Jackson tried to battle
the charges. When she appeared in family court, she brought with her
copies of medical exam reports and vaccinations dating back to each
child's birth. So obvious was her innocence of the charges that the court-
appointed psychologist recommended the children be returned to her
immediately. But the CWA had different ideas. It promised to return the

children in six months, but only if Mrs. Jackson agreed to plead guilty to neglect, despite the mass of evidence to the contrary. Even after six months, the CWA refused to let the children come home. Rather, the office insisted Mrs. Jackson undergo a psychological examination to determine her "fitness" to raise them. Probably because the psychiatrist was black, Farber tells us, Jackson confided to him her acute grief and frustration at the loss of her beloved grandchildren. The reward for her confidence? The psychiatrist's report recommended the children not be returned, and that Mrs. Jackson be immediately assigned to therapy. "Mrs. Jackson," he wrote, is currently depressed, in a rage . . . and feels everything has been taken away." This state of mind he traced not to the woman's obvious heartbreak, but to a "personality disorder."[61]

What motives do mental health professionals and child welfare agencies have when they indulge themselves in such bizarre and inhuman machinations? Profit, in part. Every substantiated case of child abuse or neglect carries the potential to unleash masses of federal, state, and private funds, not only for the child welfare bureaucracy, but for the private services it commissions—from mental health professionals to foster caregivers. Child welfare agencies are often able to cash in twice for both foster care and therapy—by billing both the taxpayers (via the use of public funds) and the accused families who can afford it. Thus, CPS does not confine its social service hawking to poor neighborhoods. Administrators, caseworkers, foster care agencies, and mental health professionals all have a natural interest in the substantiation of child maltreatment among the well-to-do, too. All benefit from "remediative" action, and from keeping many remediative services going for as long as possible. Promotions within child protection agencies, as in most bureaucracies, often depend on an administrator's zealousness in keeping large numbers of cases going and cultivating large referral networks.

To fully appreciate how much profit can be made from just one child abuse case, let's reexamine the case of James Wade, suspected of raping his daughter, Alicia. The cost James Wade bore for court-ordered "therapy" alone was $260,000, all paid, mercifully, by his Navy medical plan, the Civilian Health and Medical Program of the Uniformed Services.[62]

But before we breathe financial relief for the Wades, we must consider that besides the enormous legal fees they paid for his defense ($125,000), they were also billed—as are all middle-class parents whose children are removed as a result of maltreatment charges—for foster care charges. Although California's county-based CPS agencies call the bills for foster care they send parents "reimbursement," they are not really reimbursements at all. The state of California pays its county child protection agencies 95 to 97 percent of foster care charges, none of which it expects to see returned. When parents are billed for foster care reimbursements, child protective agencies put that money in their county's general fund. So the more kids end up in foster care, the greater the source of revenue for the county seat.[63]

Because of Alicia's age and amenable personality, we can only assume that the Wade family got off cheaply, foster care for Alicia probably running them the California standard fee of $484 each month.[64] If a child is troublesome or over twelve years of age, the price of foster care normally increases. Indeed, if Alicia had been older, or put in a group home or orphanage, it might have cost Wade between $1,500 and $3,000 a month to "reimburse" the county for her keep.[65] According to an ACLU study, the average cost of foster care per child is $17,500 per year.[66]

While all the "services" that the child welfare system forces on its clientele are a financial boon to those who proffer them, foster care is by far the most profitable. Federal funding for foster care (now supporting a third of its total cost) is uncapped, while funding for other remediative services, including counseling and adoption, are capped.[67] In many localities, child welfare agencies are even reimbursed for foster care on a per diem basis—a practice that has resulted in adoptable children being allowed to languish in foster care for years, in some cases the entire duration of their minority.[68] As Wexler notes, "If the agency goes through the equally difficult process of terminating parental rights and placing a child in an adoptive home, it gets a one time flat fee. The easiest course of action—warehousing children in foster care—is also the more remunerative."[69]

Conna Craig, of the Boston-based Institute for Children, echoes Wexler in her concern that foster care has been the unhappy fate of hundreds of thousands of eminently adoptable children in dire need of permanent homes. The foster care funding system, she writes, "gives child welfare bureaucracies incentives to keep even free-to-be-adopted kids in state care. State social service agencies are neither rewarded for helping children find adoptive homes nor penalized for failing to do so in a reasonable amount of time. There is no financial incentive to recruit adoptive families. And as more children enter the system, so does the tax money to support them in substitute care." Nationally, Craig says, the number of public agency–sponsored adoptions each year is shockingly low. Only 20,000 of the 119,000 adoptions in 1992, for example, were sponsored by public agencies. In her own state of Massachusetts, she says, child welfare agencies are known to defer requests for termination of parental rights until children reach the age of seven. Why? At that age children are deemed to have special needs, and child welfare agencies can request more funds from the federal government for their care. Older children are also less attractive to adoptive parents; thus, there is a greater chance that a child will remain in the foster care system permanently, capturing dollar after federal dollar.[70] In 1990, foster care cost the nation about $5 billion of the $7.2 billion spent on child welfare in toto. By 1993, that number had risen to $10 billion.[71] Were these impressive funds able to buy good surrogate families for children who need them, Craig argues, in a 1995 article on foster care for *Policy Review,* that money would be well spent. But unfortunately the system all too often recruits parent surrogates whose qualifications would not pass the test of private adoption agencies, and whose interest in foster children is limited solely to the income they bring from the state.[72]

The Topsy-like growth of the child welfare system is not merely the product of the self-interest and cynicism of those bureaucrats, social service professionals, and foster parents who soak it financially for all its worth. Even purged of corruption, the system would be too unwieldy to function in the public interest. Indeed, the work of most child protection bureaucrats is diminished not by bad faith but by a system bound by broad legal and financial parameters to be inefficient, and to invite confusion and mismanagement at all levels.

A quick look at the decline in standards by which caseworkers are hired shows how drastically mandatory reporting laws have fostered incompetence in the field of child welfare. In the late 1950s, when child maltreatment reports numbered around 150,000 a year, nearly half the caseworkers at public child welfare agencies had master's degrees in social work. By 1990 that figure was down to 9 percent, and only twelve states required as much as a bachelor's degree in social work. Salaries for caseworkers, always modest, have correspondingly declined over the years in real dollars.[73]

Worse, as the educational profile of caseworkers entering the system has declined, states have failed to make up the difference with training. Richard Wexler cites a 1981 study of Wisconsin's child welfare agencies which revealed that "23 percent had received no training in the state's Child Abuse and Neglect Act, 32 percent had no training in conducting investigations, and 39 percent learned no counseling techniques." As of 1990, he says, Michigan offered fifteen days of classroom instruction to entering caseworkers, but did not make this course mandatory. New York offered nothing more than a twenty-day Child Protective Services Academy training course. In Maryland, Wexler noted, "caseworkers might be on the job as long as six months before they received any training." And in California, a significant portion of caseworkers had no professional training whatsoever.[74]

Along with lack of training and low salaries comes low morale, and child welfare agencies everywhere report huge turnovers in caseworkers. Hardly a wonder, then, that along with the waste of time and energy in pursuing false and marginal reports of child abuse, the pervasive lack of competence among child welfare workers has put the very children who need the most urgent help at greater risk.

Indeed, truly abused children are more vulnerable than they ever were. Already in 1984, when child abuse reports stood at half the number they have reached today, Douglas Besharov warned in a *Wall Street Journal* feature, "25 percent of all child fatalities attributed to abuse or neglect involve children already reported to a child-protective agency." By "flooding the system with inappropriate cases," he continued, child abuse laws "made it less likely that children in real danger will receive the protection they so desperately need."[75] A 1991 National Committee for Prevention of Child Abuse study on maltreatment fatalities intimated an even clearer and more disturbing link between capricious reports and the child protective system's failure to effectively handle serious cases of abuse and neglect. Thirty-nine percent of the children who died of abuse or neglect in the two preceding years were known to child welfare agencies before their deaths. By 1993, that figure was up to 42 percent.[76]

The increasing failure of child welfare agencies to minister to the children who need them most prompts us to consider what measures can be taken to make them more responsive in emergencies. Simply raising caseworker hiring standards will probably not do it. Nor will even significant changes in the laws that have encouraged capricious reporting and child maltreatment convictions. Nor even will the most concentrated efforts to purge Child Protective Services of its nasty habits of patronage and corruption. Such reforms might give some relief for the surging numbers of innocents now persecuted by child welfare agencies, but children who are seriously abused or neglected will need something more.

In its current form, the child welfare system's remediative approaches to maltreatment are inadequate to handle problems of bona fide parental cruelty or incapacity. Curiously, the most culpable parents seem to be able to manipulate the system—usually buying time by plea bargaining and accepting the system's counseling services and parent education programs. It is just these services, however, that may constitute the most serious flaw in the system's notions of how to treat the problem of serious child maltreatment.

Indeed, the weakest link in child protective agencies' approach to abusive and neglectful parents seems to be the widespread belief that crimes against children can be curtailed through counseling efforts. Especially in recent years, growing distrust of CPS and criticism of foster care expansion have encouraged agencies to embark on "family preservation" policies that turn on therapeutic help for people who have assaulted, starved, and otherwise tortured their children—not to mention those who have recidivist drug habits. There is no proof, however, that counseling has any remediative effect on such people. Psychiatrist Richard Gelles, for example, insists that the child welfare system's psychological interventions are set up wrongly to cure "symptoms [of mental illness] that do not exist."[77] Conna Craig puts it this way: "In our social-work schools, counseling centers and government-funded research, the culture of victimization insists that the most despicable behavior by abusive parents has its causes in economics, racism, broken homes—anything but the consciences and moral choices of men and women."[78] And investigative journalist Rita Kramer has charged that recently some urban child welfare administrations (responding to criticism for destroying families) have implemented so-called family preservation policies that return children in foster care to criminal parents. These, she says, may have completed their prescribed drug rehabilitation programs and parenting courses, but all too many have in no sense been rehabilitated from their noxious substance- and/or child-abusing habits.[79]

In clear cases of serious parental incapacity or cruelty, a quick termination of parental rights and placement in a permanent home may be far more appropriate measures than counseling and foster care placement. The 1996 reauthorization of CAPTA thankfully includes a provision that allows states to refuse to reunite children with criminally abusive parents. (There are at present more than a million families who want to adopt children, according to Mary Beth Seader Stiles, of the National Council for Adoption. A large proportion of these families, she said at a 1996 Leadership Conference of the Center for Jewish and Christian Values, would be willing to parent older, special needs, or minority children.) Moreover, research on the relationship between poverty and child maltreatment clearly suggests that in ameliorating many milder cases of child abuse and neglect, it would be more effective to address the material needs of families and their want of communal supports than to provide psychotherapy.

Actually, it is ironic that so many remediative programs sponsored by CPS focus on psychotherapy, since there is some evidence that parents who maltreat their children in fact lack the mental capacities of flexibility, consistency, understanding, and organization that make for good therapy patients. In a word, they lack intelligence. In their book, *The Bell Curve*, Richard J. Herrnstein and Charles Murray point to studies which find that intelligence is a key to healthy child-rearing instincts, and that child maltreatment is predominantly found among people of low intelligence. Where intelligence is missing, they suggest, a secure social order that supports family and communal ties, strong moral values, and economically productive lives may be the ultimate answer to helping men and women be better parents.[80]

It is just such a secure and supportive social order, however, that is increasingly lacking in neighborhoods across our nation. The 50 percent surge in maltreatment deaths between 1985 and 1991 alone indicates undeniably that over the past three decades parental capacity has become an increasingly serious problem, and that child maltreatment—while hardly a pervasive social phenomenon—is also increasing.[81] What is responsible for this? In his book *Fatherless America*, David Blankenhorn successfully traces certain increased manifestations of abuse to family breakdown and the destabilization of domestic lives and community ties that has come with it. Citing both studies of domestic violence against pregnant women and studies of sexual abuse against young female children, he contends that as the number of unrelated males passing through female-headed households increases, so does the risk of domestic violence and of physical and sexual child abuse.[82]

Child abuse—overwhelmingly a problem of the poor and socially disaffected—may be largely taken as a mirror of social disorder and the attending feelings of isolation and breakdown of controls within individuals who are the most radically disaffected. A look at the most successful redemptive programs for families under investigation for child abuse and neglect suggests that this is so. Programs that consciously set out to reorder domestic lives by providing practical help, low-skill job training, values education, and moral and social support (such as membership in community and religious organizations) actually do get many parents—especially the poorest of the poor—back on track by giving them a stronger sense of security, belonging, and self-esteem.[83]

One such program is Homebuilders, an intensive six-week crisis-intervention program designed for families whose children would normally be candidates for foster care. Caseworkers are assigned no more than two families at a time, to whom they dedicate several hours a day, and are available around-the-clock. They offer not only on-the-spot advice and parent education, but emergency financial aid, job training, child care referrals, and even help with simple household tasks. The key to Homebuilders is the willingness of the caseworker to respond to the immediate worries and problems of the families with whom he or she is working (rather than focusing on personal history), and to help them in the day-to-day business of living. Homebuilders' parent training does not indulge in theoretical abstractions or psychoanalytic exploration, but rather offers hands-on solutions within the domestic environment. The National Coalition for Child Protection Reform reports that in Michigan, where the Homebuilders prototype provides a focal point of CPS's "family preservation" policy, a 1993 study found that the average cost of the program per child was $4,059—as compared with $13,021 for foster care. More important, this intervention program was found to be safer for children than foster care; children whose families had been through it were two times less likely to be in foster care one year later than children in families where parents had received more traditional forms of CPS services.

Family preservation programs designed along the Homebuilders prototype have sprung up in different areas around the country. But so far they constitute only rare if happy exceptions. It does not seem likely in the near future that such programs will be allowed to transform a child protective system that rests on such different ideological assumptions about family life. Homebuilders rests on the premise that families are innately healthy child-rearing institutions, that virtually all parents and children, however troubled, share indissoluble bonds of love, and that the majority of family crises can be overcome with simple, practical, short-term interventions. If one can take the frequency of CPS recommendations of foster care and counseling as an indication of their beliefs, it appears that most CPS bureaucrats hold little hope for families in crisis—except, perhaps, long-range psychotherapeutic intervention and surveillance. The real source of the child welfare scandal in our nation, in fact, may be the widespread acceptance in child welfare circles of theories that label families in general as pathogenic and prone to violence and abuse. Their refusal to heed evidence identifying particular family structures, situations, and dynamics that invite such violence and abuse may be a major impediment to ameliorating the problem of child maltreatment and to getting children out of threatening homes.

Parents seem to sense instinctively that child abuse is not as widespread as the media makes it appear, and that traditional American family life is not a cauldron of violence. Most of the parents I've talked to have insisted that child abuse has not much increased in recent years, but that the *definition* of child abuse has changed, and in ways that would brand their own parents' well-meaning disciplinary methods as abusive. But somehow, this view of child maltreatment is not reaching our lawmakers. Indeed, advocates for child welfare reform—especially at the state level—have had a hard time getting legislators to respond to their calls for reconstructing the system. Repeatedly they have proposed to tighten definitions of abuse and neglect, to reform mandatory reporting laws, to restore liability for bogus reporting, to curb financial incentives for foster care, to eliminate unnecessary and expensive counseling programs, and to replace them with short-term, in-home practical help for families. But politicians fearful of being thought insensitive to teeming masses of suffering children have, with only a few exceptions, turned a deaf ear.

Reforming the child welfare system may, in fact, involve first and foremost waging a battle for the minds and hearts of a powerful elite— among therapists, government officials, and the media—sold on a theory of family life that sees only pathology in intimacy. To witness the profusion of best-selling literature on family "dysfunction" and "recovered memories," the proliferation in every community of Family Crisis or Recovery Centers and co-dependency support groups, the abundance of TV news segments and talk shows centering on the theme of child abuse, and the copious photographic images of the tearful, battered child is to understand how powerful and ingrained is the distrust of that elite in the capability of parents to raise children without ruining them. Indeed, as lon as that elite continues to play chorus to a family drama of anger, violence, and therapeutic redemption, no family in America will be safe. Consider this: Every fifteen seconds, an American family is falsely accused of child maltreatment. Yours could be next.

3

Undomesticated Law

O*ne of* the questions I've asked parents as I've traveled around the country is, "How can children's lives be improved?" While I expected to hear about educational reform, safer streets, and better community supports for families, I often got a response I never expected. As a Baltimore parent commented during a focus group: "Shoot the judges and lawyers!" To which another parent responded, "Shoot the lawyers first, and then if the judges don't get the message, shoot them."

This refrain was uttered almost word for word in several cities I visited, as if parents had gotten together and rehearsed it before talking to me. Of course they were joking. But behind their joke lay palpable bitterness and fear. What, I wondered, could parents have against the legal system that prompted such a viscerally hostile reaction?

Parents perceive a disturbing trend in the law that has taken place over the past two generations. Increasingly, parents charge, the courts allow criminals to run the streets. They assert the rights of delinquents to remain in school, terrorizing their peers. They have censured religious expression in the public arena, contributing to a decay of values in schools and public life. Most important, parents say, they impede parental autonomy and authority, and then hold parents responsible for the consequences.

It is difficult not to sympathize with parents on all these counts. The last resounds particularly. Over the past generation, our legal system has steadily assailed many long-accepted parental prerogatives in the raising of children. Parents have lost considerable leeway in matters of discipline and control, and children have been granted increasing freedom to make autonomous decisions in matters of manners and morals. Today, a child who resents what attempts his parents make to control him can threaten to report them to child welfare, and after that—as we have seen—often anything can happen. A teenager can go over her parents' heads to obtain contraceptives or abortions; or if he engages in substance abuse, he can decide whether or not to put himself into treatment. A Texas father observes, "Nowadays the children have all the rights and the parents don't have any. The system is all screwed up." Or, as Hunter Hurst, of the National Center for Juvenile Justice, puts it, "We've been focusing on enfranchising youth. . . . What is a parent's real authority over a child?"[1]

One would think that the trend in lawmaking would be to decrease parents' responsibility for children's conduct in proportion to their decrease in authority. But there is a strong legal movement abroad to increase parental liability for children's misdeeds. Many states have recently toughened laws that require parents to provide restitution for property damage inflicted by their children. In the face of rising juvenile crime, there is even a trend to prosecute parents for children's crimes. In what one newspaper describes as a "general crackdown on serious juvenile crime,"[2] several states are fining parents or hauling them into jail when their children break the law. Parents have been made to pay anywhere from $100 to $25,000 for children's offenses ranging from truancy to assault with a deadly weapon. They have also been required to attend parenting classes, assigned community service work, and charged for their children's court and detention costs.

A California statute requiring parents to "exercise reasonable care, supervision, protection, and control" has been used to send parents whose children are delinquent to parent-training courses.[3] In Louisiana, if a child joins a gang, his parents can be punished. In Oklahoma, a parent whose child carries a gun to school is liable for a fine or community service.[4] In Virginia, parents whose children scrawl graffiti can be penalized up to $2,500; in West Virginia, up to $5,000. In Silverton, Oregon, and Flint, Michigan, police have cited parents whose children violated curfews and other municipal code statutes, fining them or ordering them into counseling. The Silverton law has been emulated by the Oregon state legislature and has received so much publicity it is likely to be emulated elsewhere. According to that law, if a child under fifteen breaks the juvenile code, is truant, or violates a local curfew, parents can be cited for "failure to supervise." The penalty: parenting classes or a $1,000 fine.[5]

These new edicts have been hailed by juvenile judges as the wave of the future in getting a handle on youth crime. A judge in Moncks Corner, South Carolina, provided an almost metaphorical commentary on their ostensible purpose when he ordered a child who had been charged with shoplifting, truancy, and burglary "tethered" to her mother.[6] Yet, there are no statistical indications that such laws are actually working to curb juvenile crime anywhere but in a few rural communities where they probably reaffirm a more general societal message about the importance of close parental supervision in child upbringing.[7] While the community of Silverton, Oregon (population 6,200), records a decrease in crime, in cities like Los Angeles, juvenile offenses continue to skyrocket.

A Baltimore father and police sergeant reflects on how the legal system puts a catch-22 on parents. Overzealous child protection laws, he says, have severely impeded the ability of parents to back up household rules and injunctions with meaningful punishments. Yet the state still requires parents to control children's behavior: "An officer assigned under me was arrested because his daughter made a police report when he . . . smacked her. . . . [She was] doing something she wasn't supposed to be doing. Now his job is on the line. . . . If a child goes out and does something wrong, you're responsible . . . and yet if you try to correct that child, you're also liable." James Fox, a dean at Northeastern University's School of Criminal Justice, notes that it might be more justified to "hold the peer group responsible" for adolescent crime. "They are certainly having more influence."[8]

A boy whose mother was put in jail when he broke a Roanoke, Virginia, curfew law remarked sadly, "I just left. It's not her fault. She shouldn't be held responsible. I know right from wrong."[9] And there are few more poignant indications of parents' powerlessness than the growing numbers of mothers and fathers who are enlisting the legal system to help them get children to toe the line, contacting juvenile court even before a child has committed a crime, or simply reporting seriously delinquent children to the police.[10] Some parents have shown themselves willing to put aside their own rights to due process in the interest of curbing kids they are afraid to confront. Many parents in St. Louis, San Diego, and Pasadena have consented to spontaneous door-to-door police searches in the hope that guns cached in their children's rooms will be confiscated. (In 1994, the St. Louis program alone resulted in the seizure of four thousand guns.)[11]

Juvenile judges even report that many parents openly express relief when wayward kids are summoned to court. Joseph H. Paquin, of the Superior Court of Juvenile Matters in Stamford, Connecticut, says parents have confided they are counting on him to impose the kind of authority over their children that they have been powerless to impose. "They expect us," he observes, "to put the fear of God in their child." But, Paquin warns, "What a parent expects us to do and what we can do are very, very different." [12]

Indeed, parents who might have high hopes of the juvenile justice system in setting kids right are bound to be disappointed. In many states juvenile courts afford delinquents—in the words of one investigative reporter—all the "procedural safeguards of adults . . . without the serious sanctions that make those safeguards necessary."[13] Many courts are disposed to ordering therapy and counseling for misbehaving children rather than punishment.[14] Petty crimes are often dismissed, encouraging children to engage in more serious criminal activity. And even hardened juvenile criminals seldom get their due. (In New York, for example, child perpetrators of the most violent crimes can be sent to detention facilities for a maximum sentence of eighteen months, after which time they are generally returned to the care of parents or guardians, many of whom have long since given up any effort to control them.)[15]

Hardly a wonder, then, that parents like Audrey Burnes, the single mother of a sixteen-year-old boy arrested in Stamford, Connecticut's, Southfield Village housing project for selling narcotics, have given up on the legal system. Burnes insists that the juvenile system has been much too lenient with her son, who has long since refused to follow any rules she sets for him. She would like support in getting him straightened out, she says, but the authorities refuse to monitor him properly. They even told him that they would permit him a certain number of drug-positive urine tests. "I don't know what he does when he goes out of this house," she laments, adding, "Everybody's been fair to him—he just has to want to do right."[16] Lydia Velez has also come up against a brick wall with the juvenile authorities. Her daughter, sixteen and a ninth-grader in Norwalk, Connecticut, has been chronically truant. Velez wants the girl to stay in school, but according to Connecticut's compulsory schooling law, she is entitled to quit school at sixteen. "She's 16 and doesn't know how to read," notes Velez, who expected the judge to support her by ordering the girl to stay in school. "The system has got to be changed," she says. "We the parents are losing children day by day."[17]

■ ■ ■

Curiously, while the courts often make it impossible for parents to get control over wayward children, they also display a propensity to order parents around in cases where children are clearly under adequate care and control—especially when families face the court on allegations of child abuse or neglect.

Consider the experience of Betty and Phillip Jordan, two working parents from Prince William County, Virginia. One Friday evening, the Jordans returned home to find that their ten-year-old son, Chris, had disappeared. A curt note taped to their front door ordered them to appear in court the following Monday. Apparently, a neighbor had noticed that Chris was frequently home alone in the afternoons, and called the local child abuse hotline. By the time a social worker got around to checking out the situation, it was late Friday afternoon. In a hurry to get off work for the weekend, she made no inquiries about the child's well-being. She simply chased him through his house into his backyard and hauled him away to a foster home, where he was held incommunicado for seventy-two hours.[18]

The Jordans had in fact taken sensible precautions in leaving Chris home alone. His mother came home often to be with him on her 3:00 P.M. "lunch hour," and both parents had made sure the boy, whom they considered mature and responsible, took a special course in safety for latchkey children. Nothing Chris or his parents had done was irresponsible, let alone illegal. Yet a juvenile court judge convicted the Jordans of "child neglect" and released Chris from foster care only when they had arranged an afternoon baby-sitter for him. The Jordans' request for retrial was summarily denied, so that their names were entered permanently into Virginia's child abuse registry.

What right, one must ask, had the juvenile court judge to pronounce the well-considered decisions of Chris Jordan's parents "neglectful," inasmuch as they were totally within the bounds of the law? American judges, says Mary Ann Mason, author of *From Father's Property to Children's Rights: The History of Child Custody in the United States*, have always enjoyed considerable discretion to "interpret English common law rules and their own state's legislative mandates," when deciding cases of child neglect and abuse.[19] But increasingly they are ignoring the law entirely. The recent emergence of a class of social service bureaucrats who advise the court in these matters has created a situation in which many judges have come to depend more on "expert" testimony in rendering decisions than on their study of legal statute and precedent. Indeed, in family law, as in all aspects of law, "social and behavioral science concepts and applications" are fast replacing presumptive legal rules and methods.[20] The results for families have been predictably disastrous. In the Jordans' case, for example, a number of legal statutes and precedents might have suggested a decision more supportive of their autonomy in raising their son; but the judge apparently preferred to base his ruling on a few hasty observations by a child welfare worker.

The Jordan case is hardly the worst example of the kind of injustice that prevails when courts abandon established legal procedures in determining the outcome of child welfare cases. Mary Mason asserts that because of the particular difficulties of rendering decisions in cases of sexual abuse, courts in many states have removed children from parents on the basis of "expert testimony" by individuals who have employed highly experimental psychotherapeutic methods in trying to ascertain whether children have suffered sexual abuse—among them, the use of "anatomically correct" dolls.[21] (Critics of this method have noted that the dolls are inappropriately suggestive; their oversized genitals command much more attention than they would if they were more realistically proportioned.) One can only guess what a 1994 resolution by Judith S. Kaye, chief judge of New York's Court of Appeals, to "revamp New York State's family courts" by training judges in the theory of "repressed memory syndrome" has meant for parents facing sexual abuse charges in that state. The theory alleges that repressed memories of abuse can be revived through therapy, but it has been discovered that false "memories" of childhood abuse can be easily implanted by therapeutic suggestion.[22]

What accounts for the courts' disposition to favor social science and therapeutic opinion over that of legal scholarship in making decisions that affect families? The answer is simple. For the past century, theorists of family law have become more and more preoccupied with the needs of children, and with the function of the state as a kind of "superparent" that ministers to those needs perceived to be unmet by parents.[23] Particularly in the last half century, they have wanted the courts to act as effective and enlightened instruments of child-rearing policy. For that purpose, naturally, the law books—stubborn, unwieldy, and tradition-burdened as they are—have hardly sufficed. Thus, the courts have counted on professionals in the social science fields to supply them with up-to-date "scientific concepts of proper child raising" that they might apply in judging and, where possible, rehabilitating parents who fall "below acceptable standards."[24] They have particularly relied on professionals to flesh out a reigning doctrine of family law—to determine what lies "in the best interests" of a given child.

Understandably, as the courts have become more concerned with upholding abstract standards for raising children, they have become less inclined to view the family as a sacrosanct unit, and less respectful of the emotional ties that bind family members. As early as 1978, in his study

Child, Family and State: Problems and Materials on Children and the Law, Stanford professor Robert H. Mnookin warned that in abuse and neglect cases particularly, judges were indiscriminately undermining parents' crucial position as the "presumptive locus of decision-making authority" in their children's lives.[25] Mnookin pointed to a number of legal decisions of the 1970s that, while purporting to be rendered in the "best interests" of the children involved, looked more like capricious and insensitive acts of family destruction.

Take the California case of the G's, four of whose children were removed to foster care in 1971 by the San Luis Obispo County juvenile court. Apparently, the G's, neither of whom was in good health, kept a filthy house, and their children were also frequently absent from school. The parents appealed the juvenile court's decision, asking that their children be returned to them, and a county-employed homemaker who had visited the G's on many occasions testified on their behalf. The home, she said, was indeed filthy, but did not pose any health hazard to the children, who suffered only the "minor ailments" common in childhood while in their parents' care. The children, moreover, were "happy."

While not disputing testimony that the G's loved their children and were "affectionate" parents, the appellate court nevertheless upheld the juvenile court's order. The legal basis for this ruling? The "best interests" doctrine. "The unfitness of a home for a particular child . . . is a relative concept and it cannot be determined except by judicial appraisal of all available evidence bearing on the child's best interests," the court remarked. And then in a perversely antiseptic interpolation of children's best interests, the court added, "In view of the continued inability of the parents to remedy conditions of the home . . . evidence [is] sufficient to support the findings that the minors should be removed."[26]

In another California case of the same vintage, a Czech immigrant was denied custody of her two children. During the Prague Spring turmoil of 1968, her estranged husband had abducted them and brought them to America against her will. He then died, and before she could get to the United States to claim them, the children had become wards of the state. The woman waged a three-year legal struggle to retrieve them, but the court refused to relinquish its charges. While the court admitted there was "no evidence . . . that would indicate that the [birth] mother is a bad person . . . or that she has ever done anything other than provide adequate food, clothing, shelter, attention for her children," it ruled that "the welfare and best interests of the children" to be their continued status "as dependent[s] of the court."[27]

These decisions—so distressingly contemptuous of the deep psychological bonds between parents and children—were not made in a statutory vacuum. Before 1969, the right of biological parents to raise their children was always considered to override any competing rights or interests. Parental custody was assumed to be a practically inalienable right, and no California court had the jurisdiction to remove a child from a parent without proof that the parent was either completely incapacitated or criminal. But the Family Law Act of 1969 effectively freed family courts from the obligation to take into account any presumed rights of parents in decisions regarding child placement. All a judge needed to remove a child from parental custody was a "finding" that parental custody would in some way "be detrimental to the child, and the award to a non-parent . . . required to serve the best interests of the child."[28]

One of the most damaging results of the Family Law Act was that it shifted the burden of proof in child placement decisions from establishing parental "unfitness" to establishing parental "fitness." This put parents in the impossible situation of having to second-guess both the standards of the judge and various professional evaluators, since nowhere was parental fitness itself defined in statute.[29]

After 1974 and the passage of CAPTA (the Mondale Act), most states adopted statutes that permitted juvenile court judges to remove children from their parents' homes on the vaguest of pretexts. In some states, for example, children could be removed simply on the grounds that parents were failing to provide "proper" care and attention—the definition of "proper" being entirely up to the presiding judge and the social service professionals who advised him.[30] As we have seen, the courts' unnecessary referral of children to foster care on the basis of legal vagaries is a principal defect of the child welfare system, and has only become more frequent as reports of child neglect have surged.

■ ■ ■

The parents I've talked to who speak with the most disdain about the legal system are often those who have had negative personal experiences negotiating and living with divorce settlements. When I first heard their complaints, I have to admit I listened with a less than wholly sympathetic ear. If divorces make parents so miserable, I thought to myself, why do they insist on getting them? Don't they have a choice? The more I've talked to parents, though, the more I've realized that in many cases they don't. Despite widespread knowledge of its destructive effects upon the family, a unilateral divorce can be obtained in every state with no more than a twelve-month waiting period. After surveying the research and data, Maggie Gallagher, author of *The Abolition of Marriage*, estimates that fully 80 percent of divorces are the idea of one party alone.

Thus, a substantial minority of previously married parents are simply victims of a legal system that rewards marital desertion with impunity.[31]

Moreover, since the introduction of no-fault divorce laws in the late 1960s, the courts have acted fecklessly in the issue of custody settlements. Firm guidelines in custody judgments have veritably disappeared, seriously impeding the difficult business of reconstituting families after divorce. The old legal approach was to consider the needs of the family first and foremost as a child-rearing unit. For most of this century the courts favored mothers, automatically awarding them permanent custody of their children. However unfair this "cookbook" approach may have been to fathers, the old rules had a distinct advantage: Divorcing spouses knew pretty much what to expect in the way of court decisions, and they regarded those decisions as final. Children, moreover, had the security of knowing that their reconstituted home was a permanent one, and that the close bonds they shared with their custodial parent were unseverable.

More recently, however, the law—while favoring women by acknowledging that the "primary" parent deserves some credit in the awarding of custody—has aspired to "gender neutrality," and to a more flexible determination of the "fitter" parent. This new approach to custody arrangements has resulted not only in a surge of custody disputes, but in a complicated process of marital dissolution that—despite the alleged successes of mediation—is emotionally trying for both parents and children. Instead of allowing families to dissolve with a minimum of anxiety, it renders everything negotiable, fostering a fight to the finish. Many legal experts and matrimonial lawyers are beginning to see that the new system often leaves conscientious parents feeling inadequate and betrayed, and occasionally even unnecessarily involves children in their spousal conflicts.[32]

In several states, judges routinely appoint guardians *ad litem* (legal advocates assigned to report to the court on the interests of the children) or lawyers to represent children's interests in custody suits—at parents' expense. The results have been controversial. It is by no means clear that children's ultimate interests—that is, reconstituting the family with a minimum of fuss and animosity—can be met by assigning them legal representation. The American Academy of Matrimonial Lawyers warns, "Courts should not routinely assign counsel or guardians *ad litem* for children in custody or visitation proceedings. Appointment of counsel or guardians should be reserved for those cases in which both parties request the appointment or the court finds after a hearing that appointment is necessary in light of the particular circumstances of the case."[33]

James Altham, a Connecticut attorney who is critical of the practice, suggests that the presence of children's lawyers in custody suits may exacerbate the tensions of divorce for children, as well as invite abuse of office. He cites a case in which a lawyer appointed to represent three teenagers in a Connecticut custody suit repeatedly ignored their requests to address the court on the matter of their father's visitation rights, which they felt had been unfairly restricted.[34]

Ironically, in leaving the matter of child custody up for grabs, the legal system has rendered it something of a bargaining chip in divorce settlements. In his book *The Litigation Explosion*, Walter Olson notes that custody bargaining is a major factor in the post-divorce impoverishment of women and children. Thinking it their "ethical obligation . . . to get their clients the best deal," he claims, many lawyers shamelessly use the threat of a custody trial as a way of reducing men's post-divorce financial obligations.[35] Timothy J. Horgan, a New York divorce attorney, offers this advice to divorcing men in his 1994 book *Winning Your Divorce: A Man's Survival Guide*: "If you decide not to contest custody, don't magnanimously announce your decision prior to talking it over with your lawyer. Assuming the divorce promises to be contested, threatening a custody fight may win you concessions in other areas. You don't have to follow through on your threat, but if your wife is one to whom custody is all-important, by all means 'blackmail' her. . . . You may feel guilty, but no one said the purpose of divorce was to make you feel good."[36]

Custody blackmail has become so common a cause of childhood poverty that lawmakers have begun to seek ways of mitigating its devastating financial effects. In the mid-1980s, after fifteen years of watching the welfare rolls swell with divorced women and children, a federal law required the states to draw up sample income schedules on which to base child support awards. A much-imitated 1979 California statute directs the courts to effect joint custody arrangements whenever possible, on the assumption that fathers who share caretaking and decision-making responsibilities more equally with mothers will be better disposed to provide adequate financial support for their children.

Joint custody arrangements may be helping to solve the problem of "deadbeat dads." (The 1991 Census reported that fathers awarded joint custody met 90 percent of their child support obligations, while fathers awarded visitation rights pay 79 percent, and fathers without visitation rights only 45 percent.)[37] And they have also encouraged some parents to cooperate in raising their children after divorce. But in many cases they have considerably aggravated tensions.[38] In *Divided Families*, Frank Furstenberg and Andrew Cherlin observe that especially joint physical custody (an arrangement whereby children are supposed to spend equal amounts of time with each parent) is a "high risk/high payoff strategy." "It can reduce conflict over who has custody and provide children with a continuing relationship with both parents," they say, "but it requires a great deal of communication and cooperation. . . . [It] will merely prolong and deepen conflict between parents unless they can work well together." And they warn that it is "unlikely . . . that more than a small minority of couples will voluntarily choose [it].[39]

In the late 1980s legal scholar Robert H. Mnookin and sociologist Eleanor E. Maccoby followed one thousand California families for three years after their divorces in order to find out something about the real effects of joint custody arrangements. They found that joint physical custody was all too often a legal fiction. Mothers in joint custody arrangements were as likely as not to "take on a degree of responsibility commonly associated with sole physical custody," while receiving only the amount of financial child support "appropriate for shared parental responsibility under a dual residence arrangement."[40]

Although they did not interview children directly, Maccoby and Mnookin's follow-up interviews with parents suggested that joint physical custody arrangements were particularly damaging to children whose parents were still engaged in high conflict after their divorce, and that constant shifts between homes often exacerbated conflict. To be sure, some "intensely hostile" ex-spouses in their study "managed not to draw the children into their conflict," Maccoby and Mnookin observed. But so many did involve their children that the authors warned that insofar as joint custody was "the result of encouragement by mediators, or judges for that matter, we think it unwise."[41]

Certainly any parent for whom tensions over child-rearing practices and values contributed to a divorce has to resent the recent proliferation of court-ordered custody mediation programs that push joint custody and laud the virtues of "co-parenting." Not only does such an arrangement force upon parents the unwelcome obligation to compromise their principles, but it puts children in the difficult position of maintaining two separate and often divergent lifestyles, and also presumes mothers and fathers to be equally interested in and capable at all aspects of parenthood, from emotional nurturing and educational decision-making to the provision of financial support, nutrition, health care, and discipline.[42]

It is no coincidence that upon the heels of the courts' pressures for a maximum of cooperation and flexibility in post-divorce "co-parenting" arrangements has come an increasing number of lawsuits challenging custody and visitation rights filed after the final divorce decree. Walter Olson describes a typical scenario: "The father gets his life organized, does well in his career, and perhaps remarries, while the mother struggles on in some disarray as a single parent. He then comes back to argue plausibly that he can now provide the children with a better home life than she can."[43]

The result of increased post-divorce custody litigation, Olson and other legal experts claim, has been the rise in sudden transfers of an increasing number of children from one custodial home to another in an atmosphere of resentment and hostility.

Here again, the collapse of fixed legal standards in custody arrangements seems to be responsible. In her 1986 study of the post-divorce lives of sixty California mothers, Terry Arendell notes that several women "had their primary custody arrangements challenged in the courts by vindictive husbands who seemed primarily interested in harassing them."[44] In a 1985 study entitled "Rethinking the Modification of Child Custody Decrees," New York University law professor Joan G. Wexler observed a growing trend to allow divorced parents to seek modification of their original custody agreements virtually at will, without having to prove any significant change in the circumstances in which children were living with the custodial parent. Such custody modification decrees, she observed, were handed down on the basis of "best interest" standards, even though they flew in the face of all the social science data on the optimal circumstances for children's post-divorce adjustment.[45]

One of the worst consequences of the breakdown of fixed standards and permanency in custody arrangements, however, has been the rise in allegations of child maltreatment that have accompanied custody challenges. Such allegations have evidently become especially favored grounds for legal complaint because they seem to be the only basis upon which the courts are consistently disposed to rulings that are both final and do not depend on ex-spousal cooperation. High-profile custody suits involving such allegations (such as the Woody Allen–Mia Farrow dispute) have helped convince many men and women that the quickest relief from the pressures of joint custody or generous visitation arrangements comes with a phone call to Child Protective Services.

Just how common and how frivolous are such charges? Statistics are not available, but the literature pertaining to divorce—from popular self-help guides to more scientific studies—never fails to mention that "allegations of physical or sexual abuse have skyrocketed" in cases of divorce.[46] A handbook for lawyers published by the firm of Matthew Bender entitled "Child Custody and Visitation Law and Practice" provides standard forms for legal complaints on the basis of child maltreatment. The complaints are for the most part so generic as to be applicable to almost any busy single parent at some time or another: failure "to supervise the children as to their eating regular and nutritious meals," or to provide them "adequate clothing" and "a stable environment," or entertaining friends of the opposite sex at home.[47]

If the courts have evinced consistency or stubbornness in any aspect of divorce law at all, it has been in their peculiar resistance to the notion that there may be cases other than those involving alleged child maltreatment in which the only way a child can be rescued from the ravages of post-divorce animosity is to allow the parent with primary custody full power to determine visitation rights. As early as 1973, law professor Joseph Goldstein, psychiatrist Albert Solnit, and child psychoanalyst Anna Freud advocated this as the optimal solution to custody disputes in their important work, *Beyond the Best Interests of the Child.* Asserting that a "visiting or visited parent has little chance to serve as a true object for love, trust and identification" and that "loyalty conflicts are common and normal" when children "maintain . . . contact with two . . . parents who are not in positive contact," they criticized the court's tendencies not only to encourage joint custody arrangements, but to "legally enforce" visitation rights.[48]

One case in particular goes far to vindicate Freud, Solnit, and Goldstein's views. In October 1981, two prominent Washington, D.C., surgeons, Eric Foretich and Elizabeth Morgan, conceived a daughter. It was early in their acquaintance, and Eric was a married man. A quick trip to Haiti in January 1982 enabled him to divorce his wife and make an honest woman of Elizabeth. But whatever bliss the two may have found in their illicit union did not follow them into marriage. After a stormy fourteen months and the birth of a daughter, Hilary, Elizabeth filed for divorce, making it clear in her petition that she wanted Foretich not only out of her life, but out of her child's life as well.

The final divorce decree awarded primary custody to the mother and generous visitation rights for the father.[49] Needless to say, the decree did not satisfy Elizabeth. Not three months after, she developed a sudden and profound conviction that Foretich was sexually abusing their daughter. She petitioned the court to prevent further visitation on the grounds of maltreatment, and tried in every way to block his contact with the child. Eric reacted by countersuing for permanent custody.

To judge from journalist Jonathan Groener's fascinating account of the wearying custody battle that followed, neither Elizabeth nor Eric was a very engaged parent. Both pursued demanding careers, leaving their daughter, Hilary, in the care of others for up to fifty hours a week from early infancy onward. But what they lacked in time and interest for their child, the couple made up for in seemingly bottomless financial resources and mutual hatred. For eight years they disputed Hilary's future, employing during their prolonged legal adventures no fewer than seventeen lawyers, twelve medical and mental health professionals, and two press agents. In fact, one of the most interesting aspects of the Morgan-Foretich case was its "new class" aspect—the line of paid expert witnesses in the field of psychiatry, psychotherapy, and pediatric gynecology (some of extremely dubious reputation) whom the couple paraded through court.

The Morgan-Foretich case was argued in four courts: the District of Columbia Superior Court, the District of Columbia Court of Appeals, the Virginia Federal Court, and the U.S. Fourth Circuit Court of Appeals. All the judges dismissed Elizabeth's bizarre allegations of maltreatment. (Morgan believed, among other things, that Foretich was in the habit of spanking the child on the cheek with his penis.) But by continually hearing Morgan's complaints, and then refusing to alter the original decree in any way, the courts only aggravated the couple's animosities. Neither parent was willing to accept the status quo, and that was all the court offered them.

By the third year of the Morgan-Foretich custody war, Hilary was noticeably suffering the combined effects of the prolonged legal struggle and the attendant psychological interrogations, therapy sessions, court evaluations, and genital exams—not to mention the emotional pressures of leading two separate and very different family lives. In the summer of 1987, Elizabeth revolted. Refusing to countenance any more visitation, she sent her daughter into hiding, and went to jail for contempt of court. From there she arranged for Hilary's maternal grandparents to whisk the girl out of the country.

The final resolution of the Morgan-Foretich case—decided in 1992 in New Zealand, where Hilary's maternal grandparents had finally settled with her—is of interest to us because it reminds us that children's "best interests" can only be served by lifting them from the war zone of ex-spousal animosity and litigation. In deciding in favor of maternal custody, the New Zealand Family Court judge made it clear that she did not support Morgan's child abuse accusations, nor the child's abduction. Rather, she simply sought to secure Hilary's future emotional health by preserving as much as possible the stability of her environment.

Cases like this glaringly point up not only the folly of the American courts' laxity in admitting custody challenges, but the perfunctory way in which they approach the issue of child placement in general. It should not take the wisdom of Solomon to perceive that in settling custody litigation, judges cannot simply "split the baby" and hope it will somehow be prevented from bleeding to death. And yet, over the past thirty years, it is just such a dispassionate take on family reconstitution and child well-being that has dominated legal thinking.

Notions of pain-free family breakup have become so endemic to legal thought that lawyers today rarely even speak of "family law." They speak rather of "domestic relations" law—a term that implies a certain flexibility in the organization of intimate relationships that "family law" does not. Indeed, the theoretical presumptions of family and domestic relations law are very different. Legal scholar Milton Regan, for example, describes how the emphasis of family court decisions since the 1960s has shifted from "status" to "contract" theory where families are concerned: what the legal system once saw as a virtually indissoluble social unit whose roles were heavily embedded in cultural tradition, it now sees as a soluble conglomeration of more superficial social ties that are essentially negotiable.[50]

Harvard law professor Mary Ann Glendon expresses the fundamental changes in family law in only slightly different terms. Where once family law stressed "the unitary aspect of the family," "fixed patterns of role distribution," and the assumed "hierarchical" structure of husband-wife, parent-child relationships, today it emphasizes "the separateness and individuality of the persons who are associated in families and marriages." While some legal decisions, she says, "still employ the rhetoric of family solidarity . . . if one attends to their outcomes . . . what the Court has characterized as family rights often turn out to be the rights of individuals."[51]

Whatever the vocabulary, the shift from family to domestic relations law amounts to a relatively consistent effort on the part of lawyers and judges to democratize family relationships by casting off age-old legal mandates of authority vested in parents. Typical of this is a recent case in which the Washington Supreme Court declared it was not a violation of parental rights for it to remove a thirteen-year-old girl from home on the grounds of her objection to "reasonable rules . . . reasonably enforced." The girl, who wanted to smoke pot and have sex with her boyfriend, sought the help of the court when she was grounded by her parents.[52]

Glendon recounts another 1985 case decided in New York's family court well illustrative of the bizarre legal trend against parental authority. It involved a fifteen-year-old girl who ran away from home when her mother forbade her to pursue a relationship with a twenty-one-year-old lesbian. The mother requested the court to order the child home by adjudicating her as "a person in need of supervision." But citing Supreme Court cases involving the reproductive rights of minors, the judge refused the request, claiming that the mother's effort to place limits on her child's adolescent sexual involvement overstepped her legal competence as the child's protector. The child, insisted the judge, had the "right" to "sexual self-determination." He advised both mother and daughter, whom he effectively regarded as equals before the court, to "reconcile their differences within the framework of this decision."[53]

Many parents I have talked to consider the courts' assertions of teenage sexual rights to be among the most egregious aspects of the legal system's assault on families. The courts' decisions in favor of these rights, they say, are based on assumptions about teenagers' responsibility and maturity that are belied by the statistics on teenage pregnancy, sexual disease, and childbearing. Children are in no way equipped to meet the courts' expectations of reproductive responsibility, and having been granted reproductive rights, many are ruining their lives with them, leaving parents to pick up the pieces.

Of course, not all courts have defended teenage reproductive rights to the limit. In 1993, a New York Superior Court declared a "no opt-out" condom distribution policy of the New York City schools a violation of the rights of parents. But this decision seems to have been a welcome exception in a long history of court rulings that went the other way. More typical was the reaction of the Massachusetts Supreme Court to a group of Falmouth, Massachusetts, parents who objected to the condom availability program at their children's junior high and high schools. The courts rejected the parents' claim that the program was an imposition on their constitutional right to guide their children's upbringing—this on the grounds that the program was "voluntary." "The plaintiff parents are free to instruct their children not to participate," the Massachusetts opinion read. In January 1996, the Falmouth parents appealed to the Supreme Court of the United States, but that court refused to hear the case.[54]

Beverly Peltzer, one of the plaintiffs in the Falmouth condom case, puts the issue of reproductive rights in an interesting perspective when she observes with some irony that many schools still "obtain permission from parents to dispense Tylenol or take kids on field trips," but not to hand out condoms. Handing out condoms, she says, "is certainly a more potentially dangerous situation for kids. Because along with condoms the schools are handing out a message that sex is okay." Aside from the moral and health issues, she says, there is "the possibility of emotional damage" to consider.[55]

Peltzer's comments point up the bizarre legal inconsistencies that have emerged as our legal construct of parental rights crumbles. But they also reveal the extent to which the courts have come to differ from parents in their perception of the nature of parent-child relations. Parents tend to see themselves as their children's primary protectors. They assume they have both the duty and prerogative to set limits on their children's freedom of choice by virtue of their superior wisdom and maturity. The courts, however, increasingly act on the assumption that children are competent to make their own decisions, and that the law has a compelling interest in protecting them from decisions made by others.

If ever there was a legal fiction, however, childhood legal competence fits the bill. Consider the case of eleven-year-old Gregory K., a neglected child who "divorced" his birth parents in 1992 after years in foster care limbo. This case has been held up by lawyers, children's advocates, the press, and social policy pundits as a landmark in the progress of children's rights. But what rights did Gregory K. *really* exercise when he divorced his parents?

Let's look at his situation. Gregory wanted to be adopted by his loving foster family, but Florida's child welfare authorities repeatedly delayed petitioning the court to terminate his parents' rights. Fed up with their callousness, the child turned to his foster parents for advice. They hired a lawyer and filed a suit in the child's name. The legal actions Gregory took were not and could not have been taken under his own initiative, since he could never have hired an attorney on his own, nor given that attorney directions. Rather, these steps were undertaken on the initiative of his foster parents. Luckily for Gregory, his foster parents obviously had his best interests at heart.[56]

Most legal milestones in children's rights—from assertions of teenage reproductive rights to giving children a say in custody or placement decisions—hardly add up to the liberationist exercises in self-determination that the courts and children's legal advocates make them out to be. Rather, they usually involve nothing more than a transfer of child-rearing prerogatives from parents to other adults. The chief result has been a dangerous increase in bureaucratic influence and power over children's lives.

For many American legal experts and children's advocates, President Clinton's signing of the U.N. Convention on the Rights of the Child, in February 1995, represented the successful culmination of a long-standing campaign to expand the definition of children's rights from rights of protection to far-reaching liberties of self-determination. It was seen as a crucial reinforcement in international law of American judicial trends, which have only begun to endorse the notion of legal autonomy for children.[57] And indeed, the convention grants quite broad freedoms of information, assembly, and religion to children in signatory countries. If U.S. law is made to conform to the CRC, parents' abilities to transmit to children their religious traditions, their values, their tastes, and their standards of conduct may be severely impeded.

But spokespeople for pro-family groups, like Cathleen Cleaver of the Washington, D.C.–based Family Research Council, point up that the convention has less to do with recognizing the legal competence of children than increasing the intervention of lawyers, social service bureaucrats, and government in family life. Cleaver sees the CRC's provisions as nothing less than an attempt to cast the state in an insidious dual role as part Grand High Parent, and part Big Brother.[58] Her fears are not exaggerated. Since the 1970s, theorists of children's rights have steadily advanced the notion that the child ultimately belongs to the state, not his parents—that he is "a public resource and public ward."[59] In this spirit, a U.N. pamphlet praises the convention as a "new concept of separate rights [for children], with the Government accepting the responsibility of protecting the child from the power of parents."[60]

One of the reasons the Senate has not ratified the CRC is that as people have come to sense its implications for families, popular sentiment against it has mounted. Many parents I have talked to are uneasy about the steps the courts and legislatures have already taken to promote government, rather than families, as the ultimate protector of children. A Connecticut mother put it to me this way: "Sometimes I feel my child does not belong to me; he belongs to the state." Besides the Parental Rights and Responsibilities Act now being considered in Congress, two other congressional initiatives, the Grassley Amendment to the Goals 2000 education bill and the Family Privacy Protection Act of 1995, have attempted to address parents' growing concerns that federal government agencies are using the captivity of the schoolroom to solicit sensitive information from children, and to monitor parents.

Traditionally, the courts have seen schools as deriving their authority over children *in loco parentis*—literally, "in the parent's place." They recognized no special legal entitlements of teachers and school administrators—whom they regarded essentially as parents' representatives—to challenge parental authority or contradict parents' child-rearing practices. But a 1985 New Jersey case ruled that the schools could no longer act solely *in loco parentis*, given the number of "publicly mandated educational and disciplinary policies." Rather the schools, in the view of that court, were "state actors" who "act in furtherance of [these] publicly mandated . . . policies." "School officials," the court concluded, "act as representatives of the State, not merely as surrogates for the parents."[61]

That the school now serves as the agent of the state's child-rearing ethos, and not the parent's, was also the implication of a 1993 Michigan District Court decision in the case of *Newkirk v. East Lansing Public Schools*. In 1990, Jason Newkirk was a third-grader at the Whitehills Elementary School in East Lansing, Michigan. His teacher sent him to the school counselor, Michael Fink, ostensibly to play checkers. But Mr.

Fink did more than play checkers with Jason. Despite an explicit request from Jason's parents that no counseling be performed, Fink subjected the boy—who apparently had social problems—to psychiatric treatment using a method for which he had neither been certified nor professionally trained. When Jason's parents found out what was happening, they confronted the school administration. But school authorities refused to order the counseling sessions suspended, and even withheld from the Newkirks any information about them. The Newkirks—who were forced to engage a bona fide psychiatrist for Jason as a result of psychological anxieties caused by the sessions—sued the school district. Yet the Western District of Michigan Court and the Sixth Circuit Court both ruled that the school had not violated any established right of the parents.[62]

■ ■ ■

Some of the most objectionable instances of court attempts to constrain parental influence in favor of a state-sponsored child-rearing ethos have been in cases involving religious upbringing. In 1992, a Massachusetts district attorney brought charges against David and Ginger Twitchell for medical neglect in the death of their son of a bowel obstruction. Apparently the Twitchells, devout Christian Scientists, had sought the help of their family practitioner rather than a medical doctor when their son complained of abdominal pain. When the case came to trial, a Massachusetts district court judge convicted the Twitchells of involuntary manslaughter, put them on ten years probation, and ordered them to arrange periodic medical checkups for their remaining three children. Citing violation of their constitutional right to freedom of religion, the Twitchells appealed. In 1993, the conviction for manslaughter was overturned.[63] But the Twitchells are only one of several Christian Science families for whom the practice of spiritual healing has recently meant a brush with the law.

Several journalists and legal minds have reflected on the new legal dilemmas faced by Christian Scientists, who traditionally have enjoyed substantial legal protection of their healing practices. In one penetrating reflection on these dilemmas, David N. Williams, the Church of Christ, Scientist's, representative in federal matters, charges that the recent prosecution of Christian Scientist parents is unconstitutional. The state, he says, cannot prove "a compelling interest in restricting" the practice of spiritual healing if it judges spiritual healing on its results. Indeed, the courts' recently hostile position on the matter of Christian Science healing, he says, where it is based exclusively on "*a priori* assumptions" about the superiority of medical science over spiritual healing, is a dangerous omen for the survival of religious freedom in general. "Those who are uncomfortable with [legal] provisions recognizing responsible spiritual healing for children might wish to consider the alternative," he notes. "If the state discriminated against such healing—not because it was ineffectual but only because it was not medical (at least in the conventional sense)—the result would be significant growth in the already discernible tendency for the state to become not only the prisoner but the *agent* [his italics] of the secular assumptions of a portion of our society."[64]

While the majority of us may be leery of relying on prayer as a substitute for medicine, Williams's points are well taken. Child deaths while in the care of Christian Science practitioners are proportionately no more common than under medical care, and medical insurance companies routinely reimburse the fees of the church's practitioners and nursing homes. Nor have judges who convict Christian Scientists for manslaughter or medical neglect been able to justify their rulings on the basis that medical therapies have proven more effective than Christian Science healing. (After all, children also die under the care of medical doctors.) The assumption behind their rulings is always that the state has a responsibility to uphold a *conventional* approach to the matter of health care, and this without regard to the effectiveness of alternative practices.

Indeed, what makes court rulings against parents who refuse medical procedures on behalf of their children especially noxious and threatening is that under the guise of pursuing a "secular" interest in the welfare of its citizens, the state exercises a certain tyranny on the spiritual lives of families, imposing its own subjective ethos in regard to the sanctity, the preservation, and the purpose of human life—first, by declaring the religious beliefs of parents who do not share its disposition on medical matters trivial and/or reckless; second, by forcing them to conform to the state's medical doctrine or face legal censure, even punishment; and third, by preventing them from passing these traditions on to their children. This can be clearly seen, for example, in the not infrequent cases in which courts have suspended the custodial rights of Jehovah's Witnesses who refused to consent to blood transfusions for their children. (Jehovah's Witnesses believe that to receive a blood transfusion is to risk eternal damnation, because there is a biblical proscription against consuming blood.)

But shouldn't the state intervene, one must ask, when a certain medical treatment sure to save a child's life is denied him by his parents? And what about parents who belong to less-well-known, reputable, responsible, or law-abiding religious groups than Jehovah's Witnesses or Christian Scientists; should parents who belong to marginal, perhaps

spurious religious sects be allowed to martyr their children with impunity? Should a parent unaffiliated with an established church be allowed to deny medical care to a child on the basis of what might be a
purely whimsical spiritual belief? These are difficult questions to answer. But many lawmakers and public commentators point up that (as in
all cases of neglect) in pursuing and judging cases of medical neglect,
parents' intentions and their reputations within their community must
be taken into account. Even when parents are guilty of fatal "errors in
judgment," there is no need to prolong or intensify their suffering in the
loss of a child. Indeed, the same sorts of judgment errors that lead parents to refuse medical care might lead them to the wrong doctor or to ap-
proving the wrong medical treatment. Errors in judgment are far from
uncommon among health professionals; rather, they are often the tragic
cost of advances in medicine. In a 1988 protest against "the present
trend of prosecuting Christian Scientists in medically dubious cases,"
Dr. Eugene D. Robin of Stanford University Medical School observed,
"Suppose every physician who committed an error in judgment were
brought to trial. Our already over-burdened court system would be taxed
to the limit. And suppose every physician whose errors led to the death
of a patient was sent to jail. There would be no room to imprison all of
us doctors. If we jailed all of the pediatricians who, in the past, withheld
food and water from premature babies and caused death and mental re-
tardation . . . we might destroy the prison system. If we brought to trial
for child abuse all of the neonatal anesthesiologists who withheld anes-
thesia from neonates even during major surgery because they just knew
the infants did not feel pain (they do), there would not be enough court
judges and juries to conduct the trials. I do wish we doctors would be
more compassionate and humble and less arrogant."[65]

Many commentators see the courts' interventions in the matter of
medical treatment as just one symptom of a new and dangerous trend to
disregard Americans' fundamental right to religious freedom. Yale professor Stephen L. Carter writes in his provocative book, *The Culture of
Disbelief: How American Law and Politics Trivialize Religious Devotion,*
that though the legal system claims to act neutrally in regard to religious
belief, increasingly the courts act as if religious beliefs are false. Despite
all the talk of religious freedom and tolerance, the "public square" is neither "open to religious . . . argument," nor amenable to recognizing "spiritual ways of knowing."[66] The courts, in particular, are far more willing to
impose their secular worldview on religious Americans than to defend
religious autonomy as a cornerstone of American freedom and as a central aspect of family life. The Religious Freedom Restoration Act of

1993, which was meant to address the growing problem of state inter-
ference in religious expression and practice, has thus far made very little
headway in the arena of protecting parents' rights in this regard.

The courts' impatience with families in matters of religious transmission has a long history and is only one manifestation of their impatience with the family as a repository of cultural traditions. In the second
half of the nineteenth century, invoking the legal doctrine of *parens patriae* (literally, the state as parent), the court endorsed the removal of
hundreds of thousands of poor immigrant children from their homes on
the basis that these homes were culturally—and therefore morally—inferior. About 100,000 of them were herded into so-called orphan trains,
and transported to the Midwest where they provided unpaid farm labor
to the white, Anglo-Saxon Protestant families with whom they were
placed. The aims of the courts and the private "child-saving" agencies it
entrusted with investigating families and selecting children were clear
enough: to minimize the hold of the children's culture of origin and maximize their exposure to the host culture for purposes of assimilation.
Many of the most prominent social reformers involved in this "child-
saving" movement assailed, for example, the "spiritual lifelessness" of
Roman Catholicism and openly referred to the mostly Southern European children they removed from their homes as "the scum and refuse of
ill formed civilizations."[67]

Some critics of the legal system charge that the courts still persist in
approaching child protection and placement decisions in ways that dis-
advantage minorities, and force the cultural homogenization of immigrant children. Mary Ann Mason notes in her book *From Father's
Property to Children's Rights* that children of impoverished Asian immigrants have been more vulnerable than whites to removal from their
families by social workers. The reason was that Asian families "exhibited
cultural styles that were unacceptable to the white middle classes. Many
Asian immigrant families, for example, refused to take their children to
the doctor for routine preventive care, claiming it violated their spiritual
practices."[68]

But looking at the system, it seems the problem is deeper. No longer
are the courts merely insensitive to *certain* ostensibly inferior cultures.
Rather they seem to be increasingly insensitive to the family, per se, as a
cultural entity—as what cultural anthropologist Bronislaw Malinowski
liked to term the "cradle of culture" and the "cultural workshop" of
childhood.[69] In other words, they have forgotten the vastly complex
enculturating function of family life. Indeed, except for its perverse
predilection for holding maltreated black and Hispanic children in foster care limbo rather than placing them in white adoptive homes, the le-

gal system has evinced little appreciation of the family's crucial role in childhood enculturation.

Nowhere is this clearer than in adoption law, where in their new-found concern to recognize the alleged "rights" of biological parents, judges are increasingly losing sight of the fact that the adoptive families they threaten are fully constituted social and emotional units in which the most profound cultural values are being exchanged, and the most profound cultural roles—those of father, mother, and child—are enacted.

Consider the experience of Laura and Rusty Winkler, a Minnesota couple. In August 1993, several months after the Winklers should have finalized the adoption of their five-month-old baby boy, they were forced to give him up. A county judge had asserted the right of the boy's un-married birth father to raise the child, even though the Winklers had been chosen as adoptive parents by the child's birth mother, and the biological father had not even fulfilled a state requirement to request custody within ten days of the child's birth. The Winkler family was lucky in comparison to many others. Though their struggle in the courts left them grief-stricken and divested of their entire savings, at least their baby was taken away long before he could remember his first family.[70]

Not so with three-and-a-half-year-old "Baby Richard." In 1991, Baby Richard's biological father, Otakar Kirchner, abandoned the child's pregnant mother, Daniella Janikova, and ran off to Czechoslovakia. She had the baby, and signed over parental rights, refusing to divulge the child's paternity. When Otakar returned, she told him the child had died. A few months after his return, however, the couple reunited. Daniella confessed the truth about her baby, and the two resolved to recover their child. In June 1994, the Illinois Supreme Court ordered the preschooler returned to biological parents he had never met, despite the fact that adoption proceedings were already complete and had been upheld by two lower courts. If the circumstances of the removal seem impossible to understand, so were the circumstances under which the custody suit was filed—a full fifty days after the state's legal time limit for asserting parental rights had passed. Curiously, in rendering his verdict, the judge criticized Baby Richard's adoptive family for not making arduous enough attempts to find the child's birth father and gain his consent.[71]

For John and Margaret Stenbeck of San Diego, the custody fight over their adoptive son, Michael, lasted four years. This couple were chosen as adoptive parents by the boy's biological mother, an unmarried sixteen-year-old, when she gave birth in 1991. Just around the time that Michael's adoption was scheduled to be finalized, however, a State Supreme Court ruling established a legal precedent that allowed the boy's biological father, Mark King—a former drug addict who was at one point arrested for assaulting the boy's natural mother during their short-lived relationship—to contest it and sue for custody.

For a long while, the legal system held this wretched family in a state of purgatory. In 1994, the San Diego juvenile court allowed King to block the adoption on the grounds that it would violate his civil rights as a biological parent, but they refused to go so far as to hand the boy over in custody—knowing that it was not in the child's "best interests" to be torn from the Stenbecks' stable and nurturing home. Michael became a ward of the state, the Stenbecks assigned legal guardianship, and Mark granted visitation rights.[72] It was not until King appealed the guardianship decision to the California Supreme Court, in 1995, that the case was finally resolved in favor of the Stenbecks.[73] By then, the Stenbecks, who besides Michael have another adopted son, had spent 80 percent of their $30,000-a-year income in legal fees. (The Legal Defense Fund sponsored Michael's biological father's suit free of cost.) Besides the financial costs of the lawsuit, however, there were the psychological costs. The Stenbecks both experienced recurring depression, and Michael apparently suffered periodic bouts of regression.

An increasing number of adoption disputes are at present plaguing the courts and families like the Stenbecks, who live in fear of having to relinquish children with whom they have established deep ties—children who are already full-fledged members of tightly knit families. Mary Beth Seader Stiles, former vice president of the National Council for Adoption, claims that the growing number of such cases—many instigated long after the parental rights of biological mothers and fathers have been legally terminated—are prompting some prospective adoptive parents to apply overseas, where they can be better assured of the permanence of their legal arrangements. Says Seader, "There's been a chipping away for twenty years at the permanency of adoption, or at least an attempt to chip away at it by anti-adoption groups . . . [who] believe their purpose in life should be to end adoption as we know it."[74]

Cases like the notorious one of Jessica DeBoer, transferred across state lines to her biological parents at the vulnerable age of two and a half, may be fairly unusual, but they are indicative of the increasing volatility of adoption as a social institution, where a more general trend toward legal flexibility and openness in arrangements between birth and adoptive parents has become a subject of heated controversy. Such high-profile cases as the DeBoers', in fact, have led to a public outcry for clear and uniform legal standards and procedures that will prevent children from being removed from families into which they are already well integrated. After the Baby Richard case, public furor was so great that the Illinois legislature immediately passed a law requiring the courts to stage a special hearing "to determine the best interests of the child" in cases where it has refused or annulled an adoption on appeal. But legislative initiatives in the direction of clarifying adoption law—most specifically the national Uniform Adoption Act, which would go far to establish conformity in rulings state to state—have for some reason languished.

The matter of birth parents' rights in adoption law, of course, is not a simple one. Biological ties between parents and children are, as one writer on the subject observes, "particular, specific, and most important, irreversible," and biological kinship is the very model on which we build social relationships.[75] But as it currently exists, the courts' perspective on adoption is becoming tragically blind to an aspect of family relationships that is ultimately more important than biological ties: that the day-in, day-out slogging through of time together builds indissoluble love relationships. Children are not simply *of* families, they are *in* families. The idiosyncratic rhythms, ceremonies, idioms, mores, emotional dynamics, and experiences of living *in* families determine children's characters, expectations, worldviews, and individuality as much if not more than their genetic inheritance.

In her book *Family Bonds: Adoption and the Politics of Parenting*, adoptive mother and law professor Elizabeth Bartholet launches an eloquent appeal for legal assumptions that respect the integrity of the adoptive family:

> In my view, there are many good reasons for having some presumption in favor of biologically linked parenthood. Birth parents no doubt do generally feel significant pain at the prospect of severing their relationship to the child they have created and in some sense "known" during pregnancy. . . . Our world would be sadly diminished if relinquishment were a non-event. I am prepared to think . . . that there may be some risks inherent in adoptive parenting. . . . Genetic heritage is an important influence on intellect and personality, and it may be that for many parents some level of likeness is important and too much difference is problematic. Adoption may require parents who are more open to difference, more flexible, and more imaginative than the norm. For these among other reasons, the rule giving biologic parents presumptive parenting rights . . . seem[s] to me good. . . . But we can recognize the validity of the biology-based family without denigrating adoptions.
>
> We should come to understand adoption as a uniquely positive form of family—not necessarily better than the biologic family, but not inherently inferior, either. We should make this

imaginative leap because adoption is quite obviously a good solution for existing human beings in this world, most particularly the
millions of children in need of nurturing homes.[76]

Robby DeBoer's account of the legal struggles over her adoptive daughter, *Losing Jessica*, makes an appeal for adoption law reform on exactly
this basis. The book is filled with recountings of the day-to-day experiences of family life and parenting. These experiences—lived within the
context of a self-contained cultural world that two parents have built
around a growing child—are memories etched indelibly on the characters of each family member.[77] Parents who, like the DeBoers, lose their
children in court disputes may not consciously perceive the courts' hostility to the family as an entity of cultural transmission. They likely only
perceive the huge gap in their lives—the absent footsteps of a child, and
the ache of disappointed love. But it behooves all of us who have the luxury of looking critically at cases like the DeBoers' to acknowledge that
they betray the courts' lack of appreciation for the unique role each family plays in shaping the developing human being, and the damage that
may be done to a child's emerging identity when she is ripped out of the
particular cultural environment and set of relationships in which she is
being raised, and placed elsewhere.

The legal system's increasing disrespect for the integrity of adoptive
families is only part and parcel of a far more general social trend toward
deemphasizing the family as the central influence on a child's unfolding
personality. Over the course of the past century, the family has ceded a
great deal of its influence on children's development to child care
providers, schools, social welfare agencies, and the entertainment media.
And when one considers that the courts—in both their child protective
function and in their role as the arbiters of matrimonial disputes—see a
disproportionate number of families in which parents are either unwilling
or unable to fulfill even their shrunken responsibilities for socializing and
acculturating their children, it is not surprising that judges and lawyers
would come increasingly to the conclusion that children are and ought to
be raised by extrafamilial professionals, rather than by parents.

This conclusion, however, is erroneous. In their last of three joint
studies on the child placement and the legal system, *In the Best Interests
of the Child*, psychoanalysts and legal scholars Joseph Goldstein, Anna
Freud, Albert Solnit, and Sonia Goldstein explore a multitude of cases in
which the legal system has endangered children by allowing professionals to infringe upon parental tasks, parental roles, and parental discretion. "Neither separately nor together," they warn, "do [professionals]
make up for a parent—even an . . . imperfect one."[78]

In *The Transformation of Family Law,* Mary Ann Glendon warns of the legal system's increasing blindness to the importance of strong family ties as a prerequisite for a healthy society. In upholding individual "self-sufficiency as an ideal," in disparaging the natural "intersubjectivity" of family relationships, and in encouraging state and bureaucratic intervention in family life, the law, she says, treats the family as if it were an antisocial force—a force engaged in fostering dependency and isolating individuals from the larger social environment.[79] In fact, says Glendon, it is exactly the acute interdependency of individuals in family life that makes the family a tremendous pro-social force. Families are the place where individuals can best prepare for communal responsibility and social accountability, because it is there, in an emotionally charged and self-affirming atmosphere of intimacy, that they are molded most completely to the communitarian purposes of shared lives. "There is at present in legal discourse," she laments, "little recognition that family members may need nurturing environments as much as they need rights. . . . By systematically—though for the most part unintentionally—ignoring the 'little platoons' from which . . . individuals have always drawn emotional and material sustenance, modern legal systems probably contribute to some extent to their atrophy."[80]

If families are the institution by which individuals can be most effectively woven into the social fabric, then the state's, and in particular the legal system's increasing incursions on parental authority and family stability must have far-reaching social consequences. It is no coincidence that parents lament the antisocial propensities of youth in the same breath they castigate the impositions of the courts on their child-rearing efforts, charging that their kids are "out of control," because the courts have "tied" their hands, usurped their children's trust in their competence and love, and robbed them of the security of their most intimate associations. The increasing dissociative tendencies of youth cannot be separated from a legal culture that, in its hostility to parental authority and family stability, undermines the most important source of social discipline we have—domestic lives secure in shared commitments, shared cultural values and traditions, and shared goals. One must ponder whether, were lawyers and judges to replace the "legal imagery of separateness and independence" so popular in contemporary family law with imagery more deferential to the family's communitarian purposes, we might begin to restore a measure of positive engagement in what has become a youth culture of apathy, cynicism, and pathological dissociation.[81]

Part II

PARENTING, BUREAUCRATIC

STYLE

4

Schooling for Leveling

In 1994, two years into his tenure as U.S. secretary of education, Richard Riley delivered the first address ever to our nation on the state of American education. "I suggest to you today," he said, "that the issue is not the latest ranking of schools or students. . . . The issue is not 'good,' 'bad' or 'rank' but whether we are changing fast enough to save and educate this generation of young people . . . whether education has kept up with the fundamental and far-reaching changes in the economic and social structure of this nation."

It was a familiar and tired argument, and two years later Riley himself had to admit that the American people weren't buying it anymore. In February 1996, after a 1995 Institute for Educational Leadership Survey revealed significant popular discontent with the public schools, Riley got nearer the mark. He listed four challenges ahead for American education:

> to get America reading again . . . to give parents the power to help their children learn . . . to keep our schools orderly and disciplined . . . and to recognize that we will never help our young people . . . to measure up if we lower their expectations [and] water down their curriculum.[1]

The reborn, back-to-basics Riley has had a tough time implementing his educational goals. His greatest obstacle: a mammoth educational bureaucracy of school administrators, union leaders, and state and federal Department of Education officials most of whom still believe, as he once did, in the irrelevance of academic rank and comparisons and the merit of "change"—a bureaucracy that still laments, as he once did, the "reluctance" of our nation's educational system "to give up old habits."[2]

But to what "old habits" have our schools clung? Ask parents about our educational system, and it is unlikely you will hear stories of staid old schoolmarms leading rows of neatly shorn children in the recitation of the multiplication tables. It is unlikely you will hear complaints of technological and social backwardness, outdated disciplinary methods, dusty textbooks, and musty curricula. Far from it. Most parents regret the passing of a time when order reigned in the classroom, and what you got from schools was, if not an intellectually rigorous education, at least a core curriculum directed toward functional literacy.

Our schools have changed—and for the worse, parents say. All over the country parents fret over the increase in school violence and classroom misbehavior. A Baltimore father notes, "The kids in these schools today are out of control and the teachers don't even care." A Texas father observes, "One of the things that makes it harder for parents today is when kids are in an atmosphere all day in which discipline has broken down." Parents, moreover, consistently lament the failure of the schools to turn out productive citizens who can read, write, or perform the simplest arithmetic. Another father whose job involves testing military recruits laments, "We are trying to figure out why only 15 percent of our recruits can pass the entrance exam. This is math and English at the high school sophomore level." Finally, parents accuse the schools of discouraging high standards of achievement. A Massachusetts mother regrets, "We try to model the work ethic for our children. But the work ethic is not modeled at school. Our kids are just given a nice ride. . . . The standard of excellence has completely disappeared." Even parents in highly reputed school districts tell of supplementing a lagging or incoherent school curriculum with tutoring; of evenings spent at the kitchen table ministering to children bored, confused, and even hostile to school. Have children forgotten how to learn? No, insist parents. Behind the failures of many an American child are schools that have forgotten how to teach.

The academic failures of America's schools are a matter of public record. In 1987, four years after the U.S. Department of Education published its famous report, "A Nation at Risk," a Congressional Budget Office report analyzing educational trends claimed that less than 60 percent of American seventeen-year-olds could figure out simple percentages and over 60 percent of adults in their twenties could not articulate the major argument of a newspaper article.[3] A 1990 National Assessment of Educational Progress (NAEP) report found that only one in five nine-year-olds could "perform basic mathematical operations" and that only one in eight thirteen-year-olds could "understand and apply intermediate scientific knowledge and principles." The report concluded that American eighth-graders' ability to apply the principles of science "was among the lowest . . . in the developed world."[4] A survey of high school students undertaken by Columbia University professor Diane Ravitch and the Hudson Institute's Chester Finn in the late 1980s revealed that one-third of American high school seniors did not know who wrote the Emancipation Proclamation, and that two-thirds could not place the Civil War within half a century.[5] In a 1991 international assessment of the math skills of students in industrial countries, the United States ranked "near the bottom on every test of every age group."[6] In 1993, a U.S. Department of Education study asserted that 47 percent of adults perform at low levels of literacy, 4 percent more than in 1986.[7] Finally, in April 1995, The Associated Press reported that the National Assessment of Education Progress tests showed no more than a third of high school seniors are "proficient readers," a decline of 10 percent between the years 1992 and 1994 alone.[8]

Why does the American educational system produce such sorry results? One reason, parents say, is that the schools have confused their mission. A mother observes: "My eighth-grade son came home the other day and said they had discussed sexual foreplay in his 'L.I.F.E.' class. Now he knows how to get it on with a girl at a party. What he doesn't know is what a preposition is. For that, I have to hire an English tutor at fifty dollars an hour."

An increasing number of education critics—from Columbia University's Diane Ravitch to former Secretary of Education William Bennett—would agree that the schools have wantonly abandoned academic goals for what could be characterized as life adjustment therapy. In her enlightening 1991 study, The Ed School Follies, Rita Kramer traces this propensity to the educational theorists who dictate the ways in which teachers are trained in our nation's top education schools. The overriding pedagogical philosophy promoted in ed schools, says Kramer, is that the major function of school is to make children "feel good about themselves." In visits to dozens of teacher-training institutions throughout the country, Kramer encountered a shocking lack of interest in the life of the mind, and a stubborn insistence upon deemphasizing academic training and achievement. The first task of schooling, many ed school faculty members and administrators maintained, was behavioral and social adjustment, and if a literate society must be sacrificed in the process, so be it. The head of Michigan State University's School of Education informed Kramer that the ultimate purpose of education cannot possibly be transmitting basic academic skills or nurturing academic growth, but rather must be "to foster personal and social responsibility, to learn to work with others in egalitarian ways," and to develop "a positive self-image."[9] The head of the University of Texas School of Education in Austin told Kramer that academic achievement must always take a backseat to the special form of social molding schooling involves. "You can't *not* use the schools as agencies of social change," she says. "It's too convenient."[10]

Kramer discovered that student teachers today receive virtually no training in any of the academic subjects that were once schools' *raison d'être:* reading, writing, math, history, grammar, the arts, or the natural and physical sciences. Rather, they concentrate on practicing classroom "techniques" that closely resemble psychotherapy, techniques that— while they may (in the words of ed school administrators) "facilitate" and "affirm" students, improve their "self-esteem," "get them thinking about themselves," and "change their attitudes toward themselves"—do not involve much active imparting of knowledge. As Kramer discovered, most ed school professors derogate the very idea of intellectual rigor as elitist and inappropriate to the public educational mission.

Why are education schools no longer interested in academics? Kramer traces their anti-intellectualism to the recent perversion of an old idea in American education—the idea of a civic mission. American educators have long advocated their role in preparing children for participation in a democratic society. Today, Kramer says, the most influential minds in the world of education believe that to train children for democratic life is to level them—to create a society whose members enjoy not equality of opportunity, but rather equality of accomplishment. An emphasis on academic work, she attests, is anathema to today's educational elite, because in the various accomplishment levels of academic work lies the implication that individuals bring unequal gifts to the process of learning; and today's educational philosophers believe that acknowledging those unequal gifts would be undemocratic in spirit. In the words of a Texas Southern University professor, the aim of contemporary education is to promote "equity in student achievement."[11] Even the academically oriented students in the more prestigious schools of education receive the overriding message that academic excellence is a fundamentally illiberal idea.

It is only in the context of a philosophy of education that aims at intellectual leveling as a method of egalitarian socialization that we can understand some of the recent educational developments that anger parents: the "mainstreaming" of mentally and emotionally handicapped children in regular classrooms; the gradual abolition of ability tracking, academic acceleration, and enrichment programs for the gifted;[12] the push for cooperative projects and "team" learning that increasingly replace individual work; the proliferation of therapeutic "life skills" and "human relations" courses that focus on "self-esteem," on "feelings," and on group psychodynamics; the vanishing of high culture—especially of literary classics and serious music—from the classroom; the dwindling of academic work to less than half the time children spend in school;[13] and finally the appearance of outcome-based education—a method of instruction that ties the pace of the brightest children to their slowest peers. All of these reflect the ascendancy of an educational philosophy of "inclusion" in which a far higher priority is placed on making children conform—on homogenizing them culturally, intellectually, and emotionally—than on helping them learn.

Few parents I've talked to have actively joined the fray over these specific educational issues, but to hear their views on education is to a sense a profound frustration and disorientation with the modern educational enterprise. Many parents, for example, lament that textbooks are a thing of the past. The basal readers and arithmetic texts they remember from their own childhoods, they regret, have been abandoned to an eclectic assortment of "curricular materials" that seem to lead nowhere and to disappear from the classroom as quickly as they appear. Parents are jaded by the relentless coming and going of instructional fads, and fear that their own lack of curricular overview may be related to a real lack of curricular direction. A Connecticut research scientist complains of an experimental math program in his daughter's fourth-grade classroom: "When I sit down to help my daughter with math, I don't know where to start. She brings only worksheets home, and the approach is so nontraditional that I neither have the sense of what she has learned before, nor where the individual lessons are leading." A former teacher and mother of a first-grader notes, "My son's teacher keeps talking about the curriculum, but after six months of school I can't seem to get a hold on what the curriculum actually is. I keep asking his teacher what he is supposed to *know* by the end the year, especially what he's supposed to *read*, but I never get a straight answer."

Tragically, it is unlikely that this little boy's teacher wants him to know or read anything in particular at all. She probably wants him simply to "feel good" about whatever he knows and whatever he reads. Feeling good about books, says Charles Sykes, author of *Dumbing Down Our Kids: Why American Children Feel Good About Themselves but Can't*

Read, Write, or Add, is the principal aim of every up-to-the-minute reading curriculum. Unfortunately, feeling good about reading does not make good readers. I have already mentioned that according to the National Assessment of Educational Progress results released in 1995 showed only one-third of our seventeen-year-olds attending public schools in 1994 could be labeled proficient readers; but the test also found that practically half of all fourth-graders and one-third of all eighth-graders were not able to read at the most elementary level.[14] A 1994 Educational Testing Service report found that half of our country's college graduates cannot read a bus schedule![15]

What happened to the teaching of reading? It is a casualty of educators' widespread abandonment of a phonics-based approach to reading instruction, which dates back to the 1950s, and the advent of the "look-say" method. Look-say advocates pointed to nineteenth-century research in the psychology of learning, which revealed that many adults who were fast and fluent readers had memorized the look of whole words, rather than sounding out letter combinations. They concluded that rather than learning the sounds letters make, children might be taught to read by simply exposing them to the same words over and over: Remember "See Jane. See Jane run"?

Look-say reading was a typical example, Charles Sykes tells us, of a penchant among postwar educators to "confuse the 'attributes' " of well-educated people "with the appropriate way of acquiring those outcomes."[16] It wasn't long before it became obvious that the look-say method of reading instruction was not working. In his famous critique of the 1950s, *Why Johnny Can't Read*, Rudolf Flesch warned that growing numbers of American children were not learning to read at all, and that look-say would lead only to a blight of illiteracy; but few in the field of education listened.[17] The result was the persistence of look-say reading instruction in American schools, a continued deemphasis of traditional, phonics-based reading skills, and the steady decline of reading assessment scores until the 1970s, when interest in phonics instruction revived. Unfortunately, reading assessment scores fell back again in the early 1980s as the "whole language" approach to reading gained popularity.[18]

Like look-say, whole language reading deemphasizes phonics and centers on word memorization. But unlike look-say, it stresses whole word memorization not out of the mistaken conviction that children might become more fluent readers that way, but because it presumes that learning the mechanics of reading is boring, and that it puts too much pressure on children. Whole language instruction puts positive feelings, the enjoyment of literature, and the "experience of language" before reading skills. One whole language curriculum, for example, has teachers introduce beginning readers to books by describing their topics, and then asking children to guess the words on the pages by thinking about the topics and looking at the pictures![19] The leading proponents of whole language instruction offer startling testimonials to its pseudotherapeutic and political cast. In describing the movement's roots, one whole language champion proudly notes that the method focuses "not on the content of what is being learned, but on the learner. . . . The teacher," she adds, "is viewed as a co-learner with the students. [Thus] the [class] environment is a democratic one."[20]

Some researchers say that the results of whole reading instruction have been most disastrous for immigrants and for culturally disadvantaged children who have few books and inadequate verbal stimulation at home. Robert E. Slavin, director of Johns Hopkins University's Center for Research on Effective Schooling for Disadvantaged Students, says whole reading is discouragingly laborious because it demands consistent enough exposure to English language and literature to build a large stock of recognized words in the early elementary years. Early phonics instruction is crucial in getting disadvantaged children to read fluently, Slavin says.[21] Phonics instruction also seems to be the missing link in helping learning-disabled children to read—or so their parents have told me. School reading specialists often supply the phonetic instruction that is missing in the classroom, which prompts one to wonder just how many reading disabilities are not disabilities at all, but a product of faulty reading instruction.

Even for kids from highly literate home environments and with no apparent reading problems, whole language reading instruction can be incapacitating. On Wednesday afternoons, I teach an intermediate Hebrew class at my synagogue to fifth-graders who are almost without exception upper-middle-class children of American-born professionals. Each year it takes me only a few minutes to identify the unfortunates who have been denied phonics instruction in school. These are invariably the kids who, after a year of weekly Hebrew lessons, cannot build letter sounds into words because they habitually look at whole words. Typically, when trying to read a Hebrew word, they will take wild stabs at it, forgetting to break it down into individual letters and sounds. With only an hour and a half of class time per week, I know most of these so-called whole readers will never catch on to the Hebrew language.

Writing instruction in America's schools has also suffered from the predilection of educators for replacing tried-and-true traditional teaching methods with more "therapeutic" and "democratic" approaches. The whole language approach to writing predictably downplays mechanical skills such as spelling, grammar, and punctuation for an approach that stresses originality, content of thought, freedom of expression, and the "enjoyment" of language. A sacred tenet of this approach is that no child should be required to write on a subject that is not immediately meaningful and relevant to him.

The results of this method of instruction? Here is an exercise in letter writing completed by two ninth-graders in New Berlin, Wisconsin:

> Dear School Board:
> We are writing in concern of an unfit Phyical Education Director. At New Berlin West High School we have landslides of problems regaurding Teacher's Name. The students and most of the faculty agree that she is unfit, ugly, unknolegable, underqualified and uncoordinated. This just covers the Us, we could go on forever.[22]

An unusually bad example? Surely not the product of college-bound children? Wait. The following are excerpts from letters of complaint to the dean penned by three students at a Northeastern university:

> If he wants to make a point that we'll remember, certainly a Proffessor of English can find enough vocabulary to draw from without needing to use the visualizations he chooses.
> There is a border of what is tasteful and what is unacceptable and offensive Don since has greatly crossed this border.
> [His remarks were] very unappropriated and also very affending. Well then he went back to the bowl of jello and the vibrator and that he knew allot of people who used it to massage there muscles and that he was one of them. I told him that he was wacked because there are allot of other little messages their that do the same thing.[23]

Recently, I ran across a send-home letter authored by some young, professional specialists in whole language—a "language arts" committee of middle school teachers in a Connecticut suburb:

> Dear Parents,
> One of the District's three goals this school year is WRITING.
> . . .Throughout the school year you will receive guidelines and information that will help in your understanding of the skills, assignments, and evaluation that are taking place at Cider Mill.

When teachers write so badly, it is no wonder their students follow suit. The 1992 National Assessment of Educational Progress found barely

3 percent of American fourth-, eighth-, and twelfth-graders writing at better than an "adequate" level for their grade in school.

■ ■ ■

Perhaps the most whimsical manifestations of the pedagogy of self-esteem are on display in the area of math instruction. The National Council of Teachers of Mathematics standards adopted in 1989 proclaim that the first mission of math instruction is to make the discipline emotionally appealing to children: "Affective dimensions of learning," the NCTM declares in its math standards statement, "play a significant role in and must influence curriculum and instruction."[24] Thus, the NCTM directs that teachers should concentrate less on "rote memorization of rules" and "tedious pencil and paper computations," and more on "discussion of mathematics, writing about mathematics," and "exploration of chance."[25] What about teaching children the rudiments of addition, subtraction, multiplication, and division? The NCTM standards contend that calculators render "computational proficiency" outmoded, even that "further efforts toward mastering computational skills are counterproductive."[26] The aim of math instruction, they claim, is to get children to "think mathematically."

Where they haven't been obscured, the educational outcomes of the new pleasure-seeking math have been, to say the least, disappointing. In New York City, standardized math tests have had to be adjusted to better match the curriculum; students now can earn points by demonstrating their "understanding of the process" of problem solving even if they get their calculations wrong.[27] A 1991 NAEP test showed that after six experimental years of the new math in California, the school-age population there had sunk into "the bottom third of . . . participating states" in math performance. Only one out of every twelve eighth-graders, for example, was able to add the fractions $\frac{2}{5} + \frac{1}{3}$ correctly.[28] The failures of the new math in San Diego have led to something of a parent rebellion. Michael McKeown, a scientist at the Salk Insitute in La Jolla and a San Diego father, leads a "loose coalition of some 200 parents" in fighting the trend. The group, which calls itself "Mathematically Correct," has acquired a Web page on the Internet, and has found sympathizers as far away as England and Australia. Tellingly, McKeown informed a *Christian Science Monitor* reporter in June 1996 that many of the parents in his group are scientists and engineers. "We know what kind of math you need in the real world," he says. "This isn't it."[29]

As a parent, I can attest to the incredible ways in which the new math methods cripple our children's ability to perform everyday computation. It was not until fifth grade that my daughter finally learned the multiplication tables—not because her math curriculum demanded it, but because her fifth-grade teacher was an inveterate traditionalist in such matters, and took time *out* from the prescribed math curriculum for times-table drills. While my daughter was not taught the tables until fifth grade, she had penetrated a rather sophisticated verity of the mathematics universe by third grade: She knew that multiplication is just another form of addition. How did she know that? Through games and puzzles the school math curriculum had taught her to "think mathematically." The result was that every time she had to multiply, for example, six by six, she added the numbers up, counting on her fingers: Now let's see . . . six and six is twelve, plus six is . . .

Yet the faculty of my own child's middle school proudly touts the University of Chicago math curriculum it uses for its sensitivity in "guiding the early adolescent's transition through stages of mathematical learning." As a proactive response to what its authors evidently perceive as the looming threat of pubescent mathematical Angst, this program allegedly provides a diversity of approaches to arithmetic operations from which children are encouraged to choose their favorites, and a "careful sequencing of skills and concepts built upon a variety of student experiences." Experiential math? Isn't such a belabored approach to basic problem solving a little out of line with common sense? Perhaps. But it is right in line with the pedagogical philosophy of the National Council of Teachers of Mathematics: "Self consciousness is the hallmark [of middle school students] and curiosity about such questions as Who am I? How do I fit in? What do I enjoy doing? What do I want to be? . . . From this turmoil emerges an individual, with patterns of thought taking shape."[30]

In *Dictatorship of Virtue: How the Battle Over Multiculturalism Is Reshaping Our Schools, Our Country, Our Lives,* Richard Bernstein describes a math program sponsored by the Wellesley SEED Project on Inclusive Curriculum (the acronym stands for "Seeking Educational Equity and Diversity"). SEED's director, Peggy McIntosh, sells her elementary school math curriculum on the basis that it teaches children to understand themselves "as bodies in the bodies of the world," and places them "in the deepest relationship with the invisible elements of the universe."[31] Will her program teach children basic arithmetic skills? Unlikely. McIntosh hates arithmetic problem solving because it presumes "right" and "wrong" answers, a presumption, she says, which in its very "hierarchical" nature unfairly imposes a "white," Western paradigm of "getting ahead" on an increasingly nonwhite, non-Western student population. In a democratic and racially diverse society, McIntosh insists, to concentrate on arithmetic skills is bound to demoralize children of color, who (she implies) are culturally not disposed to the notion of "getting ahead." She warns teachers against drills and tests on the grounds that in the cruel "win-lose world [of right and wrong mathematical operations] . . . there is no way the child can feel good about the assignment."[32]

■ ■ ■

Ironically, the proponents of "feel good" pedagogy often indulge in perverse exercises in negativism in the classroom. A father ruminates on the "depressing" third-grade social studies curriculum in his neighborhood public school: "In six weeks they studied the Holocaust, the civil rights movement, and migrant farmworkers. I'm thinking, here you are only eight years old. . . . You're going to feel impotent to go out and . . . face the world at such a young age." A distressed mother wonders why her daughter's third-grade class has an assignment to write a "runaway adventure" that begins: "You are a child who has run out of patience with your family. You get so angry with them that you just have to leave."[33]

Holocaust scholar Lucy Dawidowicz reports in an article for *Commentary* that a proliferation of "Holocaust Studies" units in grammar schools now typically feature concentration camp role-playing activities, where children are assigned to act out the parts of prisoners and guards.[34] Parents from all over the country have testified at U.S. Department of Education Hearings that in the course of a public education experience, their kids have been treated by the schools to films showing the burning of women and children in nuclear firestorms. Thomas Sowell, senior fellow at Stanford University's Hoover Institute, writes in his 1993 study, *Inside American Education: The Decline, the Deception, the Dogmas,* that his research assistant, "a mature, well-educated woman," had trouble sleeping after watching numerous films on a variety of subjects—from environmental destruction to nuclear war to AIDS and substance abuse—"routinely shown in American elementary and secondary schools."[35]

It is in their approach to sex education, drug education, "values clarification," and other so-called life skills courses which increasingly crowd the schoolday that educators become positively morbid. A September 21, 1990, episode of television's *20/20* investigating fashionable "death education" courses followed a public school field trip to a mortuary, where children were enjoined to touch the corpses. The many public and independent schools that use Sidney Simon's "Values Clarification" curriculum gather students in "privacy groups" to interrogate them on the following personal subjects: "What disturbs you about your parents? What is the saddest thing you remember? Tell something about a frightening sexual experience. Is there something you once did that you are ashamed of?"[36] Quest, a drug awareness curriculum, assigns the following poem as a "tickler" to fourth-grade discussion in its "Skills for Growing" program:

> James was not at school today.
> He wasn't at his desk.
> He didn't join the gang at lunch
> To play and run and laugh.
>
> He didn't join his family
> When they ate their evening meal.
> He wasn't there to kiss goodnight
> When it was time for bed.
>
> A driver who'd been drinking
> Put an end to his young life,
> And left a loss in everyone
> Who knew him as a friend.
>
> A young boy's life is over
> And who can tell me this—
> How many more can die because
> People drink and drive?[37]

Of her school's often luridly detailed AIDS lessons, the New Jersey mother of a seven-year-old exclaims, "I don't think we've considered the burden of knowledge." Another mother echoes much the same concern about the stranger-danger unit in her child's second-grade class: "My daughter refused for weeks to walk from her classroom to the school music room for pickup. She was afraid she would be kidnapped along the way!"

When she was in the fifth grade my own daughter, who is not prone to nightmares, woke up one night screaming. We finally traced her anxiety to a graphic film on molestation shown a few weeks before at school. Studies show that the younger the child exposed to such discussions is, the stronger the reaction. Professor Neil Gilbert of the University of California at Berkeley claims that about one-fifth of parents of preschoolers notice "immediate negative effects" on their children after they have gone through a school sexual abuse prevention program.[38] A University of Virginia study found that well near half the young children exposed to such curricula emerge from them with increased anxiety, and that many experience not only nightmares but bed-wetting. Hardly a wonder. Some of these programs tell children to beware not only of spankings, but of "wet kisses" and "tight hugs," even if they come from mom or dad, grandma or grandpa.[39]

Thomas Sowell says that all this amounts to a kind of shock therapy designed to shake children out of the social and political complacency they bring from home. Schools, he says, "have set sail on an uncharted sea of social experimentation in the re-shaping of young people's emotions and attitudes. . . . They [intend to] re-shape values, attitudes and beliefs to fit a very different vision of the world from what children have received from their parents."[40] Educators, Sowell contends, have a specific set of goals in this respect: to discomfit children about the security of the world around them; to break down their reserve, discretion, and sense of privacy; to discredit their faith in parental goodwill and authority; and to assault the traditional values children learn at home and at church. "Parents who send their children to school with instructions to respect and obey their teachers," Sowell warns, "may be surprised to discover how often these children are sent back home conditioned to disrespect and disobey their parents."[41]

In 1994 thousands of California parents protested to the governor when they were denied permission to see a California Learning Assessment System (CLAS) test that asked children intrusive questions about their family lives. As the protest took on steam, Governor Pete Wilson's office was barraged with up to twenty thousand telephone calls from irate parents in one week. Although a Los Angeles County Superior Court ruled that the test did not violate parents' rights, Wilson could not ignore the public outcry, and refused to reauthorize CLAS funding for 1995. Similar protests elsewhere over the increasing invasiveness of educational assessment tests and sex and drug surveys administered through public schools have even prompted Congress to begin to tighten the legal framework surrounding the issue of pupils' rights to privacy, both through the Grassley Amendment to the Goals 2000 legislation (an education bill passed in 1994 with the object of creating national models for school reform and educational standard setting) and also by way of the Family Privacy Protection Act.

Assessment tests and surveys are only the tip of the schools' inappropriate interest in the private affairs of students and their families. In Petaluma, California, for example, parents became angry recently when ninth-graders in a "human interaction" program were sent home with a worksheet on "family systems." The worksheet required the children to determine whether their families worked on an "open" or "democratic" model, or on a "closed, authoritarian" model. It also solicited information about how much money their parents made, which candidate their parents had voted for in the last presidential election, whether the children were "happy," and to what extent they felt comfortable crying.[42]

Such interrogations, which are quite common in human relations, drug resistance, and other life skills curricula, are the product of a shift in "health education" that over the past two decades has focused far more on psychosocial adaptation than on physical hygiene. As far back as the mid-1970s, a health text entitled *Health Games Students Play: Creative Strategies for Health Education* touted personal interrogations as "opportunities" for children "to generate meaningful information about themselves which can be shared by others."[43] In my own school district, "class meetings" (often led by counselors) are frequent settings in which children are invited to discuss personal information about their family lives with their classmates.

Personal confessions are often also incorporated into the academic curriculum. A book of parent testimony from U.S. Department of Education hearings reveals that the journals children keep in school districts throughout the country today as ostensible writing exercises are typically not corrected for grammar, punctuation, or style, but are explicitly defined as records of feelings. In some cases children have been solicited to write about family problems with the promise of confidentiality from their parents. While such journals are usually read only by the teacher, in a few school districts children have been required to "share" their journals with other students.[44]

Even more annoying to parents than the schools' proprietary attitude toward personal information are their assaults on parental authority. In health and human relations courses and programs parents are often referred to in derogatory and dismissive ways. A well-known high school sex education textbook—*Changing Bodies, Changing Lives*—describes parents as typically "hung up" and "having serious problems."[45] The widely used Here's Looking at You, 2000 comprehensive health education curriculum teaches kids that substance abuse is a behavioral pattern usually learned in "chemically dependent homes."[46] Parents from Oregon testified at U.S. Department of Education hearings that their elementary school children were asked in the context of a values clarification curriculum, "How many of you ever wanted to beat up your parents?" In Tucson, high school students were queried in a "health" class, "How many of you hate your parents?"[47] In the early 1990s, the drug awareness program Quest came under fire from parents. Its "Skills for Adolescence" program demanded of middle-schoolers that they list "sources of anger and frustration" and that they write a series of "blaming" statements followed by "I feel" statements. These demands, claimed parents in Oklahoma, invited kids to criticize their home lives and defy parental direction.[48] Still another drug resistance program, DARE, has been criticized for turning children into police informers who rat on parents using illicit drugs.[49]

To be fair, some life skills programs pursue their intentions quite blatantly. A newsletter from the producers of the comprehensive health program used at my daughter's school informed my husband and me: "You should be prepared for your children to come home and ask questions about your drug behavior, particularly your use or non-use of alcohol and nicotine. . . . This indeed may be an opportunity for you to examine your own behaviors with drugs."[50] My husband is a European who serves wine at dinner every night. One night, as he poured himself a glass of his favorite Sancerre, our child told him she had noticed his "habit." "But don't worry," she added, "there are many people to help alcoholics and their families." "But surely those people aren't children," my husband countered. "Oh, yes!" our daughter answered. "If a child tells a teacher or a friend, they will find someone to help."

What, we and many parents like us have asked, gives the schools the privilege to "reeducate" *us* through our children? A San Francisco mother notes with a bemused chuckle, "I thought I was raising my children right. Then I sent them to school. I found out differently from my son!" But many parents I've talked to are not so good-humored about the schools' approach—in particular, about their contentious attitude toward physical discipline. Parents see a clear connection between educators' contempt for parental authority and children's increasing disrespect. A Texas father of two teenagers relates:

"My [teenage] son called his mother a 'bitch,' and I got upset. I told him he better treat his mother with respect, and if he uses that kind of language again, I was going to slap him. So he says to me, 'If you do, I'll call the police.' Well I gave him the phone, and I said, 'Go ahead and call right now, because if you call, I'm going to give you a reason.' They teach them at school that parents don't have the right to slap them."

At the heart of parents' frustration with the schools, one senses, is a deep and seemingly unbridgeable chasm between the vocabulary of moral dictates, rules, and authority that parents think are best for children and the vocabulary of autonomy and "choices" that emanates from the classroom. Curiously, while life skills programs purport to outline the dangers of "high-risk" behavior—smoking, substance abuse, and unprotected sexual activity—most are actually quite short on straight information, and far longer on "choice" and "self-esteem" talk, emotional catharsis, exercises geared toward promoting social adjustment within the peer group, and even invitations to experiment.[51] The sex education textbook *Changing Bodies, Changing Lives* titillates adolescents with the warning, "In this book teenagers talk about the changes, choices and feelings in their lives. . . . Some quotes are quite frank, describing sexual activity or other intimate details. . . . A number of them may surprise, even shock you." But the authors make sure to remind their readers that "decisions come up daily, and you're the only one who can make them: Do you do what your friends want you to do? Do you have sex with your boyfriend or girlfriend? Do you take this or that drug?"[52]

Many life skills programs encourage children to view high-risk behaviors as personal decisions they should make all by themselves, without the influence of adults. The implication is that children should not feel bound by virtue of their emotional immaturity, their physical vulnerability, or even the legal sanctions against certain behaviors to the injunctions of parents or other adults who might tell them, "I can drink a glass of wine, or smoke a cigarette or have sex, but *you* are too young." Indeed, the "You're too young" argument is the first argument against risky behavior that life skills programs tend to discredit in their focus on "choices" and "decisions."

Most life skills programs also discredit the argument "Because it's wrong!" They aspire to be nonjudgmental and "value-neutral." Many, in fact, were originally designed on what educators call the values clarification model of instruction, whereby teachers were enjoined to encourage children to examine, assess, and reconstruct their value system as a prelude to making their own decisions. Values clarification, a technique of behavioral education that goes back to the human potential movement of the 1960s, stresses the moral independence of each individual, and attempts to foster this independence by having students share emotions, experiences, and different moral points of view in a group setting. Teachers are typically warned to beware of "advising, evaluating, or moralizing," and are instead enjoined to "ask . . . for opinions" and "promote thinking," not to preach, so that each child will develop his own personal code of morality.[53] But curiously, while these programs purport to cultivate a nonjudgmental and value-neutral environment for moral development, many clearly posit a system of what can only be termed *negative* moral imperatives, disregarding, even disparaging the institutions—family and church—that normally set the tone of good conduct. *Changing Bodies, Changing Lives* tells adolescents first that "there is no right or wrong way to have life experiences," and then implicitly compares the open and experimental sexual mores of teenagers the authors have interviewed with the "old fashioned stereotypes" and "negative attitudes toward bodies and sex" and "rules . . . about [sexual] activity" purveyed by "parents" and "religious leaders." Parents, says this textbook, should "support" teenagers as "people who are growing up and experimenting with life," since "it's part of the teenage experience to do things without being too cautious."[54] Another health education text, *Caring, Deciding and Growing,* tells kids, "A major influence on you has been the attitudes and behaviors . . . of your parents. . . . You have probably learned some fairly traditional ideas. . . . Many believe that these traditional attitudes hinder growth and development of a person because they limit possibilities."[55]

The use of values clarification in the schools is not exclusive to drug, sex, or comprehensive health curricula. To the contrary, since the 1970s it has been used widely as a classroom approach to ethics and character education, usually in an express effort to challenge the value system that children bring with them from home. In their book *Facing Value Decisions: Rationale-Building for Teachers,* the influential educators James P. Shaver and William Strong advocate values clarification as a means by which the school might counter the efforts of parents to "impose" values on their children. "The home," they contend, "is a difficult environment for a critical inquiry into values. It is too difficult for parents . . . to be analytic and to ask questions in ways that are not overt or subtle reminders . . . of what the child *ought* to believe."[56] Despite the claims to objectivity in moral inquiry, however, values clarification is prone to disorienting children's moral compass, and to promoting of the unhealthiest peer influences on moral development. The bible of the method, Sidney Simon et al.'s *Values Clarification: A Handbook of Practical Strategies for Teachers and Students,* urges teachers to engage students in peer group discussions and "trust-building" exercises designed to challenge wherever possible traditional concepts of morality and to encourage "risk taking experiences."[57] (Along this line, the Quest drug awareness curriculum enjoined teachers as late as 1989 to "push [students'] risk levels gently."[58] Simon and his co-authors also present classroom exercises that encourage kids to regard the most profound moral dilemmas as if they were trifling matters of personal taste. In one exercise, called "Values Voting," the teacher asks students to vote on such innocuous questions as "How many of you like to go on long walks or hikes?" or "How many of you like yogurt?" Slowly he or she begins to interject more loaded questions, such as "How many of you approve of premarital sex?" or "How many would approve of . . . abortions . . . [or] marriage between homosexuals?"[59]

Simon et al.'s values clarification model is hardly the worst example of the genre. A "conflict resolution" curriculum called PALS (Peers Always Listen Sensitively) used in the West Milwaukee school system poses the following dilemma to fourth- through sixth-graders: A boy wants to purchase a rowboat with some friends, but he needs ten more dollars. While he is working in his father's store, a wealthy man inadvertently hands him a twenty-dollar bill he believes is a ten-dollar bill. What should the boy do? A worksheet on the problem suggests: "You can keep the extra ten dollars and buy the boat you want. Mr. Kelly believes he is giving you ten dollars and your dad is not losing money. . . . Shouldn't Mr. Kelly share his wealth, anyway? Does he have a right to so much when all you want is a little rowboat? . . . Act out a plan. . . . Learn for the future. What would you do differently if this happened again?"[60]

As an approach to discussions of ethics in the classroom, such value-neutral approaches have recently begun to fall out of favor. In some schools, they are being replaced by slightly more directive, less therapeutic methods that stress personal responsibility and the inculcation of universally acknowledged virtues: honesty, generosity, kindness, helpfulness, justice, tolerance.[61] Unfortunately, however, too many attributes of values clarification remain firmly embedded in sex and drug curricula, where the call of the day is not "It's right or wrong" but "It's *your* decision."

Thus the undistinguished results of drug awareness program assessments, even when those programs include strong warnings about the physical dangers and legal risks of illicit drug use. One would have thought the DARE program, which stresses the health and legal consequences of drug use more than any therapeutic component, would have garnered good results. But a 1993 National Institute on Drug Abuse study in Kentucky schools found the program, which is taught by police officers and has reached 25 million schoolchildren, to have virtually no effect—positive or negative—on teenage drug use. A Research Triangle Institute evaluation of that program sponsored by the National Institute of Justice also rated DARE's effectiveness as "limited to non-existent."[62] A range of assessments of Here's Looking at You, 2000, which luridly details both the physiological and psychological dangers of drugs (to the point, even, of implicitly equating the use of caffeine with the use of cocaine in its early elementary lessons) resulted in similarly unimpressive findings.[63] In 1994, five Connecticut school districts encompassing Bridgeport and its surrounding suburbs set up a joint task force to reassess the program; two regional public school surveys indicated that it had been ineffective in tackling an epidemic of binge drinking among kids as young as sixth grade.[64] Until recently, Quest, which reaches 2 million schoolchildren internationally a year, had one of the worst records in drug education. Several in-house evaluations done in the course of the 1980s indicated that it actually increased children's dispositions to try illicit drugs. In his book *Why Johnny Can't Tell Right from*

Wrong, William Kilpatrick reports that as late as 1988, a study undertaken by Quest compared students who had been through the "Skills for Adolescence" program with a "control group on smoking, marijuana/ hashish use, cocaine/crack use and alcohol use. In all cases the Quest group showed greater increases than the controls, who either remained 'stable' or decreased their use of drugs. For cigarette smokers there was a 'much greater increase,' and for alcohol, a 'striking increase.' "[65] The Quest program at the time of the evaluation was particularly casual in its message about drug use. It has since been recast with a more forceful "no use" message, a tone far more supportive of family and church, and a community service slant. A 1992 in-house evaluation showed significant improvements in children's attitudes toward drug use.[66]

Parents are the first to admit that much of the responsibility for disorder in the schools can ultimately be traced to bad parenting; but they also insist that in their zeal to encourage moral independence and decision-making self-sufficiency, the schools encourage behavioral problems. "I had to beg them at school to help me when my son was going through that difficult fifteen-year-old stage," says the Baltimore mother of an only child who has had lots of difficulties in school. "One of his teachers knew he was cutting classes, and not only let him do it, she practically congratulated him for it."

Parents tend to see what is happening in the public schools as the product of a more general revolution in societal values that has exalted the notion of childhood independence and elevated moral tolerance over moral certitude. As one African-American mother puts it: "There was a time . . . when there was a clarity of rules. A clarity of what's right and what's wrong . . . and then somehow around the sixties . . . things got skewed, and you know everybody did their own thing, which meant they had their own set of rules."

But some critics of the American educational system insist that the schools are actually at the bottom of the general decay of morals. One of these critics is Beverly K. Eakman, whose book *Educating for the New World Order* has become something of an underground classic. Eakman claims that the great values revolution of the 1960s and 1970s was actually conceived in the schools. It was the product, she says, of a self-conscious effort by educational policy-makers to set the schools up as "agents" of a state-sponsored agenda for "social change." What would be the nature of this change? Among other things, the schools would prepare children for a planned global society in which political conformity and attitudes of tolerance would erase all possibility of social conflict.[67]

Eakman's book is hardly an exemplary work of scholarship; at times it verges on incoherence. Nevertheless, she tells some compelling stories. Among them is the story of Anita Hoge, a parent of three children in the West Alexander, Pennsylvania, school system. One day in 1984, her son, Garrett Hoge Jr., a high school sophomore, excused himself from a Pennsylvania "assessment" test to go to the bathroom. Instead, he went straight to a telephone to call home. The test he was taking, he confided to his mother, bothered him. One question had read: "The thought of working all my life depresses me. Check Yes, No, Sometimes."

It had not escaped the attention of Garrett's mother that school instruction in her rural community had of late involved what struck her as inappropriate psychological manipulation. The previous year, Garrett, a superior student, had displayed uncharacteristic bouts of anger and sullen behavior. His parents traced these episodes to an "affective," or emotion-centered, curriculum that involved "interaction therapy," and the viewing of frightening films about environmental destruction. One of the Hoges' two elementary-school-age daughters had also been upset when she was forced to participate in an experiment in "compassion": Lots had been drawn, and those receiving certain markers were ostracized by their classmates for an entire day. While still in first grade, another daughter had been forced to view explicit films about drug abuse in school. As a result, she had suffered recurring nightmares about men with needles. But Garrett Jr.'s distressed telephone call home during the assessment test was, for Anita, the latest in a string of provocations. If what he was describing was a psychological test, she knew it was being given in violation of a federal law that guaranteed her right of prior written approval of such testing; and she was going to find out more about it. Go ahead and take the test, she advised her son. But if possible, he should write down some of the questions he thought strange.[68]

The test Garrett took was the Pennsylvania Department of Education's Educational Quality Assessment (EQA), now notorious for the cover-up surrounding its illegal administration to Pennsylvania's public school students in the early 1980s, and for the outlandishness of its psychological probing. "There is a secret club at school called the Midnight Marauders," read one particularly offensive question. "They go out late at night and paint funny sayings and pictures on buildings. A student is asked to join the club. I would join the club when I knew a) my best friend asked me to join; b) the most popular students were in the club; c) my parents would ground me if they found out I joined." What possible interest could educators have in student responses to such a question? In a long and wearying investigation of the EQA, Anita Hoge, along with some other Pennsylvania parents, found out that there were actually "correct" answers to the Midnight Marauder question. State examiners wanted students to say they would join the club if their "best friend" or the "most popular students" were in it, for these responses would indicate what they regarded as a positive disposition to social conformity and peer commitment![69] Hoge's investigative group discovered, moreover, that some of the federal monies tied to the EQA test were earmarked for a remedial curriculum to be implemented in those districts where students' EQA psychological profile did not meet the standard set by the State Department of Education.[70]

■ ■ ■

Pennsylvania's behavioral experiments may have been extreme, but they are emblematic of an approach that has dominated citizenship education since the beginning of the century: Wean kids from their loyalties to families, attach them to their peers, and the result will be a more flexible, forward-looking, and unified society. This mission can be traced to the influential educational philosopher John Dewey, who believed that education was a "social process" directed toward a "particular social ideal."[71] In an industrial democracy such as America's, Dewey claimed, progress depended on generating productive and adaptable citizens. The ultimate purpose of American schooling, then, must be to prepare children for flexible participation in a complicated and fast-metamorphosing technological environment. But the job of the schools did not end with maximizing the individual's ability to adapt to change. Education, Dewey believed, must remake each individual in morals, social relations, and politics as well. In a nation of immigrants, Dewey asserted, the schools must serve as primary agencies of cultural amalgamation, dedicated to "sustain and extend" those workings of democratic life that broke down "barriers of class, race and national territory" and fostered a "broader community of interest."[72] Therefore schools should no longer focus, as they had in the past, on transmitting the knowledge and cultural artifacts of previous generations. Rather they must dedicate themselves to enlivening children's appreciation of the present. They must "add to the meaning of experience" and promote the "reconstruction" and "reorganization of experience."[73] The modern school, he said, must reject those "aristocratic" ideals of cultivation that once dominated the educational enterprise. It must erase the historical association of education with the cultivation of high-minded leisure pursuits; it must attribute profundity to the practical tasks of everyday life and work.[74] Dewey was an ardent opponent of traditional education, which, he claimed, turned the very notion of cultivation into "ornament and solace; a refuge and an asylum."

"A knowledge of the past and its heritage is of great significance when it enters into the present," Dewey wrote of the study of history, "but not otherwise."[75]

The challenge of assimilation and the perceived threat to the smooth workings of democratic life posed by each successive wave of immigrants to America in the late nineteenth and early twentieth centuries prompted many other American educators and social reformers to consider the importance of the schools' socializing mission. Struck by high crime rates and the slow process of assimilation in Southern and Eastern European immigrant communities, for example, social reformer Jane Addams saw schooling as the single hope for creating a cohesive community.[76] The kindergarten movement of the late nineteenth and early twentieth centuries was built on the premise that American educators could not "catch" a child too early to bring him "into a new social order. The kindergarten age is your earliest opportunity to catch the little Russian, little Italian, the little Pole . . . and begin to make an American . . . out of him," an early New York preschool educator boasted.[77]

So influential were such theories at the turn of the century, in fact, that it was not long before educators were busy making over what had been a varied, locally controlled, traditional, and academically rigorous public educational system in the Dewey et al. image of progress. One of the more important years for educational reform was 1918, when a commission composed of the leadership of the nation's largest teachers organization, the National Education Association (NEA), issued a statement asserting that the ultimate purpose of American schooling must be "preparation for effective living." Needless to say, the commission outlined a narrowly pragmatic definition of "effective living"; there was little room left for the simple love of knowledge or beauty for their own sake. Seven Cardinal Principles, the Commission on the Reorganization of Secondary Education decided, must dominate educational policy making: Health, Command of Fundamental Processes, Household Arts, Vocation, Civics Education, Worthy Use of Leisure, and Ethical Character.[78] The commission discredited the study of subjects that "could not be related to the present life interests of the pupil, or . . . used by him in his present processes of growth. . . . Facts, considerations, theories and activities that do not contribute directly to the appreciation of methods of human betterment have no claim."[79]

The impact of the Cardinal Principles was not immediate. But slowly, disseminated by missionaries from education schools, the new pedagogy took hold in all the major school systems around the country. By the 1930s, the studies of history, biography, and civic institutions had been largely abandoned in favor of "social studies," a new discipline that dealt primarily with contemporary problems. The teaching of many other disciplines, from math to science to English, were as well slowly transformed by the principle that intellectual rigor and high aesthetic standards were less important than social relevance and the dissemination of democratic sentiments.[80]

Needless to say, educational reforms along this line did not easily find favor with the general public. By the 1920s immigrants especially began to feel that public schooling was insubstantial and dangerously secular. They found, however, that they could do nothing about it. The old neighborhood school committees that once dotted the urban landscape had by that time been consolidated into boards serving larger areas. Ethnic and working-class representation on these boards had been eliminated, and the largely WASP civic leaders and businessmen who occupied positions on school boards tended to cede power over educational policy to the "experts"—namely the educators. School district superintendents now dictated curriculum, and parents could either take the schools or leave them.[81] Many immigrants had already left them. Out of the losing battle of urban Catholic immigrant communities with the public education establishment in the first few decades of this century emerged a celebrated parish school system.

Indeed, despite even teachers' objections, American educators of the interwar period were able to pretty efficiently metamorphose high school education into a vehicle for large-scale social and cultural homogenization. How? By the same technique they use today. As Columbia University professor Diane Ravitch notes in her 1983 work *The Troubled Crusade: American Education, 1945–1980*:

> Typically a curriculum revision program was started by an administrator who had gone to a graduate school of education, where he encountered the overwhelming [expert] consensus around the new educational trends and learned that his own school's program, no matter how successful it might seem, was outmoded. He would return to his school to tell the teachers that they were going to work cooperatively to revise the curriculum to meet the diverse needs of the growing school population and to take account of the latest findings. First, the teachers were organized into study groups, where they were directed to read current pedagogical works, such as Kilpatrick's *Foundations of Method*, Ellsworth Collings's *An Experiment with a Project Curriculum* . . . and Rugg and Shumaker's *The Child Centered School*. Outside consultants were brought in from schools of education to direct the teachers' study . . . [T]he teachers committees would then set out to re-

organize the curriculum, under the guidance of the school-of-
education expert, whose contribution was invariably described as
"an impartial point of view."

Reluctant teachers, says Ravitch, were "manipulated" into this process
via the assertions of the district administration that the process was a
"democratic" one, and that everyone was expected to participate. Of
course, the process was not democratic at all, but rather coercive. The
goals of revision were set a priori, and group dynamics were used to iso-
late dissenters. Once teachers had "participated" in the revision process,
they had an investment in the "consensus" that supported the new pedagogy.[82]

What did the new pedagogy look like? By World War II, educators
had directed curricular reform toward deemphasizing the classics and
fleshing out high school course offerings with forward-looking classes in
science and technology. Such staples of vocational and practical training
as "home economics," and "woodshop" were introduced. The American
high school became the paradigm of what would become appreciated as
distinctly American values and ideals, extolling technological progress,
secularism, and egalitarianism. In 1935, the philosopher George San-
tayana commented, "While the sentiments of most Americans in politics
and morals . . . are very conservative, their democratic instincts and the
force of circumstances have produced a system of education which an-
ticipates all that the most extreme revolution could bring about. . . . No
one dreams of forcibly suppressing private property, religion or the family, [but] American education ignores these things, and proceeds as
much as possible as if they did not exist."[83]

Still, even by the end of World War II, many American educators
worried that our nation's schools remained unreformed haunts for the
cultural ghosts of the past and the persistence of anti-egalitarian sentiments—in short, ineffective training grounds for the workforce of tomorrow. During the years 1945–46, the U.S. Department of Education
launched an investigation into vocational education along with a series
of nationwide regional conferences that resulted in yet another call for
schooling in "effective living," although this time the catchwords were
"life adjustment training." It was resolved that America's secondary
schools would prepare at least 60 percent of the student population for
nothing more than the "life adjustment training they need and to which
they are entitled as American citizens." Of the other 40 percent, 20 percent—those who were assumed to be college-bound—would receive
more substantial academic training, and the remaining 20 percent such

technical training as would accrue to future members of "desirable skilled occupations."[84]

All during the 1950s, until the Soviets launched their first satellite and jolted the American schools into reviving rigorous math and science study, "life adjustment" was the byword in secondary schools. Education critic Arthur Bestor noted at the time that the curriculum contained many "high sounding objectives, such as teaching children 'to help solve economic, social and political problems,' " but that in reality, these objectives were carried forth in an "intellectual and cultural vacuum."[85] Elementary education was also radically transformed—into a "whole program for living" in which children were to learn "human relationships" before the three Rs. An NEA curriculum development yearbook entitled "Organizing the Elementary School for Living and Learning" asked rhetorically, "Is it more important for Dick to excel everyone in his class [sic] and bring home a report card of all As or for Dick to learn how to live with the other boys and girls in his neighborhood? . . . Is it more important for Paula to learn that a quarter note gets one count or for Paula to learn the joy that comes from singing with her friends?"[86] Charles Sykes asserts it is not a coincidence that the first symptoms of attention deficit disorder—a learning disability widespread among bright American children—were discovered at the very same time that an "orgy of belongingness" replaced learning in America's elementary schools.[87]

By the early 1960s, it was evident to educators themselves that even given the recent improvements in technical education, the schools' relentless preoccupation with contemporary social relevance and social progress was becoming increasingly problematic. In 1960, Harvard professor of education Donald W. Oliver pointed up that the now-well-entrenched problem-solving approach to social studies might even have anti-democratic implications. Oliver noted a growing tendency among teachers to frame social studies lessons in ways that forced children to demonstrate common value commitments—such as "liberty," "equality," and "human dignity"—by translating these broader principles into specific behaviors and political attitudes. American educators, he charged, were running the danger of turning social studies lessons into exercises in political indoctrination: "In a word," he said, "educators offer the dictum that our goal is to make American ideals reality. . . . [But] once this is done . . . ideology emerges, and education becomes the imposition of that ideology."[88]

Yet schooling became even more intensely ideological as the decade progressed. The California-based "human potential" movement had an enormous influence on educators and educational psychologists, who seized upon its notions of "self-actualization" and its exaltation of the therapeutic "group experience" as vehicles for completing the democratization of the classroom. Through "sensitivity training"—exercises designed to help students release and share their feelings—children might be groomed to more acute social awareness and sympathy. Through the use of nondirective teaching methods, children could be awakened to the virtues of independence and self-reliance. At the heart of the human potential movement influence in education was Carl Rogers and H. Jerome Freiberg's 1969 work, *Freedom to Learn,* which soon after its publication was selling 150,000 copies a year.[89] A sharp critic of the human potential movement, Boston College education professor William Kilpatrick looks back to his days in ed school and notes:

> Rogers was largely successful in getting his ideas across—at least that is my impression after twenty years of teaching future teachers. They view their job as a therapeutic one: to facilitate self-expression, to enhance self-esteem, to be more open and non-judgmental. In short, to be more like therapists. . . . I think I understand how they feel. Those were exactly my sentiments at the time I started teaching, and in those days Rogers' theories were like scripture to me.[90]

The influence of the human potential movement was not the only factor aggravating the ideological content of school instruction by the 1970s. There was also the moral urgency of desegregation, which by the mid-1960s and the height of the civil rights movement neither the federal government nor the teachers' unions could ignore. The first substantial federal inroads into education policy taken in the 1960s, in fact, were over desegregation and the inequality of educational opportunity which beset black children in many areas of the country. Beginning with the 1965 Elementary and Secondary Education Act (ESEA), the federal government launched a veritable campaign on this issue. ESEA titles (entitlements) were mainly directed toward creating programs that would compensate for the dearth of educational resources available to minority children in the public schools. But they also financed the initial alliances forged between the schools and social service networks, and the first widespread therapeutic and behavioral experiments in schools. The latter, of course, were directed at combating the racial discrimination and social intolerance educators were convinced kids learned at home. But however noble the aim, the introduction of behavioral therapy into the classroom tipped an already precarious balance in the schools between social adjustment and social engineering, citizenship training and political thought control.

Those of us who completed high school in the early 1970s remember them fondly as watershed years in which racial injustices of the past were finally righted and students were finally taken seriously as individuals. But we also remember with less fondness that many public school administrators and teachers abdicated their responsibilities to impart knowledge as well as ideals. It was not only dress codes that suddenly disappeared in America's high schools; many graduation requirements vanished.[91] Most of the gains in freedom we thought we won at that time turned out to be illusory. The trend of curricular reform may have been psychologically solicitous, but it was politically directive and intellectually vapid. In many schools, the few traditional, in-depth academic courses that had survived earlier educational reforms were replaced by superficial "mini-courses" arranged around relevant political topics. Some teachers even actively devoted themselves to propagandizing the peace movement to the sacrifice of classroom time—something that would have been unthinkable even a decade before as a violation of educators' professional code. An acquaintance of mine remembers 1971, her senior year at an East Coast public high school, when her English teacher suspended all discussions of literature and each day led the class in a forty-five-minute chorus of "Let It Be."

Since the 1970s, ideological indoctrination and political propagandizing have sullied the educational enterprise as never before. For example, Charles Sykes has chronicled Wisconsin's Department of Public Instruction's preoccupation with inculcating feminism in the earliest grades. Its suggested "Classroom Activities in Sex Equity for Developmental Guidance" involve asking first-graders to rewrite nursery rhymes that evince "stereotyped [gender] roles." Sykes found that multiculturalism had also become something of a mania in Milwaukee, where one class of fifth-graders was recently asked to identify the subjects of biographical entries in a new CD-ROM encyclopedia by race and sex, and to measure how many inches each was allotted. They then were recruited to write letters to the publisher complaining about the unfair dominance of space given to white European males.[92]

In his searing critique of diversity education, *The Dictatorship of Virtue,* Richard Bernstein describes what happened when "multiculturalism" became the political order of the day in Brookline, Massachusetts. In 1989, he says, a well-respected advanced placement course in European history was removed from the Brookline High curriculum. Many Brookline parents became angry; not only was a fundamental college preparatory class disappearing from the curriculum, but the choices for its replacement were intellectually insubstantial and ideologically slanted. Materials for a class entitled "World in Crisis," for example, consistently referred to the state of Israel as "Palestine" and openly vilified whites, Protestants, Europeans, Jews, and Western democracy. Alternately, students could enroll in "Mind's Eye," a course that, according to the catalogue description, "grapple[d]" with such frivolous questions as "How is physics like a fairy tale? . . . Does Michael Jordan know more than Albert Einstein ever did?"[93] The disappointed Brookline parents organized to form a curriculum review committee. They were shocked to learn that in their efforts to imbue children with a greater appreciation of "cultural diversity," Brookline High instructors were teaching open contempt for Western culture and ideals. For example, a Brookline exam required students to identify the *Iliad* as the "hellenic epic which established egotistical individualism [*sic*] as appropriate."[94]

From what parents say, it seems that schools all over the country have routinely mobilized children to by no means inarguable stands on issues such as nuclear disarmament, environmental protection, animal rights, teenage reproductive rights, anti-smoking campaigns, feminism, and sexual diversity. In my own school district, the hawking of political and semipolitical causes is an everyday component of the school experience. Second-graders of my acquaintance have been enlisted to write to the President urging tougher environmental regulations; middle school students have been assigned compositions on the subject of gay rights; and high-schoolers research domestic violence and child abuse.

Even if educators always encouraged kids to take any position they like on these issues so long as they defended their stances intelligently and coherently, such assignments would still evince bias in that they promote a preoccupation with certain items on the public agenda to the exclusion of others. But instruction in contemporary political and social issues is rarely objective; typically, it results in the regurgitation of educators' opinions—opinions that are informed by the schools' links to political and professional advocacy groups. A study of environmental education texts by the Arizona Institute for Public Policy Research, for example, revealed that many of the environmental curricula used in schools were authored by advocacy groups and that, where they were, "unbiased materials are a rare exception." Charles Sykes maintains that "even textbooks from mainstream publishers take an activist rather than a scientific approach to environmentalism." In Prentice Hall's 1990 text *Your Health*, he notes, "readers . . . are urged to 'Consider joining an environmental group' and 'Become Politically Involved.' The book lists Greenpeace, Zero Population Growth, Planned Parenthood, and Earth First! as environmental organizations students could contact. (Earth First! is the radical group of environmental terrorists manqué, best known for 'spiking' trees to damage or injure logging machinery and personnel.) The same book urges students to lobby their elected officials 'to provide financial support for non-polluting transportation and energy-production technologies.' "[95]

In Addison-Wesley's widely used 1989 text *Environmental Science: A Framework for Decision Making*, Sykes adds, the authors go ideological in a big way: They label as "biological imperialism" the "human centered view" of "traditional Western teachings." They also call for the replacement of Western ethical teachings with "a new ethical system based on sustainable ethics, the reductions of arms sales and global cooperation."[96]

■ ■ ■

Unfortunately, not only the materials but the *methods* of contemporary pedagogy are turned to the purposes of political advocacy. The current educational predilection for interdisciplinary curricula is often touted for its relevance and usefulness in teaching children how academic disciplines are connected in real-life application. I by no means wish to argue here that interdisciplinary studies have no place in the schools. But many interdisciplinary programs used in schools today, particularly in the elementary years, betray the depth and discrete methodology of the very disciplines they join together, replacing serious academic work with facile political indoctrination. In a recent issue of the American Federation of Teachers magazine, the *American Educator*, Michigan State University professor of education and practicing science teacher Kathleen J. Roth critically appraised a three-month interdisciplinary unit in which she participated with a class of fifth-graders. This unit, entitled "1492," was supposed to integrate social studies and science around the theme of the five hundredth anniversary of Columbus's voyage to the New World.

Roth went into the project with a lot of enthusiasm. But she discovered that any real encounter with scientific information and methodology she tried to introduce in the classroom was eventually sacrificed to the political goals of the program: to fly the flags of "diversity" and global "interdependence." "As a science teacher I was frustrated with the constraints placed on science by the needs of the social studies concepts," Roth wrote. "Despite careful, collaborative planning, I was unable to create activities that fit the theme and connected with the social studies activities while simultaneously engaging students in active meaningful scientific inquiry. . . . We called this unit integrated science/social studies, but it really felt like social studies."[97]

The so-called studies of sea and river life and of the rain forest so popular in the early elementary years today are plagued by similar biases.

Rather than offering substantive information about ecosystems, they mostly boil down to appeals, through song and story, to save the whales, to leave the salmon stocks alone, to keep the river waters pollutant-free, or to preserve the rain forest. These goals are surely noble, but they do not answer the what, why, and how questions that science should, and they certainly do not teach scientific method. Further, they obscure recognition of the real dilemma of environmental policy-making: finding a balance between the often conflicting demands of man and his natural environment.

As much as parents may object to the politicization of contemporary education, there isn't much they can do about it. Since the turn of the century, parents have had steadily diminishing influence in educational policies. Until the 1960s, they still had a chance to take part in some policy discussions at the local level, but federal initiatives set in motion a trend toward centralization of educational policy-making at both the state and national levels that excluded parents. The increasingly centralized educational mandates of the 1970s and 1980s came to virtually dictate curriculum and educational expenditures at the local level.

No group has had greater impact on educational policies since the 1970s than the leadership of the NEA, the nation's largest teachers' union. Its ambitions can be summed up in the 1978 assertion of Executive Director Terry Herndon: "We want leaders and staff with sufficient clout that they may roam the halls of Congress and collect votes to reorder the priorities of the United States of America."[98] In fact, 1978 was the year the NEA pushed through legislation establishing the cabinet post of Secretary of Education. The night before President Carter signed the bill, an official of the organization bragged, "Here's to the only union that owns its own cabinet department."[99]

Perhaps the NEA has not quite "reordered the nation's priorities," but throughout the 1970s, 1980s, and 1990s its generous political action budget and its predilection for ambitious social crusades have helped funnel time and resources away from academics and the arts to a slew of fund-consuming and largely experimental educational mandates—from sex, drug, and AIDS education to special education and bilingual education. (Parents who wonder why arts programs are the first to be cut when local boards of education take the paring knife to bloated school budgets should know that an explosion of federal and state mandates have squeezed the local discretionary budgets that once supported the arts.)

The incredible political power of the NEA (deemed "The Blob" by former Secretary of Education William Bennett) rests not only with its ubiquitous presence in the halls of Congress, but with the close relationship between its leadership and the state and federal bureaucrats who initiate educational policy legislation. Recently this relationship became an especially pressing issue when parents watched in horror as the fever of "outcome-based education" (OBE is also known as "mastery learning" and "results-based learning") swept the country.

A federally funded brainchild of sociologist William Spady, OBE in its purest form requires every student to achieve mastery of a certain academic skill (say, simple division) before moving on to new material. Once a specific skill is taught, students are tested on it. Should any pupil fail to pass the test at an A or B level, the whole class is "remediated": that is, the entire group must repeat the material and be retested at some future date. The concept is to get every child to achieve a certain level of academic "mastery," no matter how long it takes. When students achieve "outcomes" together, supporters of OBE contend, a cooperative, productive, and egalitarian atmosphere reigns in the classroom. The OBE battle cry, "Every child can learn," is based on the idea that too many children are demoralized by grades and competition, that even more are lost to learning by the pressure to demonstrate academic competencies within inflexible periods of time, and that those children left behind in the classroom are bound to be the socially disaffected adults of tomorrow.[100]

OBE's claims to both academic and character "standard" setting initially enlisted the support of a number of powerful corporate CEOs and legislators desperate for a quick-fix solution to failing schools. But by 1994, when some form of this approach to learning had been tried in all but one state, support began to wane. Everywhere OBE was tried, it failed to yield any consistent improvement in student performance on assessment tests. And in several states parents mounted hefty protests. In Oklahoma, a multisite OBE project provoked something far less easily ignored by legislators and the educational establishment than parent anger: a television exposé.[101] In my own state, Connecticut, after the failure of several experiments in school or district-wide implementation—among them, in the well-heeled suburbs of Fairfield and New Canaan—the alarm went out, and grassroots organizations paved the way for defeat of a statewide OBE initiative.[102]

Parents believe that OBE epitomizes the worst of the educational trend toward leveling academic accomplishment as well as its insidious tendencies toward psychosocial engineering. But children as well resent what they consider a dumbing down of the curriculum to allow the least capable child to achieve the outcome.[103] Bright children who quickly master OBE academic outcomes typically spend their class time "peer-tutoring" their classmates rather than moving on. This can lead to long-term frustrations for the child who wants to and can learn. In Minnesota's Apple Valley school district, angry public high school students protested the OBE curriculum by publishing an "underground" newspaper.[104] An eighteen-year-old from Pennsylvania criticized her OBE experience for encouraging laziness and diminishing students' pride in achievement: "I don't think it prepares you for college or the real world," she said.[105]

Comedienne Tracey Ullman contends that OBE was a major factor in her decision to return to England to educate her daughter. "In California," she protested, "everything is s-o-o-o touchy feely. They are into this silly outcome based education where it doesn't matter if she knew HOW to spell her name as long as she knew WHO she was. And it didn't matter if she KNEW that two plus two was four as long as she had enough self-confidence to ASK how to get 'to the conclusion of the problem.' What a crock! She was going to end up as dumb as a mudflap."[106]

Most parent protest against OBE has not been inspired by its academic shortcomings, but by its stated therapeutic and political goals. These include teaching children to "maintain . . . emotional and social well being," instructing them in "appropriate interpersonal skills," making sure they "project anti-racist, anti-biased attitudes," and seeing that they "make environmentally sound decisions in their personal and civic lives." Are educators, parents wonder, in a position to judge just what constitutes proof of "mental and emotional wellness," "positive self-concept," "adaptability," "flexibility," an "ethical view," or a "multicultural world view?" And if children are to "establish priorities to balance multiple life roles," which priorities will the schools deem acceptable for graduation, and how will students be required to demonstrate them?[107]

The 1994 renewal of the federal ESEA bill included a provision promoting OBE in American schools; and the Goals 2000 bill has tied federal funds to the development of federal "standards" and "assessments" that many fear will be determined largely by OBE advocates. In fact, recently established national standards in language arts, compiled by the National Council of Teachers of English and the International Reading Association, read like a manifesto of the OBE movement. The goals are vague, insubstantial, and laden with touchy-feely and politically correct "outcome" language:

> Students read a wide range of print and nonprint texts to build an understanding of texts, of themselves, and of the cultures of the United States and the world. . . . Students read a wide range of literature from many periods in many genres to build an understanding of the many dimensions (e.g. philosophical, ethical, aesthetic) of human experience. Students participate as knowledgeable, reflective, creative and critical members of a variety of literacy communities.[108]

Even the federal Department of Education rejected these so-called standards as hogwash, and has withdrawn its support from them. But such setbacks are unlikely to discourage the proponents of OBE, who seem not much bothered by public rejection of their educational vision. OBE legislative proposals have been rejected or amended in Colorado, Minnesota, Kansas, Oklahoma, Pennsylvania, Wyoming, New Hampshire, Iowa, Virginia, and other states. Yet there is every reason to believe that in many of these places the more objectionable elements of this educational philosophy have taken hold in the schools anyway.[109] In 1994, for example, public outcry killed Connecticut OBE legislation, but as far back as 1986, the state legislature had already approved a long statement of educational goals entitled the Common Core of Learning, in which the philosophy of OBE was strongly represented. Of the 110 Common Core educational goals, fully fifty-one can be appropriately labeled "affective" or attitude-centered, rather than academic. Many of these goals—for example, directives to teach children to "appreciate the role and responsibilities of parents, children and families," to "understand and appreciate his/her own historical and ethnic heritage," and to "develop personal criteria for making informed moral judgments and ethical decisions"—openly intrude on the province of family life and religious instruction. Others seem aimed at fulfilling specifications that might come straight from corporate headquarters. Why, for example, should high school students be forced to "demonstrate positive attitudes toward work" or to "exhibit the interpersonal skills necessary for success in the workplace," such as "working harmoniously as part of a team" and "giving and taking direction"? Still others—directives that require kids to "develop productive and satisfying relationships with others" or "consider the range of occupations that will be personally satisfying and suitable to his/her skills, interests and aptitudes"—trivialize the most profound aspects of personality development. A high school graduate, the Connecticut Common Core of Learning goals imply, will have to prove himself not only literate and industrious, but *happy*.[110]

It is obvious that educators take the Common Core affective goals very seriously. A slew of counseling and behavioral programs pervade Connecticut's kindergarten through twelfth-grade curriculum, from "conflict mediation" and "developmental guidance" to drug-, sex-, suicide-, and stress-prevention education. In its official "Statement of Philosophy" my own school district makes no bones about the mission of education:

> Children . . . today will be adults in a period of unprecedented social and cultural change. The goals of public education must be directed toward helping individuals to be open, to be flexible and

adaptive enough to respond positively to a world of change in which interpersonal relations become paramount. . . . Human relations cannot be left to chance. Conscious efforts must be directed toward higher levels of openness, understanding and communication among all persons regardless of their cultural, ethnic, racial and social differences.[111]

Walk into any school in my district, in my state, and you will hear echoes of this philosophy. Listen to a guidance counselor in a lower Fairfield County middle school not far from where I live: "Where child development is concerned, we have to be proactive rather than reactive," she says. "Kids face a lot of transitions today, from death or divorce in the family, to increased pressure in school. We have to teach these kids strategies of coping with transitions, and constantly reinforce the idea of peer support groups. . . . We want them to know that there is always someone to turn to, and that they can emerge from change in a stronger way." In this counselor's mandatory "developmental guidance" classes, which meet once a week for forty minutes, kids talk over problems they may have adjusting at home or in school and receive training in stress and conflict reduction. It perhaps need not be said that this training turns on the single axis of achieving maximum peer group solidarity. Through role playing and memorizing formulas meant to deflect the emotional intensity of conflict ("I feel badly when you . . .") kids are supposed to learn how to communicate with each other, trust each other, and lean on each other in times of need.

The hardier souls among the children I have asked about the usefulness of such exercises display open contempt for them, labeling them "dumb" and "a waste of time." They contend that no "coping," "stress reducing," or "conflict mediation" techniques they learn at school speak to the real situations of their lives. The more sensitive children, however, indicate that such classroom therapeutic encounters can be destructive. A Connecticut mother recalls that her son came home upset one day after a counselor offered students in her son's sixth-grade developmental guidance class jelly beans if they "shared" a private problem with their classmates. "Everybody likes jelly beans, so most of the kids just made a problem up," she recounted. "But then there was this one little boy in the class who started confiding his real problems and crying. It was embarrassing for everyone, and he got made fun of afterwards."

When she was in the fourth grade, my own daughter came home one day from school in tears with the request that she be removed from "class meeting." At class meeting that day, it turned out, the counselor had tried an exercise in group dynamics that had gone terribly wrong. Each child was asked to mention a "quality" he or she possessed. When the turn of one hyperactive and sensitive little boy came, he blurted out, "I guess I am annoying." The class whooped and cheered, and the counselor responded by asking them in what ways the child was annoying and how they might "help him to be less annoying." The ensuing roast lasted several minutes, and my child watched in growing distress as that little boy dissolved into tremors. Admittedly, the counselor handled this situation with inexcusable incompetence, but is not such an exercise in and of itself dangerous? Put another way: Which classroom activity has a greater chance of hurting children emotionally—setting them to analyze a sentence or setting them to analyze a personality?

It is no accident that the way schools manage kids is becoming increasingly difficult to distinguish from the way corporations manage employees. The mutual influence and interplay between industrial and educational psychology is perhaps clearest where the organizational structures of industry have been imported wholesale into the classroom—that is, when some school districts, for example, have adopted the motivational theories of industrial psychologist W. Edwards Deming, championing plans for "total quality management," allowing children to perform "quality control" assessments and soliciting student input into curriculum development.[112]

But there is a far more widespread and spurious connection between educational and industrial psychology today—the tendency of both to rest on the assumption that human productivity is greatest where the needs and interests of individuals are submerged to the needs and interests of groups, and where the individual is manipulated to adapt to the demands of group solidarity. It is beyond the scope of this book to comment on the effects of this psychological approach on productivity within the industrial sector. But in schools, the increasing preoccupation with group psychodynamics and their ostensible relationship to personal motivation and productivity is troubling.

First there is the recent rage for collaborative learning, where children are assigned joint academic projects, and are also required in some cases to take on assigned roles within the group—as the group "encourager," the group "mediator," and so on. Collaborative learning has a long history that, like almost every other driving force in education, can be traced to the educational theories of John Dewey. But it owes its recent push to educational philosophers who note its similarity to state-of-the-art models of corporate systems management. Indeed, in some suburban school districts where many parents are corporate employees, educators have attempted to "sell" cooperative learning on the grounds that it prepares children for a good fit into corporate life, making "team players" of them.

Parents, however, aren't uniformly buying. Some of them contend that by relegating teachers to the function of classroom "managers" and exalting pupils to roles as learning "partners" and "peer-tutors," collaborative learning impedes the progress of slow learners and frustrates as well as overburdens bright children. At a recent meeting about gifted children in my school district, one mother of a middle school girl noted, "Everyone knows that in collaborative learning the major part of the work is not done by the group. It's done by the brightest member of the group. And that child seldom gets credit." Her comments seem to be borne out in a 1992 research project that involved interviews with gifted children on their collaborative learning experiences.[113] The social message of collaborative learning—that everyone is responsible for the progress of the group—is contrary not only to the reality children see around them at school, but the one they will face in the workplace. As an acquaintance of mine, the mother of two high school boys, puts it, "These kids spend so much of their school time on team projects. They are sometimes even graded as a team. But are they going to take their SATs in teams? Are they going to be accepted to college in teams? Are they going to support a family in teams?"

Even the most ardent proponents of cooperative learning have had trouble explaining emerging evidence that this educational method may actually diminish self-esteem and impede positive attitudes toward learning, particularly when children do not receive "mutual support" from their peer relationships or put mutual effort into teamwork.[114] But an even more glaring danger is that educators have become so preoccupied with the collaborative learning process that some forget what children are supposed to learn in school *besides* collaboration. In *Circles of Learning: Cooperation in the Classroom*, three of the foremost gurus of cooperative learning, David W. Johnson, Roger T. Johnson, and Edythe Johnson Holubec, inadvertently provide an example of this pitfall when they describe what they consider to be an exemplary English grammar lesson plan:

> John Dugan, in his 11th grade English class in Suffern, New York, begins a unit on grammer [sic] with teaching students a set of leadership skills. He structures *positive interdependence* by giving students the assignment of (1) mastering the leadership skills and (2) ensuring that all members of their group mastered the leadership skills. The leadership skills he teaches are:

1. *Direction Giving:* Gives direction to the group's work by:
   a. Reviewing the instructions and restating the purpose of assignment.
   b. Calling attention to the time limits.
   c. Offering procedures on how to complete the assignment most effectively.
2. *Summarizing:* Summarizes out loud what has just been read or discussed as completely as possible without referring to notes or to the original material.
3. *Generating:* Generates addition [*sic*] answers by going beyond the first answer or conclusion and producing a number of plausible answers to choose from. The process he uses to teach the skills is as follows. First, he explains the skills. Second, he models the skills by demonstrating them. He then asks the class to generate a series of phrases that could be used to engage in the skills such as "One way we could do this is . . ." . . . He next selects three students to role play a group session in front of the class in which the leadership skills are used.[115]

Hey, wait a minute! Wasn't this supposed to be a *grammar* lesson?

Besides collaborative learning, the schools borrow other personnel management techniques from industrial psychology, among them an approach to discipline that sees conflict as a group rather than an individual problem. Increasingly, teachers punish an entire class of children for the misbehavior of one child, rather than single out anyone. This approach, my own daughter attests, "gives the bad kids the pleasure of knowing they've ruined it for everyone else." The idea behind it—to go by informal explanations I've held with elementary school teachers in my own school district—is the conviction that disobedience or naughtiness are signs of incomplete social integration.

In a growing number of schools, children actually receive training in conflict mediation techniques, "negotiat[ing] a constructive resolution" to whatever conflicts come up on school grounds. Rather than focusing on who may be right or wrong, this training focuses on getting each party to a conflict to express their feelings and engage in "creative problem solving." In this view, the "mediation" of schoolteachers and administrators is an undesirable alternative to be resorted to only when children cannot solve disputes themselves or when "peer-mediation fails."[116]

How does this cumbersome approach to discipline work in the real world of schools and kids? When she was in fourth grade, my daughter ran into a little problem. A girl in her class stole something from her. It was an inexpensive item—a pencil sharpener—but it was my daughter's, paid for out of her allowance money at the school store, and painstakingly decorated by her with new markers. To see it brazenly displayed on another child's desk was painful to her, but when she confronted the culprit, she met mockery and rebuke. She and I both appealed to the teacher and the principal. Both refused to get involved. The principal insisted that his intervention in the matter "might backfire," causing my daughter to "lose" the other child's "respect." He suggested, instead, that the girls "work it out" themselves. They did. Both agreed there had been a regretful misunderstanding, and that the pencil sharpener belonged to my daughter; but not before the pencil sharpener had disappeared into thin air. A year and a half later the girls still aren't speaking to each other.

This is a small incident, but typical, I think, of educators' wrongheaded approach to those misdemeanors of childhood that, if left unresolved by assertions of authority on the part of adults, are bound to skew children's perceptions of justice. Many parents I have talked to have remarked on the propensity of schoolteachers and administrators to refrain from punishing or ostracizing children who prey on other children. Considering this, it is hardly surprising that stealing is rampant in high schools, that young men and women are stabbed and shot in the presence of school faculty on school grounds, that—denied adequate protection and moral guidance from educators—ever-younger children are acting out the roles of criminals and vigilantes in the classroom. Take the New Orleans third-grade girl who explained to police that she brought a .357 Magnum pistol to school because a boy was harassing her, and school officials had ignored her pleas for protection.[117] Such stories are no longer atypical. A 1993 National Center for Education Statistics survey found almost half of high school students reporting weapons in their schools, and 40 percent reporting gangs.[118] A 1993 Youth Risk Behavior Surveillance System survey by the U.S. Department of Health and Human Services found 22.1 percent of high school students reporting having carried a weapon to school in the thirty days prior to the survey—ostensibly "for protection" from the very school comrades to whom their teachers so avidly socialize them.[119] According to Bureau of Justice statistics, 3 million crimes occur each year on or near school grounds. Almost 2 million of these are crimes of violence: rape, murder, assault, or robbery. In a 1992 survey of seven hundred cities by the National League of Cities, only 11 percent reported that school violence is not a problem.[120] And a more recent Gallup poll indicates that 25 percent of children "regularly fear for their safety in schools."[121]

Just as disquieting in my view is the schools' profound disregard for the inner life of the individual, which they subjugate to the dynamics of group interaction. School psychologists and counselors seem less and less interested in helping any but the most troubled children on a one-on-one basis. Children with everything from family crises to social and psychological problems are typically not helped individually in schools, but rather brought together in groups to discuss their dilemmas and come up with "strategies" for coping with them.

By teaching children to air the most profound feelings of love, insecurity, betrayal, and fear indiscriminately, such practices diminish and diffuse the intensity of emotional life. One need only spend a little time in an elementary school classroom to see that some behavioral programs work on the premise of emotional conformity. A good example comes from the widely used Here's Looking at You, 2000 drug education program, which introduces the therapeutic vocabulary of "grief" and "coping" to second-graders by exhorting pupils to "pretend your pet has died." After discussing their "feelings" about the imagined loss with the teacher, the class is urged to sing a song to cheer themselves up: "If you're sad and you know it, shed a tear."[122] Similarly, in "death education" units, teachers have asked six-year-olds to design their own coffins using shoeboxes, to write their own obituaries, and to coin a suicide note.[123] What can be the ultimate effect of such exercises? Only to harden the feelings, to desensitize children to the deep and perhaps overwhelming emotions that might attend their reflections on life and death in times of personal tragedy. These exercises quite obviously are intended to foster a matter-of-fact disposition toward the human condition—the kind of disposition that, if I may paraphrase the Gospel of St. Luke, will enable our future citizens to "Leave the dead to bury the dead . . . and proclaim the Kingdom of Productivity."

Whatever their success in fostering our future citizens' "adaptability" and "flexibility" to changing circumstances, there are indications that the ramifications of such psychological experiments are dangerous. A number of cultural commentators have lamented the curious emotional indifference of today's youth, their conspicuous lack of individuality, and their sometimes pathological suceptibility to gang-think. Journalists report with growing consternation stories of remorseless adolescents who get a high out of doing evil with their friends. Eleven high school youths assault a Central Park jogger in an episode of "wilding." Three high school boys in Atlanta torture and kill a fifty-year-old victim of multiple sclerosis, then sit down to a meal of macaroni and cheese in his kitchen.[124] A Michigan girl shoots a seventy-three-year-old man after an argument, then brings his body to show off at a party.[125]

Could it be that in their determination to loose children from family loyalties and to promote the peer group as a source of both emotional support and social approval, educators have inadvertently promoted such hideous behavior? Could it be that in their zeal to lay bare children's inner lives for scrutiny and refitting, they are selling children's souls to their peers? Some parents think they are. Home schooling parents often point up what they consider the unhealthy ways schools socialize kids. African-American home schooling mother Donna Nichols-White told *Time* magazine, "When people mention the problem of gang membership, I mention that the common factor amongst all gang members is they attended school."[126] Curiously, former guru of the human potential movement Dr. Roger Coulson has acknowledged a connection between behavioral education and increasing juvenile violence and disaffection, and has disavowed it as psychologically manipulative, destabilizing, and morally confusing. Social policy-makers who bemoan the propensity of teenagers to succumb to unhealthy peer pressure ought to consider rethinking the schools' herding approach to socialization and returning the focus of education to academic achievement, leaving children's psychosocial development to the family.

If you suspect me of overstating the problem, walk down the streets of your city or suburb. Contemplate those many groups of identically dressed, identically walking, talking, and acting teenagers who gather there—from the "home-boy" and *Clueless* clones (whose vocabularies are not coincidentally limited to the ultimate leveling phrases: "like," "you know," and "As if!") to gun-toting and baby-carrying babies. Contemplate the outbreaks of ethnic, racial, and misogynist violence in neighborhoods where children have taken courses in "tolerance" and "self-esteem," but have been given no rules to live by. Consider just briefly the deliberate sins of our schools, perpetrated daily on a captive audience of 45 million American children: They undermine family intimacies; they impede parental authority; they disorient the moral compass; they trivialize feelings and emotions; they frustrate intellectual development. All in all it adds up to what can only be labeled a vicious assault on the emerging individual. Is it really so amazing that our youth is in trouble?

5

Sex Ed in the School of Hard Knocks

When **I** was in grammar school in the 1960s, sex education was a matter of one or two delicate films on the physical signs of "growing up." In fifth or sixth grade girls and boys were herded into separate classrooms, many times in the company of their parents. There, in industrial-gray footage and solemn tones, we were introduced to the world of reproduction. That was it. Not exactly titillating material. But those were the days when teenage boys and girls still glanced shyly at each other across dance floors, before carnal knowledge had become an educational cause célèbre. Instruction in human sexuality was still largely a family matter, and a measure of sexual innocence well into early adulthood was considered desirable.

By the 1990s, sex education was a different story altogether. Most schoolchildren were no longer allowed to get through puberty wondering over the mysteries of physical love. First-graders shouted the names of their genitals and explored masturbation in "talks about touching." Boy-girl pairs of fifth-graders defined "cunnilingus." Seventh-graders slipped condoms over bananas. High school students passed "finger cots" around the classroom and discussed the merits of brachiopractic intercourse. Sex education had given way to no-holds-barred "sexuality

149

education" for every age group.[1] A 1993 ABC television special pretty accurately captured the current sexuality education scene when it featured a cheerful group of eighth-graders, armed with condoms and dental dams, instructing their peers in AIDS prevention.[2]

Of all parents' disenchantments with the "life adjustment" focus of the educational enterprise, no aspect has created as much public furor as sex education has. Public outrage led to the forced resignation of United States Surgeon General Joycelyn Elders in December 1994 for her remark advocating the teaching of masturbation in schools. And parents across the country have organized protests against condom distribution, sexual-diversity education, HIV/AIDS education, and other items on the sexuality education agenda.

Nowhere has parent impatience with sexuality education earned as much media atttention as in New York where, in the fall of 1992, tensions between former New York City Chancellor of Schools Joseph A. Fernandez and frustrated minority parents of the city's outer boroughs prompted something on the order of a parent revolution. Resentments began brewing when, in the fall of 1991, a "condom availability" program was instituted in the high schools that afforded no "opt-out" provision—that is, parents were not permitted to exempt their children from receiving condoms in school if the children asked for them. Many parents, seeing the program as an affront to their authority, urged their community school boards to protest and began organizing among themselves.

By spring, parents had another bone to pick with Chancellor Fernandez: the city's new AIDS/HIV curriculum, which, parents charged, stressed condom use over sexual abstinence and contained unacceptable levels of sexual provocation and vulgarity. There were lessons that taught children as early as fourth grade about anal sex, condoms, lubricants, and dental dams, introduced radical gay organizations such as Act Up, and advocated mutual masturbation as a safe alternative to intercourse.[3]

The conflict came to a head the following fall, when Fernandez, defying the Board of Education's resolution to change the curriculum, sided with its authors. To require teachers to stress abstinence in AIDS education, he said, constituted an unconscionable "morality oath." Thousands of angry parents—overwhelmingly black and Hispanic—stormed the steps of City Hall, proclaiming that by skirting the issue of sexual morality, the schools were encouraging teenagers to behave irresponsibly.[4] A month later, two thousand black and Hispanic parents hit the streets again, this time in a march on the Board of Education headquarters in Brooklyn to protest a multicultural elementary school curriculum written ostensibly with them in mind. Educators touted the "Children of the Rainbow" curriculum as a paradigm of sensitivity to ethnic diversity. But parents noted with discomfort and dismay that it also evinced a preoccupation with promoting sexual diversity. For example, the curriculum exhorted teachers to refer to lesbians and gay men in "all curricular areas" (including science and math) as early as kindergarten; and it recommended readings in the early elementary grades parents felt violated childhood innocence—among them, a book describing a lesbian couple's artificial insemination (*Heather Has Two Mommies*) and a father's homosexual affair (*Daddy's Roommate*).[5] Reverend Michael Faulkner of Manhattan's Calvary Church captured the spirit of that second march by referring to the "Children of the Rainbow" curriculum in the context of a school district AIDS policy that seemed to him a wanton attack on sexual continence and family values: "We will no longer tolerate those destructive ideas that are destroying our families. . . . Our children should not be treated like animals. Abstinence is not a dirty word."[6]

The latter protest, organized by a broad coalition of community groups, many of them grassroots parents organizations, was parents' most impassioned and outspoken response yet to sex education in the age of AIDS. It cost Fernandez his job. And it probably influenced a December 1993 State Appellate Court ruling (*Alfonzo v. Fernandez*) that found the city's no-opt-out condom distribution policy to be a violation of parental rights. While it didn't solve the problems of provocative sex education in the New York schools, it did away with the controversial "Rainbow Curriculum" and eventually resulted in an HIV/AIDS curriculum that was more responsive to the wishes of parents and communities and included a strong abstinence message.

Similar protests have sprung up in opposition to sex ed programs in cities and towns across the country, from Los Angeles and San Francisco to Baltimore, Bridgeport, Connecticut, and Fairfax County, Virginia.[7] A number of them have been successful, but because few have attracted any degree of media attention—and because most parents haven't hit the streets in protest—some commentators have assumed that only a vocal minority of American parents oppose the generally liberationist sexual ideology of comprehensive sex education programs. Charles Sykes, for example, asserts, "Parents who grew up in an age when sexual norms were in flux and when traditional notions of morality were dismissed as priggish and judgmental . . . cringe at the thought that they might be becoming their own mothers and fathers, those museum pieces of sexual repression and badgering."[8]

But what parents say about sex and AIDS education reveals that they are worlds away from the current educational "wisdom" in their perspective on child and adolescent sexuality, whether or not they are out marching in the streets.[9] Indeed, the state of sex education in the schools is among their most frequent complaints. A suburban Massachusetts mother insists, "I'm not sexually hung-up, and I don't really know any parents who are. But [the sex educators] have got the playing field all wrong. We want to protect our eight-year-olds, and they want them to be erotic." An Austin mother declares, "I don't think it's appropriate for someone to teach my daughter to use a condom . . . forget it! It's my responsibility to teach my child about sex, and nobody is going to take that away from me." And a Baltimore father of three observes, "That campaign for condoms in the schools—now, I know things are out of hand, but . . . the attitude [of educators] is they're going to do it. It's telling them, 'Go and have sex and use a condom and go your own way.' You can't send a message like that to kids."

When asked who should teach children about sex, parents unequivocally answer, "Parents!" When I ask why, they invariably reply that parents put sexual information in a moral context that the schools cannot or will not offer. Yet educators like Dr. Robert Spillane, superintendent of the Fairfax County Public Schools, stubbornly contend that "parents shouldn't be involved in family-life education."[10] How did we come to such a pass?

It was in the 1970s, it seems, that the schools first determined to tackle something beyond the transmission of basic information about reproduction. Many educators were fresh from college campuses, where they'd embraced the doctrines of sexual liberation. With missionary zeal, they assumed the task of disseminating these doctrines to their students, whom they saw as victims of the repressive sway of their parents. The federal government sped their campaign. By the end of the decade a national evaluation of the goals of sex education programs in American high schools revealed that the catechism of sexual liberation was already well entrenched in the educational system. The most "exemplary" sex education programs, the study declared, were on the way to fostering significant "changes" in "sexual attitudes and behaviors" by promoting "a reduction of sexual guilt" and "an acceptance of alternative lifestyles." The report did note that the values conveyed in sex education classes were "not supported by all members of society"—that, indeed, they were "in conflict with the belief held by some people that sex should be enjoyed only within the context of marriage."[11] But most educators dismissed parents' objections to the new sex education curricula as the crotchety railings of a sexually unenlightened generation, and to the extent that they seriously considered the contradiction between the sexual mores taught in many homes and those being promoted in the schools, they deemed it to be healthy.[12]

By the mid-1990s, it would seem, much of the new generation of parents—many of whom had cohabited before marriage and had even had children out of wedlock—would have been at ease with the ideology of a 1970s-style sex education curriculum. (The younger among them had, of course, undergone it firsthand.) But the sexual codes propounded at school and at home continued to diverge. In part, this was because as baby boomers aged, their values changed. In becoming parents, to borrow family scholar Barbara Dafoe Whitehead's term, they crossed a "cultural divide." They realized that the "values . . . of expressive individualism . . . that served in singlehood no longer serve . . . in parenthood." They no longer saw sexual liberation as an unmixed blessing. What if one of their children contracted AIDS? Got pregnant? Was emotionally devastated by a failed relationship? No wonder, as Whitehead points out, that parents consistently point to the culture's celebration of sexual freedom as a "major obstacle to child-rearing."[13]

As parents' attitudes have changed, however, the ambitions of sex educators have grown. They have extended their domain from the high schools down to the earliest grades, and expanded their mission from the dissemination of information and attitudes to hawking condoms, all under the rubric of "early" and "comprehensive" sexuality education. As of June 1996, condoms were distributed in more than fifty urban communities and more than four hundred schools.[14] Mandates that promoted the comprehensive sexuality education model proliferated. Seventeen states required comprehensive sex education in all public school districts, starting in kindergarten; thirty more advocated it as an approach to required kindergarten through twelfth grade AIDS/HIV education.

Two aspects of comprehensive sexuality education particularly distress parents. They believe that it prematurely introduces children to sexual information, especially on sensitive topics such as sexual orientation, or frightening topics such as sexual abuse. They also fear that sexuality education may inappropriately titillate children. In discussing sexuality education, especially in the early elementary years, they invariably invoke their own childhoods and express regret and discomfort at how much more explicit classroom sexual instruction is today.

A look at one of the major blueprints for comprehensive sexuality education curricula currently in use—the "Guidelines for Comprehensive Sexuality Education" published by the Sexual Information and Education Council of the United States (SIECUS)—suggests that parents' discomfort is amply justified. The SIECUS guidelines have been endorsed by more than seventy prominent research, educational, medical, and social welfare organizations, including the American Psychological Association, the American Library Association, the American Medical Association, and the National School Boards Association; and more than twenty thousand copies have been distributed to state departments of education, school districts, and schools across the country for use in teacher training and curriculum development. But despite the seals of professional approval they bear, the SIECUS guidelines, which purport to offer children the "information" and "options" necessary for a "healthy" sexual and family life, actually serve up a potpourri of platitudes and directives that are at once banal, developmentally premature, sexually stimulating, scary, and conspicuously lacking in models of emotional and social stability. Here are some "developmental messages" suggested by the SIECUS curriculum for children ages five to eight:

- On values: "Individuals and families have different values."
- On the definition of family: "A family consists of two or more people who care for each other in many ways. . . . There are different kinds of families. . . . Individual families change over time."
- On abstinence: "Intercourse is a pleasurable activity for most adults."
- On human sexual response: "Both boys and girls may discover that their bodies feel good when touched."
- On masturbation: "Touching and rubbing one's own genitals is called masturbation. Some boys and girls masturbate. Masturbation should be done in a private place."
- On sexual abuse: "Sexual abuse occurs when an older, stronger or more powerful person looks at or touches a child's genitals for no legitimate reason."
- On sexual identity and orientation: "Most men and women are heterosexual, which means they will be attracted to and fall in love with someone of the other gender. . . . Some men and women are homosexual, which means they will be attracted to and fall in love with someone of the same gender."

Developmental messages for nine- to twelve-year-olds evince a similar propensity for shallow philosophizing and sexual suggestiveness, and for burdening kids with information unsuited to their developmental needs or understanding:

- On values: "Values help people decide how to behave and interact with others."
- On human sexual response: "Boys and girls become capable of *more complete* [my italics] response to sexual stimulation during adolescence and adulthood."
- On reproduction: "Sexual intercourse provides pleasure. Whenever genital intercourse occurs it is possible for the woman to become pregnant."

- On shared sexual behavior: "Couples have different ways to share sexual pleasure with one another. Being sexual with another person usually involves more than sexual intercourse."

For twelve- to fifteen-year-olds, the "developmental messages" amount to inviting sexual experimentation while seriously downplaying the physical and emotional risks of casual sex:

- On sexual response: "Sexual response varies from experience to experience and throughout life. . . . Orgasm is an intense pleasurable release of sexual feeling or tension experienced at the peak of sexual arousal."
- On sexual dysfunction: "The way a person feels about self and sexuality affects their [sic] ability to function sexually."
- On abstinence: "Teenagers considering sexual intercourse should talk to a parent or other trusted adult about their decision, contraception, and disease prevention."
- On contraception: "Young people can buy some contraceptives in a drug store, grocery market, or convenience store without a doctor's prescription. . . . Abstinence, withdrawal, and natural family planning are methods of contraception that are always available and free. . . . Each contraceptive method has advantages and disadvantages."
- On sexual identity and orientation: "Some young people have brief sexual experiences with the other gender, but they mainly feel attracted to their own gender. When a homosexual person accepts his/her sexual orientation, gains strength and pride as a gay or lesbian person, and tells others, it is known as "coming out."[15]

It's hard to imagine how these developmental "messages" translate into classroom lessons and exercises, but they seem likelier to confuse than to inform, to unnerve rather than to build sexual confidence. The clearest overriding message seems to be something on the order of "Get sexual, and then worry about the consequences." Yet the SIECUS guidelines are pretty mild in comparison with other state-of-the-art approaches to comprehensive sexuality education, probably because they are only guidelines and not a fleshed-out curriculum.

A prominent new sexuality education curriculum for the lower grades recently piloted in New Jersey—Rutgers University's "Learning About Family Life"—explains sexual relations to kindergartners in this way: "When a woman and a man who love each other go to bed, they like to hug and kiss. Sometimes, if they both want to, the man puts his penis in the woman's vagina and that feels really good for both of them."[16] The well-known high school textbook *Changing Bodies, Changing Lives* advises boys, "If you are having intercourse with a girl and want it to last longer, you can stop thrusting for a few moments when you feel yourself getting aroused. If the girl is on top and controlling the movement you can ask her to stop for a minute or to move more slowly."[17] In an AIDS video sponsored by the Massachusetts Department of Public Health, a nurse lines up kids holding flashcards that depict fourteen steps for condom use, among them: "talk with partner," "decision by both partners to have sex," "buy the condom," "sexual arousal," "erection," "intercourse," "orgasm/ejaculation."[18]

In public and private schools, sex educators often go even further. In the spring of 1992, I talked with an AIDS/HIV instructor employed by the New York Bureau of Jewish Education; he purported to "get beyond the euphemism of sexual language" by engaging seventh- and eighth-graders in New York schools and synagogues in recitations of street names for a variety of oral and anal sexual acts. Planned Parenthood of Bergen County, New Jersey, offers a sex ed "Workshop for High Risk Youth" in which high school kids are asked to recite a litany of coarse names for the male organ—*prick, dick, cock, schlong, dong, wiener, tool, pecker,* and so on.[19] Sexuality education consultant Deborah Roffman, who is on the faculty of several independent schools, starts her sexuality education classes with the following exercise: "Turn to the person next to you. Make eye contact. Say 'Hello, penis.' Shake hands and return the greeting: 'Hello, vulva.' "[20]

In the early 1990s, the New York Association of Independent Schools trained sexuality education teachers to conduct "limit setting" role-play in the classroom by teaching adolescents such hygiene-conscious slogans as "No glove, no love!"[21] In Fairfax County, Virginia, the comprehensive sex education program for high-schoolers during the 1980s included instruction in "methods of orgasmic response"; kids were encouraged to share "what turns them on" in group discussions, and "suggestive" and "explicit" materials were distributed in order to stimulate sexual fantasy.[22] And in researching *Why Johnny Can't Tell Right from Wrong,* William Kilpatrick came across: a filmstrip produced by the Unitarian Universalist church for use with students from fifth grade up that featured a male-female couple performing oral, anal, and vaginal intercourse and a male couple performing oral and anal intercourse; a pamphlet for eighth-grade classes in the Buffalo schools that advocated "fisting" (brachiopractic intercourse) and "talking dirty" as safer alternatives to oral, anal, and vaginal intercourse; and a homework assignment to masturbate given to juniors at a Massachusetts high school.[23]

Need it be said that romance, love, and family life play very minor roles in these particular approaches to sexual instruction? Many sexuality education experts contend that love interferes with kids' judgment during the sex act. Sexuality educators William A. Fisher and Deborah M. Roffman argue that only by discouraging amorous behavior—by "breaking through fantasy and emotional barriers" and instilling a series of "rational . . . behavior sequences" involving "negotiation skills" and "explicit scripts"—can we hope to get kids to use contraception and prophylactics consistently. In other words, only by encouraging teens to separate sexual acts from love will we enable them to protect themselves from pregnancy and sexually transmitted diseases.[24]

Therein lies part of the reason why more parents don't protest comprehensive sexuality education: educators like Roffman and Fisher present their methods as sexual disease and pregnancy prevention programs. Parents are well aware that, as sexuality educators would say, adolescence is "a risky time."[25] They know that kids today have to deal with a powerful media culture of sexual imagery as well as raging hormones, and they are frightened by reports of skyrocketing rates of teenage pregnancy and sexual disease, including AIDS. Perhaps, they think, matters have become so urgent that sexual morality and models for family living are luxuries we can't afford. If comprehensive sexuality education will keep kids alive, parents are willing to believe it's necessary, no matter how uncomfortable they are with the values propounded.

But sexuality educators not only exploit parental fears; they also contribute to the very problems they purport to combat. For example, a number of critics of sex education in the late 1980s and early 1990s contended that there was a distinct relationship between the fortunes of comprehensive sex education programs and rates of teenage pregnancy and sexual activity. For over a decade before the introduction of comprehensive sexuality education in the early 1970s, they noted, teen pregnancy rates had been falling. But with the infusion of federal funds into comprehensive sex education, pregnancy rates rose rapidly. In the 1970s alone, the teen pregnancy rate rose from 88 to 111 per 1,000 women, and the percentage of girls between fifteen and nineteen years of age who had engaged in intercourse skyrocketed from 27.6 to 42.2.

What happened next makes it difficult to attribute those increases to other factors, such as the general loosening of sexual mores in the culture at large. In the early 1980s, the Reagan administration blocked federal funding for comprehensive sexuality education and passed federal regulations requiring parental notification when contraceptive services were rendered to teenagers. Teenage sexual activity and pregnancy rates dropped radically. Among young black women, the group most vulnerable to early, out-of-wedlock childbearing, sexual activity rates fell by mid-decade to below pre-1971 levels.[26] As funding for comprehensive sex education resumed in the mid-1980s, pregnancy and teen sexual activity rates shot up once again.

In a 1989 study conducted under the auspices of the Department of Health and Human Services, researchers Stan E. Weed and Joseph A. Olsen analyzed data collected over a period of ten years by the Centers for Disease Control, the Guttmacher Institute (the research arm of Planned Parenthood), the U.S. Census Bureau, and a number of Title X and Title XX (Family Planning Clinic and Adolescent Family Life Act) programs. They discovered that the "greater teenage involvement in family planning programs," the higher teenage pregnancy rates—even when they controlled for such factors as urbanization, race, poverty, and geographic mobility.[27] No studies directly implicated sex education in rising rates of sexually transmitted disease, but indirect evidence abounded. During the late 1980s there was a rapid rise in the incidence of chlamydia, genital herpes, genital warts, and syphilis among teenagers.[28] The links between increasing early and promiscuous sexual activity in women and rises in incidents of STD-induced infertility and cervical carcinoma were particularly disconcerting.[29]

As early as 1979, a study of the effects of comprehensive sex education on teenage sexual attitudes hinted at the problem: The provocative nature of school sex education, the researchers concluded, makes students more tolerant of their own and others' casual sexual activity, and their relaxed attitudes in turn might increase their vulnerability to pregnancy and disease.[30] Certainly the goal of reducing this vulnerability all too often seems to have been forgotten. By 1982, Hans H. Neumann, M.D., medical director of New Haven's Department of Health and a specialist in venereal disease, lamented after researching comprehensive sex education programs in the United States and Sweden, "What we have . . . in many of our schools are far reaching human sexuality programs exploring such areas as masturbation, sexual techniques, homosexuality and rape. The goal of reducing teenage pregnancy [and sexual disease] has been all but lost in favor of 'educating' students to achieve sexual adjustment."

Neumann offered New Haven as a case study in the failure of comprehensive sex education. One of the city's three public high schools had instituted a comprehensive sex education course in 1971, while "the other two high schools offered little or no sex education." Yet by 1982 the high school with the broad-based program had a disturbingly high pregnancy rate, higher than those of the other schools.

The crux of the problem with comprehensive sex education, Neumann asserted, was freewheeling classroom sex talk that broke down all barriers of social and sexual inhibition. Inhibition, he pointed out, is the safety valve that keeps teenagers from the obvious risks of casual sexual involvement. If masturbation was, as sex educators deemed it, a "private" subject, "inappropriate for living room discussion," what were high school kids in mixed-sex classrooms doing talking about it? There was an inherent contradiction, Neumann maintained, between educators' desire to reduce teen pregnancy and health risks and their determination to "create . . . a generation of sexual sophisticates."

Neumann's recommendation: Keep sex education focused on the cold facts rather than the hot fantasies. Classes, he said, should offer "basic instruction in anatomy, reproduction, VD prevention and hygiene." They should be led by health care professionals qualified to answer medical questions, and most important, they should be segregated by sex. He cited an "overwhelming" response in favor of this last point on questionnaires completed by a group of high school girls who had participated in a discussion of a sex-related topic in a co-educational classroom.[31]

Many in the medical and scholarly communities echoed Neumann's assertion that preventing risky behavior and promoting sexual adjustment among teenagers might be mutually exclusive goals.[32] But sex educators continued to insist that in a sexually liberated society, teenage sexual activity was an inevitable fact of life, and that sex education was needed to deal with its unwanted consequences. They defended themselves against accusations that they were contributing to the problem by pointing to studies that cited other factors in the rise of teenage pregnancies: family breakdown, poverty, low self-esteem, and sexual imagery in the media. They also stressed that sexuality education programs had to be taught by qualified instructors if they were to be effective. But they defended instructors' practice of emphasizing the pleasures of sexual experience as well as the risks; otherwise, said SIECUS board member Pamela Wilson, "today's young generation will grow up to be anxiety-ridden" and "sexually dysfunctional." In other words, sex educators were in classrooms not so much to police public health as to counter negative ideas about sexuality children learn from "parental instruction": that sex is a "taboo topic," that the "human body is shameful," that the "genitals are nasty," that "roles for boys and girls are rigidly determined."[33]

■ ■ ■

With the controversy over comprehensive sex education in mind, I decided to take my own look at such a program in a predominantly white, middle-class community. I wanted to test the model in a place where poverty, unemployment, crime, drugs, and family breakdown—the symptoms of inner-city social disintegration that might contribute to rates of teen pregnancy—were not too much in evidence. I settled on Falmouth, Massachusetts, which had a long-standing comprehensive sexuality education program that was touted as among the most progressive in the country.

Falmouth is a community of pristine streets lined with colonial-style homes and upscale boutiques. With a year-round population of only 27,000 (slightly more than 5,000 of whom are children), it's a quiet town, with a large proportion of retirees. But Falmouth is also home to a world-class institute of marine studies and summer home to many artists and professionals. Hardly a wonder, then, that the town is on the cutting edge of sex education, with a curriculum designed in the spirit of the SIECUS guidelines and one of the most radical condom availability programs in the nation; it was the first program to encompass junior high as well as high school, and the first to offer condoms to children as young as twelve years old without parental permission.

By the time I visited Falmouth, in the fall and winter of 1992–93, mandatory eighth- and ninth-grade health classes that included sex education had been in existence for eight years. I was unable to attend the eighth-grade class, but I did attend several sessions of the ninth-grade class. Sex education in the ninth-grade "Health Issues" class was ostensibly directed toward abating "high-risk behavior" among teenagers and counteracting "negative" information or misinformation about sexuality kids might be gathering from the media and their friends, or bringing from home. According to the school district health coordinator, Helen Ladd, the program stressed "sexual decision-making skills" and "values clarification" rather than morality.[34]

The language of the program was frank, but as far as I could tell it was not vulgar. Yet the material was quite plainly structured in ways that inevitably made the "choice" of sexual activity look more viable than celibacy. While students were told in explicit detail and over a period of many weeks how to stimulate their partner's erogenous zones and initiate a variety of sexual acts safely, only forty-five minutes each semester were devoted to the topic of sexual abstinence. While conception and childbearing were discussed, marriage was never mentioned as a prerequisite to parenthood. Family life was touched upon, but as in other health courses in Falmouth, almost exclusively in a negative way—in units on battering, incest, substance abuse, and (in the case of the eighth-grade series of units on human sexuality) on parent-child conflict. The gamut of sexual orientations (including bisexuality and transvestitism) was introduced, along with clear warnings against developing prejudices about any of them.

Whatever the original intentions of its authors, one thing about the Falmouth curriculum stood out quite clearly: Though it was absent in morals, it was full of behavioral imperatives, all of them aimed at inculcating a specific set of sexual mores and an equally specific etiquette of sexual behavior. In short, it was designed to get teenagers to be open to sexual experience without making themselves vulnerable to exploitation, pregnancy, or disease.

Picture twenty fourteen-year-olds in a Health Issues class, a wrap-up on a unit on "date rape." They file in, a motley assortment of tall and short, dark- and light-haired, chubby and thin. With one prominent exception, a blonde in tight jeans, a low-cut shirt, and an impressive dose of eyeliner, they do not look very sexual. In fact, many of the boys appear to be only on the verge of puberty. Conversation seems sex-segregated as they sit down; girls socialize with girls, and boys with boys. A short, husky boy who looks especially young—the single African-American in the class—asks me why I'm there. I explain that I'm there to observe. "Oh yeah? Are you a reporter?" he asks. "In a way," I answer. "I'm a researcher." This seems to satisfy his curiosity, and he turns around.

The discussion is led by two affable teachers, a heavyset man and an athletic-looking woman. In the last class, the students saw a dramatization of date rape on film. They've also received a handout about "sexual misunderstanding" entitled "If a Girl . . ." A table lists certain female behaviors—"wearing sexy clothes," "flirting," "using four-letter words," "letting [a boy] touch her breast," "says 'no' when making out"—and the different meanings they may carry for girls and boys. The handout concludes enigmatically, "Because of these differences in interpretation, [sexual] misunderstandings can arise. . . . We just have to get around them the best we can, and that means taking some risks. . . . So maybe David's wrong about Wendy being interested in him. But maybe he's not. He'll never know unless he's willing to take a risk."

Today the students are asked to identify "attitudes" that might reduce the incidence of date rape. The class, about evenly divided between boys and girls, is conspicuously silent. I wonder if the mixed message they have received from the film and the handout—feel free to take sexual risks, but watch out for date rape—is holding them back. "Come on," urges the male teacher. "What can we do to prevent what we saw in the film—to prevent date rape? How do we communicate?" One studious-looking girl raises her hand. "Verbally?" she tries. "Right!" says the teacher. "And?" He signals a triangle with his hands and mouths the letter "A." Someone answers, "Assertive communication." "Right," the teacher says again. "Remember we talked about 'I' statements? What would be a good example of an 'I' statement?" The black student answers jokingly, "I am somebody." Tittering is heard, and the rustling of binder pages. The kid tries again. "I'll beat you down if you don't stop!" Everyone laughs except the teachers. The difference between assertiveness and aggressiveness is discussed. The teacher warns against "ultimatums."

A worksheet is passed out, entitled "Sexual Assault Activity 3." The assignment reads, "What are some attitudes or beliefs that society needs to reduce sexual assault?" The kids are asked to work in groups of three to come up with at least one attitude that might prevent date rape. The teachers meander around the classroom, supervising.

One girl begins, "Well, one attitude could be that most men are rapists." The female teacher says, "Where did you get that impression?" The girl blusters, "You told us!" She looks through her notebook and reads what she says are the teacher's words. "No, no," the teacher corrects her. "I said last class that most rapists were men, not that most men are rapists!" "Oh," replies the girl, at a loss for another "attitude" to jot down.

The black student is having difficulty with the assignment. "What's wrong with date rape?" he asks the female teacher. "I can do whatever I want with a girl! I'm stronger." The teacher, who seems reluctant to condemn this attitude, asks him why he would want to force himself on a girl. "So there will be more babies in the world," he answers. The male teacher comes to the rescue. "How would you like it if someone said that about your mother or your sister?" he asks. The student recoils, chastised. I reflect upon the irony of a sexuality educator being forced to invoke the "repressive" code of family life in order to teach what is probably the most important lesson a child can learn about male sexual conduct: Never treat a woman in a way you would not want your mother or sister to be treated.

The sexily dressed blonde is also having problems with the assignment. As the male teacher passes she catches his eye. "I don't know . . ." she says, glancing up provocatively. "I mean, girls get horny, too, don't they?" The teacher moves on, giving her a look signifying that he is not impressed. The class regroups to exchange the "attitudes" they came up with. The most well received of these boil down to "open communication," "mutual respect," "gender equality," and the blond girl's second, more demure assertion that "Just because a girl's got a reputation doesn't mean she wants to have sex every time she goes out." Several of the boys, however, don't agree that these "attitudes" can actually reduce the incidence of date rape. They especially contest the attitude that "men and women are equal" and that there should "be no issues of power in the relationship." One tall, serious-looking boy asks the teachers in so many words how one can have an attitude that is based on what seems to him an obvious untruth. "Men are stronger than women," he insists, and to prove it he refers to the film the class has just seen in which a man has used his physical superiority to have his way. "Women aren't physically equal. . . . It'll never happen." That issue is not resolved when the bell rings, but the teachers compliment the kids on a "super job."

The next class is dominated five to one by girls (a proportion that I am later told is the result of tracking the children according to test scores in English and math). When the discussion starts, it is clear that most of the girls have been unnerved by the film. Again the male teacher asks about attitudes that might combat date rape. A wiry brunette raises her hand tentatively. "Never be alone with a boy." Both teachers look slightly distressed, but pass over the remark with the comment that there might be ways in which one can avoid date rape and still date. A girl with red hair and freckles who looks young for her fourteen years raises her hand. "Bring a gun on dates," she ventures, her voice quietly resolute. The teachers choke back laughter, but none of the students even crack a smile.

The teachers try again. Haven't they talked about mutual respect? About open communication? About assertiveness? About equality? About gender roles that encourage men to be sexual aggressors and women to be passive? The students obediently write these things down in their notebooks and begin to come up with answers that are more acceptable to their instructors, but there is a rote quality to their responses, and I am overwhelmed by a feeling of sympathy for them. In my day, I think, a universally accepted ethic of teenage sexual continence prevented most high school girls from having to negotiate their way through "misunderstandings" about whether they were going to sleep with their dates. And if they were psychologically coerced or taken by physical force, it wasn't date rape, it was statutory rape or just plain rape, in which case the legal implications were obvious.[35]

These kids, I think, live in a complicated world—a world of too many scripts and too few rules. They are not getting what they were intended to get from the date rape unit—namely, initiation into a sexual utopia in which boys and girls respectfully negotiate foreplay before moving on to the main act. Rather, they are getting the message that it is a sexually rapacious world out there, where girls are sitting ducks and boys pounce at will. Do they ever long for a set of unambiguous dos and don'ts of sexual behavior?

I asked the school nurse, Shirley Cullinane, to paint me a picture of the current dating scene at Falmouth High. She estimated that about half the students were sexually active. The other half, she intimated, did not date much, because in many high school circles dating seemed to presume sex. Many boys and girls, she said, were promiscuous and boastful about it, but quite a few girls had complained to her that they felt pressured to have sex. One student claimed she had sex with a boy solely because she was afraid of angering him. "I happen to know this boy," Cullinane said. "Anger is not good with him." She summed up, "The girls are intimidated by the boys. Some of the [older] boys have four and five girls." Why did the girls stand for being treated as nothing better than concubines? They seemed, especially the younger girls, to value the attention and the social prestige of dating, even if it involved unwelcome sex.

Did Cullinane talk to any of the kids about the possibility of a dating life without sex? Not directly, she said. But she often told kids about her own innocent high school years, and about her celibate two-year courtship with her husband-to-be. These stories, she insisted, were like fairy tales to the kids. "They think I'm lying . . . when I say I was a virgin when I got married. . . . They think there is no way you can go out with a man for two years and not have sex with him."

I asked whether parents made any attempt to teach kids about abstinence. Cullinane said that many Falmouth parents were divorced and had "live-in girlfriends or boyfriends," so it was difficult for them to act as paragons of sexual propriety. Yet, she said, "It's the kids who are most promiscuous." Indeed, she admitted many kids feared revealing to their parents that they were sexually active. Many girls come to her when they find out they're pregnant. "I always ask, 'Have you talked to your mom? You've got to talk to your mother.' And they always say, 'Oh, I can't tell my mom about it.' But many times the mothers will turn out to be supportive. . . . Family Planning . . . counselors will often go talk to the parents, go home with a [pregnant] girl if her parents know. . . . But we've had a lot of abortions go out of here, and the parents have never known. . . . It costs them three hundred, four hundred dollars, but the girls won't ask for help."

Cullinane told me that whatever her personal views of their sexual behavior, she has never advised kids to stop having sex, "because they'll do what they want anyway." We live in a time, she says, in which there seems to be a complete collapse of behavioral standards, among adults as well as children. Kids "think it's okay to do what they want," she remarked sadly, "because everyone else does."

Whenever Cullinane could, she urged kids she knew were sexually active to take precautions against pregnancy and sexual disease by using condoms. She was happy that the school district had instituted a condom distribution program. But if the kids wouldn't listen to the message "Don't have sex," why did she think they would listen to a message about condoms? "It all comes down to education," said Cullinane. "You know how when smoking became a serious problem in this country and they started hitting every corner of the earth with 'Don't smoke' . . . it eventually seemed to sink in so that my generation doesn't smoke. I think if we really push and push. . . . I'm on this task force that's trying to educate the town—the adults—about AIDS. But these kids have to be educated, the kids more than anyone, because they're the ones who are so promiscuous."

Considering their relentless faith in "education," it may seem curious that school health professionals like Cullinane never entertain the possibility that repeating the message of sexual abstinence might be as important to teenage sexual health as repeating the message about abstinence from smoking. To the contrary, the schools' campaign on sexual health could be aptly compared to offering children cigarettes with filters. For years condoms have been hailed and unveiled in Falmouth Health Issues classes, and in January 1992 the Falmouth School Committee, acting on a Massachusetts State Department of Education directive, approved a policy of making condoms available to kids from the seventh grade up. As in other communities, however, while educators and health professionals lined up behind the policy, Falmouth residents were by no means united with them. No other school decision, in fact, has ever elicited more controversy. When the public got wind of the coming initiative, in the fall of 1991, angry parents of junior high and high school students called the PTO and school administrations, and a group of parents circulated a petition protesting the policy. By spring, they had collected 3,200 signatures against it, and the town government was forced to call a referendum.[36]

At the referendum, the condom policy slipped by on a margin of just over 3 percent—slightly more than two hundred votes. Even today, five years later, opponents of the policy never fail to point out that in precincts with higher proportions of public school clientele the policy was voted down, and they claim that it was only thanks to a strong turnout in the Woods Hole community, where there is a large population of young singles, that it passed. Yet there was a core group of condom supporters in the PTO who actively campaigned for the policy. They, like the school health faculty, seemed certain that condoms were the only answer to a growing public health problem, even if they disapproved of casual teenage sex.

In January 1993 I talked with fourteen parents who were in the vanguard of support for the condom program. Almost everything they had to say about teenage sexual behavior and about the comprehensive sex education program in their schools echoed the opinions and concerns I have heard elsewhere around the country. They thought that sex education was ideally their job, and not the job of the schools. They were open about sexuality at home, and eager to transmit a positive message about sexuality as well as to impart accurate sexual information and a sense of sexual responsibility. Several lamented that in an age of sinking sexual morals they felt isolated in the task of conveying high standards of sexual behavior. "Parents have to do everything," lamented one mother. "Society does nothing." They complained that kids today are "too fast" sexually. One black woman—who, besides having children in the high school, worked in the school office—said, "I don't think they [high school kids] should have any involvement in sex per se other than the knowledge of it at this point. . . . But you've got these kids going at it in the hallway of the school . . . like this was some kind of love tunnel or something."

Several parents mentioned that their children had come to them for help in dealing with peer pressures to be sexually active. One mother said, to the amusement of the other parents, that she told her children, "If someone wants you to do something you don't want to do, tell them your mother won't let you." Another mother said, "I don't think my son is sexually active, but I tell him if he ever finds himself in the heat of passion . . . to stop and just imagine your mother is sitting on your shoulder."

Many parents worried that too many adolescents reduced sexuality to a casual, mechanical act. One woman emphasized the importance of "teaching young people that this is the way our Creator made us. Our sexuality is really our spirituality." Another mother said she wanted her kids "to know that in my view sex . . . belongs in marriage."

The parents praised Falmouth's sex education program, principally for providing sexual information and support to children who might come from homes less enlightened than their own. But some felt that the curriculum introduced the subject of sexual orientation at too young an age. A few complained that lurid discussions of sexual disease—especially AIDS—left their adolescents unnecessarily frightened. Particularly disturbing to many of the parents was the derisive attitude some of their boys displayed toward homosexuals after AIDS victims were brought into the classroom as testimony about the ravages of the illness. Several mothers felt that premature classroom discussions of homosexuality in general had tapped into their sons' adolescent fears of both identification and confrontation with homosexuals. They worried that these discussions might backfire, encouraging homophobic acting out.[37] The same woman who wanted her children "to know that in my view sex . . . belongs in marriage" commented that kids "tend to sit in judgment about homosexuality . . . they're very conservative. I have a much more liberal attitude than my kids."

The fathers I spoke with among the pro-condom contingent agreed that classroom discussions of homosexuality were unproductive, but they worried less about the boys' lack of comfort with homosexuality than about what they considered to be the ideological agenda underlying an inappropriate focus on homosexuality. One father was disturbed that classroom discussions allowed homosexuality and heterosexuality equal time. "I don't know if I can support the idea that homosexuality is just another lifestyle," he said. "I think there is a difference between accepting people as . . . human beings and saying that homosexuality is just the same as anything else."

Given their reservations about the comprehensive sex education program, why were parents so anxious to get behind the condom availability program? The threat of AIDS. The woman who appealed for a reminder that sexuality is linked to spirituality put it succinctly: "It used to be the very worst that happened [to kids who had sex] is they got pregnant and ruined three lives. Now they can end those lives."

The fear of an AIDS epidemic among adolescents was so profound that parents opposed to the condom policy had found it difficult to engage parents in favor of the policy in discussion of the deeper moral implications involved. For the pro-condom contingent, condom availability was not a moral issue but a public health issue. Opponents of the policy often found themselves constrained to debating the issue on medical grounds—by pointing up rates of condom failure, for example—rather than asking whether condom availability might impede parents' ability to enforce high standards of sexual conduct, or what might be the effects of the implicit message that casual, premarital sex is okay for kids as long as they use a prophylactic.

Many of the parents I spoke with described the program as a "safety net" for an increasingly promiscuous adolescent population who were not getting the guidance at home that they themselves were providing for their own children. Said one Falmouth father, "There are . . . significant numbers . . . of kids out there who are missing some kind of parenting they should be getting. The schools have to step in." But how can parents who emphasize their role as standard-setters for their children's sexual behavior view the standard-crushing school environment as an adequate surrogate for parents who are not doing their job? Do parents really think it is enough for *other people's children* to receive sexuality training devoid of any firm convictions about the relationship between

the sex act, love, and family life? Do they ever consider a possible connection between the sexual attitudes explored in comprehensive sex education classes and the increasingly promiscuous sexual culture they
so fear?

James Remillard, a leader of Concerned Citizens, the watchdog
group that formed the core of opposition to condom availability in Falmouth, didn't blame parents for this lack of perspicacity. He noted that
the school "presents its sexuality education program to parents as primarily informational, not ideological. They say to parents, 'We're professionals.' And parents believe it, because they want . . . to trust the
schools." But he worried that Falmouth educators might not be as professional as they claimed. He cited an incident that had occurred in December 1992, when the Falmouth schools' health faculty distributed a
forty-minute survey on the subject of drugs and sex to students in the
seventh through twelfth grades.

The survey—the third of its kind in three years—was ostensibly
drawn up to gather data that might help to secure special health education grants from government and private foundations and to determine
"priorities" in the school district's health programming.[38] It was administered without informing parents. But a copy of the questionnaire got into
the hands of a parent who found it highly offensive. Some of the questions about student sexual behavior were leading in the extreme—calculated, in Remillard's words, to "manufacture rather than gather" data. Of
thirty-nine questions addressing the sexual behavior of children as young
as twelve years old, twenty-four assumed that children were sexually active. For example, the question "When did you first have sexual intercourse?" listed various grade levels as possible responses, but gave no
opportunity to answer "never."[39] Any sexually abstinent teenager who
took the survey, Remillard remarked, was bound to feel "isolated . . .
from [his] peers and unconventional."[40]

Alarmed, Concerned Citizens sought the help of Judith Reisman,
president of the Center for Media Education and co-author, along with
Edward W. Eichel, of *Kinsey, Sex and Fraud.* Her evaluation of the doc-
ument: that it evinced utter "disregard for scientific standards," "violated
scientific protocol," was constructed in a way bound to "contaminate the
data," and was filled with questions that "loutish[ly] . . . put the 'burden
of proof' on . . . youngsters to disclaim their part in antisocial, illegal and
humiliating activity."[41] It was also insensitive, Reisman pointed out, sin-
gling out a question that read, "What is the sex of the person(s) with
whom you have had sexual contact?" Not only did the available answers
("A. Male; B. Female; C. Both") again assume sexual activity, they also

implied consent among a population of minors, some of whom might have been sexually abused or coerced.[42]

At a public hearing, Concerned Citizens approached the Falmouth School Committee armed with Reisman's and three other professional evaluations that were sharply critical of the survey; they requested that it be invalidated. The request was granted, but the committee took the opportunity to invite the district health coordinator, Helen Ladd, to refute charges by angry parents that the survey might be an indication of a highly flawed curriculum. Ladd publicly outlined that curriculum, which she insisted was neither assuming nor encouraging risky behavior, but rather focused on "self-esteem," "communication," "decision-making," and "responsibility."[43]

But just how much self esteem, communication, decision-making, and responsibility have Falmouth High School students learned through comprehensive sexuality education? No statistics exist, but the anecdotal evidence of widespread sexual coercion suggests that, at least for the female students, the program's record on self-esteem and communication is a sorry one. There is statistical evidence that the "responsibility" and "decision-making" aspects of the program have not fulfilled expectations. Despite the longevity of the comprehensive sexuality education program, which virtually defined sexual responsibility as protection from pregnancy and disease, teenage pregnancy rates were rising by 1992 at the rate of 10 percent a year, about three times the national average of around 3.3 percent. According to a March 1993 report sponsored by the Falmouth-Mashpee Teen Pregnancy Prevention Coalition, there were "increasing numbers of single mothers under age 19, and the average teenage mother is giving birth younger."[44] The incidence of sexually transmitted disease among teenagers showed a similarly alarming trend. There had been an epidemic of syphilis among Falmouth teens in the late 1980s. Now they were in the grip of an epidemic of chlamydia; rates of that disease had gone up 200 percent in the fifteen- to nineteen-year-old age group between 1989 and 1991 alone.[45]

Of course all this was before the condom availability program had existed long enough to evaluate its impact on the schools' efforts to combat teenage pregnancy and STDs. But there is little indication that as the district has settled into its condom availability policy, this has made a difference. I was unable to obtain statistics on teen pregnancy rates (including aborted pregnancies) after 1992. But in 1994, the most recent year for which data is available, live births to teenagers—which had fluctuated in the period between 1990 and 1992 between a low of thirty-eight and a high of fifty-eight, numbered fifty-one. (According to

Massachusetts public health records, public assistance paid for prenatal care in thirty-one of these cases.) When I recently called the director of Falmouth-Mashpee's Early Childbearing Program to ask her about these statistics, she indicated that teen pregnancy remains a serious problem in Falmouth. As of April 1996, she was carrying a caseload of thirty pregnant and parenting girls; several babies, she contended, had been conceived on school "snow days" during the previous winter. The chlamydia epidemic among the fifteen- to nineteen-year-olds had stabilized, but at the highest levels of the decade.[46]

The new data has not surprised me. In the winter of 1993, it was already apparent that condom availability in the Falmouth schools would probably not have much of an impact on teenage STDs and pregnancy. The health coordinator, Helen Ladd, had warned me that she would "be hesitant to sell my program on the basis of numbers." The school nurse had contended that after one year of the program Falmouth High students were using condoms only sporadically. How did she know? The kids told her, and she was having considerable trouble giving condoms away. At the start of the program, she said, she gave out approximately five condoms a week, mostly to girls who came to her office to request them. But by the eighth month of the program, despite her consistent offers to kids she knew were sexually active and were not using condoms, she was able to give out only two—both to the same freshman male.

Were the kids too shy to take condoms from someone they knew? Hardly, Cullinane thought, since some of the girls came into her office "five and six at a time . . . and sit around . . . talking about . . . oral sex." Some kids refused her offers of condoms on the grounds that they dull sexual feeling. But most insisted they "trusted" the people with whom they were having sexual relations to be free of sexual diseases. And some girls, she said, "think it's cool to get pregnant. It's a grown-up thing to do." The Falmouth case seems to confirm the findings of sex education researchers Weed and Olsen that

> [a]dolescents simply lack the developmental capacity and maturity to engage in the rational decision making process required for effective contraceptive use. . . . For some teens the prevalence of risk taking, combined with a sense of infallibility about immediate and personal consequences, could easily override their inherent (but undeveloped) logic and their perception of negative consequences.[47]

The Falmouth experience also echoes the results of studies indicating that despite a widespread campaign in American schools and media urging consistent condom use, almost half of sexually active teenagers remain unresponsive to the message.[48]

But most important, the Falmouth example points up some of the greatest weaknesses of endeavors in behavioral education that rest upon neither a firm consensus of values between parents and educators, nor on sound notions of child and adolescent emotional and intellectual development.

In an article on comprehensive sex education in New Jersey published in the *Atlantic Monthly* in October 1994, Barbara Dafoe Whitehead indicates that the problems that haunt Falmouth haunt other school systems where talk of sexual "choices" is rife and where exaggerated notions of teenage competence, independence, and capacity for responsible decision-making reign.

New Jersey has unusually high rates of teenage pregnancy. And these sorry statistics, says Whitehead, are linked as much to the state's approach to sex education as to its troubled urban socioeconomic profile.[49] Educators and social welfare professionals in New Jersey, she contends, no longer support the "sexual moratorium" that has traditionally held sway from the onset of physical maturity to the attainment of economic and "social maturity" in modern society. Such a moratorium would normally afford young people "the opportunity to acquire the competencies and credentials of adulthood before they took on the responsibilities of . . . parenthood." But as things stand, the professionals have abdicated authority over teenage sexual behavior, Whitehead charges, releasing many vulnerable, poor adolescents to the "burdens and responsibilities of too-early adulthood."[50]

Of course, sex education is only one factor among many in our culture that seem bent on undermining children's delicate and immature psychosexual constitutions and thrusting them into responsibilities they cannot handle. A hypersexualized media and the irresponsible lifestyles of too many adults—many of them parents—contribute to the problem, as does a legal culture that seems to be more interested in protecting children's rights to sexual self-determination than in shielding them from sexual exploitation. (At least half of all children born to teenage girls are fathered by adult males, according to a national study undertaken by the Alan Guttmacher Institute.[51]) But sex education seems to be one arena where small changes can make big differences in teenage behavior, and where those changes are relatively easy to make.

Take the positive record of abstinence curricula, for example. Abstinence curricula were developed as a result of the Reagan administration's Adolescent Family Life Act of 1981. They typically provide the same information about reproduction and the risks of teen pregnancy and sexually transmitted disease the comprehensive sexuality education curricula do, but always with an emphasis on abstinence before marriage and on the eventual rewards of monogamous marital relationships. Advocates of comprehensive sexuality education have contended that many of these programs "rely on instilling fear and shame in adolescents in order to discourage premarital sexual behavior," exaggerate the physical and psychological risks of early sexual activity, encourage intolerance of homosexuality, fail to provide teenagers with adequate information about contraceptives, and promote gender stereotyping.[52] Some of these charges may be true in some cases. But whatever their flaws, these programs seem to be far more effective than comprehensive sex education in fighting teen pregnancy and sexual disease. While no large studies of abstinence education have been done, smaller studies indicate some impressive results. For example, between 1984 and 1988, the San Marcos school district near San Diego brought a pregnancy rate that had reached nearly 20 percent down to 1.5 percent with an abstinence education program devised by a Washington State firm called Teen Aids. A controlled five-year study of twenty-six schools using the now-well-known Sex Respect abstinence curriculum showed the pregnancy rate of teenage girls who had participated in the program to be 44 percent lower than among girls who had not.[53] (It should be noted here that the Sex Respect curriculum is not a self-selecting one, like many of the voluntary abstinence clubs that are developing in schools around the country. Its efficacy, therefore, in reducing pregnancy seems to be of real significance.)

Abstinence programs are only slowly catching on, but their presence and their apparent success has probably been a factor in the very recent preoccupation among comprehensive sexuality educators with providing clearer support for abstinence, at least for younger teenagers. A growing number of comprehensive sex education programs now include training in sexual "refusal skills."[54] Most such programs are based on a model developed in 1985 by gynecologist Marion Howard, director of a reproductive clinic for teenagers at Grady Memorial Hospital in Atlanta, which combines information on reproduction, sexually transmitted disease, and contraception with role-playing exercises and assertiveness training. The exercises are designed to make kids comfortable with resisting unwelcome pressures to engage in sex. (Howard developed the refusal skills training component of her program when, disappointed with the results of a more conventional sex education program she had instituted in Atlanta's junior high schools during the late 1970s, she surveyed one thousand teenage girls about what they most wanted to learn in sex education. The most frequent answer: "how to say no without hurting the other person's feelings.")[55]

Predictably, when abstinence support is grafted onto sexuality education programs that also support the "choice" of being sexually active, results are mixed. A study of 758 California high school students by the research group ETR Associates compared a group that had received comprehensive sex education with one whose sex education curriculum included strategies for reducing sexual pressures. Eighteen months after finishing their respective sex education courses, the students who had learned refusal skills were 25 percent less likely to have begun sexual activity—an improvement on comprehensive sexuality education to be sure, but not as good a record as abstinence-only programs can claim so far.[56]

Whatever continued research shows, the return of abstinence support to schools in any form is encouraging. Comprehensive sexuality education advocates like Peter Scales, director of the Center for Early Adolescence at the University of North Carolina, may insist that adults don't have "the credibility" to advocate abstinence, but there is a great deal of evidence to suggest that today's teenagers are yearning for directives from adults to say no to sex. A SIECUS study of 1994 found that more than half the teenagers who have had intercourse wish they had waited longer. And recent advertising campaigns encouraging sexual "temperance," among them the Southern Baptist Church–sponsored "True Love Waits" campaign and the state of Maryland's "Virginity Is Not a Dirty Word" campaign, have been huge successes with teenagers. (The latter, reports the *New York Times,* was thought to be responsible for a 10 percent decline in Maryland's teen pregnancy rate between 1992 and 1994 alone.)[57]

There is also recent evidence that were schools to take a stronger stand on teenage sexual abstinence, they might prepare our youth for far more pleasurable and guilt-free sex lives than they are being prepared for today. Despite the claims of sexuality educators that traditional sexual values lead to unhappy and repressed sex lives, a recent study by the National Institute for Health Care Research found that "sexual responsiveness is significantly affected by the relational context in which it occurs" and that "the people who report the most satisfaction with their sex lives are the faithfully married." Why? Partly because married couples enjoy "freedom from fear of comparison, rejection and disease."[58] Indeed, if the trend to abstinence support continues, we may see not only a sorely needed reinforcement of family values in schools, but a new kind of teenage sexual liberation—liberation from sexual exploitation and the disappointments of ill-considered sexual decision-making, liberation to lives of greater adult sexual fulfillment.

6

The Workfare/Day Care Trap

During the winter of 1995, a new, Republican-dominated Congress set its paring knives to the welfare system, determined to trim federally run entitlement programs by transferring them to state control. The reaction in liberal circles was relatively quiet until the school-meal program came up on the block, eliciting cries of "Enough!" from child advocates, educators, Democratic politicians, and much of the media. For nearly fifty years the free lunch program had been a symbol of national concern for the welfare of children.[1] "The American public expects us to cut spending and downsize government," claimed one Democratic congressman, "but I don't think they expect us to make war on kids!"[2]

Spokesmen from the Children's Defense Fund predicted dire consequences should the federal government relinquish control of the program. Vermont governor Howard Dean, Democratic chairman of the National Governors Association, reflected, "I think America has a national interest in its children; . . . the same benefits and strength and support that a child from Minnesota deserves . . . a child from Alabama deserves.[3] The President chastised Congress that it was being "tough and cruel on kids." Public protests emerged in almost every state as if the Republican plan was to rip food out of the mouths of babes.

In fact, the plan was to "allow governors to coordinate school lunches with all the other nutrition programs that Republicans plan to devolve to state control," on the assumption that the closer the administration of such a program is to its beneficiaries, the more cost effective it will be.[4] School meal programs were one of the few entitlement programs the Republicans never had any intention of phasing out; indeed, they had raised the federal contribution to them by 4.5 percent, 1.4 percent more than had been suggested by a Democrat-dominated Congress.

Ironically, the debate over school meals may have turned on the completely false assumption that the American people are uniformly behind them. In July 1993, the school board of Meriden, Connecticut, prompted by vocal opposition in the community, rejected for the fourth time in eighteen months a state mandate requiring the district to offer free or reduced-cost breakfasts to seventy-one poor children at the John Barry Elementary School. The vote set off a battle between the town of sixty-thousand and the state of Connecticut that culminated in a court order to institute the program.

On the face of it, the town's opposition was hard to comprehend. The mandate, after all, was intended to furnish needy children with the morning sustenance they needed to learn. Furthermore, the breakfasts were to be financed entirely from federal and state grants. But the recalcitrant citizens of Meriden had reasons for resisting. The existing free and reduced-price lunch program, they maintained, was a prime example of government waste. It was costly and poorly managed; administrators verified income data on only 3 percent of applicants; the food served was neither nutritious nor appetizing, so that much of it went straight from plates into garbage cans. And though the lunch program was ostensibly paid for out of state and federal funds, it still incurred operating costs for the town. Meriden already faced a declining tax base and a budget bloated with social programs imposed from above.[5]

There was another issue at stake that had nothing to do with money, opponents of the program insisted: a way of life dear to Meriden's large population of second-generation Italian and Polish immigrants. For these hardworking, middle-class citizens, most of whom grew up in very poor homes, serving breakfast was "the job of parents, not schools." Jim Tavegia, a state legislator from Meriden and one of the principal spokesmen against the program, summarized the views of many of his constituents: "Why disrupt healthy patterns of family life among poor people? We are absolving poor parents of an important responsibility. . . . First we serve free lunch at school . . . then free breakfast at school. . . . Next we'll be setting up beds!"

Indeed, not one of the mostly Hispanic parents whose children were slated as beneficiaries of the program spoke publicly in favor of it, and several had called the school board president to tell him they resented the implication that they were not giving their children breakfast in the morning. The truth was that only one or two children actually came to John Barry School hungry each day, and they were already being provided for without a special government program.

William Lutz, one of the minority on the school board who supported the breakfast plan, revealed why—even given a noticeable lack of support from the poor—the state would not back down. The breakfast program, he contended, was not just a matter of government charity; it was an experiment in offering extended school services, a concept that would soon spread to schools with more affluent student populations. "We are hoping that the costs of serving free breakfasts will eventually be offset with paid participation by children from more prosperous two-income households," he said, adding, "Families don't eat breakfast together anymore. . . . Many kids who eat breakfast alone at home would welcome the opportunity to sit down to a muffin and a glass of milk with their friends at school."

The Meriden school breakfast controversy is a revealing example of the current tension in our society over the growing institutionalization of children's lives. Government and an interested group of professionals zealously pursue an agenda of expanding direct "services" to children who may or may not need them, while many proud and loving parents struggle against the bureaucratic stream to maintain strong bonds with their children. The Meriden dispute points up the tendency in our culture to tip the child-rearing balance that once favored families—in this case, by two meals to one—over bureaucracies.

Schools increasingly function as clearinghouses through which social and health services are urged, even forced on children and families. Recently the community of East Stroudsburg, Pennsylvania, was rocked by scandal when the J. T. Lambert Intermediate School ordered genital exams performed on fifty eleven-year-old girls, many without their parents' permission. The object: to search for genital warts and evidence of sexual abuse. Katie Tucker, the mother of one of these girls, told the *Washington Times*:

> They were told they needed to take off their clothes and just leave their underwear on. They were standing in line, perfectly embarrassed, and then they found out the doctor was doing genital exams. The girls were scared. They were crying and trying to run out of the door, but one of the nurses was blocking the door so they couldn't leave.

My daughter told the other nurse . . . "My mother wouldn't like this. I want to call her." And they said, "No." And my daughter said, "I don't want this test done." And the nurse said, "Too bad." [They] put the girls in a room and had them lie down on a table, spread-eagled, with nothing covering them. . . . The girls had no idea what they were doing. The doctor didn't talk to them. She just did the genital exam and didn't say one word. . . . All my daughter could do was stare up at the ceiling. And it hurt. And it still hurts.

When parents protested, school officials insisted the exam fell "within the parameters" of guidelines set for them by the state, which included a mandate to procure a "medical examination and comprehensive appraisal of the health" of schoolchildren at certain ages.[6]

Parents of two teenage girls in Toccoa, Georgia, are suing their school district because in the summer of 1995 they came upon a bag of condoms in their daughters' room. Apparently the girls had been taken by a school counselor—during the school day, without the parents' knowledge—to a clinic where they were prescribed birth control pills, tested for AIDS, and examined for cervical cancer. The school authorities' explanation? "We're simply trying to do what's best for the students."[7]

In well-heeled Fairfield County, Connecticut, parents have fought the introduction of student advisory programs that promise to go beyond academic guidance to encompass more personal mentoring responsibilities. Their objections boil down to the sneaking perception that it is a mistake to cede family functions to bureaucracies. In the words of one mother, "I don't want a schoolteacher parenting my child. It's my job to parent him."

But the schools, with a battalion of social service staff within their walls, are already supplanting the family in a variety of functions. To date, 1,625 programs in forty-three states and the District of Columbia are expanding schools into one-stop shopping centers that provide a full complement of social services—meals, health care, counseling, family planning—to children and adolescents either on site or through school-linked "integrated social service" networks.[8] They also monitor families, on the assumption that (in the words of the Education Commission of the States) "the focus of services must shift from easing the latest crisis a family is facing to preventing family crises from occurring."[9]

The notion that parents are incapable of raising children without the help and oversight of an army of social service professionals provided by the schools is rapidly gaining currency. In a September 1992 issue of *The School Administrator,* former Surgeon General Joycelyn Elders touted the extensive family planning and mental health services at Little Rock's Central High.[10] In the same issue, two San Diego educators reported on their district's efforts at "Spinning a Family Support Web Among Agencies and Schools."[11] In 1993, Herbert Grover, Wisconsin's superintendent of public instruction, suggested that the "definition of education" must "include a child's continuing intellectual, physical, emotional and social development and well-being." Wisconsin's schools, he maintained, must thus provide "full-time preschool child care, before- and after-school child care, parent training . . . early childhood education programs and health, mental health and social services" and even "home visits to parents."[12] Finally, a 1993 report by the North Central Regional Educational Laboratory held that school–social service links should "go beyond cooperation and coordination to collaboration, and that they should be "comprehensive; preventative; family centered and family driven; developmental . . . ; integrated; flexible; sensitive to cultural, gender, ability and racial differences; and outcomes-oriented."[13]

In Illinois, pro-family groups defeated a legislative proposal that would have enabled the state Board of Education to set up a program to send state employees into homes of "parents of children in the period of life from birth to kindergarten" for purposes of parent supervision and training—and without soliciting their consent.[14] This seems to have been the most radical and far-reaching state-sponsored parent-monitoring attempt to date, because it would have granted social service access to every home in Illinois, whether parents were willing or not. Still, all over the country the mechanisms for supervising parents and strong-arming them into the state's parenting vision are rapidly falling into place, probably because parents who are "offered" services—especially poor parents—are reluctant to refuse them for fear that they might be subjected to investigation for child abuse.

Perhaps the best known of the school-linked social service programs is Missouri's Parents As Teachers program (PAT), which sends social service professionals into 160,000 homes to instruct mothers and fathers in government-approved methods of parenting. The schools keep records of the parents' competence and the children's development. Not only does the program embody a frightening potential for thwarting family privacy and autonomy; it also displays the typical propensity of professional interventions in family life to create the need for still more interventions. PAT's health screening program, for example, found "potential" physical or mental disabilities in 37 percent of the children screened between 1989 and 1990. According to investigative reporter Angela Dale, one hearing and vision screening technician involved in the program "was told he must produce a 20 percent failure rate" on the tests he administered, though he claimed the average failure rate for such tests is somewhere between 2 and 6 percent.[15]

Educators themselves are not uniformly impressed with the explosion of social services in schools. Although the nation's largest teachers' union, the NEA (National Education Association), has supported them, the AFT (American Federation of Teachers) has been somewhat critical. AFT president Albert Shanker notes, "If you put all the services in the school, there's a tendency for the teachers to say it's not all that important for this child to learn algebra; it's more important for the child to be healthy."[16] At a time when the schools are failing at their basic function—to produce literate citizens—it does seem unwise to turn them into social service clearinghouses.

Not surprisingly, school-linked social service programs have been directed primarily at the poor, with substantial funding coming from government programs such as Title I, Even Start, Head Start, and Medicaid. Many attempt not only to provide family counseling and health services but to get children into preschool as early as possible. The call of the day among social service professionals is "early intervention," a term that encompasses not only parent training and family monitoring efforts, but also early childhood schooling.

Bowling Park Elementary, in Norfolk, Virginia's, inner city, is among six hundred schools that operate on a model of "cooperative management in which parents, teachers and mental-health counselors . . . focus on building close-knit relationships with children." In practice, that can mean monitoring parents' competence and children's development from birth, with parental "consent" of course. "Parent technicians" visit infants and toddlers in their homes, take parents on field trips (in two instances to local prisons, where they were warned, in one principal's words, that "this is where their child is heading"), and invite them to school-sponsored exercise, parenting, and adult education classes.[17] All-day, year-round preschool begins at the age of three, on the assumption that "schools are being called on to be those 'surrogate parents' that can increase the 'teachability' of children who arrive on their doorsteps in poor shape." (This, at least, is the assessment of Joy G. Dryfoos, who has written about full-service schools.)[18]

Nowhere, however, are the cross-purposes of parents and professionals so evident as in the recent government push to expand day care and early preschool programs for the poor, at a time when middle-class parents are reassessing the supposed social and educational benefits of group care for young children. Many of the parents I interviewed for this book expressed serious reservations as to the benefits of preschool. The well-publicized phenomenon of "kindergarten burnout" has discouraged many parents from pushing academic achievement on young children. But parents also have reservations about leaving young children in a group of peers during the day, whether for educational purposes or not. A Baltimore mother, herself a child care worker, says, "We didn't have to deal with society until we were about six years old. . . . A lot of kids are . . . dealing with society and outside forces at two years old. . . . They're forcing the children into education and social activities and sports and all those things so much earlier. Not that all those things are bad, but I think that if they were home-oriented longer, it would be better for them."

Whatever parents may think, there is a strong contingent in government and social services that is determined to push young children out of their homes and into the peer group setting. Recently, the Centers for Disease Control set out to organize an intensive early-intervention research project in fourteen cities entitled Project BEGIN—Bringing Early Growth (and Development) Into Neighborhoods. Originally the project—which, it was hoped, would serve as a national model—was slated to bring low-income children between twelve and thirty-six months into full-day "child development" centers where they would be placed in groups of eight, with two adults overseeing each group.[19] An extensive array of social services was also planned for the mothers of these children. Not surprisingly, it turned out the idea was economically unfeasible, and the authors of the project, in conjunction with child development consultants from around the country, are presently renegotiating its design.

But the Department of Health and Human Services has undertaken an enterprise in many ways similar. The Zero to Three Initiative, a Head Start program directed at infants and toddlers from impoverished homes, is purported to answer the problem of school preparedness that the original Head Start program never solved. To be fair, Zero to Three is not a monolithic program; rather it has emerged as a set of community-based projects that link kids with child care and early education, parents with a variety of social service resources, counseling, and parent education. But a principal component of the initiative appears to be projects and referrals that look a lot like day care and early-childhood schooling for kids still in diapers. Why? Acknowledging the failures of the older Head Start program for three-, four-, and five-year-olds, Professor Ed Zigler of Yale contends, "Waiting for children to turn three in order to be eligible for Head Start is waiting too long." Bob Hochstein, of the Carnegie Foundation for the Advancement of Teaching, theorizes, "Head Start's success rate will bloom once it expands its focus to include the most critical years of a child's brain development."[20]

The problem with such rosy prognoses is that the verdict on even the highest-quality group care experiences in early childhood—whether in a day care or preschool environment—is very discouraging. Several studies in the 1980s indicated that grouping very young children together for extended periods may pose unnecessary threats to their physical well-being—for example, a heightened risk of contracting cytomegalovirus (CMV), which, when transferred from children to their pregnant mothers, can lead to birth defects. The American Academy of Pediatrics warns that outbreaks of gastroenteritis, bacterial meningitis, and hepatitis A are common in group day care. A 1984 study noted that small children in day care environments were twelve times more vulnerable than children who were cared for at home to the influenza B virus, which sometimes causes meningitis. Respiratory illness and giardiasis are among other diseases heavily associated with group child care.[21]

But the primary argument against group child care rests on its psychological and social risks. A recent University of Texas study of three hundred third-graders compared children who had experienced full-time group day care in their infant and preschool years with those who were cared for at home. Both parents and teachers claimed that kids raised in group environments exhibited poorer peer relations, work study skills, levels of cooperation with adults at home and at school, grades, and self-images. Researchers found that these "negative effects appeared particularly pronounced for children placed in full-time non-maternal care in infancy," and that "despite all the current talk about 'quality' child care . . . high-quality nonmaternal care appeared to cause the same pattern of harmful effects as low-quality care."[22]

A 1985 study published in *Child Development* concluded that the early day care experience had long-lasting negative effects on self-discipline. This study compared a group of five-year-olds who were raised from the age of three months in a high-quality day care program run by the University of North Carolina with a group who were kept at home for the first five years of life. The former group were far more likely to display aggression with their classmates and teachers and to avoid schoolwork.[23] Several other studies of university-sponsored, high-quality group day care programs indicate that the younger the child, the more detrimental the group care experience. A University of Illinois study of children from stable middle-class families, for example, found that "repeated daily separations experienced by infants whose mothers are working full-time constitute a 'risk' factor" in psychological health and development.[24]

In his study *High Risk: Children Without a Conscience,* psychologist Ken Magid sees a connection between early institutional child care and increasing childhood violence, criminality, emotional disorder, and even psychopathic behavior. He asserts that an increasing number of children suffer a "character disturbance" called antisocial personality disorder (APD), the symptoms of which are emotional detachment and uncontrollable inner rage. The origins of APD, says Magid, can be traced to disruptions in parent-infant bonding.[25] Among the chief causes of such disruptions: divorce, abuse, neglect, and group rearing initiated too early in a child's life.

Magid believes that our society is much too nonchalant about the strain early day care experiences place on the crucial bonding process between parents and children, especially when that process is already strained by family breakdown or dysfunction, or poverty. With their high personnel turnover and emotional aloofness, most day care arrangements are inadequate for young children whose family lives are less than ideal. But any long-term nonparental child care in the first three years of life, Magid warns, puts children at risk of insecure attachments: "After reviewing all the literature," he concludes, "no child should be left for any significant period of time during the first year of life. After the initial attachment period, parents can safely use substitute care if they follow careful guidelines. Parents should remember that bonding breaks and trauma can occur during the second or third years as well."[26]

The classic signs of APD—early harbingers of the criminal personality—can be seen, Magid says, in the increase in aggression among young children. To illustrate his point, Magid offers a scenario recognizable to any American parent:

> You've just walked into a waiting room in a pediatrician's office. . . . A little boy playing in the center of the room attracts your attention; in fact, it would be impossible not to notice him. He is zooming around the room, playing with first one toy then another. . . . He is an extremely beautiful child . . . with a captivating twinkle in his eye. You figure your child is about the same age as he, guessing him to be about 4 years old. Your little girl has picked up a toy truck and sits down to examine it. But before she gets all the way down to the floor, this little boy . . . has run over and yanked it from her hands. . . . As you sit with your mouth agape, he hits her with the truck, smirks and runs to the corner, where he immediately drops the truck and begins climbing on chairs. He pays no heed to your child's cries, acting like he doesn't even notice. Despite his mother's pleas the child does not stop his antics or even acknowledge her.[27]

What parent today has not encountered that familiar little "terror" of a child who hits, spits, screams, threatens, and generally wreaks havoc with impenetrable self-assurance and pleasure! When finally forcibly restrained by an adult and given a talking-to, his eyes harden, his lips purse in an inscrutable smile. When one meets the parents of such children, one is often surprised to find them loving, concerned, frustrated, and anxious to correct their child's failings. Where, one wonders, do such children acquire their hostility? The answer may lie in the overcrowded or otherwise unloving child care situations in which they have been forced as infants to fight for attention, and in the contradictory messages about acceptable behavior that they have received from parents and daytime caretakers. In fact, aggressiveness has also been observed in children whose working parents have left them with baby-sitters for long periods of time.[28]

The possible clash between "professional" and parental approaches to discipline is one of the seldom-discussed stresses day care places on children. In their 1978 study, *Infancy: Its Place in Human Development*, Harvard psychologists Jerome Kagan, Richard Kearsley, and Philip Zelazo observed, "Many day care workers, trained in a philosophy of permissiveness toward aggression and emotional spontaneity, are reluctant to punish every misdemeanor. . . . The parent with an articulated ideal and coherent philosophy of child rearing . . . might view the day care environment as dangerously indifferent" to behavioral development.[29]

My talks with parents indicate that few view day care as conducive to the consistent discipline they want for their children. They are concerned about not only discrepancies in standards of behavior but the absence of strong parental role models and the kind of engaged parenting that is the sine qua non of a strong value system. As a San Francisco father who teaches high school physical education observed, "When the parents are not there the kids lose their identity; that's why they get lost so easily. . . . Being a role model is not, you know . . . being on TV or being a great athlete. It's just being there for your kids."

Parents also contend that group rearing subjects children too early to the conformist influence of their peers. They are right to be concerned. In their book *Preschool in Three Cultures: Japan, China and the United States*, Joseph J. Tobin, David Y. H. Wu, and Dana H. Davidson observe that while American preschool teachers pay more lip service to individuality than do their colleagues in Asia—stressing their effort to help children become "uniquely themselves" and "self-actualized"—they cannot help but promote the group experience, because the very nature of preschool *is* the group experience. "Our sense," the authors observed, "is that American, Japanese and Chinese preschools' approach to balancing groupism with individualism and equality differ more in theory than in practice. In all three societies, preschool children spend most of their day as members of groups. In addition to the explicitly group-oriented 'small group' and 'large group' activities scheduled each day . . . the children spend much of the rest of the day in group activities that are not labeled or thought of as such."[30]

Many preschool teachers seem to promote a philosophy of social interaction that explicitly encourages peer pressure and discourages individuality. A Washington, D.C., Head Start teacher apologized to a reporter for a four-year-old in her class who remained in a corner, painting quietly, while her classmates jostled one another for their favorite toys. "Michelle is shy," her teacher said, attributing a trait she clearly viewed as undesirable to the child's until recently home-bound life: "These kids need to start our programs at a younger ages."[31] But why should a child like Michelle begin Head Start at a younger age? To be socialized earlier into becoming a toy-grabber?

Many advocates of expanding day care and preschool argue that even if group care poses some social or psychological risks for children, it can provide intellectual stimulation not available to children in their own homes—especially to disadvantaged children. The principal impetus for Zero to Three and a host of other more localized initiatives that combine "enriched developmental experiences" for children with literacy and child development education for parents—from the Child Opportunity Zone programs of Rhode Island to the Success by Six initiative in Iowa—is to improve the cognitive abilities of children considered by virtue of their family background and home situation at risk of reduced cognitive functioning. But while no study has linked early group care with *poor* cognitive functioning, even the most highly touted early-intervention programs have failed to demonstrate any long-term positive effect on either IQ or school performance. A consortium headed up by Irving Lazar of Cornell University summarized the results of eleven well-known early-intervention programs of the 1960s and 1970s, including the Perry Pre-School program in Ypsilanti, Michigan, and the Abecedarian and Milwaukee projects. Their 1982 report found these programs to have little or no permanent effect on intellectual ability—at least that measured by intelligence tests. True, children exposed to these high-quality early educational experiences registered on the average a "net gain in IQ of more than seven . . . points . . . soon after completing one of these . . . experimental preschool programs," but within two years this gain declined to three points, and later seemed to disappear altogether.[32]

The most successful of these programs, the Perry Pre-School program, has often been cited for long-term gains in social adjustment if not in IQ scores. Allegedly, those enrolled in the project in the early 1960s were twice as likely to demonstrate functional literacy, to have graduated from high school, to have attended college, to be gainfully employed, and to have avoided teenage pregnancy as men and women from the same socioeconomic background who had been in a control group. Yet many scholars contend that some of these gains "fall short of statistical significance."[33] (The Ypsilanti project involved no more than 123 children in both the experimental and control group.) They also point out that the project required so much money and personnel that it could never be replicated on a mass basis.

Since 1989, the federal government has funded an early-intervention "demonstration project" entitled the Comprehensive Child Development Program (CCDP) in twenty-four sites around the country. The program was conceived along the same lines as these earlier projects, providing developmental activities for children from birth to the age of five for at least three and a half hours three days a week. But it provides much more intensive counseling and educational services for parents than previous early-intervention projects. The American Enterprise Institute's Douglas Besharov, who has written extensively about early intervention projects, noted in a recent *Wall Street Journal* article that the CCDP has "enjoyed extremely high levels of funding," yet the program has not been able to improve children's "physical health, cognitive development or socio-emotional development."[34]

Why are such extensive early-intervention education programs being pursued, despite the conspicuous dearth of evidence that they are likely to improve disadvantaged children's prospects? Mainly because they are predicated on the ill-conceived conviction of educators like Anne Mitchell, of the Bank Street College, that, "the most complete intervention we could design for at-risk young children and their families would be a comprehensive package that combines full-day, year-round early childhood programs that are in the best senses both custodial and educational, with parent education/family support programs that have a strong employment training component."[35] Such theories of custodial government are not without their dangers. In their book, *The Bell Curve: Intelligence and Class Structure in American Life*, Richard J. Herrnstein and Charles Murray write that many in the social welfare system have "lost faith that remedial social programs work" and have begun to assume that the specific problems of the underclass that decrease parental capacity—crime, family dysfunction, unemployment, and drug use—can only be addressed through massive state intervention, providing poor children with the full range of custodial care that parents would normally provide—from food to medical care to instruction in "hygiene, sexual socialization, and socialization to the world of work."[36] They warn, however, that in the context of our democratic traditions, these interventionist social programs have "totalitarian" implications.[37]

■ ■ ■

In light of the failure of early-intervention models, and their disturbing political implications, what can be done to improve the prospects of the increasing numbers of children born to poor, single, teenage mothers locked into cyclical patterns of welfare dependency and family dysfunction?

The first thing we may have to do is relinquish the present early-intervention models, which almost without exception have turned on the notion that at-risk children are better off separated from their mothers during waking hours. Interestingly, the first intervention programs (and those with the most hopeful results) involved only minimal parent-child separation each day; the Perry project, for example, was a two-and-half-hour, five-day-a-week program for three- and four-year-olds. But over time, social service professionals have proposed ever longer and earlier separations of parents and children. Some early-intervention programs—like the Comprehensive Child Development Program, or another sixteen-city demonstration project, New Chance—which provide educational and job skill training for AFDC (Aid to Families with Dependent Children) recipients while their children are given high-quality day care—claim that "being a good parent requires a healthy degree of self-respect . . . and . . . self-respect . . . means being economically self-sufficient," but they are plainly less interested in producing good parents than in producing economically viable parents.[38] Even those social programs expressly focused on "promoting parenting skills and positive parent-child relationships" rather than preparing parents for functional literacy and jobs often engage in day care and preschool referrals, and seldom involve intensive parent-child interaction. Thus, they tend to relegate infants and toddlers who are greedy for love, attention, and engaged and experienced hands-on parenting to the doubtful comforts of institutional affection.

It may not only be the children who suffer disruptions in bonding during long daytime separations from their mothers. Women who do not enter motherhood with self-confidence and adequate parenting models from their own past may well lose interest in the welfare and development of children from whom they are kept apart. The large body of research on separation anxiety in working mothers supports the view that maternal attachment increases with the time a mother spends with her baby, and decreases when she spends less time.[39] Thus, programs that essentially relegate parents to the role of part-time caretakers may inadvertently subvert the parental competence and healthy family functioning they purport to promote. Certainly these programs have not been found to reduce the high rates of clinical depression that beset disadvantaged young mothers. Perhaps that is because in discouraging full-time mothering they are not ministering to the unfulfilled emotional needs that drive many young women to childbearing in the first place.

Early-intervention programs for at-risk children that turn on the idea of hands-on parenting are rare. One of these is South Carolina's Resource Mothers program, which links pregnant teenagers with experienced mothers in their neighborhoods for discussions and training in hands-on parenting. In her book, *It Takes a Village and Other Lessons Children Teach Us*, Hillary Rodham Clinton claims that this program has had an "impact both in improving the health of babies and in reducing the incidence of child abuse" in that state.[40] The approach seems eminently sensible. Having older local mothers give younger mothers-to-be advice is very different from subjecting them to the professional monitoring of outsiders. In my own experience, advice from other mothers— especially from older women who've seen it all—has been much more meaningful to me in the day-to-day business of parenting than advice from the "experts."

Elizabeth Gill, a guardian *ad litem* for the 17th Judicial Circuit Court in Florida, recognizes the built-in irony of the classic early-intervention approach to family life—particularly the discrepancy between the purported aim of early-interventionists to improve parent-child relationships and the absence of parents in the environments they are increasingly creating. Noting that "early intervention efforts often complete the disintegration of poor families by attenuating the bonds between mothers and their children," Gill believes that "If we really want to help families, we've got to nurture those bonds."[41]

Gill plans to undertake a bold experiment in Broward County, Florida, directed mainly toward teenage mothers who are under investigation or at risk for child abuse or neglect. Unlike the Head Start parent-child centers in her area, which provide mothers with hands-on training only one day a week, Gill's centers will require mothers to stay with their children most of the day, taking primary responsibility for caring for their babies as they receive training in child development, literacy, housekeeping, cooking, nutrition, games, sports, art, music, and core values. The centers will be staffed not by professionals but by well-respected neighborhood women who have raised families successfully. A trained nurse will be available for half a day each week, and a teacher will monitor the girls' academic progress one day a week.

■ ■ ■

O*ne of* the big problems with trying to sell social programs that presume or require parental involvement is that a broad coalition of interest groups on both sides of the political fence is invested in the full-time participation of women in the workplace. Until the 1980s day care was primarily the cause of the left. Among the most ardent supporters of government sponsored day care and preschool expansion in the 1960s and 1970s were feminists impatient with traditional gender roles in marriage and child-rearing and determined to free women from the drudgery of housework, child care, and restrictions on their career opportunities. Feminists have had an enormous investment in positive outcomes of day care research, and they remain the first to dismiss any negative findings as a "backlash against the women's movement."[42]

But in the last decade, the political right—once the ardent defender of traditional mothering roles—has also become invested in promoting day care and other methods of institutional child-rearing. Noticing that nearly half of AFDC recipients had been on the welfare rolls before, conservative politicians determined to get these women—the great majority of them never-married mothers—off the dole and into the workplace.[43] They have supported schemes that would combine child care provisions with job training and/or placement, even for women with preschool children. Indeed, conservatives were instrumental in passage of the 1988 Family Support Act, which in establishing the JOBS program (Job Opportunities and Basic Skills) required states to "replace the existing AFDC program with a new Family Support Program which emphasizes work."[44] Thus was "workfare" born—a job-training and placement scheme intended to encompass every welfare recipient with children over the age of three.

But five years of the Family Support Act and its workfare experiment did little to shorten the welfare rolls. Never-married mothers of preschool children were particularly resistant to the workfare/day care initiative.[45] By the 1994 elections, many conservatives, fed up with what they saw as the incurable economic irresponsibility of welfare recipients, were advocating even more extreme visions of institutional child-rearing than day care. In December 1994, Newt Gingrich, newly elected speaker of the House of Representatives, proposed that the entire welfare system be dismantled. AFDC welfare benefits, he proposed, should be eliminated entirely for underage single mothers and limited to transitional help for older single mothers. He suggested that the children of parents who therefore might not be able to provide for them be consigned—via processing by the already overburdened child welfare system—to orphanages.

The left and the right have had, of course, very different motives for their efforts to promote working mothers and institutional child-rearing. The left has seen in the working woman and the day care environment the possibility of molding the childhood personality away from the dependencies, special interests, intimacies, and preoccupations of nuclear family life, thus creating—in the words of one feminist—"new forms of community" and an essentially post-family social order.[46] The right, on the other hand, has promoted institutional child-rearing as a technique for cutting the losses of contemporary family fragmentation and dysfunction, particularly among the underclass. Throwing up their hands in frustration at the failures of the welfare state and the disintegration of the black family in particular, conservative politicians have sought to force single mothers into work as a first step toward reestablishing greater personal responsibility and social discipline in the inner cities.

It has been very discouraging to those of us convinced of the integral relationship between children's well-being and parent-child bonding to watch the left and the right exchange institutional child-rearing schemes. But it is also a telling commentary on the extent to which even our most conservative leaders are prone to losing their focus on family when it comes to the poor. In their preoccupation with the principles of fiscal accountability and individual economic responsibility, the right assumes that children's well-being in inner cities will improve when we have restored the work ethic among underclass single mothers. But they are probably wrong. Improving inner-city children's chances may have far more to do with promoting a *family* ethic than promoting a work ethic.

Soon after Gingrich came up with his orphanage plan, David Blankenhorn, president of the Institute for American Values and the author of *Fatherless America*, commented with sadness in the *Los Angeles Times*, "The proposal to build more orphanages is similar to our current strategy of building more prisons. Both ideas assume that more brick-and-mortar structures, staffed by public or quasi-public employees can fill the vacuum in our society created by the growing collapse of parental capacity and the disintegration of the married-couple child-raising unit." The real issue in the welfare debate, Blankenhorn insisted, is not how to get poor women into the workforce, but how to provide a more solid family structure and more opportunities for parental engagement to the children of the poor. We should pursue family policies that encourage marriage and responsible fatherhood, Blankenhorn argued. "As a national strategy for reversing the decline of child well-being, the fatherhood idea is far more consistent with the better angels of our nature than either the prison idea or the orphanage idea."[47] Blankenhorn made an important point. Knowing, as we do, that even the most extreme material want in childhood is a far less accurate predictor of wayward behavior than are deficiencies in family structure and parental engagement, it is irresponsible of government to pursue any other social policy than one that attempts to shore up family structure among the poor. Especially wrongheaded, then, is any solution to welfare that will ultimately rob children already bereft of fathers of the consistent attention of their mothers.

Thankfully, as the welfare debate settled in 1995 and 1996, the right (probably influenced less by statements like Blankenhorn's than by its determination not to burden the federal budget with the building of orphanages) eased its support for orphanages. But the welfare reform bill ultimately signed by the President in 1996—in its preoccupations with work requirements, child protection, and child care funding—betrayed both the Democrats' and the Republicans' fundamental lack of interest in strengthening families rather than government services. Indeed, limiting AFDC cash assistance and establishing work requirements for single mothers after two years of payments amounts to a perversion of the original mission of welfare. The system, after all, was created in 1935 as a safety net for single parents (at the time, widowed mothers) who wanted to stay home to nurture their children in the early years of life.

It remains to be seen whether welfare reform will succeed at least in the difficult but crucial task of combating an epidemic of illegitmate childbearing among poor women, and—particularly alarming—among poor teenage girls. Conservatives have made much of statistical findings implicating the system in perpetuating a vicious cycle of illegitimacy and social disorder in inner-city neighborhoods. Studies comparing the welfare benefit structure to rates of childbirth among unmarried women in different states (for every 10 percent increase in AFDC payments in recent years, there has been a 5 percent increase in extramarital childbearing) show that government disbursements to the poor have encouraged out-of-wedlock childbearing.[48] As Wade Horn, director of the National Fatherhood Initiative, notes, welfare entitlements not only came to serve as social insurance for promiscuous women, but were structured so as to render marriage "an economically foolish choice" even for poor women in stable relationships. If a welfare recipient with two children married a minimum-wage worker, their combined income would decrease thirty percent. If she married a moderate-income worker, their combined income would be reduced by 17 percent.[49]

But while the 1996 compromise bill will require each state to set numeric goals in combating illegitimacy, while it will encourage young women to identify the fathers of their children, while it nominally requires teenage mothers under the age of eighteen to live with their parents (there seem to be plenty of loopholes here), and while it sponsors abstinence education, its provisions are still wholly inadequate to reconstruct a culture of marriage among the poor.

In focusing on paternity establishment especially, lawmakers have—as usual—taken the easiest, most cowardly, and undoubtedly least effective way out of the mire of family disintegration. Wade Horn noted already in the winter of 1996 that policies which focus on "paternity establishment and child support enforcement" instead of marriage are bound to backfire. "As word circulates . . . that cooperating with paternity establishment but failing to comply with child support orders may result in imprisonment or revocation of one's driver's license, many [men] may simply choose to become less involved with their children."[50]

What could Congress have done differently? For starters, little effort has gone into addressing the sinking job prospects of the men who father the children of welfare mothers. Men who have a hope of supporting families are far more likely to marry than men who are out on the street. As far as I know, only one program offers men the kind of job training and placement opportunities that have been offered through workfare to women. Mayor Stephen Goldsmith's Rebuilding Families Initiatives in Indianapolis include programs that sponsor school-to-work training for inner-city youth and match unemployed fathers with job training programs and jobs in the private sector.[51]

Indeed, there might have been more responsible and child-friendly possibilities for welfare reform than were offered by the 1996 welfare bill. What if we had continued to guarantee government subsidies to poor single mothers without demanding that they work for benefits until their children reach school age? What if we had demanded from poor mothers of young children not work for pay but adequate mothering? This could have been done by dismantling what has become a highly specialized and mainly clerical welfare bureaucracy and returning to an older model of AFDC aid in which a social worker was assigned to each AFDC recipient family and given some discretion to replace cash benefits with in-kind provisions if money was being wasted, and to assist clients in managing their homes, caring for their children, and planning for eventual participation in the workforce. Giving a social worker access to an AFDC client's home on a regular basis need not mean the kind of coercion that social service professionals regularly exert on the poor today, by prescribing what is usually unproductive counseling, therapy, or parenting instruction. Nor need it mean launching an AFDC client's preschool children into the morass of a social service network that can offer no more than a pale substitute for parenting. It can simply mean providing meaningful help to families in the immediacy of the home environment. Such a reconstructed welfare system would no doubt have helped many young and insecure single mothers gain the kind of self-confidence through their role as mothers that might actually expedite their entry into the workforce.

What if, furthermore, we had re-created the AFDC system in a way that actually rewarded couples for marrying and staying married—for example, by giving married couples preference in assigning public housing? What if Congress had resolved to shore up the AFDC-UP program, the heavily restricted welfare program that provides aid to two-parent families? What if we had determined to subsidize for the first time the 20 percent of poor families in which both parents are present and one is a full-time wage earner? Such a system would at least encourage poor women to marry before having children. Even if in many cases these were "marriages of convenience," they would reduce welfare caseloads by ensuring that a larger number of fathers would acknowledge paternity and be accountable for child support. And such a system would go a long way toward reversing the inane biases of the current system against both marriage and work.[52]

A welfare policy that rewards both marriage and working fathers would, in fact, be a boon for poor children of both married and single parents. There is ample evidence that the worst pathologies of inner-city youth—such as drug dealing, gang life, and teenage pregnancy—are directly related to the conspicuous absence of healthy male role models in their homes and neighborhoods.[53] Irwin Garfinkel and Sara S. McLanahan of Washington's Urban Institute observe, for example, that fatherless teenage girls are more than two and a half times as likely to bear children out of wedlock as teenage girls raised with fathers in the home and more than twice as likely to bear children as teenagers.[54] William Galston and Elaine Ciulla Kaymarck of Washington's Progressive Policy Institute have argued that the statistical connection between crime and fatherless families is so strong that it "erases the relationship between race and crime and between low income and crime."[55] James Q. Wilson, James Collins Professor of Management and Public Policy at UCLA, observes, "Neighborhood standards may be set by mothers but they are enforced by fathers, or at least by adult males. Neighborhoods without fathers are neighborhoods without men able and willing to confront errant youth, chase threatening gangs . . . reproach delinquent fathers . . . [and] control boys on the street."[56]

Beyond its potential to heal many of the social ills of inner-city neighborhoods, a welfare policy that favored married couples with young children—and especially those families with only one income—would also be likely to encourage healthier notions among poor women about their child-rearing obligations to society. Less than a third of all married mothers work full-time, a fact that clues us in as to the profound pressures of maternal obligations and the extent to which married mothers—by virtue of their release from much of the financial pressure of child support—have the luxury of meeting these obligations.

At present, however, even the most conscientious single mother faces an insoluable dilemma. If she stays home with her children, she suffers the humiliation and social disrepute of welfare dependency. If she goes to work, she leaves her children to be raised by others. If she does not already worry that leaving her child or children in child care may work to their detriment, it will not take long before her anxieties are aroused. AFDC recipient Monica Powell told a reporter for *U.S. News & World Report* that she had "dropped out of her job search to stay home with her five year old after her daughter starting talking about French-kissing boys and going to a club 'to get a groove on with a man,' language she picked up at a child-care center."[57]

I am convinced that no program of welfare reform can alleviate the misery of inner-city childhoods until American politicians and intellectuals drastically rethink the premise that supporting young children financially is a greater social good than doing the actual work of rearing them. Almost without exception, the mothers I have spoken with contend that mothers should be at home with young children. Yet their testimony also suggests that there are few social circles in which mothers—single or married, rich or poor—are not made to feel socially inferior (or worse, socially useless) if they do not work at least part-time outside the home. In all but the most conservative sectors of American society there is a pervasive belief that a working woman is a liberated and happier woman, and that a woman without a salary is ultimately a slave to whoever supports her children, whether it be her man or her government. Even President Clinton's former family policy advisor William A. Galston, a notable defender of the family, contended at a conference of the Council on Families in America in 1996 that "few Americans" would want to return to the at-home mothering model of the 1950s. Any family policy appropriate to 1990s, he declared, must accommodate the "right" of women to participate in the workforce.[58] This odd *Arbeit macht*

Frei mentality is nowhere more uncompromisingly articulated than by privileged feminist ideologues like Betty Friedan, who hold up the model of the working mother as the epitome of women's liberation, and insist—as she is reported to have done at a conference on family issues in the early 1990s—that the working mother "does not need a husband; she needs a support system."[59]

Friedan has hit upon a profound, if horrific self-fulfilling prophecy. The fewer mothers who marry, the fewer of them will remain at home to raise their children. Thus the greater will be the need for child care services, the greater the expansion of the custodial state and its wanton assaults of children's and families' well-being. Naturally the weaker the family and the more developed the resources of institutional child-rearing, the more pressures on women to cede their child-rearing responsibilities to government.

■ ■ ■

How did it happen that mothers were expected to participate in the labor force outside the home in the first place?

Once upon a time, when our economy was primarily agrarian, the home was the center of work and family life. Mothers and fathers played fairly equal, if clearly differentiated, roles in child-rearing (women seeing to the custodial tasks of child-rearing and the nurturing of their children, men to children's education and training). Children helped out with economic production. With the increasing industrialization of the nineteenth century, men increasingly left home in order to earn their bread, and their participation in homemaking and child-rearing diminished. As goods and services—clothing, household products, even schooling—traditionally produced at home became available for purchase, women's responsibilities diminished as well.

Technology continued to streamline domestic tasks in the twentieth century; at the same time, some of the emotional responsibilities of family life became the province of professionals. In *The Second Shift*, sociologist Arlie Hochschild notes that "tasks women used to do at home have also gradually come to be done elsewhere for pay. Day care for children, retirement homes for the elderly, homes for delinquent children, mental hospitals and even psychotherapy are, in a way, commercial substitutes for jobs a mother once did at home."[60]

As domestic work diminished, home life no longer offered the challenges it once did, and the professionalization of many once domestic functions gradually led many women to feel that child-rearing was no longer the proper province of parents. As early as the 1950s sociologists noticed that many prosperous middle-class mothers were depending upon schools, clubs, and summer camps to raise their children for them.[61] In their exhaustive study of life in a Canadian suburb in the 1950s, *Crestwood Heights,* John Seeley, R. Alexander Sim, and Elizabeth W. Loosley offer some touching and disturbing examples of the extent to which a smug professional class of child-rearing experts, determined to "propagate current ideologies in education and child-rearing," were able to render "highly literate" women profoundly insecure—even superfluous—in their role as mothers:

> The school . . . is more certain of its methods than the parents are of theirs. . . . At Home and School meetings it was not uncommon for parents to ask teachers what the proper hour for bed should be, or how to prevent a child's telephone conversations during homework. The parents of one kindergarten child were contemplating a move . . . which was not undertaken until the teacher had given it as her opinion that the change would not be detrimental to the child. . . . Parents are educated by the school for their cultural obligation toward the child, which approaches, increasingly, the role of trusteeship for the school. . . . A favorite ingroup joke of Crestwood Heights teachers states that "the ideal child is an orphan."[62]

By the early 1970s many middle-class women not only were convinced of the superfluity of stay-at-home mothering; they felt compelled by market pressures to work for pay—partly in order to purchase the very goods and services they once provided for themselves. Many eagerly rushed into the labor force with dreams of the good life. A great many of them were disappointed to discover, when they became mothers, that family life and household tasks, however shrunken, still demanded far more time and commitment than a working life allowed them. In 1988, a working mother with a full-time job worked an average of 57.3 hours a week on the job and at home, while a housewife worked an average of only 32.2 hours a week. That left the housewife with twenty-five hours more per week in which to interact with her children.[63]

Time-pressed lives and attention-starved children have led many American women to reassess the wisdom behind the working mother model. The fifteen-thousand-member national support organization Mothers at Home reported in a 1989 public policy pamphlet entitled "Mothers Speak Out on Child Care" that "the exceptionally candid letters we receive from mothers across the nation confirm . . . that most mothers today either do not need or do not want substitute child care. Firsthand experience with day care has shown mothers that it doesn't do the job; that no matter how 'quality' it becomes, it will never do the job."[64]

Aware of the conflicts women had about child care, some feminists of the 1980s attempted to make the movement more responsive to many women's aspirations for lives closer to home and children. In her 1981 book, *The Second Stage*, Friedan herself appealed for according family life a more prominent place in feminist doctrine.[65] But in general the "mommy issue"—especially as it relates to work-family conflicts—is a problem that the feminist movement has cavalierly brushed aside. Felice Schwartz, a longtime feminist and founder of Catalyst, a nonprofit group that promotes women in the workplace, came under strong criticism from the National Organization of Women and under widespread attack from feminists when she published work in the late 1980s and early 1990s advocating the creation of a career track for women that would allow them to take leaves of absence to raise young children. In her 1996 book, *"Feminism Is Not the Story of My Life,"* Elizabeth Fox-Genovese captured the alienation today's working mothers feel from feminism, mainly as a result of such traditional feminist hostility and insensitivity to family issues.[66]

For the most part, feminism has remained deaf to the large numbers of women I've talked to who remember with fondness and some nostalgia that when they got home from school, "Mom was home." Many of these women feel guilty their own children do not enjoy what they took for granted in their own childhoods—the consistent presence of a parent in the household. A Baltimore mother remembers, "You know, when I grew up, the mother always stayed home and did everything for the kids. . . . She was there to show some kind of example." A Texas mother relates, "My parents divorced when I was eighteen and my brother was four—and he's, like, raised in a different family, because my mother was working and there was no parent at home with him. And he is spoiled. . . . My mother felt so guilty that she let him have his way with everything."

As Fox-Genovese puts it, "When we consider the lives of women and children, the feminist hostility to the 'mommy track' seems puzzling at best, irresponsible at worst." Traditional feminists, with their professional child care "scenarios," she implies, are snobs who lack "any sense of who will really take care of the children, unless, of course, you assume that children do not need much attention beyond that which can be provided by servants."[67] In fact, Fox-Genovese's characterization of feminists as spoiled is painfully accurate. Consider the tired, self-obsessed arguments for careerism and communal child-rearing that journalist Ellen Willis pursued in a 1994 *Glamour* article entitled, "Why I'm Not 'Pro-Family' ": "I don't doubt the fragility of today's family life is hard on kids. . . . On the other hand, children are more narcissistic than most adults ever dream of being—if my daughter had her way, I'd never leave the house. They too have to learn that other people's needs and feelings must be taken into account."[68]

For women like Willis, who teaches journalism at New York University and no doubt gets tremendous emotional satisfaction and even significant material reward from her work, labor outside the home constitutes a woman's "right," a measure of her "happiness," and a symbol of her personal "freedom." A career satisfies her "needs" and "feelings." But if women like Willis are happier for their careers, are their daughters? And how representative is Willis? Most working mothers I've talked to do not think their jobs provide sufficient emotional compensation for the impediment they constitute to their work as parents. They feel their children's need for them is not "narcissistic" but an authentic demand they have a terrible time satisfying. A San Francisco working mother relates, "Personally, I'm feeling guilty with my kids. . . . How many hours do I spend . . . *productive* hours, with my kids?"

Heidi Brennan, director of social policy for Mothers at Home, says her impression in corresponding with hundreds of women about work-family issues is that American mothers as a whole have been "coerced against their will *into* the workplace." She adds, "There is a complete disconnect between the views of policy-makers and real people on the issue of working mothers." Policy-makers believe there is a dichotomy of opinion about at-home mothering between working and nonworking mothers, she says. But if there is a dichotomy, it is between elite working mothers (that is, professional women) versus the rest of the world. Many more women, Brennan claims, would stay home if there were more social support and less financial penalty for the decision to do so.[69]

Certainly the parents I have talked to are convinced that children suffer when both parents work, even when they are cared for in their own home by nannies or baby-sitters. Some parents I spoke with have consciously made financial sacrifices to stay home with their children. A Texas mother decided "after trying to work when my children were small that it really wasn't worthwhile. . . . They don't get your values; they get the baby-sitter's values." A San Francisco father said, "Financially we felt it when our kids were small . . . we really felt it . . . [and] we struggled through it. . . . But my wife was there when the kids came home, and it worked out nice—someone else didn't raise them." A Baltimore mother confessed that she "wanted to go back to work once my children were school age. But I realized that's when you really have to be home, to supervise them after school."

Working mothers echoed these sentiments, and many said they wished they could quit work. They found that their participation in the workforce has yielded more stress, more worries, and more domestic strife than they remember their nonworking mothers having faced. An African-American working mother of two teenage boys notes: "My mother was home with us. She could enforce the rules. I tell my son, don't go out till I get home, don't look at TV, make sure your chores are done. . . . He comes from school at two-thirty, three. . . . By the time I get home it's five-thirty, it's almost too late. . . . He's done everything by then that I told him not to do!"

Hardly a wonder, then, that a 1994 Labor Department survey found that while 79 percent of working women liked their jobs, only 15 percent contended they would continue to work full-time if they could afford not to.[70] Far from achieving the happy independence feminism promised, working mothers labor under tremendous emotional pressures. Arlie Hochschild describes how women under the work gun often become "the target of children's aggression . . . the family 'heavy,' the 'time and motion' person of the family and work speed-up . . . hurry[ing] children through their daily rounds."[71]

When Hochschild went out in the late 1980s to talk to women and men in two-income families, she was dismayed to note that even successful career women suffered unbearable tensions between their roles as mothers and their roles as wage-earners—tensions that expressed themselves in chronic fatigue, illness, and depression. These tensions, she noted, might have been relieved were husbands more willing to pick up the slack, but men seemed reluctant to do their share, consigning women to a "second shift" of household and child-rearing burdens that made their lives a never-ending cycle of pressures.

When men remained uninvolved in homemaking and child-rearing, working women—strained beyond their limits—were also disengaging themselves from homebound demands. "In the race against time," Hochschild lamented, both parents often "inadvertently cut back on children's needs," "cutting corners" on both physical and emotional care. "Trying to rationalize her child's long hours in day care," Hochschild noted, "one working mother remarked about her nine-month-old daughter that she 'needed kids her age' and 'needs the independence.' It takes relatively little to cut back in house care, and the consequences of skimping on housework are trivial, but reducing one's notions of what a baby needs—imposing the needs of a fourteen-year-old onto a nine-

month-old baby—takes a great deal of denial and has drastic consequences."[72]

Hochschild's prescription for picking up the parenting slack focuses
on calling for more help from working husbands, and better child care
options. Despite the intractable conflict she unearthed between the
work schedules of two-income parents and their ability to minister to
children's needs, she remained convinced that for women, the laboring
life was an opportunity, a magnificent revolution "stalled" by the rem-
nants of household oppressions.[73]

But even in marriages where men are willing to take up a more significant share of the "second shift"—as in many marriages of people I interviewed for this book—it has become increasingly clear to both fathers
and mothers that given the intense negative pressures on children from
outside the home, at least one parent should devote the major portion of
his or her energies to watching and raising the children.[74] Many two-
income parents I've talked to worry that the lack of parental presence in
the home during the daytime leaves children, in the words of a Texas father, "to their own devices with simply too many options." Such children, parents say, often develop problem behaviors out of sheer
loneliness. A New Jersey mother puts the problem in a nutshell: "The
feeling a child has when no one is at home. . . . There has to be something hollow inside."

In a 1989 study involving five thousand eighth-graders in Los Angeles and San Diego, "latchkey" children were twice as vulnerable to substance abuse as were children who were supervised by adults after
school, a fact which many experts link to loneliness as well as lack of supervision.[75] To some extent after-school programs might be the answer,
but given children's—even older children's—needs for down time and
interaction with their parents, a more efficacious solution to the "home-
alone" syndrome might be the "home with mom (or dad)" answer. (A
1990 Search Institute survey revealed that about half of all sixth-graders
and 60 percent of high school seniors are home alone for two hours a
day or more.) As we will see later, the recent trend among parents to supervise their children in the workplace after school reflects their growing
conviction that signing their kids up for after-school activities is not the
ultimate answer to the problem of after-school supervision.

Given their awareness of the negative impact on their children, why
do mothers work? Overwhelmingly, because of financial pressures. Many
of the parents I've talked to find that even with two incomes, it is hard
for them to make ends meet. The median income of the American family in inflation-adjusted dollars was no more in 1993 than in 1973; in

fact, real wages for males fell from a median of $34,048 for full-time work to $30,407. In an age of rapid technological change, jobs are no longer as secure as they once were. At the same time, the cost of college and—where public schools have failed—private school strains even high-earning households. The average mortgage takes almost double the bite—up to 40 percent—out of family income it took twenty years ago.[76] And taxes have risen from an average of about 2 percent of family earnings in 1950 to more than 30 percent today. Meanwhile, almost a third of men between the ages of twenty-four and thirty-four do not make enough money to maintain a family with two children above the poverty level.[77]

While working fathers do not experience as great a strain between the demands of work and family as working mothers do (most married men still see their primary role as financial provider, a role they view as "overlapping" with, rather than "conflicting" with, parenthood, according to David Blankenhorn, author of *Fatherless America*),[78] they also feel palpable tensions today between their obligations to work and to family. According to a *New York Times* survey of 1990, 72 percent of working fathers considered themselves "torn by conflict between their jobs and the desire to spend more time with their families." A poll conducted by the *Los Angeles Times* revealed that 57 percent of fathers felt that they did not spend enough time with their children.[79]

Hardly a wonder. The father of the 1990s is much more apt than the father of the 1950s to allow work pressures to infringe on domestic ritual, even though he is aware that he is putting his job before the kids. In fact the father of the 1950s, much maligned for his alleged detachment from the home and child-rearing, was the most domesticated in our century, according to Blankenhorn. William Whyte's 1956 work, *The Organization Man*, Blankenhorn contends, was actually a critique of the "turn toward familism among 1950s fathers," which to Whyte reflected "a decline of the Protestant ethic and . . . an overall weakening of the American male character."[80]

Most of us who are raising children today remember fathers who showed up at the dinner table at a preassigned hour without fail. How many of our children can boast the same? Says William R. Mattox Jr., director of research and policy for the Family Research Council and a specialist on work and family issues:

> Contrary to the assertions of professional children's advocates in Washington, the number one problem facing American children today is not lack of subsidized day-care centers, nutrition pro-

grams, or after-school care for "latchkey" kids . . . [or] even economic poverty, although 20 percent of American children live below the official poverty line. The biggest problem facing American children is a deficit of another kind . . . a lack of time with and attention from their parents. Parents today spend 40 percent less time with their children than did parents in 1965. . . . In 1965, parents on average spent approximately 30 hours a week with their kids. By 1985, parent-child interaction had dropped to just 17 hours a week.[81]

A Texas father I spoke with compared his own childhood to that of his children:

Kids today are dropped off at seven, before school starts, they're in school all day, they stay in the after-school child care until five-thirty. Mom or dad comes and picks them up, then they go home, homework and shower, eat supper, go to bed. They don't have that unstructured time anymore . . . that interaction with the family where just everyone is sitting in the house doing their own thing— maybe talking, you know, the kids playing. . . . I don't know that that happens much. . . . I know I had a lot of that.

Part of the reason for what has become an intense competition between work and family time lies with the realities of the modern global marketplace. American corporations have been forced to push working parents to their limits, without regard to the attendant strains on family life and stability. In my Connecticut town, which has a large population of corporate employees in middle management, the average resident stays less than three years. The corporate penchant for frequent transfers creates a situation that even wives who do not work outside the home find extremely unsettling. An acquaintance of mine in a nearby town, the mother of a child about to enter elementary school, divorced her husband because she could not endure their frequent moves, and felt her daughter would suffer from the lack of a stable communal environment.

In the late 1980s and early 1990s, many large corporations bent on expansion were eager to attract qualified labor by offering employees family-friendly perks—among them day care, telecommuting, and flex-time options. Not surprisingly day care subsidies and on-site day care centers proved less popular in the long run than telecommuting and flex-time arrangements. In general, management found day care expensive, many parents seemed reluctant to take advantage of either subsidies or on-site day care centers except in emergencies, and employees who were not parents found support of day care inequitable.[82] Flex-time and flex-place arrangements, however, proved more attractive for the majority of businesses. They seemed to increase productivity, were bottom-line-friendly, and did not invite conflicts between parents and nonparents regarding equity in benefits. (Studies of home-based telecommuting show an increase of productivity from 20 to 40 percent, as well as enormous time and money savings in the long freeway commutes that separate affordable family housing with corporate office complexes.)[83]

But downsizing has stalled or slowed business's eagerness to pursue such family-friendly policies. Bill Mattox, of the Family Research Council, notes that in a time of shaky job security employees are far less assertive in pushing a pro-family agenda, for fear that their coveted jobs will go to hardworking singles who have no family responsibilities.

And there are indications that despite the bottom-line benefits of telecommuting and flex-time, some of the nation's largest corporations insist on pursuing family policy avenues that will assure them closer surveillance of employee activity, no matter the costs. The American Business Collaboration for Quality Dependent Care, launched in 1992, is an alliance of twenty-one corporate giants—including Aetna Life and Casualty, Allstate Insurance, American Express, AT&T, Bank of America, Deloitte and Touche, Hewlett Packard, IBM, Johnson & Johnson, Mobil, Price Waterhouse, Exxon, Xerox, Citibank—who by 1996 had committed $127.4 million to "develop and strengthen school-age, child care and elder care projects in communities across the country." Funds from the project will be used to finance day care centers, to train day care workers, to standardize and accredit after-school child care programs, to extend child care hours in existing programs, and to set up voice messaging systems in schools so that parents do not have to take the time out from work to meet teachers face-to-face.[84]

It does not take much insight to see that the goal here is to trap parents in the workplace for as long as possible each day. Of course corporate managers are for day care rather than flex-time and telecommuting where it allows them to assign their employees overtime, "vary their work schedules, [assign] travel on business, and participate in additional schooling or training sessions after work hours."[85] A recent DuPont employee survey proudly noted that the company's dependent care policies (which provided backup care for ill children and reimbursements for child care while traveling on company business as well as child care referrals and some flexible work practices) enabled the average manufacturing employee to put in a forty-seven-hour week, with managers typically working fifty-five hours per week. While it was reported in the

DuPont study that employees found it difficult to " 'get everything done' for work and family," and that working mothers with working spouses spent "103 hours per week (out of a total of 168 hours a week) on a combination of work, commuting, child care, household and personal chores," the company congratulated itself on earning greater employee commitment by way of its "work/life" programs. "We've always said that people are our most important asset," effused John A. Krol, president and CEO-designate of DuPont. "This study demonstrates that when a company acts . . . by responding to employees' concerns, it is not only good for our people but it's good for business."[86]

In December 1995, I read with dismay a story in the *Christian Science Monitor* that told of high workloads and low employee morale at many companies during the holiday season. Several corporations, the report said, had found it necessary to stage seminars to help employees cope with work-family stresses. The object of these seminars? To get workers to relinquish feelings of guilt for cutting corners on family time and holiday preparations. The thought of *relieving* work pressures at the holiday season in the interest of family time apparently did not occur to the personnel managers who set up these stress seminars; nor, obviously, did it occur to them that for employees, the hours spent in such quasi-therapeutic exercises might be spent more rewardingly with their families.[87]

Big business's determination to increase short-term productivity, even at the expense of family life, is apparent in the Family and Medical Leave Act, which suffered acutely from the advice of the big businesses whom it pretended to obligate in the name of family time. This bill, which enables men and women who work for companies with fifty or more employees to take a three-month leave without pay for childbirth or family illness, guarantees their position and medical benefits only if they return to work after their reprieve. As conservative author and syndicated columnist Maggie Gallagher remarked to me when the act was passed in the spring of 1993, it was "perfectly named, since it encouraged new mothers to leave their families." David Ruben, a liberally aligned contributing editor to *Parenting* magazine, was not much more impressed. He noted in an August 1993 article, "This law is no panacea for hard-pressed working families. . . . Because the leave is unpaid, it's a sure bet that many parents won't be able to afford the time off they're entitled to."[88] Both were right. A 1996 survey revealed that only two-fifths of those who took maternity leave under the act stayed home an entire three months with their new babies, and one in eight women who took maternity leave had to request public assistance for lack of financial resources.[89]

Talking to parents in two-income families reveals that fitting family life into an increasingly demanding and incompassionate work culture is among the most frustrating challenges of their lives. In response, increasing numbers of them are setting their sights on a fuller family life and more time at home with their kids, even when that means significant financial sacrifice. Indeed, as we shall see in Chapter 9, even if government and business have not yet gotten the message about the failure of our workfare/day care mentality, parents have.

7

Material Kids

W_hen_ **I** first went out to talk to parents about raising kids in the 1990s, I was struck by the resemblance between their comments and the New Left critique of the consumer culture in the 1950s and 1960s. In his ground-breaking 1963 book, _Culture Against Man,_ for example, Jules Henry had spoken of "the urgencies of consumption, and the feeling that hard work was not worth the effort." A New Jersey mother told me, "They want and want and want. They want everything and they don't want to work to get it," and a Texas father observed, "Kids are jaded. . . . It's 'What's next, what's next?'" Henry lamented the breakdown of "the ancient impulse controls"; a Baltimore mother recounted:

> A couple of years ago . . . [my son] wanted a Starter jacket, and that's when the headlines hit in the news that people were getting shot and killed for Starter jackets in the schools. . . . This whole thing with the jacket was the worst time of my life, because I feared for his life when he got the jacket. But he said "Mom, please understand I am living in this world. You're afraid of it, but this is _my_ world."

205

Henry observed that we were "shifting from a society in which Super Ego values (values of self-restraint) were ascendant to one in which more and more recognition was being given to the values of the Id (values of self-indulgence)."[1] A San Francisco father told me, "We are bringing [problems] on ourselves. . . . We're moving right along with technology and making changes, moving away from the church, moving away from standard social values."

Parents are worried about the urgent covetousness and lack of impulse control that can prompt seventh-graders to shoot one another over sneakers and jackets. And though in my conversations with parents many have insisted that a great deal of the problem could be solved if money-obsessed parents stopped trying to "keep up with the Joneses" through their kids—if they turned off the TV, took away the video games, restricted allowances, and said no to the latest fads in dress, music, and gimmick toys—parents also realize that the problem is a much larger one. It involves battling a culture in which material acquisition has become the very definition of the good life.

Parents today are deeply ambivalent about what money buys for their children. On the one hand, many are proud to be doing better financially than their parents, and are happy to provide their children luxuries they did not have as children. In a San Francisco focus group, an African-American father observed, "You know, I work, and my wife, too—we really work for our kids, and anything that I possibly can get within reason, I just get it, and I give it to them. It's not this big 'earn' thing." A Japanese-American mother added, "If one of my boys wants an eighty-dollar sweater, I'll get it for him. I *need* to get it, you know? They are good boys."

On the other hand, many parents remember growing up less dependent on material things, and consider their children spoiled. An African-American mother says:

> My son has to have Calvin Klein jackets. . . . It could look like garbage, but if it's got the name on it . . . he'll take it. See, when we were kids, we were so poor—I always tell everybody we were so poor we couldn't even afford the "or" in poor; so we were *po'*—okay? We'd go to the Salvation Army and get school clothes. . . . My mother would bring them home and wash them and iron them. . . . My kids think that is the funniest thing—(*mocking*) "You wore 'em, Mom?" Well, you wore 'em or you went naked! We didn't have any choices! That's why I get to the point sometimes where [I say to my children], "You don't have any rights in my house . . . [except] to be clothed and fed and cared for."

Parents like this one would hardly wish material want on their children. But they are plagued by the effects on children of a society obsessed with things.

Parents resent consumer culture, for example, for destroying the most basic pleasure of childhood—that voyage of discovery that used to be called "play." Parents everywhere worry over the tendency of their children to bore quickly (a boredom they do not remember in their own childhoods). And they are especially disturbed by the dependency of young children on mechanized entertainment—on videos, video games, and other electronic gadgets that simulate an electronic reality rather than stimulating children to explore the world around them. One mother worries, "It shortchanges them in the long run to have all these technical things. They don't learn to be creative." Another laments, "There is no inventive play. . . . When I share some of the games I used to play as a kid they like them, but they don't know them on their own. When kids come over, they want to play Nintendo; they want to watch a movie."

Most parents I've talked to sense that the failure of children to indulge themselves in free play—their seeming inability to organize time that has not been organized for them—is only a symptom of the extent to which childhood itself, as a distinct phase of life, is disappearing under the weight of unwelcome cultural pressures. Once, parents say, the cultural environment protected and cherished childhood as a time of relative freedom from structure and social pressure. But children are no longer—in the words of one mother—"allowed to be children." Adults are intervening in and structuring childhood play at earlier and earlier stages in children's lives. And that means that childhood play has become increasingly fraught with pressure.

Some of the fault lies in the influence of a society whose fetishes for technology and professional sports have colored parents' child-rearing priorities. A father who coaches girls' soccer on Saturday mornings observes, "Some parents sign up kids for the soccer league who obviously don't want to play. . . . It's a status thing, and they push the kids hard." But structured play is also a consequence of living in a society in which children can no longer roam the streets safely. A mother remembers, "You looked forward when you were a kid to going across the street, or to the park or to your friend's house. But . . . [kids] can't do that anymore. My son begs me to go out. I'll let him go three houses up, but I'm watching him all the way, and if this kid is not home, [he's to] come right back."

The world in which on Saturday mornings children set out on neighborhood adventures has disappeared. Saturday soccer leagues have replaced the spontaneous neighborhood games that kids organized and ran themselves. When children play, it is generally under adult direction. These structured games, parents claim, are ultimately destructive to a child's burgeoning sense of initiative. "Something is wrong with this country when kids are sitting there saying, 'Who's going to tell us what to do?' " comments a father, and his peers agree. Another father remarks, "My son is into baseball, soccer, team activities, which is good. But then on the other hand I would like him to learn to sometimes just hang out."

In parents' minds, television is a culprit that has conditioned many children to sedentary habits and to the lowest common denominator of adult taste in entertainment. Many parents suggest that TV is the creator of a new archetype: the couch-potato child: sexually precocious, cynical, materialistic, culturally rootless, and overweight. Afternoon and prime-time television programming, parents complain, even commercials, offer too much information inappropriate for the eyes and ears of children. An African-American father says, "Everything on television is about sex! Sex, sex, sex! You look at a commercial, one little soft drink commercial, and there's this woman there with her lips all over the can." Another father says, "The other night we watched *60 Minutes,* which is supposed to be prime-time [family-oriented] programming. Well, they had this segment on prostitutes in Thailand. And I've got to explain [this] to a six-year-old!" A mother complains, "With the TV you have no control. The news is the horror story of the week, and the movie of the week is always two people in bed with each other and no [deeper] context."

The overwhelming majority of parents I talked to insist they try to monitor and restrict their children's television viewing, but it isn't easy. What was once "family hour," reports the *Wall Street Journal,* has been invaded by "steamy romance" and "sexual innuendo" on shows ranging from *Melrose Place* to *Roseanne.*[2] In an era when two-thirds of American households have three TVs or more, and more than half of ten- to sixteen-year-olds have TVs in their own bedroom, the kids can easily sneak off to another room to watch something mom and dad might not approve of.[3] Many parents express nostalgia for a time when there was only one TV to a household. But consumer pressures on their children, scattered family lives, and their own increasing dependency on the tube for information and entertainment, they say, have created a situation in which each family member has his own TV and indulges his own viewing preferences.

In 1987, a survey undertaken by the American Academy of Pediatrics found that children between the ages of two and twelve watched on average twenty-five hours a week of television. William Lutz, author of *Doublespeak: From "Revenue Enhancement" to "Terminal Living": How Government, Business, Advertisers, and Others Use Language to De-*

ceive You, says that this number of hours translates into approximately 100,000 advertisements viewed before first grade, and 350,000 before completion of high school.[4] Parents can't control—or even anticipate— the content of advertisements, but many do try to hone their children's abilities to assess how advertising preys on them. An African-American mother of three relates, "When they had cereal with the little trinkets inside. . . . I was saying to my children when they would ask for the cereal, 'You know, this little trinket will not work. It will fall apart. I am going to buy one box, and don't ever ask me again.' It was something that lit up and the thing didn't light up; it fell apart. And you know they really *saw* it." Many parents express relief that schools are now teaching courses in critical television viewing.

I personally find it curious that during the 1980s, while a consensus was building to restrict advertising during children's programming, educational television began to tap into advertising forms, building merchandising empires on shows like *Sesame Street* and *Barney* and creating shows like *Reading Rainbow* that were little more than a string of glorified advertising segments. The parents I've talked to, however, still regard educational television as the saving grace of a "confusing" and "scary" medium. Comparisons of public and commercial television prove that of the 40 percent of TV child characters who exhibit antisocial behavior, only 5 percent can be seen on public television.[5]

Most parents are not prudes. They have nothing against provocative entertainment if it is clearly aimed at an adult audience (and served up in an appropriate time slot). Many point to shows like *Roseanne* as an improvement over the bland and highly unrealistic entertainment they watched as children. But much of the material commercial television directs at children, parents complain, offers them what amount to negative and bizarre behavioral models even when they are not explicitly violent. A father notes, "The kids [on TV] smart off. I mean, if you've ever watched *The Simpsons*. . . . Well, the kids think it's funny, and it *is* funny, but it's *not* for children. . . . I watch it with my kids, and explain to them . . . that real kids don't act like those kids."

Of course, television is not the only huckster selling materialism and "attitude" to the young. Children's books now come with matching dolls, sheets, and wallpaper. Film icons and rap CDs are served up with hamburgers in fast food restaurants. Designer clothing fads rip through high schools, and even curricular materials at school sometimes bear the logos of the growing number of soft drink companies or banks that sponsor educational programs. Is it any surprise that children grow up with the perception that life is about how you look and where and what you buy, and that its rewards come as fast and furiously as the images in a

Coke commercial? "We live in a fast food society," sums up a Texas father of two teenagers. "I mean, immediate gratification. And a lot of that has to do with the media."

None of this is new, of course. Ever since the 1920s, when Walt Disney merchandised Mickey Mouse watches to pay for his experiments in animated films, children have been the specific targets of advertising campaigns. Most parents remember the teen magazines of the 1950s and 1960s, purveyors of whole constellations of vogue in fashion and entertainment. Children's merchandising is not an evil in itself, nor would parents so resent it did they not feel that it has become the *primary* influence on children's taste and character. They sense that children today have little alternative to the fixations of consumer culture—first, because of the way television has taken over the home, and second, because the media seems determined to disorient children's moral compass.

Some parents go to considerable lengths to combat the former. "The first thing I do when I get home," declares one father, "is turn off the TV. I refuse to compete with the TV." But where, parents are asking, are the family shows of yesteryear—models of stable lives and enduring values for children? Abandoned, for the most part, to portrayals of alternative households and lifestyles. Where are the movies that offered wholesome adventure and true suspense? Abandoned to sexual explicitness and gore. When even *Seventeen* magazine, the venerable arbiter of consumer and entertainment taste for "nice" girls, hawks the song "Teenage Whore" on a film soundtrack that allegedly offers a "cohesive and creative attempt to reflect 'you,' " and goes on to entice young women "to shock your parents by searing your flesh with sexy tribal scars"—"now that even *nice girls* get tattoos"—what, parents wonder, is the world coming to?[6]

Besides making them materialistic, parents claim, the media desensitizes children. Children often laugh at scenes of disturbing violence in movies or on TV. A mother of three remarks, "My son—he's a very sensitive kid underneath, when he's not being macho . . . he's not a big TV watcher; he watches Nickelodeon and things. . . . But when there *is* violence on TV, like on the news or things, he'll make jokes or make some cynical remark about it. . . . And it really bothers me that he doesn't have that sensitivity that younger kids should have."

Are parents right? Is the media dehumanizing our youth? In a quiet, suburban high school in Dartmouth, Massachusetts, two fifteen-year-old boys charge into a social studies class and stab a fellow student to death. In San Antonio, Texas, a thirteen-year-old girl participates in the brutal beating and gang-rape of a peer. In a Kansas City, Missouri, movie theater, a fifteen-year-old boy opens fire on his mother with a handgun. In Bath, New York, a fourteen-year-old boy bludgeons and strangles a preschool child to death. In Wenatchee, Washington, two twelve-year-olds murder a migrant worker. In a small Pennsylvania town, two skinhead teenage brothers murder their parents and younger sibling. The press reports with increasing horror that young people who kill often appear not only to be remorseless, but to love the notoriety they get through the media. When, in 1993, seventeen-year-old Raul Omar Villareal of Houston was informed he would be charged with murder after taking part in the gruesome rape and strangulation of two high school girls, he allegedly bragged to a friend, "Hey, great! We've hit the big time."[7]

"Teenagers don't invent violence, they learn it," observes David Gelman in a *Newsweek* commentary on the explosion of violence among youth.[8] Indeed they do, but where? Commentators point to a body of evidence that suggests the rise in teen violence is related to growing chaos in and disintegration of family life. In a September 1994 *Commentary* article, University of California at Los Angeles professor James Q. Wilson noted that more than half of the young people who are incarcerated for long periods of time in juvenile institutions come from families with a history of criminal behavior.[9] Gelman, however, primarily blames the "culture of violence" on the entertainment media—where rap chants like "Beat the bitch with a bat!" compete with cinematic montages of "blazing guns, exploding cars and heads, and bodies hurtling out of windows."[10]

Parents seem to agree with Gelman that teen rapists and murderers are at least as likely to have learned their behavior from the "virtual reality" of TV, movie, and computer screens as from their families. There is no question that a family history of crime, as well as family breakdown, is a strong predictor of delinquency in youth, that children whose home lives are less than supportive are far more vulnerable to the destructive influences of the culture. But broken or otherwise dysfunctional families surely do not bear all the blame for rising teen crime, especially given that divorce and illegitimacy have been growing steadily since the 1970s, while crime by children and teenagers began to accelerate disproportionately only within the past decade. Even parents in healthy, intact families complain that their children are increasingly insensitive and disposed to aggressive behavior.

University of Illinois psychologist Dr. L. Rowell Huesmann observes, "Serious aggression never occurs unless there is a convergence of large numbers of causes, but one of the very important factors we have identified is exposure to media violence."[11] Indeed, several recent studies link rising teen violence to a culture of aggression manufactured by the media, among them the 1991 book *Deadly Consequences*, by Harvard School of Public Health professor Deborah Prothrow-Stith.[12] But parents do not need proof from academics to perceive the threats of violent and sexually provocative entertainment—from television, movies, video games, and music—to their children's moral and social development.

One fall day in 1994, an acquaintance of mine, the economist and social theorist Sylvia Ann Hewlett, walked into her fourteen-year-old son's bedroom to find him doing homework to the strains of rapper Snoop Doggy Dogg. She could not understand many of the lyrics, but what she could understand disturbed her greatly. She asked her son to write down all the words. A lyric from the song "Ain't No Fun," for example, proclaimed, "I know the pussy's mine." The song went on to say that after sex, "there's nothin' else to do with it."[13] What bothered Hewlett about the music, she observed in an informal statement before the Council on Families in America, was not only its violence and misogyny, but the fact that boys and girls barely on the cusp of puberty had ready access to it at neighborhood record stores.

Hewlett is not alone among public figures in her shock and frustration at the spiritual desolation and obsessive vulgarity of teen culture today, nor in her fear that under its influence, children's better natures will be overtaken by cynicism, cruelty, and fear. In recent years, many figures have called attention to the irresponsibility of an entertainment industry that seems intent on filling children's lives with images of violence and models of human degradation. Dr. C. DeLores Tucker, chair of the National Political Congress of Black Women, made the news in 1995 when she confronted Time Warner's board of directors at a shareholder meeting about their marketing and distribution of Snoop Doggy Dogg's album. Her own attention had been turned to gangsta rap when her seven-year-old began to use the word "motherfucker" indiscriminately in conversation. Since then she has joined Senator Joe Lieberman and former Secretary of Education William Bennett in a campaign against obscene lyrics and the other major corporations that market them: Sony, BMG, PolyGram, and EMI. Among the targets of their fury: " 'Death metal' songs distributed by Sony, which describe in graphic terms a bloody rape of a woman with a knife and a child molester's wish to use the severed head of a young girl to masturbate."[14]

In his book *Hollywood vs. America,* film critic Michael Medved turns his attention to the peculiarly perverse role models of today's teen culture. In what is perhaps the most powerful moment of his argument for a return to decency in entertainment, Medved juxtaposes the sweet sentiments of Elvis Presley ("Love me tender, love me true, all my dreams fulfill") in the early days of rock 'n' roll with the more recent lyrics of the rap group N.W.A. (Niggaz with Attitude), who command,

"Come here, bitch, and . . . lick up the dick!"[15] The Rolling Stones, Medved observes, may once have been "the most notorious of . . . rock 'n' roll bad boys," but even their much talked about ode to promiscuity, "Let's Spend the Night Together," would probably be too mild for today's music market. "It's hard to imagine the members of Mötley Crüe or Metallica willingly spending an entire night with anyone," he notes wryly. To conform to contemporary tastes, the Stones would probably have to retitle the song, "Let's Spend Ten Hostile Minutes Together (So I Can Degrade You and Beat You Up)."[16]

While a Geto Boys album of 1990—distributed, again, by Time Warner—had women's rights advocates frothing in anger because it included a song in which the narrator "whipped out the machete" and "sliced [a woman] up until her guts were like spaghetti," Medved points out that male performers have not had a monopoly on sadistic sexual fantasies. Madonna's ode to sadomasochism, "Erotica," was a surprise hit in 1992, and Courtney Love, lead singer of Hole, is among the stars of "slut rock."[17]

Several years ago, before she became our nation's second lady, Tipper Gore wrote a book exposing the growing preoccupation with obscenity in music and other forms of popular culture entitled *Raising PG Kids in an X-Rated Society*. Since the ascension of her husband to the vice presidency, Mrs. Gore has toned down her campaign against youth culture considerably, but the continued sales of her book is proof of many parents' gratitude for her poignant and sensitive appeal to the entertainment industry "to halt [its] moral and artistic decline."[18] The organization she founded, the Washington-based Parents' Music Resource Center (PMRC), still labors to keep parents up-to-date on the teenage music market.

Along with the national Parent-Teacher Association, in fact, the PMRC was the first public interest group to attempt to restrict children's access to pornographic music. In the mid-1980s the two organizations approached record executives asking for a set of industry-wide standards for rating music lyrics similar to that used in the motion picture industry. Unfortunately, they were met with charges of "cultural terrorism" from rock celebrity and industry spokesman Frank Zappa. (Apparently, it did not occur to Mr. Zappa that an industry engaging in mass distribution of songs that exhorted children to "shoot to thrill" might itself be more appropriately accused of cultural terrorism.)[19] In 1989, four years after a Senate Commerce Committee hearing on the matter and much public pressure, the major record producers finally budged a bit on the issue. They agreed voluntarily to label albums containing violent or sexual material with a "Parental Advisory—Explicit Lyrics" sticker; but they refused to set industry-wide standards for determining what, in fact, *constituted* explicit material. So there has been no improvement in the content of the music nor, it seems, much progress in restricting children's access to it. While a growing number of stores refuse to carry stickered CDs or tapes, much objectionable material remains unlabeled, and some parents contend that a labeling system alone only earmarks for children the raciest, and therefore the "coolest," CDs.

The PMRC is today one of several watchdog groups that actively monitor the music industry and its exploitation of the youth market. (Representatives of a number of such organizations recently participated in a joint public protest with C. DeLores Tucker and representatives of the NAACP and National Baptist Convention against Tower Records, which included Tha Dogg Pound's offensive album *Dogg Food* in its 1995 Christmas advertisements.) But the battle against obscenity in music directed at the teenage audience will be a hard one to win, largely because parents are far more concerned about pornography in the visual than in the aural media. In an age of headphones, generous allowances, and independence from an early age, parents have remained generally unaware of what their children listen to, and slow to wake up to its dangers. Ironically, it has been particularly hard to publicize the problem of obscenity in rock music because generally newspapers refuse to publish violent or pornographic lyrics. The recording industry pursues its teenage audience as a segregated one, and it has been able to put out a noxiously antisocial product while evoking little public protest precisely because the mainstream media shields *adults* from it.

Among the hundreds of parents I have talked to, I have heard far fewer complaints about sex and violence in popular music than the same in television, movies, videos, and computer games. Even parents who are well aware their kids are listening to the late Tupac ("If you really wanna fuck me, I'm ready") Shakur or Snoop Doggy Dogg often behave as if listening to this music is less harmful than an hour or two of steamy soap operas or Kung Fu films.[20] Do parents find visuals more provocative than music? It is hard to know. But many I have talked to have no compunction about restricting teenage television, video, and movie viewing, yet they set no restrictions on purchasing and listening to music. "We have one rule in our house," says a Connecticut mother of three teenage boys whose music collection boasts Tupac Shakur, Snoop Doggy Dogg, and Metallica, among others. "If you are old enough to listen to this music, you're old enough to keep it away from your younger brother and sister." Another mother says that while she actively keeps her two teenage girls from R-rated films, she only asks that they avoid "vulgar language" in their record purchases. Her thirteen-year-old's tape collection, however, includes punk rock group Green Day's recording, *Dookie*, which features a song about masturbation that includes the lyrics "I'm so damn bored I'm going blind!/And I smell like shit!"[21]

Many hit rock lyrics today are not particularly obscene or disgusting, just extremely depressing. For example, on the 1995 recording *Garbage*, the alternative group Garbage sings, "My only comfort is the night gone black. . . . I'm high upon a deep depression."[22] In "Bomb," on the 1994 hit recording *Sixteen Stone*, the group Bush sings, "Blow me away, see if I care."[23] Nine Inch Nails and Marilyn Manson are other good examples of the many groups who purvey a sound as nihilistic and deliberately repulsive as their lyrics. Of course, ever since the publication of Goethe's *Sorrows of Young Werther*, young people are drawn to the marketing of world-weary sentiments and despair. But the effects are more difficult to gauge when the audience has not been provided with the intellectual equipment to distinguish aesthetic sensation from mere sensationalism, art from junk.

It is not within the parameters of this book to delve into the crisis of public taste that has left popular entertainment in the demoralizing fix it is in today. (This is a subject on which Michael Medved has already spoken eloquently, and which Martha Bayles has handled admirably in her penetrating criticism of the pop music industry, *Hole in Our Soul: The Loss of Beauty and Meaning in American Popular Music*.[24]) But to talk to parents about teen entertainment is to sense not only their intense frustration with the ubiquity of violence and pornography, but their feeling of essential powerlessness to do anything about it. The prospect of waging war against popular entertainment seems like taking on Don Quixote's proverbial fight against the windmill. For each offensive movie, film, or video game the entertainment industry ends up apologizing for— like Michael Jackson's 1991 music video "Black or White," which featured images of the rock star simulating masturbation and smashing a parked car until public furor prompted an edit of the more offensive scenes and a public apology from Jackson himself—the industry churns out countless more. Faced with a nearly universal glorification of "sex, drugs, and rock 'n' roll" by the entertainment industry, parents have few alternatives to offer their children other than a hollow comparison of *Beavis and Butt-head* with *The Flintstones*, or 2 Live Crew with the Temptations.

Those of us who are raising children today grew up in an environment in which popular culture may have been less vulgar, but it was hardly less shallow. Like our children we were generally denied the exposure and rigorous intellectual training that results in aesthetic discrimination. Even the lucky elite who received such an education in the

1950s, 1960s, and 1970s were just as likely to reject it for its elitism as to incorporate it into their lifestyle. The twenty-fifth anniversary of Woodstock recently reminded many of us of our own youthful attractions to an "alternative" culture that promised liberation not only from what we regarded as outmoded bourgeois sexual norms and social conventions, but also the stale and superficial fare of television, movies, and Muzak. The world of the 1980s and 1990s is certainly more brutal than the one I remember; there is more drugs, more sex, more suicide—probably there are even a lot more cars being driven by teenagers. But the same problem—as reporter Donna Gaines captures stirringly in her 1989 study of suburban New Jersey teen culture, *Teenage Wasteland*[25]— haunts it: the lack of viable alternatives to the inanities of what is generally regarded as "clean" popular entertainment. The kind of entertainment that got the *Good Housekeeping* seal of approval could not—even in my day—attract the curious and questioning minds of adolescents or disguise what we recognized as an intellectual and spiritual void. Given our failure to educate our children's tastes to something above the level of banality, it is not surprising that they find alternatives below that level.

My generation's allegiance to the socially critical aspects of the rock 'n' roll movement may in itself be the reason we are having big problems getting control of a teen culture run amok in our homes. Certainly these attachments are complicit in our inability to make the kind of aesthetic judgments on gangsta rap, on gang-rape rock videos, and on on-stage demonstrations such as the rock group W.A.S.P.'s famous "Fuck Like a Beast" show (in which members of that death metal rock band mocked a chain-saw rape) that would label them once and for all as socially destructive obscenities, and therefore as outside the pale of commerce in a civil society. So far, public protests have focused on consumer protection and corporate responsibility (on appeals to the entertainment industry to clean up its act or at least put warning labels on their products), rather than on enacting and enforcing public decency laws. It is not that we have completely forgotten what public decency is, but we no longer have tools for applying those notions to the arts and entertainment industries.

I have often wondered how long it would take me to get arrested if I were to stand in front of a Tower Records store handing out dirty pictures underscored with obscene language to the preteen girls who pass me by. Probably about as long as it takes for an alarmed citizen to make a phone call to the police, and for the police to dispatch a car. And yet, Tower Records *sells* records to preteen girls containing dirty pictures and obscene language, all the while claiming for their product First Amendment protection to freedom of speech and artistic expression.[26] Martha Bayles suggests in *Hole in Our Soul* that in focusing their efforts on "consumer advocacy" letter-writing campaigns and boycotts, activists such as Tipper Gore and C. DeLores Tucker have made a grave tactical error, by implicitly acknowledging the products themselves as forms of artistic expression. Few leaders in the campaign against pornography in popular entertainment, Bayles complains, have had the "wherewithal to tackle the cultural question"—namely the question of what separates a daring work of art from trash.[27]

Similarly, the debate on falling standards in the TV industry has been waged and won not on the premise that gratuitous violence and vulgarity (in other words, junk of a singularly harmful nature) should be jettisoned from the tube, but rather on the idea that labeling objectionable material, moving it out of prime time, and enabling parents to block access to it via V-chip technology is good enough. But if we insist on substituting V-chips for reinstituting broadcasting standards on the airwaves, we are not going to get very far in cleaning up what has become a sorely polluted cultural environment. To use an analogy: What is a more intelligent approach to the problem of dirty air: air quality regulations, or the distribution of gas masks to people who insist they need to breathe?

It will take much more than even jettisoning offensive material and reinstituting broadcasting standards to combat the precipitous decline in entertainment. It will take a massive campaign for the rebuilding of audience taste. In television this would mean prescribing a number of hours devoted to the kind of high-minded cultural and educational programming we can be proud not only to show our children, but to watch ourselves. As I complete this manuscript, the Federal Communications Commission has finally, after a long and wearing internal battle, adopted a policy of requiring just three hours per week of educational children's programming from noncable broadcasters, and this with a rather loose definition of educational programming.

■ ■ ■

Many parents attempt to make up for the inordinate influence of an aesthetically and spiritually deficient media culture by encouraging their children to read good books, by sending them to church and religious school, and by signing them up for music and art classes. Often the quality of instruction offered by the institutions they enlist disappoints them. But in school things are even worse. A single, working mother in a New York City suburb remarked to me: "At my son's fifth-grade parent-teacher conference, the teacher mentioned how great it was that he liked to read. I asked her what he read in school, and she said, '*Garfield.*'" Well, I was shocked and quite perturbed that she meant to praise my son for reading

Garfield at school. I asked her if she would consider putting a piece of good literature his way."

In a misguided effort to make school "relevant" to children's lives outside of school, educators often bring popular culture into the classroom in the form of literature, music and social instruction. In fourth grade, for example, my own child was assigned to write a "rap" poem as part of her language-arts program. Not surprisingly, children take this emphasis on popular culture as an endorsement and end up clinging to the tastes of the marketplace rather than expanding their horizons toward more sophisticated work with a longer shelf life.

Already in the early 1980s the schools were served notice of the destructive results of their efforts. In 1981, the National Assessment of Educational Progress lamented the dearth of historical knowledge of the arts among high school students. They lacked familiarity with even the most famous works of Western art and music, not to mention ethnic art forms. In fact, they seemed to prefer advertising graphics to art, and to "favor mimetic criteria (the closer to reality something is, the better it is)" in judging art. Most students appeared to be "unable to go beyond the look of a painting's subject matter in order to make judgments about the merit of a work. They are essentially artistic literalists. . . . Their responses to works of art shallow, narrow and uninformed."[28]

The arts have long since disappeared from many urban public schools. But today, even in affluent suburban schools, arts education is based far more on contemporary models taken from popular culture than on historic models of high art or folk culture. In fact, in their efforts to achieve a curriculum that emphasizes "self-esteem" and "multiculturalism," public schools often offer children only the most derivative forms of popular culture, rather than an authentic encounter with Western, Asian, or African aesthetic traditions. I don't know how many times in my own child's school career I have sat through interminable concerts of songs all about global understanding, love, and getting along together—songs that are nothing more than pale imitations of Broadway and Hollywood melodies with a few rock and rap influences thrown in. Each time I listen to these cornball confections (sung, I might add, with very little joy), I wonder whatever happened to the spirituals and international folk songs I remember singing in school with delight.

When the schools offer only the most banal models of the kitsch the popular culture is awash in, how are parents to direct them toward an appreciation of high art and authentic folk art? And if the classroom is truly the place for an honest encounter with ethnic pluralism (and most of us who still believe in public education believe that it should be), then the schools are failing children miserably. When I ask the white kids I know what they think of when they think of "black American" music, for example, almost none of them mention anything besides rap and reggae. Their ignorance of jazz, blues, and all the other contributions of African-Americans to American music is a sad commentary on an approach to education that emphasizes tokenism over substance and a true catholicity of spirit.[29]

In his recent work, *The End of Education*, cultural critic Neil Postman notes that in "studying the creative arts" we learn the value of diversity as an "inescapable side effect." He writes:

> Imagine a concert that features Luciano Pavarotti, Placido Domingo, and José Carreras. Zubin Mehta conducts; Yo-Yo Ma and Itzhak Perlman are soloists. Imagine that, after the intermission, Leontyne Price sings Wagner. . . . Besides the fact that it would be nearly impossible to get tickets for such a concert, it would also be impossible for those who got in not to notice the contributions of people from all over the world. . . . But the audience has not come for a lesson in diversity or even, if you prefer, the universality of Western music. Neither do people go to museums and plays and read novels and poetry to learn about the cosmopolitan nature of artistic creation. They do these things to nourish their souls. Art, it has been said, is the language of the heart, and if we teach about music, painting, architecture, and literature in schools, we ought to be doing it to help our youth understand that language so that it may penetrate to their hearts.[30]

One reason our public schools fail as aesthetic educators of the young is their fear of exploring Christianity as a deeply rooted source of aesthetic inspiration. They go out of their way to ignore two millennia of Western visual and musical art inspired by Christianity, out of an exaggerated fear of compromising the secular character of public education with references to the Christian religion or religious symbols. Educators are not entirely to blame for their profound lack of sensitivity to the ties between Western art and Christianity; they are afraid of lawsuits like the one launched in 1995 on behalf of a Jewish high school student who protested the religious exclusivity of the material sung in her Utah high school chorus.[31] The result, however, is that in all too many public school districts children are robbed of an integrated understanding of the Western cultural heritage and deprived of aesthetic models that would help to combat the more perverse influences of popular culture.

The parents I've talked to are bitterly divided about how to interpret the schools' general retreat from Christian aesthetic heritage. Some are extremely angry and resentful. Others, however, take it as an indication of the educational establishment's increased multicultural sensitivity. Many Jewish parents in particular note with relief the disappearance of carols and crèches from the schools at Christmastime, and the consequent appearance of Stars of David and songs about Chanukah.

What they may overlook in their relief at having menorahs placed beside Christmas wreaths, however, is the lack of serious attention given to *any* religion or religious symbols. A Connecticut mother says:

> It irks me that the public schools are happy to discuss all the secular and useless aspects of religious holidays, but not the deeper significance of those holidays. What they are doing is worse than leaving religion alone. They are debasing religion. There is more to Christmas that Santa Claus, and more to Chanukah than dreidels, but you wouldn't know it to send your children to school. I think they've misinterpreted the notion of separation of church and state in public education. The idea is not that there should be no religion in the schools, but that there should be no *discriminatory* religion.

Far from promoting deeper ecumenical understanding, the schools' handling of the major religions—from Judaism and Christianity to Islam and Buddhism—has actually impeded it by promoting only the shallowest display of religious symbols and discouraging any real discussion of the moral and spiritual imaginations of the peoples for whom these symbols have meaning. While children in American schools are constantly told that American life is the product of a myriad of rich ethnic influences, they receive no real instruction about these influences. They typically do not study, for example, the religious philosophies that motivate the array of distinct ethnic groups who call themselves Americans. (They do not even seriously study foreign languages—one way American children could be exposed to different ways of thinking in preparation for leading productive and tolerant lives in a "global" or "multicultural" society.)

Neil Postman believes that rather than being hostile to religion, public schools have much to gain by undertaking instruction in comparative religion. Religious narratives, he points out, tell "stories of how different people . . . achieve a sense of transcendence." It is quite impossible for anyone to claim to be educated who has no knowledge of the role played by religion in the formation of culture, Postman argues. Therefore it is a shame that "public schools are barely able to refer to religion in almost any context."[32]

But in fact it is not religion per se that the schools neglect, but *main-*

stream religious imagery and religious references, except in the most superficial context. For example, since the 1960s, the public schools have explored Native American art, folkways, and spiritual imagery. Originally this was done with the intent of providing children with an understanding and appreciation of the worldview and aesthetic sensibilities of precolonial American peoples—in other words, as one strand among many in American artistic and spiritual experience. But as serious discussion of Christian and other mainstream religious symbols and ideas has disappeared from schools, Native American culture has been emphasized more strongly. In a study of widely used grammar school textbooks, New York University professor of education Paul Vitz found that the average American child who attended public school received far more instruction in Native American spiritual beliefs than in the religions of the West.[33] Although it provides a useful model of a truly integrated study of art and belief, the almost exclusive emphasis on Native American imagery and spirituality gives it a prominence that does not realistically mirror its influence in the larger culture.

Recently New Age spiritual concepts and practices have been finding their way into the schools. It is hard to assess how influential this movement has become, but William Kilpatrick, author of *Why Johnny Can't Tell Right from Wrong,* says the movement has "made considerable headway in the Pacific states, and that many of its tenets—the quest for "the mystical experience of wholeness," for "self-transcendence," for "healing" the "Whole Earth" and for replacing patriarchal religious traditions with "non-patriarchal forms of spirituality"—coincide with the "goals of multiculturalists, environmentalists and some feminists." New Age influences, he argues, can be seen in the widespread use of "guided imagery" exercises in self-esteem, drug-awareness, and stress-reduction curricula, and New Age themes are making their way into classroom reading material.

Teachers who explore these ideas and approaches in the classroom may view them as harmless. And indeed in the watered-down version in which it reaches the schools, Kilpatrick points out, New Age philosophy amounts to nothing more than a few shallow borrowings from the "more bohemian forms of Eastern Spirituality—Taoism and Zen Buddhism"— refracted through the lens of the human potential movement of the 1960s. But nevertheless it can be dangerous. Exhorting children to function as their own "spiritual guides" rather than offering moral direction, focusing on fantasy rather than the imposition of intellectual discipline, New Age spiritualism deceives children about the tough demands of life and learning.[34]

Here again, in their treatment of religion and the spiritual quest, schools seem to be working against the rich, pluralist heritage of the public and toward cultural homogeneity. Indeed, the schools further the destruction of culture that the media begins. It has always been a mission of the public schools to expedite the process of assimilation and Americanization for immigrant children. But today they may be divesting all our children of the minimal cultural and spiritual vestments they bring with them from home.

■ ■ ■

*M*any *parents* blame contemporary religious institutions for failing to offer children a compelling alternative to a culture of materialism, secularism, and homogeneity. Religion, an overwhelming majority of them contend, is one of the most important components in healthy family lives, giving families "a sense of unity" and helping each generation to pass along its culture to the next. A San Francisco woman whose parents immigrated from Greece recalls how her church helped her children solidify ties with their ethnic community:

> I'm not the most religious person, but I think church was a very important part in a child's life. If nothing else, have some fear, have a believing . . . in a bigger being . . . Christ or Buddha or whatever . . . having some structure! My children went to Greek school on Saturday; Sunday they were in Sunday school. And it was a wonderful structure. They hated it at the time, but they're looking back today and they say it was a wonderful thing. They're not the most religious kids today, but they have a fear of God, a respect, and it's a wonderful thing as a community.

But if the average American family, as many parents contend, "has gotten away from religion," it is also true that the kind of vibrant religious life parents remember from their own childhoods is difficult to find these days. While many parents see their churches as the only remaining tie between young people and their cultural roots, others complain that church is becoming like the proverbial supermarket white bread—more fluff than nourishment. Many second- and third-generation ethnics believe that deculturation has invaded the very core of their communal life: the church. Their churches, they complain, have turned away from traditional ritual, in many cases abandoning the language, music, and ceremonies of worship that sustained them in childhood. Some parents observe that in their efforts to be relevant and attractive in a secular society, churches have become practically secular institutions—more focused on providing social activities, political advice, and psychological support than spiritual inspiration and comfort.

Some parents report that they are in effect replacing what it is missing in church by setting aside certain evenings each week for family devotionals. The Connecticut mother who lamented the schools' neglect of substantial discussion of religion said, "I was raised Episcopalian, but the church I remember as a child is not the same church I go to today. The other day I went to Mass, and there was this woman sitting next to me who mentioned she had converted, and I thought to myself 'Why? What did she convert to?' It took all of my strength not to say to her, 'Well, this used to be a great church, this used to be a great *religion,* but it isn't anymore!' "

One of the biggest failures of churches today, say parents, is the casual approach they take toward religious education. The churches, many parents charge, are complicit with the schools in pushing a therapeutic curriculum of contemporary "relevance" and "positive feelings," emphasizing finger painting and fuzzy feelings over sacred images and texts.

In a 1992 article in the magazine *First Things,* Nancy W. Yos, who grew up in the Midwest in the mid-1970s, depicts the intellectual and spiritual emptiness of her own Catholic education, despite twelve years of instruction that included four years at a Catholic high school:

> I remember that we drew and colored pictures for the first several years of CCD [catechism classes], that even as late as the first day of our eighth-grade CCD class, our teachers asked us what we would like to do, and if we would like to color. . . . I remember in high school, the second half of our sophomore year religion class was devoted to "Sex, Sexuality and You." That was a purple-covered textbook . . . and in it was a drawing of an erect penis. . . . Our junior and senior year religion textbooks were called *Deciding* and *Relating.* . . .
>
> Until the past few years, when I began to try to educate myself . . . I did not know the difference between Gospels and Epistles. I did not know which were the holy days of obligation, nor when they occur. I did not know how to say the Rosary, nor what its decades represent. . . . I knew almost nothing of the Church calendar, of its seasons and feast days. . . . I did not understand what was signified by the word "Passions," nor did I know why a lamb was supposed to represent Christ in this connection. . . . I was ignorant, and remain basically so, of the gigantic topic of Church history.[35]

A Catholic mother recently described to me her decision to take over her child's religious training:

> One day I substituted for my daughter's fourth-grade religion class. I asked the kids to tell me some things Jesus had said. Not one child could repeat a single phrase Christ had uttered, not even "This is my body; this is my blood," which they hear at Holy Communion each week. The kids have this vague idea that Jesus was a good guy; but they don't really know anything about Him. That's how far the religious school curriculum has been watered down.

As a religious school teacher in a Reform synagogue, I share this woman's consternation with the quality of religious education. Two years ago I attended my own synagogue's children's service on the Jewish New Year and was shocked to find that the rabbi did not give the traditional Torah reading: the Binding of Isaac. When I asked him why, he explained that the story was "a little too frightening for children."

The growing reluctance on the part of clergy and religious educators to confront children with God's exceedingly tough demands on those human beings who decide to serve Him—specifically the quite formal and specific demands He makes through Scripture—has to take its toll on children's moral development. When religious educators exhort children to "do unto others" without offering them substantive examples of the challenges that their biblical ancestors faced in "doing unto others," how can they prepare children for the real trials of living moral lives?

From 1980 to 1990—roughly the period during which the allegedly progressive "self-esteem" model of education established itself across the board in our nation's religious schools—church attendance among high school seniors dropped from 43 to 30 percent, and the number of high school seniors who listed religion as an important element in their lives dropped from 65 to 56 percent.[36] One young man of my acquaintance recently told me that "coloring-book CCD" had turned him off religion in high school, but that his decision to attend a Jesuit college eventually drew him back into the fold. "It was there I finally got my questions answered. Until then, when I would ask 'Why?' nobody explained."

I teach Hebrew to fifth-grade bar and bat mitzvah candidates, the majority of whom have never attended a traditional Jewish Sabbath service with a Torah reading, have never held a Bible in their hands, could not quote one phrase of Jewish wisdom if their lives depended on it, and have only the foggiest notion what the Jewish holidays are all about. Most of them have had six previous years of religious school in which every Sunday brings a fight *not* to attend. I like to think it is a turning point in their religious education when at the beginning of every year I assign two or three readings in the Pentateuch. Suddenly a new seriousness of enterprise emerges in the classroom, for these are kids who have never before been entrusted with reading and interpreting an authentic religious text.

Doubtless it would be a mistake to inflict on children too academic an approach to religious instruction, but to keep them in crafts and sanitized versions of Bible stories forever—to deny them substantive background and knowledge of the intensity, emotional depth, and richness in human experience that religious texts reveal—is to give them the false impression that there is nothing beneath the surface of religious ritual, nothing with which to grow in moral and spiritual understanding. Mainstream clergy fret about the vulnerability of young people to coercion by religious cults, but few of them contrast the spiritual and moral direction cults provide with their own churches' neglect of the young. When the churches leave the great spiritual questions of life—the nature of good, evil, heroism, and villainy—to the Walt Disney Company and the Power Rangers, what can they expect children to reach for when they outgrow juvenile entertainments?

The propensity of religious educators to ignore children's spiritual and moral hunger—to allow, as it were, secular culture to rush in where angels fear to tread—was brought home to me in a recent discussion I had with the principal of a well-attended Reform Jewish Sunday school in my area. She confessed to me that she had made a mistake in setting the curriculum for a new high school religious school program. After considerable efforts to find a textbook "appropriate" for high-school-age religious school students, she chose a book that discussed "decision-making strategies" regarding sexual involvement and drug use. It was not long, however, before she realized that "when these kids came to class, they didn't want to talk about sex or drugs. They wanted to talk about God. They had a lot of questions about religious philosophy, so that's what we ended up discussing."

I fear that few religious educators today would be so responsive to the urgency of adolescents' need for spiritual instruction. For many, it seems, the job of religion is to complete the job of cultural assimilation begun by the media and carried on by the schools. The tenor of Reform Jewish education—which still boasts the highest membership of the four major Jewish denominations—has become so secular that many Jewish leaders are worried. In a book appropriately entitled *Putting God on the Guest List,* for example, Rabbi Jeffrey Salkin has appealed to Jewish parents to stop leading their children straight from the pulpit to the disco, and to "reclaim the spiritual meaning of your child's Bar Mitzvah" (the ritual marking passage into adulthood).[37]

In a recent article in *Commentary,* Irving Kristol, publisher of *The Public Interest,* ruminated as to whether the lax commitment of Jewish educators to religious tradition—specifically the penchant of Reform Judaism to a political rather than pastoral focus—might threaten the very existence of the American Jewish community. Jews, he noted, are marrying outside the faith at alarmingly high rates, and only a small minority bring non-Jewish wives and husbands into the fold.[38] But the synagogue is hardly alone in suffering a decline in membership. There is every indication that the massive exodus from mainstream Christian churches and the draw of charismatic Christian, Jewish, and Muslim sects have a lot to do with the penchant of today's mainstream clergy for substituting political sermons for pastoral concerns, for urging children toward personal expression rather than giving them a solid spiritual and scriptural foundation, and for denying church members and their children the comfort of a deeper connection to their past by preserving rituals.

The mainstream Christian churches are particularly prone to soft-pedaling dogma and tradition where they might direct followers of one faith to take a different path from those of other faiths. The churches seem to have taken the cue that it is impolitic to maintain the "truth" of a particular religious faith because it leaves followers of that faith open to charges of elitism or bias. Many churches back off even from making pronouncements on morality, for fear that such declarations are too narrow and judgmental, and that in affirming traditional moral doctrine or biblical injunctions, they will drive potential worshippers away from already half-empty pews. Thus, the liberal Christian denominations have caved in on the issue of affirming traditional family structure, for fear of alienating divorced, single-parent, and gay members of their congregations. Professor Don S. Browning of the University of Chicago Divinity School writes that the churches have lagged far behind politicians and public policy-makers in addressing divorce and illegitimacy as factors in the decline of social well-being. Instead, he notes, a Presbyterian Church report negatively "depicted the [traditional] family . . . as a patriarchal institution—violent, unequal and rapidly becoming a passing sexual arrangement." A report from the Evangelical Lutheran Church in America called *The Church and Human Sexuality* not only "ignored the national debate about the situation of children, the absence of fathers and the emerging culture of non-marriage and divorce," but "was tentative about the relation of procreation and marriage, implying that in some cases it was justifiable to intentionally break them apart."[39]

Gilbert Meilaender, professor of religion at Oberlin College, observes also that too many church statements on the subject of family structure have made "a virtue of . . . [the] necessities" of divorce and illegitimacy, issuing statements that purport to recognize the equal value of a "diversity" of family structures, and that declare that family "roles should never become more important than the persons involved." Meilaender charges that in their "focus on quality of relationship rather than structure," many churches have exacerbated the tendency of individuals to fall prey to the unhealthy secular notion of family as "a locus of self-fulfillment for singular individuals." This notion, he says, ignores the importance of duty and continuity not only in promoting children's well-being but in realizing the Christian view of love and family life.

Many Protestant churches, Meilaender contends, have sidestepped their moral duties by choosing to view family breakdown and the loosening of family bonds as an opportunity, rather than a tragedy. They tend to emphasize the aspects of Jesus' life and preachings that derogate narrow family loyalties in favor of the universal community of Christian brotherhood. Meilaender argues, however, that this view is shortsighted and ultimately a misreading of Jesus' message. Jesus may have said, "Whosoever does the will of God is my brother, sister, and mother," but he mentioned family bonds precisely to invoke the strongest possible metaphor for the ties that bind people together. What many liberal denominations miss in turning away from discussions of family structure, Meilaender contends, is that Jesus regarded the family as the very model of communitarian purpose and love on which the Kingdom of God must be built. When that model is weakened or disappears, so ultimately does the Christian community.[40]

Similarly, feminist critiques of the patriarchal aspects of the Judeo-Christian traditions have led theologians to avoid the familist metaphors (the Holy Family) and gender-specific language (God the Father) that have traditionally given worshippers the power to conceptualize the power and greatness of God. The transformation of God the Father into God the Parent—surely among the least powerful members of the contemporary human species—can only be understood in the context of the larger movement to marginalize the Christian faith's most powerful symbol of penance and self-sacrifice: the cross. The cross, says the University of Chicago's Don Browning, has increasingly become a "no-no" of religious discussion in mainline Christian faiths. Feminists, he claims, have rightly pointed to the use of the symbol in traditional theology to justify a "Gestalt of exploitation." Contemporary Christian theologians, he says, are uncomfortable with its "more masochistic expressions,"[41] and would rather emphasize the rewards and reciprocity, rather than the sacrifices, of Christian love.[42]

Christians may, however, pay a huge cultural price in abandoning the powerful symbolism of the cross. I volunteer to help out with a PTA-sponsored art appreciation program—an informative and well-presented series of audio-filmstrips and prints of mostly nineteenth- and twentieth-century European art that is one of the few opportunities children in my school district have to encounter masterworks of Western art. Three years ago, I went into my daughter's third-grade class to show a presentation on self-portraits. I decided to linger on a work by the famous Jewish Postimpressionist Marc Chagall, because I saw something significant in the corner of his fanciful self-portrait—an image of Christ on the cross.

In an effort to engage the children in a discussion of the image, I casually asked, "Who is that in the left-hand corner of the painting?" The "discussion" stalled right there. Only one of the twenty-three third-graders even recognized the figure of Christ. That child was my daughter, the single Jewish child in the class. Now, I know most of these children; and I can say with certainty that at least three-quarters of them attend church and Sunday school regularly. Why did they not recognize the figure of Christ?

One might charge that the image of the crucified Christ was out of context in a public school classroom, and that in any case, children who attend Protestant churches would not have been exposed to the religious imagery associated with Catholicism and Greek or Russian Orthodoxy. But I believe the real reason is that today children—and this includes Catholic children—are increasingly denied the narrative of the Crucifixion. Why? Because, in the words of the radical feminist theologian Mary Daly, it concerns a "uniquely male . . . reification" of God, because it is a concrete reminder of the wages of sin and the brutality of Christ's punishment for *our* sins, and because it is a story of redemption through sacrifice. It is a story, moreover, that affirms the ultimate dignity of suffering. In short, it is a symbol of a theology of duty and sacrifice that religious reformists of the past thirty years have determined to cast upon the garbage heap of history as too negative, as the product (in Mary Daly's words) of a "prison" of "static, timeless" rules and "self-destructive dichotomies."[43]

Perhaps contemporary theologians believe that they have replaced the old theology with a more upbeat, positive, and plastic theology—one more adaptable to contemporary democratic life, and one that more fully celebrates the joys and fulfillments of life and love. But this new theology is dangerously tolerant of the fluidity of contemporary life and family styles, and of the temptations of consumer culture. It is a theology (in Mary Daly's words) of "self-communicating Be-ing,"[44] a theology of self-actualization that assures us that life is what *we* make of it, not what God has told us we should make of it. It is a theology that allows us—if I may paraphrase Neil Postman's observations about the religious component in television advertising—to confine our moral parables to exorcising the evils of bad breath, yellow floors, and having bought the wrong traveler's checks; to build our "visions of Heaven" on the sale of the "right" insurance and on the purchase of the "right" car, without ever having to examine how close we are living to God's vision, or to weigh our lives on the scales that were once revered in the Western world as the ultimate standard—namely, the lives of Jesus and of Moses.[45]

Curiously, in a chapter called "Beyond Christolatry: A World Without Models," in her enormously influential 1973 book, *Beyond God the Father,* Mary Daly prophesied the very experience I had in my child's third-grade class: "A logical consequence of the liberation of women," she wrote, "will be a loss of plausibility of Christological formulas which reflect and encourage idolatry in relation to the person of Jesus."[46] Those church-attending "Christians" in my daughter's third grade who did not recognize the figure of Jesus are products of just that "loss of plausibility of Christological formulas." They are already living in the utopia Daly envisioned less than twenty-five years ago, a world liberated from religious "models" and religious idolatry. (They are not, of course, living in a world liberated from *non*religious idolatry. I would not want to know how quickly those kids would have recognized the figure of Michael Jackson had *he* been painted in the corner of Chagall's self-portrait.)

It would be unfair to blame the churches entirely for what has become increasingly apparent is the failure of spiritual development in America's youth, or even to insist that all churches are passive complicitors in the disintegration of the family. There are many churches—particularly fundamentalist denominations—that offer an uncompromising spiritual vision to their young members, and that remain loyal friends to the family. But as the traditional Christian symbols of sacrifice and commitment disappear from worship in many of the mainstream faiths, we have cause to worry. For the majority of Americans worship itself is increasingly irrelevant, and with it the rituals and traditions of faith that have held families and cultures together for centuries. Thus many of today's youth are being deprived of a rich and meaningful spiritual, aesthetic, and cultural heritage, a heritage that goes far beyond faith in specific church doctrines, but touches upon the very essence of the human experience. One does not have to be a practicing Christian, for example, to appreciate the crèche as a cultural reflection on the miracle of birth; nor must one believe Jesus to be the son of God in order to be

touched by the Pietà as a reflection on the power and redemptive potential of sacrificial love. If these uplifting symbols disappear, what will we
find to replace them?

Parents are disappointed in the churches, but they continue to view
them as the greatest hope for restabilizing the family and redirecting a
youth lost to a culture of violence and vulgarity. In the words of an African-
American mother, "The church has more power than the government or
anything. The church can help. . . . The family that prays together stays together." Increasingly, liberal and conservative politicians alike view the
leadership of churches as essential to the reconstruction of a decaying
civil society. Recently Senator Dan Coats of Indiana has introduced congressional legislation for a charitable tax credit designed to direct "funding
and authority into the hands of institutions with the power to reclaim our
lives and humanize our society"—namely the churches Americans trust to
offer the kind of "healing power of true compassion and spiritual hope,"
that will "turn an addict into an example . . . a troublemaker into a peace-
maker . . . a criminal into a man or woman of conscience."[47] Similarly, in a
1993 address, President Clinton challenged a national convention of the
African-American Pentecostal Church of God in Christ: "Who will be
there to give structure, discipline and love to these children? You must do
that, and we [government] must help."[48]

Some observers do not hold out much hope that the churches are
up to the task the politicians are prescribing for them. In commenting on
the President's 1993 address, Don Browning warned that while "some
individual churches" had "strong programs" to address the social malaise
destroying children and families, church leadership seemed in general ill
equipped for the huge task the American public and politicians are determined to set for them. As of 1995, Browning said:

> Neither Christian conservatives nor liberals were doing the socio-
> logical analysis or theological reconstruction required to create
> programs and concepts needed to address the complexity of the is-
> sues facing American families. Neither liberals nor conservatives
> had a grasp of family history, how it had developed in the West,
> and how religion, culture, and economic trends had interacted to
> create modern industrial and post-industrial family forms. . . . Un-
> til deeper historical, cultural and theological understanding and
> reconstruction is attempted . . . confusion is likely to continue to
> plague the family debate in American . . . religious life.[49]

In the last year or so, a few religious leaders have begun to address
the kind of inner "reconstruction" of which Browning speaks. In the

spring of 1996, a conference of religious leaders from a number of Christian denominations and Jewish sects organized by the Washington, D.C., based Center for Jewish and Christian Values met to discuss the implications of family breakdown, the dissolution of the marriage bond, and the growing involvement of the custodial state in the raising of children, and finally the influence of the entertainment media in devaluing human life.[50] This ecumenical effort to restore the voice of the clergy as a voice of leadership in combating the larger crisis of moral and cultural decay in America is encouraging indeed.

Perhaps, in the end, we will be able to turn to the churches to refill the spiritual and cultural vessel of childhood that the secular pressures of American life have emptied. After all, they were the last of America's institutions to succumb to those pressures. Rooted in communities and in distinct ethnic traditions, they still are in a position to provide families—both dual and single-parent families—what many urgently want: social supports and tangible models for living richer lives. And churches still have the unique capability of giving children—even children who are growing up without families—the sense that their lives, no matter how hard or senseless they may seem, have a purpose. Perhaps Pope John Paul II describes best the very special and urgent role of the churches today, in a chapter of his book *Crossing the Threshold of Hope* entitled "Is There Really Hope in the Young?"

> *What are young people of today like, what are they looking for?*
> . . . [Y]oung people are always searching for the beauty in love. . . . If they give in to weakness, following models of behavior that can rightly be considered a "scandal in the contemporary world" (and these are, unfortunately, widely diffused models), in the depths of their hearts they still desire a beautiful and pure love. . . . Ultimately, they know that only God can give them this love.[51]

Part III

THE FAMILIST

COUNTERCULTURE

8

Alternative Schooling

R*ecently,* I asked a home schooling mother what initially prompted her to take what most of us would consider to be a radical step. "For me it was simple," she said. "I can't entrust my garbage to the town's waste removal system, so why should I entrust my *child* to its school system?" How many parents put their kids on the bus to school each day with the sinking feeling that the hours spent there will be at best a waste of time, at worst a ruinous misadventure? I confess to having stood at the top of our cul-de-sac wondering whether it might not be more directly in my child's interests to let the yellow bus pass by, and take her education in hand myself.

Somewhere between 900,000 and 1.2 million children do let the school bus pass every day.[1] They are the children of America's home schooling families. Their numbers have multiplied exponentially in the past two decades (from 12,500 in the late 1970s, according to a *Time* magazine report),[2] and their retreat from institutional schooling can tell us much about the kind of soul-searching the anti-family culture has prompted.

Many home schooling parents believe, and fervently, too, that the only viable answer to raising kids in a culture they find increasingly hostile to their child-rearing work is to buck its trends. If educational institutions can no longer be trusted to reflect their values and educational standards (so goes one argument) then families must withdraw from those institutions and become educationally self-supporting. A home schooling mother puts it this way: "I would like to send my kids to school. I *believe* in school. But I just can't believe in the schools available to us."

Home-schoolers, says Maureen Carey of Holt Associates, a Cambridge, Massachusetts, home school resource corporation, are people who are "taking charge" of family lives that everywhere else are "out of control." A growing number of parents, she says, perceive that school is "a terrible waste" of childhood and family time, and that schools are "less about learning than about control." Traditionally, says Carey, home-schoolers have been radical nonconformists, people who "never bought the system." But increasing numbers of parents, she says, are tiring of conformity. Citing statistics that indicate home schooling will continue to grow, Carey notes, "Parents feel like an oppressed minority. They find it hard to identify with prevailing cultural values."[3]

According to the Home School Legal Defense Association, the numbers of home-schooled children are increasing presently at a whopping 25 percent a year. Ten years ago the movement could have been characterized as marginal—a strange mixture of mostly fundamentalist Christians and a few inveterate hippies—but a "new breed" of home-schooler is now emerging, well-educated urban and suburban professionals whose motivations may be neither religiously nor socially radical. And while a 1992 summary of several demographic studies of home schooling families shows that 75 percent are Christian and regularly attend church and 90 percent can be categorized as "white/Anglo,"[4] home-schoolers are becoming more diverse by the day, their ranks swelled by parents who are simply "fed up with the schools" and are "fuelling the search for public-school alternatives."[5]

This trend is the product of more than a frustration with overcrowded classrooms and disappointing academic results in public schools. It reflects a deepening polarization between parents' and educators' notions of what desirable results would be and how to achieve them. Indeed, it reflects a breakdown of public consensus on the deepest questions of moral and civic life: how to raise decent and productive citizens. It is also a dramatic statement of a new kind of commitment to family life, and of a conviction that a rich family life is our greatest reward. Home schooling is one aspect of a new vision of family life that equates family time with children's well-being, and that puts family intimacy and parent-child bonds before self-realization and economic gain.

Home schooling families typically have more children than families who send their children to school. They boast a higher degree of parental involvement in the home, usually with an at-home mother functioning as teacher.[6] While most are not poor, few are wealthy. In 1992, about a quarter had incomes of less than $25,000 a year, and only 20 percent incomes of more than $50,000 a year. The average home schooling family, the summary concluded, had a slightly lower family income "compared to the nation at large."[7]

Steve Stecklow, author of a recent *Wall Street Journal* report on home schooling, asserts that many of the home schooling parents he talked to don't so much harp on the failures of school as wax poetic about the pleasures and rewards of close family interaction. These parents, he says, would be loath to send their children to any school, even one with an excellent academic reputation. "Some mothers remarked to me that they just enjoyed having their kids around the first five or six years, and for that reason wanted to keep them at home."[8] Yet Stecklow points to a growing network of resource and support groups, and extracurricular and sports activities organized locally by home schooling families as evidence that home schooling parents are not, as some critics charge, simply retreating from society, or raising a generation of social misfits.

In my conversations with home schooling parents, I have been struck by the extent to which they defy their stereotype as overprotective control freaks. In fact, many home schooling parents see the *school* as confining and controlling. The home, they say, is a far healthier environment for cultivating individuality, independence, and special talents. Former teacher David Colfax and his wife, Micki, whose four home-schooled boys have gone to Harvard, point out that in institutional schooling, the child "is age graded, sorted, labeled, and resorted according to currently fashionable criteria . . . processed, over the years, much like a can of soup or a piece of hardware." The public school curriculum can never compete with home schooling, he insists, because it is by the very nature of institutionalization a compromise—"a hodge-podge of materials and assumptions resulting from the historical interplay of educational theories," as well as "organizational . . . and political expedience."[9]

Many times the initial impetus to home schooling comes not from any theoretical presuppositions about the educational system as a system, but merely from the realization that a child's particular educational needs—a gift, a particular learning style, a "learning disability"—are not being satisfied by schooling. One home-schooled teenager in Massachusetts reports that her grammar school teachers despaired she would ever read when her mother removed her from school at the age of nine. "In one year at home," she says, "I went from a nonreader to reading at the level of a senior in high school." The father of an eleven-year-old violin prodigy told me that home schooling wasn't his idea, but his son's: "It got to the point where he felt that school was in the way of his music. He couldn't spend seven hours in school and then come home to four, five, six hours of practicing, not to mention his desire to pursue other interests. . . . He wanted to practice; and we wanted him to be happy. It was a matter of optimizing time."

Naturally, home schooling is not always a resounding success. Some parents who remove their kids from school find the task of supervising their children's academic progress overwhelming and eventually return them to school. But they return them better for the effort. Says Virginia mother and journalist Cheryl Ann Hughes, who interviewed many home schooling mothers on behalf of the national organization Mothers at Home, "Even when mothers send their children back to school, they are much better advocates for them. They've had a great opportunity . . . to really get to know their own children . . . to know what motivates them, and *how* to motivate them."

One important survey revealed that parents' frustrations with the kind of social experience the schools provide was at least as significant a factor in the rise of home schooling as disappointment in the regimentation or results of academic programs:

> Most home-schooling parents see the home school as a means of protecting their young from the rivalry, ridicule, competition and conflicting moral values they believe are associated with much of the socialization that takes place in schools. . . . This attitude does not preclude [their] children from associating with other children; most parents encourage social encounters . . . [but] they want their children to be family socialized . . . [to have] their family be the center of the children's social world.[10]

Indeed, home-schoolers see their way of life as an optimal path to social integration, primarily because it recognizes the importance of family interaction in the process. They have a clear idea of the social mission of family life—that the family is where all social interactions begin and are modeled. Both the academic and social successes of home-schooled children results, Cheryl Ann Hughes observed, "show us that the learning experience they give their kids encourages earlier independence and responsibility."[11]

The essays by home-schooled teenagers in the 1993 *Real Lives:*

Eleven Teenagers Who Don't Go to School offer testimony to what liberation from the school can mean not only for kids, but for their communities. Rebecca Merrion, a fifteen-year-old from Danville, Indiana, writes:

> Volunteer service is one reason why I am not going to school. I like the feeling I get from giving my time to less fortunate people. If I was in school I would not have enough time for my volunteer work, and I think that volunteer work should be a part of everyone's lives. . . . I have volunteered with homeless shelters, with Habitat for Humanity, and I visit several elderly ladies who live in our community—like my 97-year-old friend Beulah, a spry lady who learned to drive when she was 71![12]

Besides being active in community life and having the time to pursue special interests and hobbies—from the arts to animal husbandry to marine biology—several of these teenagers have ventured far away from their home base in search of knowledge and experience. One sixteen-year-old embarked on a bicycle journey through South America. If anything, the essayists featured in *Real Lives* tend to look compassionately upon their schooled peers as "prisoners" of a generationally segregated world of institutional unreality. Kids in school, they say, are kept from living the kind of activist, in-the-world lives that home-schooled teenagers take for granted.

How does the average home schooling family fare in teaching academic skills? In November 1990, the National Home Education Research Institute prepared a report on standardized test results of 4,600 home-schooled children, 80 percent of whom were given either the California Achievement Test, the Iowa Test of Basic Skills, or the Stanford Achievement Test. In every subject, from reading and math to science, social studies and language, home-schooled kids scored "on the average at or above the 80th percentile," a full thirty points above the average school-educated child.[13] More recent tests, including a 1994 study of 16,000 home-schooled students who were given the Iowa Test of Basic Skills and a 1992 survey of 10,750 children who took the Stanford Achievement Test, confirm that the average academic performance of home- schooled children is well above average, with most children scoring in the 70th percentile in language, math, and reading. In statewide assessments, home-schoolers' performance on standardized tests has ranged from slightly above average (in Alabama) to the 85th percentile (in Oklahoma), and in a California assessment, home-schooled children ranked on a level with children who attended private schools.[14]

How does one explain such success, when most home schooling parents are not certified as teachers? Developmental psychologist Benjamin Moore may have touched upon the key when he observed that home schooling "parents . . . have enough concern for their children to take on the task of systematically teaching them" and that they are allowed an emotional "partiality" toward their pupils that institutional schooling cannot permit.[15] As home schooling parent and longtime high school English teacher David Guterson observes, the most important variable turns out to be "that all home schoolers come from families devoted to the education of their young."[16]

Parents' attitudes appear to be a key component in the success of any educational enterprise. Since the publication in 1966 of James Coleman's study, *Equality of Educational Opportunity*, which linked children's success in public school with the educational backgrounds and socioeconomic attainments of their parents, a number of research studies on effective schools point to the importance of both family background and parental support and involvement in schooling. Educrats have interpreted these findings to mean that educators must co-opt parent support and involvement in children's schooling in order to achieve successful educational outcomes.[17] Indeed, recently the U.S. Department of Education has embarked on an almost hysterical crusade to get families involved in schools. But the nascent home schooling movement has drawn the inverse conclusion: If the family is such an important influence on educational success, it must also be the best-equipped source of the educational experience.

This was the conclusion reached by John Holt, who began his long research and writing career as an advocate of public school reform. But after many years of observing the incapacities of the classroom to respond to children's different learning styles and backgrounds, he came to believe that meaningful school reform in the sense that he had campaigned for it was an "illusion." Formal education was ill equipped to realize his dream of a spontaneous, child-directed, and engaging classroom learning experience. Parents, however, seemed to be able to provide exactly this experience, without formal training as educators. Holt was struck by the fact that almost all the parents he met on his travels who had withdrawn their children from the schools had managed to provide their children with intellectually stimulating and emotionally satisfying educational experiences, no matter the level of their own educational attainments.[18] This seemed to indicate—in contrast to some of the educational research—that parental educational achievement and socioeconomic status were less crucial factors in childhood educational success than parental support and involvement, and that families with backgrounds of low educational accomplishments did not hopelessly consign their children to low educational achievement.

Holt started a home schooling newsletter called *Growing Without Schooling* and began to correspond with parents, advising them and providing them with a theoretically consistent framework for their initial struggles with the school and legal systems. The spontaneous "unschooling" movement, as he termed it, seemed primed to recapture constitutionally guaranteed personal liberties in opposition to institutional life and government regulation. Education, Holt came to believe, should never involve compulsion because it was essentially a private act. "A person's schooling," he said in summing up his educational philosophy, "is as much a part of his private business as his politics or religion."[19]

But Holt also liked to call home schooling "unschooling" because the type of home education he supported was radically individual—a revolt, in itself, against the trend toward conformity in modern institutional life. Although he supported all home-schoolers, regardless of their approach, he was not a particularly avid proponent of the many standardized curricula used by home schooling parents. Rather he encouraged a more informal approach to the learning process, urging parents to teach to their children's interests and let them take the lead in determining the lessons of the day. In this, Holt remained true to a radical Rousseauian educational philosophy that saw curiosity as endemic to childhood and held that learning must be adapted to a child's disposition, inspiration, and life experience.

A goodly number of home-schoolers today consider themselves spiritual descendants of Rousseau and Holt. Says one of them, "Most people think that home schooling is Mommy and kiddie at the kitchen table, but that is the least of what it is or should be." In other words, many home schooling parents do not sit their children down to an hour of math, an hour of English, and so on, but structure schooling not only around their children's learning styles and passions, but around the day's tasks and amusements.

Even families who structure their lesson times do not necessarily rely on prescribed curricula. A 1990 nationwide study commissioned by the Home School Legal Defense Association found that parents "handpicked the major curriculum components" of 67.4 percent of home-schooled children. Less than a third of the families surveyed used multisubject curriculum packages. Some religious home-schoolers use denominational curricula. (A Catholic woman who home-schools in my hometown says she uses the Seton curriculum, which she finds strong in both academics and catechism, but she refrains from sending her child to the local parish Sunday school, because her parish does not offer the quality and depth of religious training she seeks for her child.) Many textbook publishers report a surge in review requests and orders by parents, another indication that parents are scrutinizing materials and tailoring them to their children's needs.

In a way, home schooling is an answer to what one scholar of the family has identified as the consistent failure of contemporary education to convey to children "the abiding cultural heritage which gave meaning to their parents' lives."[20] The most eloquent advocates of home schooling have repeatedly pointed out that whether it is pursued in a structured or unstructured way, home schooling has been the source of an intellectual and cultural revival within their households. Parents who home-school consistently praise it because it benefits *them* intellectually and morally—not just their children. When mothers and fathers who have long since completed their formal education are required to explain the principles of long division, lead discussions of *Tom Sawyer,* conjugate French verbs, trace the migration of salmon, or even explain why egg whites expand when they are beaten, they learn along with their children. But more importantly, parents who home-school consciously accept more fully their responsibility "to set an example in the conduct of their own lives." This means not only taking seriously the intellectual development of their children, but incorporating all the best habits of learning to make the home an "educationally enhancing environment."[21]

■ ■ ■

The relative ease with which parents can now pursue home schooling obscures the ferocity of the battle for home schooling rights waged in the early days of the home schooling movement. During the 1960s and 1970s home schooling families often ran afoul of compulsory school attendance laws, their children labeled "truants." Many of them were forced to battle criminal charges in court, and there were even cases of children being carted off to foster homes by welfare workers. Several landmark court decisions in the late 1970s, however, changed the legal landscape for home-schoolers.

Probably the most significant of these for the average American—because it involved no struggle over religious rights—was handed down on November 13, 1978, by the Massachusetts Superior Court in *Perchemlides v. Frizzle.* Well-educated, liberal, middle-class, and harboring high standards of achievement for their children, Peter and Susan Perchemlides had been drawn from hectic Boston to the bucolic university town of Amherst, Massachusetts, partly in search of good public schools. But their youngest child, Richard, eight years of age in 1977 and intellectually precocious far beyond his years, did not fare well in the elementary school, turning suddenly and uncharacteristically shy.

The Perchemlideses attributed Richard's sudden change in character to the pressures toward conformity and the anti-intellectualism of the school system, tendencies that went against the grain of his personality and family background. In the words of Susan Perchemlides, her son came, as a result of his school experience, to believe that he was "supposed to be into TV and games and not aware of the world around him, that he [must be] most comfortable with kids his own age and [have] a developing consumer consciousness." The schools, Susan further charged, were so intent on the teaching of "social skills" to the detriment of academic learning, that Richard had lost all interest in school. Peter Perchemlides tried to change the situation through involvement in the public school planning committees, but to no avail.

Determined to restore their child's lost sense of himself, the Perchemlideses resolved to educate Richard at home. They were amply equipped for the task. Peter had a Ph.D. in biochemistry, and Susan had successfully undertaken the home schooling of their two elder sons for four years before the move to Amherst. But when they approached the Amherst school district with a detailed home schooling curriculum in language arts, science, mathematics, music, and health, the superintendent dismissed their application as a capricious exercise of "pet educational theories." He found it particularly objectionable that neither parent was a certified teacher and that their curriculum contained no "group experience."

While they appealed to the town's School Committee to review their plan, the Perchemlides family was surprised to find that neither they nor their legal counsel nor anyone who might speak on their behalf was invited to any of the five review meetings held by that committee. Rather, in April 1978, the school district answered their appeal by filing criminal charges under the state of Massachusetts truancy statute and ordering their child back to school. The Perchemlideses in turn filed a civil suit against the School Committee in which they charged that the committee's attempt to force their child to school was a violation of their constitutional rights to freedom of conscience and privacy. The state, asserted the Perchemlideses' legal defense, had no right to enforce a set of social values on Richard that he and his parents found unconscionable.

The case is of interest not just because it epitomizes the growing antipathy of American parents to the social aims of contemporary education, but because the court's decision clearly articulated the rights of parents vis à vis the legitimate interest of the state in assuring that children are appropriately schooled. Judge John Greaney found that in refusing the Perchemlides family's home schooling plan, the School Committee did infringe on their rights inasmuch as it sought to "eviscerate" a constitutionally protected educational alternative by imposing unreasonable objections to it. "The state has an interest in regulating the education of school-age children," Grealey affirmed, but only insofar as it must "see that children are educated to . . . bonafide academic and curricular standards." It did not have the right "to reject an alternative to public education solely because it did not mimic public education in its socialization aspects. He added, "Under our system, parents must be allowed to decide whether public school education, including its socialization aspects, is desirable or undesirable for their children."[22]

The vehemence with which many school systems reacted to the home schooling alternative in its pioneering years (the Perchemlides case was by no means atypical of the protracted legal struggles of home-schoolers in the 1970s) reveals much about the threat educators perceived in home schooling. In a valuable exposition of the implications of the Perchemlides case written in 1983, when home schooling was still in its infancy, cultural critic Stephen Arons asserted that the movement threatened the educational establishment by implicitly attacking its claims to professional status and by challenging the indispensability of school services to families and children.

But Arons also noted that the legal battles waged over home schooling were emblematic of a much larger conflict between families and schools. His talks with a number of public school parents involved in protests against the system over curricula and socialization issues revealed a pervasive fear that children were "growing up amidst a rubble of collapsed cultural meanings and dysfunctional social values," and that the schools were complicit in this collapse and dysfunction.[23] In a time of "cultural uncertainty" and "transition," Arons contended, children were increasingly becoming pawns in a power struggle between parents and schools over exactly what constituted appropriate education. What should children learn? How should they be taught? What values ought education to promote?

Today, these same issues are more alive than ever. At their heart is a contest over what have become two distinct political cultures in our nation: the political culture promoted by extrafamilial child-rearing institutions versus the political culture promoted by families. The first is a culture of conformity, of homogenization, collectivization, peer-orientation, and a dictatorial vision of political activism; the second is a culture that values individuality, pluralism, privatism, intergenerational interaction, and grassroots political activism. While the decision to home-school is seldom a consciously political one, home schooling parents are, in fact, implicitly choosing sides in what is fast becoming a struggle between an "official" and a popular ethos of civic education. The decision to home-school represents an implicit judgment against the "official" ethos in favor of the popular one. Indeed, every day a child spends schooled by his parents is proof of one more family's crisis of faith in a system that increasingly pits government-sponsored child-rearing institutions against families in a battle for the souls of children.

Today, when home schooling is legal in every state, many parents who choose it are barely aware of the more subversive implications of their choice. But once they have home-schooled for a while, they are bound to be reminded. Christopher J. Klicka, executive director of the Home School Legal Defense Association, says it is still relatively common for home schooling families to suffer social worker "harrassment"; even though they no longer violate criminal truancy laws, home schooling families are often reported by the school authorities and even neighbors suspicious of the practice to child welfare authorities. Most states subject home schooling parents to restrictions or to the fulfillment of certain conditions. Many of these are reasonable enough—requiring parents to register with the educational authorities, to teach certain basic subjects, to permit the school district to test children once a year or review a portfolio of work. But a few states make things more difficult for parents. In California, for example, there is no home schooling legislation at all, so that it is necessary to register one's residence as a private school in order to home-school. A few states restrict home schooling to parents who have college degrees, or even require teacher certification; parents who do not fulfill these requirements must seek an exemption on the grounds that they are keeping their children home for "religious" reasons.

A number of court and legislative moves in recent years have threatened the home schooling movement. In February 1994, when Capitol Hill was debating the reauthorization of the Elementary and Secondary Education Act (ESEA), a last-minute amendment by Representative George Miller of California requiring every teacher in a nonprofit school to be certified in every subject taught brought home-schoolers to arms. The amendment was in fact a national version of several recent unsuccessful initiatives in various states to require parents without certification to hire certified teachers for home-schooled children.

The ESEA amendment was ignored by the press, but news travels fast over the Internet; statewide home schooling networks, which typically function as clearinghouses for educational resources as well as lobbying organizations, sprang into action. For a week congressional offices were flooded with telegrams, calls, and faxes protesting the effect such legislation would have on the future of home schooling. Many members of Congress reported that it was the biggest response to an issue they could remember. The amendment was defeated by a vote of 424–1.[24]

The response to the proposed amendment alerted legislators to home-schoolers as a powerful if small special interest group. But they would be well advised to recognize its deeper political implications as well. Home schooling families do not only *propound* an alternate vision of the civic mission of schooling, they *live* an alternate vision of civic activism that is fast becoming a model for families. In his book *Family Matters: Why Home Schooling Makes Sense*, David Guterson puts it this way:

> Schools have not been effective agents of [political] consensus building. . . . [But] home-schooling can do much to promote the process of building a national consensus, beginning of course, by inspiring a consensus about the importance of family life. A home-schooling society might also nurture the kind of independent-minded, critical electorate our republic now desperately needs; it might infuse our tired democracy with a new, grass-roots energy . . . inspire a broader commitment to community service and allow for the maintenance of different cultural traditions within the American setting . . . [and] generate a new respect for diversity in values, pursuits and principles. . . . All of this, of course, is speculative and utopian. It is also worth considering.[25]

■ ■ ■

Home schooling is only the most radical example of a general educational counterculture that has erupted in resistance to the political and social pressures of public schooling, and to the larger anti-family pressures of the culture. While nowhere is the tension between parents and public education more glaringly obvious or dramatically demonstrated than in the rise of the home schooling movement, the ideological tensions between parents, public schooling, and the more general cultural environment are also manifest in the turn to private schools.

Researchers in education conclude that the last two decades have witnessed the most widespread retreat from public schooling since the emergence of the Roman Catholic school system a century ago.[26] It is hard to know exactly how many families can be counted in the public school exodus—just how many products of public school education have sought alternatives to public education for their own children—but they seem to be in the hundreds of thousands, and they are certainly not all upper- or even middle-class. An increasing influx of poor and immigrant families in recent years to private schooling has changed the socioeconomic profile of private school clientele.[27] Many more would choose private schools if they could afford it, a response confirmed in every one of my focus groups.

But it is not the established secular independent day and boarding schools—even those on the East Coast renowned for educating our elite—that have been the principal beneficiaries of public school falloff. The National Association of Independent Schools (NAIS), the network that links many of the nation's most prestigious secular private schools, reports that enrollment in well-established independent schools has increased, but only by a little more than 12 percent since 1980 (16 percent from 1991 to 1996). This translated to about 45,000 children—hardly a drop in the gigantic bucket of public school flight.[28] In New York, New Jersey, Connecticut, Massachusetts, Maine, New Hampshire, Vermont, and Rhode Island—a region known for excellent private schools—enrollment increases were either unsteady or relatively negligible over the entire decade between 1985 and 1995.[29] Indeed, in New York City several long-standing day schools were struggling to keep their heads above water in the early 1990s. Plunging enrollments and diminishing financial resources forced a few to close, others to merge.

Boarding school enrollments were also on the decline, dropping 5.5 percent nationally between 1987 and 1992 (NAIS affiliates reported that between 1988 and 1990 alone, boarding school enrollment plunged more than 10 percent in New York State). Some boarding schools have saved themselves by abolishing boarding or making it optional, or by marketing themselves aggressively overseas.[30]

To some extent, demographic and economic factors have constrained the growth of independent schools: a diminishing youth population during the 1980s, the economic recession of the late 1980s and early 1990s (which came at a time when educational costs were drastically increasing), and the flight of affluent families from many of the urban centers where independent schooling has traditionally been concentrated. But those factors don't explain the demise of the boarding school. Even the venerable English "public school"—the epitome of private, elite education—appears to be in trouble, according to a recent article in the *Christian Science Monitor*.[31] Why?

The fact is, parenting styles are changing at the higher levels of society; except perhaps for the wealthiest of the wealthy, parents are living cozier, more child-oriented lifestyles, choosing to keep their kids at home rather than ship them off to boarding school for someone else to bring up. The same motivations that increasingly keep parents away from boarding schools are likely slowing growth in secular independent schools. Despite the efforts of independent schools to reach out to a broader socioeconomic base, most parents who choose private schooling seem to be looking for something beyond old names and academic prestige in their search for educational alternatives. Increasingly, they are searching for more closeness with their children, and a deeper sense of identification with their children's school. In short, they are searching for community.

American families—both rich and poor—are banding together to create new educational institutions rather than relying on established ones—whether in the public or independent school system. A plethora of private schools ranging from fundamentalist Christian to Afrocentric, many existing on the proverbial shoestring, are growing out of ethnic and church communities, suggesting a conscious desire among a growing number of parents to create schools that will better reflect their moral values, spiritual worldview, and cultural traditions. The fast-growing movement to form "charter" schools (271 of these parent-driven alternative public schools were opened between 1992 and 1996) and the dozens of private secular schools operated by parents that are springing up around the country reflect the same ardent desire for community, approached from the opposite direction: Here the school is likely to form a base for communal interaction, rather than its crown, uniting parents of perhaps diverse cultural and socioeconomic backgrounds around shared educational values and pedagogical aims.[32]

From cities and suburbs to rural areas, American parents seem to be demonstrating their conviction that fresh alternatives are needed to turn schools into institutions that have meaning for them as well as their children. The new schools that are forming evince an enormous variety of pedagogical approaches, but they have a few telling characteristics in common: They are almost always small, with a student population of fewer than two hundred. They boast a high ratio of teachers to students, enabling each child to secure plenty of individual attention. They emphasize a stable and weighty academic curriculum. They consciously root children in a cultural tradition. They almost always welcome, even require, parental involvement. And most important, they are uncompromisingly supportive of family life and parental authority, while helping the families they serve to form a community of shared values, goals, and priorities.

Denominational schools have led the recent boom in nonpublic education, as part of a general trend toward a more fundamentalist religious ethos. Most prominent in the denominational school movement are the Christian schools, which—curiously—originally sprung up primarily in the South out of resistance to the desegregation of public schools. Between 1965 and 1982, the evangelical school population grew from fewer than 100,000 children to around 700,000. Not surprisingly, during the years of desegregation Christian schools were generally regarded as academically inferior and provincial, as well as racially intolerant. But by the mid-1990s, 75 percent of Christian schools were racially integrated, and many had also developed reputations for academic excellence.[33] A *Wall Street Journal* article of 1994 reported that more than 1 million children were being educated in more than ten thousand evangelical schools, and the number of students was rising at the rate of 10 percent a year.

In her 1988 study, *Keeping Them Out of the Hands of Satan*, sociologist Susan D. Rose traces the renaissance of fundamentalist Christian schooling to a religious reawakening in American family life. This is a time of cultural disorientation, Rose says, when "the rapid rate of social change and the competing demands of families, work, church, education and peers take their toll on individuals who are trying to find their way in the world." Americans, she contends, are "searching for coherence . . . meaning and direction" in a society where "cultural reality becomes increasingly defined at a corporate, consumer level."[34]

As Rose penetrated the culture of Christian schooling, talked to parents and teachers, studied the curriculum, and analyzed the pedagogical methods used, she began to understand—if not wholly sympathize—with its attractions. Moreover, she discovered that evangelical schooling was anything but monolithic. Different schools emphasized widely different pedagogical approaches. Her analysis came to focus on a school affiliated with a charismatic church that boasted many of the "child-centered" and exploratory classroom activities that have typified twentieth-century progressive education, as well as another school with a more conservative pedagogical bent. The latter concentrated heavily on individual work, placing students in separate cubicles and requiring them to do much of their work independently. What these two schools had in common, however, was their emphasis on religious training and the transmission of religious values. Both provided the kind of socially, intellectually, and morally integrated educational experience rare in public and even independent schools today. Both provided children with a clear and highly structured worldview—a worldview that complemented and supported the shared values of family and church community and provided a strong alternative to the influences of consumer culture.

What most distinguishes the evangelical school movement and probably accounts for its increasing popularity among parents is the extent to which both its pedagogies and its child-rearing values uncompromisingly defy many of the failed experiments touted in public schools. Against whole language and theoretical math, the Christian school—however child-centered the classroom—typically offers instruction in phonics[35] and arithmetic operations. Against the ethical relativism promoted in public schooling, the evangelical school posits the notion of moral absolutes. Against public schooling's peer direction, the evangelical school posits a hierarchical natural order in which elders hold legitimate and unchallengeable authority over young people. Against public schooling's spiritually blind trust in technocracy, the evangelical school posits the power of prayer and spiritual revelation. Against public schooling's self-esteem curriculum and academic levity, the evangelical school posits a philosophy of personal humility and a curriculum of academic rigor. To public schooling's wearisome training in psychosocial adaptability, the evangelical school responds with an immutable social vision grounded of "coherence" and "belonging" in the institutions of family and church.[36]

Educators in evangelical schools tend to have a humble assessment of their proper place in children's lives. Instead of appealing to children over their parents' heads, as so many public and independent school educators do—and instead of seeing their work as a corrective to parents' misapprehensions or mistakes—they emphasize their allegiance to parents' authority in children's lives. For evangelical educators, the school occupies the lowest place in a hierarchy that descends from God to church to family to school. As Rose observes, "teachers are considered to be the servants of parents" in evangelical schools.[37]

Parents who have left public schools for Christian schools often say that their trust in the educational mission of the school has empowered them in dealing with their children's teachers. At the same time, teachers' deference to parents as the ultimate authorities in their children's lives appears to increase parents' respect for teachers' professional judgments and encourages parents' openness to advice.[38]

■ ■ ■

It might be expected that all private schools would maintain a respectful stance toward parents' authority, since parents, after all, are the clients of private schools. But as we have seen, independent secular schools are growing much more slowly than denominational schools, and part of the reason may be that recently they have become just as prone to pedagogical experiment, behavioral faddism, and the cult of "professional expertise" as are the public schools.

Parents who send their children to independent schools have informed me that even the most exclusive and highly reputed private schools have become arenas of contention between educators and parents. The chief causes of conflict, not surprisingly: comprehensive sex education, condom distribution, the moral failures of values clarification courses, behavioral and therapeutic curricula, the shallow and heavily ideological thrust of social studies courses, literature courses, and multicultural approaches, even the failure to transmit basic skills. If what these parents tell me is true, what accounts for the success of such schools in testing? Maybe that the average private school parent is prosperous enough to supplement failing school programs with tutoring. (When I had my child in a New York independent school, I was shocked to learn how many of the other parents were hiring after-school tutors in the basics for children who had allegedly been admitted to school under selective criteria.)

Open political and sexual advocacy is far more likely in independent than in public schools, since there still exists a modicum of constraints on public school teachers in many communities to at least *affect* neutrality. For example, such controversial annual school rituals as "coming out" days (school celebrations of homosexuality) seem to have had their origins in the independent rather than in the public high schools.[39]

Similarly, in private schools pedagogical experiments can often get more seriously out of hand, as apparently happened with the Emily Fischer-Landau project at Manhattan's famous Dalton School between 1984 and 1992. Financed by the dyslexic scion of a wealthy New York family, this $2 million research program for the diagnosis and treatment of learning disabilities was intended to set up an educational model that could be emulated in the public schools. But what resulted was an educational fiasco.

For eight years running, each incoming kindergartner at Dalton was given a battery of tests for possible learning deficiencies, typically administered without notice by strangers who took children out of their comfortable classrooms and into the school's dark basement. Not surprisingly, many of the children did not perform well, so that within only a few years, a third of the kindergarten students at Dalton were being labeled learning disabled—children, it should be mentioned, with an average IQ of 130. It was not long before fourteen full- and part-time learning specialists were employed administering "remedial help" to these unfortunate children. By 1992, half of the kindergarten to third-grade "lower-school" population had spent some time in remedial programs, and the classroom teachers were complaining that LD specialists were disrupting their classrooms.[40]

Now, the Dalton School is one of the most selective private schools in the country. Its parent body consists of some of the wealthiest and most prominent New York professionals. Imagine the consternation of these people when they were notified of the possibility that their children had learning disabilities such as "sequencing ability deficits" and "visual motor" difficulties. Intimidated by the cult of expertise that surrounded the Emily Fischer-Landau project but not satisfied to leave their children's fate to the special education faculty, many engaged private tutors and psychotherapists. Former Dalton school psychologist Dr. Gail Furman contends that many of the learning specialists and psychologists involved in the project took full advantage of their ties to the school's well-heeled parent body, charging fees of up to $200 an hour for after-school tutoring and counseling, and cultivating referral networks through their Dalton association. "If you're a . . . specialist on the Dalton list, it can make a person's career. . . . It's worth a lot of money," Furman remarked to a *New York Times* reporter.

But while the greedy "professionals" benefited enormously from the project, and while the disabilities program burnished Dalton's reputation in the outside world (during the course of the project, Dalton administrators were popular lecturers and advisors on the subject of learning disabilities), half of Dalton's students languished. The familiar pitfalls of educational experimentation—shoddy research instruments, bureaucratic arrogance, and a cavalier confusion of children with guinea pigs—were derailing the self-confidence and academic progress of a truly gifted student body. The screening instrument for LD diagnosis employed by the project staff, it turned out, was faulty, the remedial work assigned ill-conceived and in most cases unnecessary. The Emily Fischer-Landau "experts" had even neglected to set up control groups. One Columbia University School of Education researcher who worked on the project for over four years admitted sheepishly to an investigative reporter that as an exercise in educational research the project was worthless: "In the field of education, there is this problem with research. People don't think of setting up controls. It's not like science."

In 1992, the disabilities program ended abruptly with a teacher revolt, the parting of the lower school principal, and the dismantling of the Emily Fischer-Landau project's board of directors, which not only controlled the project, but had begun to show aspirations to run the whole school. It is important to recognize that in a city in which many independent schools were struggling in the early 1990s, the professional hubris manifest in the Emily Fischer-Landau experiment would probably have dealt a death blow to a school that did not have Dalton's blessings of ample endowment, and whose student and parent bodies were less self-consciously select than Dalton's. But the school seems to have survived the crisis, although it brought a considerable amount of negative publicity.

■ ■ ■

Excesses like this one help explain why many parents have turned to home, denominational, or parent-run schools rather than to independent schooling. But they do not explain the strange predicament of the Catholic schools, which one would think would be among a very attractive alternative to failing public schools, especially for inner-city children. Despite the high academic prestige of the Catholic schools, and their emphasis on values education, they have suffered drastic enrollment declines in the past thirty years, from 5.6 million in 1964 to 2.5 million in 1994.

These declines, Catholic educators say, can be traced to a falloff in religious observance among middle-class Catholics of European descent, as well as to their flight from urban centers to the suburbs, where fewer Catholic schools exist. While the blacks and Hispanics who followed the European ethnics in inner-city neighborhoods did seek out the Catholic schools, the schools have not been able to sustain themselves. The disappearance of teaching orders, the consequent expenses incurred in hiring lay faculty, and the increasing indigence of the neighborhoods they serve have put the parish school system under unbearable financial pressures, and many fully enrolled schools have been forced to close.[41] The demise of the inner-city parish school has been a great misfortune to minority communities, not only because it was well known to be the school of choice in both the Hispanic and black communities, but because a number of statistically valid studies have touted it as the hope of inner-city minority youth. In study after study, Catholic schools appear to be far more effective than public, independent, and even non-Catholic denominational schools in preparing disadvantaged children for college.[42]

The parish schools that have survived may still be in some sense neighborhood schools, but they serve a far higher proportion of non-Catholics than ever before.[43] In many inner-city neighborhoods, non-Catholic blacks are lining up to get into parochial schools, even parochial schools whose material resources are far less impressive than those of the public schools, and whose class sizes are higher. (In 1986, 61 percent of the black population of inner-city Catholic schools was non-Catholic.)[44] Although surveys of the black clientele of Catholic education indicate they are in general more prosperous than the Hispanic (lower-income blacks are apparently less likely to send their children to private schools than lower-income whites or Hispanics),[45] it is clear that hundreds of thousands of black and Hispanic inner-city families are making significant financial sacrifices in order to afford the average elementary school tuition, which, as of 1990, had topped $1,000 a year.[46]

What gives Catholic schools such solid educational results, especially with kids from lower socioeconomic backgrounds? In contrast to inner-city public schools, they seem to have stronger administrative leadership, more community involvement, and greater responsiveness to the needs of students. They allow their teachers more input in school governance, have higher academic expectations of even the weakest students, and spend more time on academic tasks. Catholic schools provide a consistently orderly and disciplined environment for academic concentration—one that starkly contrasts with the high rates of violence, disorder, and absenteeism in inner-city public schools.

But most important, Catholic schools support families. As a survey of parochial school parents sponsored by the Catholic League for Religious and Civil Rights explained the schools' popularity: "School officials are perceived by the parents as being responsive to the preferences of parents. This includes the inclination of officials to act according to the preferences of the parents, even when those preferences are not explicitly expressed, because they share common attitudes toward school issues."[47] In other words, Catholic schools are the schools of choice for many inner-city families—including non-Catholics—because these schools endorse the values that parents want to encourage in their children's upbringing. Indeed, researchers have found that values education is the principal reason that lower-income parents, particularly lower-income African-American parents, choose Catholic schools; higher-income parents are far more likely to point to the academic advantages.[48] A non-Catholic African-American mother I spoke with in a Baltimore focus group explained her and her husband's choice of a Catholic school in those very terms: "Our daughters' school supports our values. We looked very hard for this school."

When a 1982 study by James Coleman, Thomas Hoffer, and Sally Kilgore entitled *High School Achievement: Public, Catholic and Private Schools Compared* pointed up the superiority of Catholic education for children from lower socioeconomic backgrounds, supporters of the public schools balked. Coleman and his associates asserted not only that Catholic schools got better results than public schools, but that the Catholic schools more effectively approximated the stated goals of public education: racial and socioeconomic integration and equality of achievement. A lot of effort has since been expended in trying to explain away the superiority of Catholic education for low-income children by claiming that the process of admission to Catholic schools is selective—in effect skimming off the cream of low-income youth from each neighborhood. If the public schools weren't doing their job, went the argument, it was because they had to serve *all* children, no matter how disadvantaged, troubled, or lacking in intelligence, whereas the Catholic schools had the luxury to select their clientele and to expel troublemakers. Moreover, parochial schools were dealing not only with a smarter student body but with parents who cared enough about education to evaluate the options available to them.

But several studies emerged during the 1980s that debunked the idea that Catholic schooling worked solely on selectivity. These studies, in fact, advanced greatly the debate on exactly what characteristics might make schools successful even for students who come from severely underprivileged backgrounds. Coleman, Hoffer, and Kilgore had already noted that disparities in achievement between students from lower and higher socioeconomic backgrounds disappeared the longer disadvantaged kids stayed in the Catholic school system. The same year that study was published, another work appeared that suggested the Catholic schools had answers to the puzzle of low minority achievement that could benefit public schools. Andrew Greeley's survey of fourteen thousand minority students, half of them in Catholic high schools and half in public high schools, found that the greatest improvement in achievement levels occurred among the most disadvantaged students attending Catholic schools, the very poorest of the poor whose parents had the lowest levels of education. Surely these students were not favored by any process of "selection," Greeley pointed out in his book *Catholic High Schools and Minority Students*. Rather, the schools themselves were doing something that worked to lift disadvantaged children out of the mire of poverty and ignorance: namely, setting high academic standards, imposing effective discipline, practicing quality instruction, and demanding hard work in return.[49]

Moreover, a 1982 analysis by James Cibulka, Timothy O'Brien and Donald Zewe of fifty-four inner-city private schools, almost all of them Catholic, showed that they were only marginally selective in their admissions processes and almost never expelled students. In their work, *Inner-City Private Elementary Schools: A Study*, these researchers noted that poor children in Catholic schools did better on national assessments than their peers in public schools, and exhibited far fewer disciplinary problems. The researchers attributed this success to the "sense of community that existed among faculty, students and parents." These schools, they asserted, highly valued parent-teacher communication, sought parent input, and supported parental priorities in their approach to both intellectual and moral development.[50]

A 1984 survey of parochial schools' effectiveness published by the National Catholic Educational Association[51] should have laid to rest once and for all the assertion that Catholic schools were successful because they were selective. This study, which focused on variables of achievement *within* the Catholic school system, discovered that discrepancies in achievement levels between students from upper- and lower-class families were prominent only in those Catholic high schools that allowed students a choice of whether to take advanced classes in math and science. Performance in core academic courses—the courses required of all students—revealed no significant variables that could be traced to family life, even among the most disadvantaged students with the most disorderly family lives. "Academic policy is a key factor in . . . achievement," the report concluded. "Where choice occurs . . . as in the number of mathematics and science courses taken . . . the effects of social class [on achievement] loom larger."[52]

Since then two major studies on the impact of Catholic schooling on low-income and minority students have appeared. A 1986 study entitled *Catholic High Schools: Their Impact on Low-Income Students* emphasized the importance of clear academic focus in the achievement of disadvantaged students, and a 1987 study (by none other than Coleman and Hoffer) entitled *Public and Private High Schools: The Impact of Communities* acknowledged the crucial role of "social capital" in Catholic schools' success with such children—namely the extent to which the personal touch, and the sense of community and oversight generated in these schools, helps disadvantaged kids along. These studies point up not only the strong relationship between academic demands and performance, but also the importance of the school as a community of shared values and aspirations that, when it forms an alliance with parents, has the capability of exercising a strong positive influence on child development.[53]

All in all, the research on Catholic schools implies that the most effective schools—regardless of the population they serve—demand a lot from their students, cater to spiritual and moral as well as mental development, and function as extensions of the family. Especially when they serve an embattled population, schools must be able to supplement the direction, control, and emotional support that may be missing in family and surrounding community life. Verne Oliver, former principal of New York City's progressive independent Lincoln School, has for nearly a decade been involved in a foundation-supported scholarship program that places at-risk minority children in Catholic schools. What do these children get in the Catholic schools that is missing from the public schools? "Love," says Oliver, or something very nearly approximating love: a haven in a heartless world. The commitment of administration and faculty to each pupil is evident in clear disciplinary policies, in the transmission of respect for property and authority, in the emphasis on intellectual rigor, the well-defined structure of school life, and in the attention paid to moral and spiritual development. All of these things provide a caring school atmosphere that mimics the best of what family life can offer, she says, and does much to compensate for neighborhoods and homes marked by disorder, failure, and brutality.[54]

■ ■ ■

Thankfully the lessons learned from parochial education have not been entirely lost on public educators. In recent years the public schools have tried to broaden the range of alternatives for minority students and to be more responsive to the needs and educational priorities of all parents. They have introduced variations on the theme of school choice, allowing parents to choose favored schools within districts, or to arrange interdistrict school transfers to magnet schools offering special courses of study or a particularly academic focus.

In twenty-three states, new legislation has made it possible to establish alternative charter schools, the single biggest trend in schooling.[55] Legislation has been typically weak in the sense that it often provides only minimal funding, little or no seed money, and still less support in hiring faculty when unions make it difficult to secure teachers. The number of charter schools allowed has also been typically limited by state legislatures, probably because much of the educational establishment opposes them; but by 1997 more than 480 charter schools had opened.[56] These schools—invariably small, administratively flexible, and parent-driven—are exempted from many of the administrative rules, union restrictions, and curricular mandates that impede efficiency and block innovation in public education. They tend to be specialized in their academic focus, and many are pedagogically experimental.

In the case of both magnet and charter schools, there are some that aim to attract a diverse ethnic and racial population by bringing inner-city students to the suburbs, or vice versa. Others, however, are self-consciously neighborhood schools content to cultivate local reputations for safety, academic excellence, and parent involvement. In the inner cities, the latter seem to be preferred. The reason? Attempts to integrate whites from outlying districts into alternative inner-city schools has often meant restricted access for local students.

New York's alternative public education provides a good example of the kind of success alternative public schools can boast. That city's school system remains ravaged by a top-heavy bureaucracy, crippling union rules, time-robbing nonacademic mandates, inflexibly fixed funding designations, patronage, and corruption. Nevertheless, its historically important academic magnet schools—the most famous being the Bronx High School of Science and Peter Stuyvesant High School—still attract bright adolescents of all races and social classes from the city's five boroughs. Indeed, the tough admission policies and shining academic reputations of the city's academic high schools have been a draw even for wealthy children who have spent their elementary education in independent schools.

Moreover, in the past two decades the Department of Education has quietly allowed some experiments in school choice that have yielded remarkable results. The most famous of these occurred in East Harlem's School District Four, where between 1974 and 1982 Seymour Fliegel, former head of the New York City Office of Alternative Schools was able to reconstruct the school system of one of America's poorest communities. In instituting a new system whereby parents and children were able to choose from a district-wide list of alternative schools rather than simply be assigned to a neighborhood school, Fliegel and some innovative teachers and administrators turned the district, once New York's worst educational failure, into a success story that within five years was sending some of the city's most disadvantaged children to college. And school reading scores in the district climbed in the period between 1974 and 1982, from ranking last among the city's thirty-two districts to ranking fifteenth.

Fliegel and several hand-picked school administrators applied a philosophy of school reconstruction to which an increasing number of dedicated school reformers are subscribing. On the theory that in a small school dedicated to the interests and ambitions of its pupils and their parents "no one gets lost," Fliegel replaced the large, factorylike schools in the district with little, academically specialized schools, several of them often grouped together in one complex. The schools were then allowed to compete for their student bodies, and those that failed to meet the interests and expectations of the neighborhood parents and children folded. Those that have met the demands of the community—that met, in Fliegel's words, the "critical tests of achievement and attractiveness"—have survived and prospered.[57]

The District Four experiment, recounted in a recent book by Seymour Fliegel and James MacGuire, entitled *Miracle in East Harlem*, produced some of the most exciting models of alternative education in the country—among them the progressive Central Park East School, whose principal, Deborah Meier, received a MacArthur Foundation "genius" grant for her achievement in building what is now perhaps the most famous elementary school in the country. Meier is now engaged in a $25 million project sponsored by the Annenberg Foundation to raise the number of alternative New York schools to one hundred. But not all the successful schools of District Four are similar to Meier's forward-looking model. Indeed, the success of Fliegel's "alternative" plan lies in its very real offer of *varying* pedagogical styles to parents and children—from

traditional classroom approaches and academic focuses to radically experimental ones. The result has been a district that not only boasts decent scores on standardized tests and low dropout rates, but schools
notable for their disciplined and orderly atmosphere. Why? Because parents are able to choose schools that most closely match their own child-
rearing approaches and their children's learning styles; schools that are
client-friendly and responsive by design.

In Los Angeles, the Vaughn Next Century Learning Center is one of
ninety California charter schools. In a poor and predominantly Hispanic
community, eight parent-teacher committees manage the school and
parents sign a contract committing them to thirty hours of volunteer
work each year.[58] In Freeland, Michigan, principal Ron Helmer has converted his own garage into a Math and Science Academy for thirty-nine
children.[59] In Chicago there has been a major school reform movement
abroad for almost a decade now, with an emphasis on parent input.
Since 1988, each of that city's schools has had a governing council of six
parents, two community representatives, two teachers, and (in the high
schools) one student representative who, along with the principal, have
decided on the spending of discretionary monies (which can be as much
as $1 million for high schools receiving Title I federal funds) and have
drawn up plans for school improvement. By 1994 one-third of Chicago's
schools had been restructured as a result of this degree of autonomy, and
although there was, in the words of one school reform advocate, considerable "resistance," and a danger of not being able to "sustain the mo-
mentum" of reform "over the long haul," a lot had been accomplished.[60]

Alternative innovators in the public school system like John Elwell,
director of New York City's Center for Educational Innovation, believe
that schools directed with strong parent input represent the hope of urban public education. The best inner-city public schools, Elwell says, are
those which are "parent-driven and parent-protected." Elwell looks to
parents, in fact, as the most likely saviors of the public school system in
troubled urban centers. He points to the growing number of schools
started by parents in New York City, for example the Manhattan School
for Children in New York's District Three. A few years ago, he says, some
parents on Manhattan's Upper West Side "wanted to send their kids to
the school across the street but didn't like what was going on inside." So
they got together and decided to revamp the neighborhood school. "We
found a teacher to work with them and they created a new school in an
old building."[61]

But this small elementary school serves a highly educated middle-
class community with a clear sense of educational aims. Are parents from
poorer neighborhoods truly capable of rescuing their schools also? Do

they have the wherewithal to start new schools, and determine educational directions? And who will save those public schools whose clientele are children from families so crushed by poverty, drugs, and dissolution that they cannot properly keep a home, much less participate in their children's education?

In some new, experimental schools that cater to the most disadvantaged populations, teachers and administrators have noted that they have a far greater chance of reaching kids when they muster up as much parental involvement as possible, and compensate for what they can't muster up by providing something of what kids are missing at home. Manhattan's Wildcat Academy, a high school serving 125 of the New York City's most "troubled" kids, requires parents to meet with faculty when their children—who invariably have been expelled from other schools in the city—are referred for entrance. Only about 50 percent of the parents show up for the conference. But those that do find they are co-opted into a well-organized "conspiracy" of "benign surveillance" that will eventually turn their child's life around. For those teenagers whose parents don't care—and there are many—teachers and administrators step in. Kay S. Hymowitz, a Manhattan Institute fellow and writer for New York's *City Journal*, reports, "They will confer with a student's boss, take a cool-down stroll with a student when he is jumpy, and, if necessary, accompany him to a court hearing. When summer comes, students who are not working or visiting relatives are looked after in a combined school-job program. Graduates are not merely sent off with a handshake and a diploma. The school helps find them jobs or provides the support they need to enter college—arranging for SAT exams, visits to campuses, and help in filling out applications."[62]

Wildcat Academy is a demanding program alternating a week of work with a week of study. It provides chronically truant and often violent adolescents with emotional support, tight supervision, strict rules, and consistent and caring discipline from 9:00 A.M. to 5:00 P.M., often for twelve months a year. The philosophy of the school: to bring marginal kids into the mainstream by teaching them through experience that there are palpable rewards in hard work and responsible behavior. The Wildcat Academy has a small but devoted faculty, and because it remains an alternative school unencumbered by bureaucratic and union rules and regulations, it has a staff that has the freedom to pitch in with everything from custodial and administrative work to counseling. The school's small size, its emphasis on individual attention, respect for, care, and mentoring of its pupils creates a sense of cohesion, a kind of family atmosphere that gives pupils without family a sense of family support and purpose. Director Amalia Betanzos affectionately speaks of "coddling" her Wildcat students, a surprising term in the context of a school filled with kids who have earned reputations for fierceness at other schools. But as one observer, journalist Kay S. Hymowitz, notes, Wildcat is a place where "discipline and clear expectations are tempered by personal affection and respect . . . the traditional prescription for child-rearing at its best."[63]

All is not lost in the public schools. The establishment of alternative public schools, a growing public school choice movement, even cooperation in some school districts—notably in California—between administrators and home-schoolers who wish access to some school resources and extracurricular facilities show that public education is not quite the impenetrable fortress of contempt for parents and their values that it was even a few years ago. If the family-hostile bent of the public school system has not yet been shattered, it has at least been cracked. Public educators, it seems, are starting to relearn the lessons that should have guided them all along: that genuine educational standards must be set by the parents who know kids best, and not by the state; that the foundation of learning is nothing other than discipline tempered by love and respect; and that only by supporting family values, mimicking family structure, and re-creating a family-supported school community can schools do their proper job.

9

The New Familism

As *part* of an assignment for her fourth-grade class, my daughter was asked to interview one of her parents about his or her job. She chose to interview my husband, whose job, by many people's standards, is considered unusual: He is a house-husband. I was not present for their conversations, but I was amused to read in my daughter's finished report that my husband experiences "high job satisfaction," and that what he "likes best about his work is the independence." This is an opinion he seems to share with a growing number of male and female colleagues: at-home parents.

The National Center for Fathering notes that the total number of at-home dads "involved in primary child care" in 1991 while mothers worked came to 3,385,000, and that 20 percent of preschoolers that year were in "father care"—a jump of 5 percent since 1986.[1] It is hard to know how many more fathers have become primary caregivers since then, but anecdotal evidence, most especially increasing coverage of at-home dads in the press, points to a steady increase in the trend.

A new survey on the guys once deprecatingly referred to as "Mr. Moms" was released in 1996 by DePaul University's Dr. Robert Frank and Roosevelt University's Dr. Michael Helford. The survey focused on

371 men who spent at least thirty hours per week taking care of their children. Most were home not simply because they were unemployed, but by choice. A father from Georgia who quit his job as a teacher to stay home with his kids explained that neither he nor his wife liked "having to take the kids to day care every day and hearing second-hand what new progress they had made." Another father, an electrical engineer, said, "I quit my . . . job 18 months ago and haven't looked back. . . . We had a 17-year-old daughter, a five-year-old son and a six-month-old son we had adopted as an infant. The baby was in day care. My wife made more than 60 percent of the household income. More than half of my share went to day care and before and after care. What's wrong with this picture?"[2]

Like my husband, more than half these men reported that they were "extremely satisfied" in their role as primary caretaker of their children. They did report problems, however, especially feelings of isolation, and a perception that society did not take their work seriously. Peter Baylies, publisher of a small but fast-growing newsletter, At-Home Dad, puts it this way: "When a father goes to the supermarket with his child, people will look at him and assume he has the day off from work or got laid off. They don't view him as a full-time father."[3]

The 350 at-home mothers interviewed by Darcie Sanders and Martha M. Bullen for their 1992 book, Staying Home, sounded astoundingly similar.[4] Many of the women identified "being my own boss" as among the principal benefits of being at home, and they too complained of isolation and the feeling that society did not value the work of at-home mothers.[5] But clearly the benefits outweighed the drawbacks: 59.5 percent noted that staying at home had a "positive effect on their self-image"; 75 percent observed improvements in their relationships with their children; and more than half observed improvements in their marriage. A significant number claimed their spouses helped more with child care and household tasks than they had before. And while staying at home clearly required financial sacrifice, the average decline in household income reported by these nonworking mothers was just over $9,000 a year, less than the amount of money—including child care, clothing, transportation, and income tax—that it probably would cost them to go to work in the first place. A whopping 97.8 percent said that if they could "revise history," they would "choose again to stay home" with their children, and although almost three-quarters of the women had professional training or college or graduate-level degrees, more than 60 percent of them had no firm plans to go back into the labor force. They had chosen their work, liked it, and were not terribly anxious to give it up—except, perhaps, in order to go back to school.

For most families, the financial sacrifices of at-home parenting are probably greater than these women reported. Respondents to the Frank and Helford survey, which encompassed at-home moms as well as at-home dads, reported that when fathers stay home it costs the average family about $26,600 a year in income; when mothers stay home, about $24,000. Nevertheless, a growing number of families are making the decision to renounce second incomes, either wholly or partially, for the sake of their children's well-being. Of nearly 14 million couples with children where both work for pay, reports the National Center for Fathering, only a little more than 5 million work full-time day-shift jobs.[6] In 1991, the Department of Labor reported that for the first time in the twentieth century the number of women of childbearing age who worked had dropped, with some 320,000 leaving the workforce for home.[7]

It's hard to get at the real numbers of women who are leaving the workforce, because the Department of Labor counts as "working women" those who work for pay as little as one hour per week and those who work without remuneration in family businesses or farming fifteen or more hours a week. But in a 1994 interview, National Bureau of Labor economist Howard Hayghe said that the trend to at-home mothering was palpable in the large numbers of women who were "finding alternative methods of employment that are allowing them to stay home more with their children. They're finding part-time work, home-based businesses and free-lance work."[8] Support organizations for at-home mothers confirm Hayghe's analysis, asserting that a large proportion of their members do earn at least some money. Mary James of the 325-chapter MOMS Club claims that fifty-eight of the sixty women in her chapter alone did some work for pay from home.[9] But these organizations also report surges in their membership—women who clearly regard their primary "job" as mother and housewife and are consciously making the transition from work to home-centered daytime lives. Between 1994 and 1996, for example, the membership of Formerly Employed Mothers At the Leading Edge (FEMALE) nearly doubled,[10] as did Mothers of Preschoolers International between 1991 and 1994.[11]

As we have seen, many parents have grown critical of a culture of child-rearing by proxy. The increase in at-home parenting by both women and men reflects a large and rather sudden attitudinal shift among Americans. For more than two decades, for example, the number of women who claimed they would quit their jobs to stay home with their children if they could afford it held steady at about 30 percent. Suddenly in the late 1980s and early 1990s that number rose to 56 percent.[12] A 1993 Family Research Council–Voter/Consumer Research poll found that nine out of ten dual-earner married couples believe children do best when their mothers are home. A 1991 poll of fathers found that 75 percent would exchange fast career advancement for more family time, and a 1987 *Fortune* magazine survey found 30 percent had done so.[13] According to another 1993 Voter/Consumer Research poll sponsored by the Family Research Council, most working people would even trade early retirement for more time to devote to raising children.[14]

This attitudinal shift has been labeled by family scholars and journalists "the New Familism." Barbara Dafoe Whitehead summarizes its implications succinctly:

> [The] generation that invented singlehood as a "lifestyle," that cohabited and delayed marriage and childbearing . . . [that] a decade ago . . . were some of the most committed exponents of careerism . . . has now settled down into family life. . . . If there is a single common experience that contributes to The New Familism, it is parenthood. . . . As the baby boom generation becomes involved in parenthood, we see a reassessment of work life. . . . More and more parents of young children are realizing that work life and family life conflict, that time is scarcer than money, and that time and attention are the chief currencies of family life.[15]

The New Familism, indeed, has meant a significant philosophical shift for baby boomers—a shift, as Whitehead notes, that separates parents from nonparents and challenges a constellation of theories of self-actualization that are still propagated by much of the intellectual elite. Typical of these is the work of psychotherapist and Radcliffe Affiliate Scholar Rosalind C. Barnett and Boston University journalism professor Caryl Rivers, who in their 1996 book, *She Works/He Works: How Two-Income Families Are Happier, Healthier, and Better Off,* advise women to "relax," trust the child care industry, and go fulfill themselves in the workplace. Parents, they insist, worry unnecessarily about their children, harbor unrealistic expectations of "perfection" as parents, and are unnecessarily "concerned" about "disaffection" in family life. Were they to think more about themselves and less about kids, everyone would be better off. Women who don't work, they remind us, have higher chances of suffering depression and low self-esteem.

But parents no longer cotton to the argument that just because "in other cultures where children have many caretakers they do just fine," they will do just fine in our culture,[16] or that staying home means surrendering to financial dependence, boredom, frustration, depression, and low self-esteem. Many mothers assert that if it is indeed true that at-home mothers are more susceptible to depression than working mothers, the solution may not be continued participation in the labor force but increased social supports that diminish the isolation of at-home parenting.[17] Debbie Sawicki, an Illinois mother and national director of FEMALE, says her organization is particularly concerned with resurrecting the image of at-home mothering as socially productive work. "What we are doing, what every at-home mother does is more important than running a Fortune 500 company," Sawicki says. "It is a tall order to raise children in this society."

Easing the transition between work and home and bolstering the self-esteem of at-home mothers are only a few of the FEMALE's aims. It also advocates for family-friendly workplace policies—including job-sharing, part-time hiring, flex-time, and flex-place arrangements—and sponsors not only play groups but activities for mothers, like book discussion groups. "Our main focus is on mothers as *women*, and not as mothers," says Sawicki. "We see that a lot of women need the company of other adults once in while without their children, something they don't get a lot of at home."[18]

A number of the mothers' organizations that have cropped up in the past decade are dedicated to providing the kind of "survival skills" and social supports that are hard to come by in a society that places little value on the work of parenting. Some of these organizations, such as FEMALE, MOMS Club, Mothers at Home, and Lawyers at Home, seem preoccupied with rescuing at-home mothering from its image as socially and intellectually "lightweight." MOMS, a California-based organization started in 1983, encourages its member chapters to engage in service projects for the community and offers exercise groups. The National MothersCare Network, a federation of full-time mothers groups, was formed in 1994 with the explicit purpose of acting "as a watchdog against what members feel are inaccurate and derogatory portrayals of stay-at-homers."[19]

"There is a bogey woman out in the woods, who, when we begin to doubt our gains, keeps us modern women in line," says Maggie Gallagher in her witty 1989 social critique of feminism, *Enemies of Eros*. "She has big, yellow, guilt-inducing eyes; her skin is hidden beneath a grotesque growth of polyester. She has the figure of a wounded penguin . . . [and] a wall-to-wall orange-carpeted ranch house cage . . . [where] . . . little screaming demons . . . slobber and spit up and destroy."[20]

Advertisers have observed that the stay-at-home mother of today is hardly the "captive squirrel" of Dorothy Dinnerstein's *The Mermaid and the Minotaur*, caught in the "treadmill" of waxing and rewaxing her "intrinsically vinyl floor."[21] Because she is more likely to have professional training or a career behind her, she is more sophisticated than her mother was; she dresses more fashionably, she exercises to stay in shape.

She is far less likely to care than her own mother did about whether the kitchen floor shines or the front stoop is swept. She's "relaxed" about "scrubbing," notes Susan Small Weill, an advertising strategist with the Seiden Group who draws up campaigns trying to reach this woman, "because she's not at home for that."[22]

But if today's at-home mother is working hard to look like a good cultural fit—slim, healthy, relaxed, savvy, the kind of woman who might grace the cover of *Self*—she's not. She is a countercultural icon, if there ever was one, living a countercultural trend. And she knows it. She is a woman whose major concern is not herself and her own advancement, but others and their advancement—a woman who refuses to bow to the social forces telling her, in the words of social critic Mary Eberstadt, to continue "putting children last."[23]

Sanders and Bullen found out some interesting things about the women they interviewed who had returned home to raise their children after working. Only 5 percent said their workload or work schedule was a primary reason for quitting, and less than 3 percent listed concerns about finding or affording child care. The majority of respondents returned home because they "felt it was the best way to raise" their child (26.5 percent), "because they "didn't want to miss" their children's childhood (22.7 percent), and because they wanted to raise their children with their "own values" (19 percent).[24] Similarly, a 1993 survey of 21,000 Canadian workers found that the most common reason women stated for quitting work was "not enough time with children."[25]

Men, it appears, are far more apt than women to quit jobs primarily because they are unhappy with their work. And even women who report job satisfaction do not appear to be as emotionally attached to their work as men are. A 1995 survey by the Families and Work Institute found 55 percent of American women bring home half or more of family earnings; but as the earning gap between working women and men closes, women still tend to put family first both in their estimation of personal success and in their worries about work; 26 percent of women respondents to the Families and Work Institute survey, for example, noted as chief among their work-related worries either balancing work time with family time or dealing with the effect of work pressures on their families. In comparison, 19 percent worried about benefits, and only 10 percent about "lack of advancement opportunities for women."[26]

■ ■ ■

The New Familism is perhaps even more evident in the increasingly inventive ways parents combine work and parenting than in the trend to full-time parenting. Caroline Hull, managing director of the Connexus

Group, a firm that advises corporations on developing flex-time and flex-place work policies, observes that the population engaged in some or all home-based work increased from 24.9 to 38.4 million workers between 1988 and 1991.[27] Who are these at-home workers? The great majority seem to be individual entrepreneurs rather than corporate employees. As of 1995, according to FIND/SVP, a New York–based market research organization, there were 15.6 million home-based businesses in the United States and 8.2 million telecommuters, in addition to more than 16 million people who did catch-up corporate work after hours in home offices.[28]

Yet Joanne H. Pratt, a management consultant and researcher, observes that although telecommuting not only gives parents flexibility in combining work and family obligations but generates additional working hours, corporate culture is still resistant to full-time telecommuting. "Technology is driving us in the direction of home-based work," she notes, "but the attitude of corporate management is still 'Come to work and be counted.' "[29] But even if telecommuting were implemented on a broad scale in the research, marketing, and information sectors, in fields like the service industries and manufacturing it will never be feasible. Some people will always have to come to work and be counted. Thus, the child care preferences of parents who do work away from home are important to note. A 1991 study found that 28 percent of preschool children whose mothers worked were cared for by their fathers, although only 20 percent of those fathers were primary caretakers, and only 16 percent of these men were at home all day. This suggests the prevalence of "tag team" arrangements between parents, in which dual-earning couples stagger work shifts in order to split child care responsibilities relatively equally between them.[30]

About 20 percent of preschoolers with working mothers are cared for by other relatives while their parents work—mainly, it seems, by grandmothers—and many working mothers strongly prefer such arrangments to child care centers, family child care, or other nonrelative child care arrangements. Indeed, the fact that 51 percent of all preschoolers with employed mothers (about three of every ten preschoolers) are still cared for by child care providers unrelated to them may have less to do with a slight preference for nonrelative child care than with the unfeasibility of tag team arrangements for the vast majority of families and the unavailability, in an age of geographic mobility and economic insecurity, of other family members prepared to baby-sit. In a 1994 Families and Work Institute survey of 820 mothers in the Los Angeles, Dallas/Fort Worth, and Charlotte, North Carolina, areas, the great majority of mothers who had chosen relative care said that having a caretaker who was a member of the family was a top consideration, and they were the least likely of any group to "prefer another [child care] arrangement" to the one they had. The report noted, ironically, that when viewed objectively (in terms of the quality of the child care environment), relative care was not necessarily better than nonrelative child care, but that mothers who chose it were "comfortable" with it regardless of quality, explicitly because providers were family.[31]

Parents' desire to keep their kids close to the nest is a significant factor, then, in their child care choices. And it is the key factor in another emerging trend: thousands of parents are taking their children to work with them—not only as an emergency solution when trusted child care arrangements fall through, but as a habit. In a *New York Times* article, Louis Uchitelle reports that the practice is most common among factory workers, whose children, according to union officials and factory owners, "congregate by the thousands after school in the lobbies and on the lawns" of their parents' workplace. Of course, parents have other motivations for taking their kids to work than wanting them near: concern about after-school loneliness, neighborhood crime, television, and peer influences. Or they may be disappointed in the offerings of after-school programs but reluctant to leave children to their own devices, especially when in many jurisdictions parents who leave children under the age of twelve at home alone run the risk of being reported for child neglect.

Indeed, though experts may decry what they consider to be an "unstimulating" environment for children, parents and many corporate managers contend the practice saves endless telephone calls from work as well as minimizing the distractions caused by anxiety about children's welfare. Some parents—particularly divorced or single working mothers—not only argue that "the alternatives are potentially more damaging" but say children "gain from watching their parents work." One divorced working mother in New York told Uchitelle that she had started bringing her son to work when an after-school child care program at his public school folded, but had since become a strong advocate of the practice. "We spend quite a few quality hours together," she said. "The only time we are not together is when he is in school. That puts my heart at ease."[32]

Some companies "look the other way" at the presence of children in the workplace, trying not to encourage it. But others have taken note of parents' wishes, establishing emergency child care centers or officially sanctioning children's presence in parents' offices. The San Jose National Bank, for example, allows new mothers to bring their babies to work until they are six months old. It is one of several California companies experimenting with a "Babies in the Workplace" program.[33]

■ ■ ■

Recent changes in the way parents balance work and family obligations are not the only indications of a New Familism. Other recent trends reflect a shift in parents' values. Family researchers and journalists have noted that divorce rates have leveled off and that many Americans are making special efforts to increase unstructured time spent with their children.[34] More parents are "hanging out" with their children rather than arranging planned activities for them.[35] And the family dinner—once thought on the verge of obsolescence—is making a comeback as a focal point of the day and a sacred arena for family interaction. A 1995 Families and Work Institute survey found that two-thirds of families with children up through high school eat dinner together at least five times a week. Anecdotal evidence suggests that many families are consciously resurrecting the communal dinner after finding that their relationships had suffered from its absence.[36]

Especially children of the "baby bust"—the twentysomethings reared in a culture of dual-income families and divorce—seem to be ardently rejecting what they consider to be the skewed values of career- and self-obsessed parents. They insist they will make a serious commitment to marriage and to child-rearing.[37]

In a March 31, 1995, speech to the Council on Families in America, Rutgers University professor David Popenoe noted that several other pro-family social trends are emerging. First, there is a consensus among Americans that social programs such as welfare must be reformed in ways that will encourage the rebuilding of intact families. Second, secularism has run its course, and Americans are exhibiting a renewed interest in religion, spirituality, and church membership. Third, the economic downturn of the late 1980s and early 1990s has toned down some of the more decadent expressions of affluence and converted many onetime trend-setters to more homespun comforts and values. This renewed interest in the quality of family life, Popenoe predicted, is bound to increase as social scientists continue to reinforce the link between weak family bonds and the social malaise of youth.

Popenoe went on to describe research that has begun to underline the importance of distinct mothering and fathering roles in child-rearing. Several scholarly studies of the 1980s affirmed the biological basis of gender differences and their healthy influence on children. In an era when ideals of parenting have become increasingly androgynous, many men are finding it difficult to meet society's demands to relate to their children in more nurturing, traditionally feminine ways.[38] Children of both sexes benefit from the typically contrasting male and female styles of child-rearing—a father's teasing "rough play" and no-nonsense discipline, and the gentler, more cautious approach typical of mothers—and miss each when it is absent. Both are crucial as models for the developing childhood personality.

But despite its hopeful expectations, Popenoe cautioned, prospects for the New Familism are not entirely rosy. Many of the younger people who form its core, Popenoe insists, lack the role models in childhood that have traditionally helped people overcome challenges and adversity in marriage and achieve marital constancy. Much of the renewed American interest in religion and spirituality is New Age spiritualism that is conspicuously anti-traditional, culturally rootless, and relatively silent on the importance of marriage and family. And while family scholars like to point to studies in evolutionary psychology, anthropology, and sociobiology that emphasize the universality of marriage as a child-rearing bond, the importance of distinct mothering and fathering role models in the home, and especially of paternal investment in child-rearing, that same research has tended to highlight how ill disposed men are to monogamy.[39]

Other scholars and social commentators who have noticed the New Familism also recognize its caveats. In his 1992 book, *Our Journey Home*, Family Research Council president Gary Bauer expressed high hopes for the New Familism as a grassroots movement. "The daily papers are filled with stories about child abuse, drunkenness, violence and family disintegration, but these are still the exception, not the rule," he observes. "Baby boomers, usually thought of as liberal and hostile to traditional values, are leading the charge back home."[40] But Bauer concedes that support for strong family values is as scarce in the universities and among the opinion-making intellectual, professional, and monied elite as it is in Hollywood. There is still enormous hostility to the kind of changes our society needs to make in order to create a more wholesome environment for child-rearing.

Perhaps the most disturbing deficit of the New Familism in the eyes of sharp-eyed cultural observers is the extent to which American parents acquiesce to the role of disenfranchised minority, retreating from civic activism. In general, says David Blankenhorn, president of the Institute for American Values and author of *Fatherless America*, Americans seem to have "surrendered the keys" to what is becoming an increasingly family-hostile culture.[41] Statistics on civic participation in the baby-boomer age group support the conclusion that Blankenhorn's observation is tragically accurate. In the past generation there has been a disturbing drop in membership in civic and political organizations. The voting rate among baby boomers, who constitute the bulk of the parent population, is approximately 38 percent, markedly lower than that of the preceding generation.[42] Membership in the PTA has declined by more than half in the last thirty years. The ranks of volunteer service organizations like the League of Women Voters and the Red Cross have also declined significantly, as has attendance at town and school meetings (down 39 percent from 1973 to 1993) and political party volunteerism (down 56 percent in the same time period).[43]

Single parents or parents in dual-earner households may be too harried to get involved in community affairs, but their involvement rarely increases when they leave the workplace for home. Darcie Sanders and Martha M. Bullen report that of the women they surveyed, only 5.9 percent did more volunteer work as at-home mothers than as working women, and only 1.3 percent were more active in the PTA (6.4 percent said they were schoolroom mothers or aides). While almost a quarter of these women belonged to a church or synagogue, and 37.8 percent were members of mothers groups, play groups or support organizations, only 0.7 percent belonged to a local political organization.[44] Indeed, so great, apparently, is civic apathy among parents in my own small New England town that only one-third of public school parents went out to vote for the school budget last year, a bad showing that led to its defeat by a well-organized and politically activist contingent of senior citizens.

Several family scholars, among them economist Sylvia Ann Hewlett, reflect that if civic involvement is the key to realizing family interests in public policy, civic apathy among parents may be the biggest obstacle ahead for pro-family interests. Parents are a minority; as of 1990, only 35 percent of American households had children, as compared with 60 percent in 1960. But that does not explain why they enjoy so much less political power and social and economic privilege than, for example, retired Americans. "To a distressing degree," Hewlett comments, referring to the results of this disparity in political activity, "public policy is being used to transfer money from the needy young to the comfortable old."[45]

Jean Bethke Elshtain, professor of ethics at the University of Chicago, would agree. Only through the active participation of parents and families in civic life, she insists, can we hope to improve the well-being of children and properly sustain the social institutions that have traditionally supported and completed the child-rearing work of the family; and yet increasingly, the voices of parents recede from town halls, community associations, and club rooms behind the walls of homes.

Why is the "civic dimension of family life," to use Elshtain's well-chosen words, no longer so apparent and compelling to parents? It is not that parents don't care what happens in their towns and communities, suggests Elshtain, but rather that they feel alienated by the dominant values of the culture. "The reciprocal relationship between family and civil society," she contends, "is now overwhelmingly negative."[46] From my experiences talking to parents, I would agree with her. Parents feel isolated from society and civic institutions; as a Texas father put it, "We are little islands out there." Overwhelmingly, when I asked parents what government could do for families, I got the same response: "Nothing."

Elshtain sees the isolation of families as part of a decline in American habits of civic association—one that has separated politicians and civic institutions from the people they serve by creating a vacuum of communication and a "culture of mistrust, cynicism and scandal." Once, American families regularly participated in town meetings, philanthropic or church organizations, and block associations. They helped to build communal institutions that were sensitive to local concerns, values, and traditions, and able to pick up the pieces when families themselves failed children.

But baby boomers, more career-oriented and self-centered than previous generations, withdrew from the civic arena creating a vacuum in community-based initiatives. Into that vacuum moved advocacy groups formed to promote narrow agendas to the larger public. They neither required nor encouraged political dialogue and compromise, as the old community networks did. Meanwhile there was a proliferation of "support" groups—a form of association that, despite its appearances of intimacy, often thrives on anonymity. Initially an outgrowth of the encounter group and group psychotherapy, support groups were essentially the antithesis of community associations, designed to allow individuals to "focus on themselves in the presence of others," rather than on their community.[47]

This withdrawal from community involvement and political exchange was paralleled by the increasing centralization of nationally based volunteer organizations, which more and more began to set their agendas from the top down, often exerting dictatorial control over the activities and projects of local chapters. Even the most mainstream of them—the League of Women Voters and the Parent-Teacher Associations—have become caught up in the tide of political advocacy, marshaling the support of their local leadership base for controversial political agendas far removed from the preoccupations of local constituencies.

The PTA, for example, now does not even bill itself as an educational association for parents, but rather as "children's advocacy" organization run by parents in conjunction with teachers. Indeed, it has become the parent-volunteer arm of that union behemoth, the National Education Association. Not that the PTA was ever particularly dedicated to heeding local parent constituencies in the matter of educational

policy; the organization was formed more than a century ago for purposes of "parent education" by the wealthy, prominent, "progressive"
women known today as the foremothers of the turn-of-the-century "social reform" movement.

Educational policy analyst Charlene Haar, author of a forthcoming
book on the PTA, notes in a recently published historical overview that
from the beginning the two organizations were entwined. As early as
1920 the national office of the PTA was housed in the NEA building in
Washington, D.C. The 1927 PTA convention program hailed the NEA's
"seven cardinal objectives of education" and called on delegates to adopt
resolutions based on them. PTA news was often disseminated through
NEA publications.

Unfortunately, in 1968 the NEA convinced the PTA leadership to
declare neutrality in school board–union negotiations, thus effectively
banning the organization from the "arena of debate on important education issues."[48] Since then the PTA has become increasingly servile to the
teachers' union—so servile that a 1994 PTA publication, *The Parent
Teacher Organization*, boasted: "Cooperation with the National Educational Association is carried down from the national to the state, district
and local levels."[49]

Not surprisingly, the PTA's loss of independence and its consequent
increasing ineffectuality as a parent organization has taken its toll on
membership rates, which between 1966 and 1982 fell off drastically,
from 12 million to only 5 million. In 1974, PTA national president Lillie
Herndon admitted that the organization had not recorded the ages and
professional composition of its membership for four years. The reasons
were transparent: The organization did not want to acknowledge how
many parents were leaving and how many teachers and nonparent "children's advocates" were joining.[50] Today the organization still keeps no
demographic information on its membership, which—despite a second
baby boom and modest dues—has increased to only 6 or 7 million. As
Haar observes, "Public resentment against skyrocketing costs and dismal
educational results has caused parents to demand more voice in education policy-making. Parents are rebelling against policies which scorn
their values and squander their tax dollars."

The failure of the PTA to "provide parents with a useful role in education policy-making" is a source of frustration for many mothers and
fathers who prefer to forgo membership rather than attend PTA conferences that ignore the academic deficiencies of the public educational
system, feature seminars on HIV/AIDS awareness, oppose school-choice
legislation, and pander the latest trends in parenting advice.[51] Worse,
however is the control the national PTA attempts to exert over local

chapters, which has come to border on bureaucratic parody. Recently, the PTA central leadership ordered local chapters, for example, to refrain from using the phrase "room mother" to refer to the parents who organize class parties and field trips in elementary schools. Instead, there are now "room representatives" whose function is to act as "liaisons" between individual parents and school PTA boards. Technically a parent-member of a particular PTA chapter is not supposed to approach a member of his or her school PTA board on any issue without going through his or her "room representative"—a rather amusing and off-putting directive when one considers that in the average small American town the people on one's own school PTA board are often friends and neighbors who would hardly resent a phone call.

Less amusing are PTA elections, in which the present leadership of the organization typically puts forth a single slate of candidates, carefully screened for ideological conformity to NEA goals. So shameless is the PTA about its NEA loyalties, in fact, that in 1994, just after the California PTA helped the California Teachers Association defeat a private school voucher initiative, a PTA executive boasted, "PTA volunteers defeated Proposition 174; all the California Teachers Association did was put up the money!"[52] (The union dedicated $13 million to defeating the initiative, at a time when the state's classrooms were severely underfunded and overcrowded—often lacking in basic educational materials.)

At a convention workshop, another PTA leader warned local delegates, "We will pull the PTA Charter if any unit goes beyond the PTA agenda—as we would have with any PTA that supported [school] vouchers."[53] Such undisguised demand for what the Nazis liked to term *Gleichschaltung* (complete ideological and administrative conformity at every level of an organization, in every locality) effectively prevented any open debate in California's suburban public schools on the plight of inner-city parents.

The California voucher initiative is a typical example of the PTA leaderships' penchant for toeing the NEA line even at the risk of muzzling public debate and undermining public trust. In a state where property taxation has been severely curtailed, the voucher initiative would likely have put too great a strain on the public school system, but it deserved discussion—and if not in the PTA, then where? When the PTA declined to provide a forum for debate, it sent a contemptuous message to California parents of color that was only partially modulated when the California Teachers Association scrambled to support limited public-school-choice legislation in that state.

In my own community, rising public resentment of the PTA is palpable in the letters of complaint published in the local newspaper. Many mothers join the organization upon arriving in town, hoping not only to volunteer in the schools, but to have an influence on school policy. They are almost always disappointed. One mother wrote of how she and her children were "heavily criticized by the PTA Council members and treated with great disdain by the teachers" after she spoke out against PTA-supported positions at a public hearing on the local school budget, although she received "a great deal of support and congratulations from parents."[54]

Parents' frustration with the state and national PTA has led many local school parent associations to disaffiliate or not to affiliate in the first place; the independent Parent-Teacher Organization, or PTO, is becoming ever more prevalent. Tina Eberly, for example, started an elementary school parent group in 1995 in the town of Lisbon, North Dakota. When considering PTA affiliation, she worried that PTA dues money might go to lobby for policies the parents in her school district could not support: "I had no idea they were so politically involved," she noted to a reporter. "I don't think many of the parents [here] care to be involved in political and social issues. . . . We're more concerned with the education of kids . . . in our school system."[55]

Many educational researchers have lamented a phenomenon that is becoming widely known as "parent dropout." According to a recent study by Child Trends, a Washington, D.C., based research group, parent involvement in PTA meetings, school open houses, science fairs, and other school activities recedes sharply by the time their children are in middle school.[56] To some extent parent dropout is a natural phenomenon. By middle school, children are making an effort to establish an autonomous identity, and are less communicative about what is happening at school. They may even view the presence of parent-volunteers at school as an imposition on their independence. And to some extent parent dropout is an unavoidable consequence of an educational system that teaches children to view their parents as unnecessary appendages to a life focused around the authority of the school and the peer group.

But parent dropout in the middle school years may also be a product of frustration with just such existing organizations like the PTA that purport to represent parents' interests in school affairs, but really don't: a consequence of too many unthanked volunteer hours, unanswered queries about school policy, and ignored requests for educational change and accountability. I have dwelled on the PTA not to scapegoat that organization, but to point up one of the chief villainies in the general decay of civic life in our country, especially in the conspicuous decline of parental involvement: the failure of our major civic organizations to respond to the real needs and concerns of families. We know that schools that demonstrate respect for parents' values and judgment have high parent involvement. The same has to apply for parent-volunteer organizations. Those that do not demonstrate respect for the views and priorities of parents cannot expect to maintain an active base of volunteers for long.

The PTA is not the only victim of powerful special interest and political advocacy groups. The League of Women Voters today all too often circumvents two-sided debates in its ostensible efforts to inform citizens on vital policy issues—educational and otherwise—affecting families; instead it often substitutes panels of government officials or "experts" who promote one-sided public policy agendas. Similarly, the philanthropic National Federation of Women's Clubs entered the political fray of the 1990s via the by no means inarguable feminist "consciousness-raising" efforts in the areas of sexual harassment, abuse, and date rape; I resigned from my own NFWC chapter when in the spring of 1995 I entered a meeting and found at my place a flyer urging me to attend a rally opposing Newt Gingrich's Contract with America as "a contract against women." Several women at my table commented that this "official position" made them feel uncomfortable. (I live in a very conservative town.) I'm no great admirer of Gingrich, but I don't need the Women's Club to give me my marching orders against him—especially when they are not preceded by an open discussion among members.

How can civic organizations expect members to accept political positions assumed on their behalf? Many would claim that they conduct membership surveys, but typically these surveys are skewed in a way bound to produce the desired results. A recent League of Women Voters "poll" on school-choice legislation in Connecticut, for example, was not a poll at all, because it asked no questions; rather, it presented a "concurrence"—a series of statements "based on the League of Women Voters New Jersey position" on school choice—with which Connecticut League members were asked to agree or disagree. The New Jersey League had declared its opposition to vouchers on the basis that "public education must be fiscally and educationally accountable" to citizens, and school vouchers would be the equivalent of throwing public money at schools that did not have to be fiscally and educationally accountable. Taking this deceptive position as the foundation for their poll, the Connecticut League asked its members a series of leading questions (e.g., "Should the system of elementary school education be educationally accountable?") designed to get its members to "concur" with their peers in New Jersey.[57]

Increasingly, local policy-making has become skewed in favor of the positions of powerful political advocacy groups and professional elites, many of which are not only promoting their own opinions through local civic organizations, but pushing agendas they have long since worked out with government bureaucrats and politicians in Washington. The disappearance of informed and open debate at the local level of civic organizations has severely impeded the democratic process, but the agenda-pushers' desire to achieve consensus has hardly been fulfilled. Rather, government policies have been implemented without compromise, because ordinary citizens have been denied the resources to penetrate and shape them. The result is that an enormous amount of resentment has fomented "against the system," and large numbers of citizens have been driven into polarized opposition.

For many of the parents I've spoken to, American life has literally become a "system"—a Kafkaesque constellation of hostile forces that seems inflexible and impervious to the wants and needs of the average citizen. "We're looking at the system we live in," observes a San Francisco father. "We're trying to fight it, period."

For the past few years, the liberal press has chronicled with trepidation the success of the right wing in elections for everything from school board posts to congressional seats. They cannot understand the metamorphosis of Pat Robertson's Christian Coalition from a fringe group of poor Southern whites to a broad-based, middle-class movement claiming adherence by up to a third of the voting population.[58] To me, the success of the far right seems obvious enough. Many parents look around at rising social chaos and the implementation of social policies with which they cannot identify and simply close ranks.

The parents I have talked with over the last few years are afraid their children are being led into lives of desperation and destructiveness. They see "the craziness out there." They see the moral fabric of society disintegrating before their eyes. They see their teenagers seduced by smut and they see the proliferating street violence that makes house prisoners of younger siblings. They see civilized social intercourse undermined by profanity; humility, chastity, and discretion mocked as weakness and repression; discipline derogated as abuse; devotion to family disparaged as co-dependency; a culture of marriage promoted for people of the same sex, but not for people of opposite sexes. They see an entrenched educational and child welfare bureaucracy prepared to sever their ties to their children at a moment's notice, a legal elite that claims their children as state "resources" and "wards."[59] They see a public moral code that levies no heavier injunctions on children than to tell them not to smoke, and if they do drugs, to keep the needles clean. At the same time they see a society impinging on honest efforts to rear children who will not murder and steal. Is it a wonder they are driven to moral panic?

Nor do the electoral gains of the Christian fundamentalists reflect the true extent of parents' disaffection. As the American Enterprise Institute's Benjamin Wattenberg has noted, the political contests of the next few years are bound to be fought on the ground of values, which most parents clearly perceive to be in crisis. The political party that addresses this crisis will win parents' hearts.[60] But so far, with most politicians apparently deaf to this concern, the grassroots pro-family movement has been dedicated more to countercultural retreat than to political activism. It is the retreat of the preoccupied, consisting of "evasion" techniques designed to provide wholesome childhoods to beloved children despite an unwholesome cultural environment. It is the opposition of nonparticipation, of privatization, which—despite occasional frustrated outbursts of contention—works mainly by manipulating the system to get kids into the "right" school, the "right" play group, the "right" neighborhood, or the "right" afternoon activity to keep them out of trouble. It is a strategy of sandbagging, of disappearing—behind suburban hedges or urban apartment doors—to draw up game plans for survival.

But the potential political force of alienated middle-class parents and desperate working-class parents should not be underestimated. The choices they are making—in schooling, in social contacts, in community associations, even when they are choices of retreat—have profound political implications. In re-creating family-based communities from the ground up and forming alternate networks of association, parents are increasingly in a position to have a significant impact on issues of concern to them.

The electronic media, paradoxically, has proved to be a friendlier force for public participation in political and social debate than most newspapers and magazines, let alone most civic organizations. TV and talk radio producers, with their love of controversy, have at least encouraged the kind of lively debate on pressing family issues conspicuously lacking in the so-called public forums of town halls and legislatures. Instead of bringing about an Orwellian nightmare of government control, notes Wall Street Journal editorialist John Fund, the electronic media—including cable television, interactive television, and the Internet—may offer our one great hope for resurrecting public debate.

The alternative media and new technology are revolutionizing the way information is exchanged and the way issues, from education to taxes to health care, are debated. Americans have a greater opportunity than ever before to find out what is going on and to make their voices heard.[61] There are five times as many radio talk shows today as there were seven years ago. The Internet offers at least five thousand electronic discussion groups and 2,500 electronic newsletters, with round-the-clock access. For the past few years, the electronic media, from America Online's "Home Schooling" and "Full-Time Dad" forums to the "Parentsplace" World Wide Web site, have been giving time-strapped American parents a way to exchange information, advice, and opinions on education, work/family issues, the media, and other important subjects.

It has also given them an effective means of political lobbying. In February 1994, a last-minute congressional amendment to the Elementary and Secondary Education Act that would have required private school teachers and home schooling parents to be certified by the government was defeated when word went out to over 200,000 parents over the electronic grapevine. A similar electronic alert helped defeat funding for CLAS, the California Learning Assessment System exam, that year. If there ever is a parent revolution, it may just begin on-line, where an increasing number of parent activists find like-minded cohorts, debate issues with people of different opinions, compare notes on victories and defeats, and fire off manifestos.

On May 4, 1994, at 11:02 A.M., Cindy Duckett, for example, unleashed via Prodigy Interactive Service an open letter to Kansas legislators that has since traveled a veritable underground railroad among grassroots parent activists. The subject: the defeat of a parental rights clause in an education reform bill up for consideration by the Kansas legislature.

> Dear Representative: I certainly was relieved this morning when I read in the paper an article entitled "House Nixes Parents' Rights Clause." You see, I had kind of taken for granted that my husband and I did have primary control over the care and upbringing of our children. What a load off my back to find out someone else had that weighty responsibility. . . . Now, I'm not sure who it is that has this control, but I would guess that it must be the State. . . . [As] control without responsibility somehow doesn't seem fair . . . here are a few areas of responsibility I most willingly hand over to you as the one who has primary control over the care and upbringing of my (oops!) your children.
>
> Let's talk about food. Our grocery bill is approximately $150 a week. I suppose if we really scraped, my husband and I could eat for $50 . . . so that leaves you $100 a week to cover. We appreciate school lunches and breakfasts. Could you please serve supper, too? Perhaps then we'd only need about $50 a week or so to cover the cost of snacks. Clothing costs will be more than food. I'll try to

shop the bargains, but could you send $300 a month? I know that
seems high but you have 5 children residing at our house and at
least three will need new coats next winter. . . .

Oh, one thing you might be saving for is college. Our first
daughter will start in 5 years. We'd like her to go to a really good
school, but since you're in control, we'll try to respect your
wishes. . . .

Parents like Cindy Duckett may soapbox, commiserate, inform, and
organize via modem, but that does not mean they have abandoned
old-fashioned political activism or face-to-face community-based net-
working for the anonymity of cyberspace. The New York parent demonstrations of 1992 and the impressive turnout of black men committed to
stronger family lives at the Million Man March in Washington, D.C., in
October 1995 are proof that "parent power" is more than a matter of
megabytes. A growing number of grassroots organizations offer support
to families, look out for family interests, and even lobby for family-
friendly public policy changes on the national front, adopting the same
political advocacy methods used by the promoters of bureaucratic child-
rearing.

Some, like the fifty-year-old, forty-thousand-member La Leche
League, concentrate on promoting parent-child bonding in a society that
discourages it; others, such as the previously mentioned FEMALE,
MOMS, and the Christian organization MOPS (Mothers of Preschoolers International), offer everything from practical advice, social opportunities, baby-sitting co-ops to Bible study groups, community service
projects, and advocacy.

MOMS, the community service and support organization for at-
home mothers, started in 1983 with fifty chapters and now has 325
chapters in various areas of the country. Founder Mary James epitomizes
the defiant spirit of the parent activist: "Many mothers' groups presume
that mothers at home need either teaching or tender care, such as the local support groups started by hospitals' mental health outreach programs. We believe that mothers at home are neither stupid nor insane,
and should be treated as adults who have made an honored sacrifice to
help their families and society."[62]

The increasingly gray area that separates parent support organizations and pro-family advocacy on the local and national scene is apparent in the agenda of several support groups run by mothers. (Fathers'
support organizations do not appear to have entered the arena of public
policy advocacy except in promoting "fathers' rights" in custody situations.)[63] Parents' Place, a San Francisco–based support organization for

parents of preschoolers, works to fight violence and sex in the media, speaking out and urging parents to speak out when they encounter provocative or frightening imagery, and offering workshops for Bay Area parents on how to talk to young children about such images.[64]

FEMALE, as I have mentioned, is active in work-family issues. Mothers at Home has also established a public policy department for research, public information, and lobbying. Its directors have taken public stands for measures that would promote at-home mothering—including policies that would make home-based employment easier and remove tax incentives for day care—in addition to providing day-to-day support for mothers. They eagerly promote their positions among the Washington political elite, but they just as eagerly read mail and accept suggestions and submissions from readers across the country for their publication, *Welcome Home*. With their dedicated volunteers and openness to input from parents, such organizations are well poised to introduce family policy initiatives.

Though parents are latecomers to the political advocacy scene, they are beginning to fight fire with fire—to take up the tools and techniques that others have used to influence politicians and policy-makers in directions they consider to be unproductive and unresponsive to their interests. Still, they are hampered by a lack of time and money. For that reason, the spate of countercultural family advocacy organizations run on a more systematic basis by ministers, educators, psychologists, and social scientists that have sprung up may be more successful in fighting the family-hostile cultural and political establishments.

These new advocacy organizations run the political gamut, from the liberal New York–based National Parenting Association to the conservative Eagle Forum. A few of the most influential and popular organizations—Dr. James Dobson's Focus on the Family, for example, and Dr. Bob Simonds's Citizens for Excellence in Education—are avowedly conservative and Christian. Others, like the Virginia-based parental rights organization, Of the People, and the Pennsylvania-based National Fatherhood Initiative, are nonsectarian and nonpartisan efforts to reflect and promote the broadest possible consensus on policy issues of import to parents and families.

Despite the differences in their ideological starting points, the most successful of these organizations have some striking things in common. They insist that strong, healthy families are integral to a strong, healthy society that has children's well-being at heart. They also assume that any government-sponsored policy directed toward children must be judged in the context of its impact on the quality of family life and parent-child interaction. They are concerned to preserve family autonomy, and want to work toward solutions to work-family conflicts that will favor family time. They are increasingly suspicious of proxy-parenting; instead of advocating more day care centers for working mothers, for example, they would choose to advocate for sequencing opportunities and more flexible work schedules for parents, even for recognition of parenting as a profession in its own right.

Their leadership, furthermore, is committed to cutting through the rhetoric of family pathology purveyed by the professional elites. Assuming the competence of ordinary men and women to raise children well, they see the recent rise of family violence not as an endemic problem of family life, but as a reflection of the enormous pressures on families levied by a family-hostile culture. These organizations are not out to blame the family for the ills of society, but to shore up the family and enhance community support for engaged parenting. Their object is to minimize government intervention and to maximize parental empowerment in the child-rearing process. Most important, they are working hard to draft public policy proposals based on the real desires of families, instead of merely assuming what families might want or need from government.

Economist Sylvia Ann Hewlett contends that talking to parents and children has been a large part of her work as president of the National Parenting Association. While Hewlett, as a liberal, may be more trusting of the professional elites than many of her more conservative colleagues among family advocates, she insists there can be no possibility of reshaping family policy in ways that will solve the crisis of childhood other than "putting parents in the driver's seat," as the principal initiators of a "new wave of community-driven responses" to social problems.[65] Similarly, the National Fatherhood Initiative, a firmly centrist organization, went straight to the public for an exchange of ideas in 1995, holding community forums across the nation on the subject of the disappearing American father.

As a conservative, Christian ministry offering individual help and counseling to families facing the challenges and crises of contemporary life, Focus on the Family may be more limited in its appeal, but it prides itself on being in touch with millions of ordinary individuals. Its research arm, the Family Research Council, is meticulous in seeking out family policy approaches that mirror the concerns and opinions of Americans across the religious and political spectrum.

And it seems there is, after all, a broad public consensus on family issues, however much it has been ignored by bureaucrats and politicians. In a series of polls sponsored during the early 1990s by the Family Research Council and undertaken by Voter/Consumer Research, 69 percent of respondents believed, for example, that the "key to improving the well-being of children is greater parent involvement in children's lives and not more government services to children." (The strongest support for this idea came from married parents with children, but singles were not far behind.)[66]

They overwhelmingly viewed the impact of the federal government and entertainment industries as negative forces in the lives of children, and regarded "direct, personal investment in children's lives as more important than political involvement on behalf of children or material substitutions for parental time."[67] When they were asked to view the issues of divorce, unmarried parenthood, and day care through the eyes of children, they came down overwhelmingly on the side of two-parent homes and parental involvement, with 83 percent saying that "it is better for a child to be born into a two-parent family than to a single mother" and 87 percent claiming that "young children fare better when they are primarily cared for by their own mother rather than by a day care provider."[68]

Other points of general agreement: Three-quarters said they would "rather live in a place that strongly upholds traditional family values than a place that is very tolerant of nontraditional lifestyles."[69] Most believed that the family is eroding—not merely "changing." (Interestingly, African-Americans were the most likely of any racial group polled to believe that children today have it rougher than their parents did when they were children.) The majority of Americans would trade early retirement tomorrow for family time today. And most respondents would rather have lower taxes and fewer government services than higher taxes and more government services.[70]

But while it appears that there is unity among a cross section of Americans—parents and nonparents—on general family policy issues, there are also signs of a "family gap," an emerging voting pattern that separates parents with children at home from other segments of the population. The family gap was first traced in the 1992 presidential election, when political analysts scrutinized the demographic profiles of Bush, Clinton, and Perot supporters. These analysts found that Clinton, whose campaign proudly stressed that he was a baby boomer and an involved dad, was curiously not elected by his peers. A Wirthlin poll conducted by *Reader's Digest* in 1993 found that parents between the ages of twenty-five and fifty-four with children at home were the least likely Americans to vote the Democrat ticket.[71] It further revealed that neither race, ethnicity, religion, gender, age, education, nor marital status was as great a determinant of choice of candidate as the presence of children in the home.

The success of the GOP in the 1994 congressional elections reinforces the notion that political conservatism has taken hold among the very parents who were the children of the 1960s. So, also, do the results of the 1996 elections, in which widespread GOP congressional successes have been traced to the essentially conservative political dispositions of suburban parents—in particular those traditionally liberally aligned women the media refer to as "soccer moms." (Indeed, Clinton's 1996 success with this group has been largely attributed to his efforts during the campaign to reinvent his public image as a concerned parent and values conservative.) How is baby boomer conservatism to be explained? Father Richard John Neuhaus, editor of the religion and public policy journal *First Things*, has suggested that the defection of baby-boomer parents from their former liberal political allegiances has a lot to do with what the baby-boom generation recognizes as the institutional child-rearing failures of the liberal society. Today's baby-boomer conservative, Neuhaus observed, is nothing other than a former liberal "with a daughter in high school."[72]

But the new conservatism among baby boomers has economic as well as ideological roots, I think. Parents are the hardest workers in our society. Typically, they bear the greatest tax burden of any portion of the population. Yet they are the constituency least likely to benefit from present government entitlements and tax breaks, which are heavily focused on the elderly and the unemployed. (Although Clinton in 1992 received only 33 percent of the votes of married parents between the ages of twenty-five and fifty-four, he received 48 percent of the votes of those over fifty-five.) As we have seen, parents are perhaps the most likely of any demographic group to be abused by big-government bureaucracies, and the least likely to benefit from government services.

Some of the more recent legislative initiatives parents have inspired and supported are good indications of the extent to which parents are beginning to grapple with their peculiarly ungratifying status as a population alternately ignored and oppressed by government. Take Florida's "Spanking Bill of Rights," for example, a parent-driven legislative initiative that turned into a heady legal contest between parents and child-rearing professionals. Uneasy with the state's vague child abuse laws and disturbed by reports that its Health and Rehabilitation Services had launched child abuse investigations in and even removed children from homes where they had been spanked, parents appealed to legislators in the early 1990s to clarify the parental right to impose reasonable corporal discipline on misbehaving children. (Ironically, Florida is one of twenty states that have statutes clearly granting *teachers* the right to paddle children, but the rights of parents are hardly so clear.) A bill introduced in 1994 by State Senator James Hargrett attempted to rectify this situation by affirming the right of a parent to employ corporal punishment, provided such discipline did not involve "willful or intentional acts" of injury, and that it did not result in "significant bruises or welts." The bill passed both houses of the legislature and enjoyed considerable popular support, but under pressure from child welfare advocates, Florida's governor vetoed it. In April 1995 a revised version of the bill designed to prevent serious nonvisible injury to a child was passed again by the Florida Senate. It finally made it through the House in May 1996 and became law in June, but without the governor's signature.[73]

Struggles like these indicate that any parental rights movement promises a fractious political contest between parents and professional elites. As of fall 1996, the Parental Rights Amendment and the congressional Parental Rights and Responsibilities Act, both of which reflect the desire to establish legally "the fundamental right of a parent to direct the upbringing of a child," were meeting powerful opposition from professional advocacy groups.

As I complete this manuscript, the battle lines have been clearly drawn: On the one side a powerful contingent of political and professional advocacy organizations, ranging from the American Civil Liberties Union and People for the American Way to Planned Parenthood, the Colorado Education Association, the National Organization for Women, and the League of Women Voters, is determined to convince the public that parents don't need rights and would only abuse them. On the other side is a motley if determined group of citizens worried about the forces that increasingly impinge on their ability to raise decent children.[74]

Parental rights may or may not be the issue that finally moves a silent majority of parents to political involvement. But the accelerating debate surrounding parental rights initiatives will surely bring to the fore many principles that unite parents and can form the basis of a more family-friendly family policy agenda. American parents want relief from the pressures of the family-hating culture. They want more family time, and more parent-child interaction. They want less government intervention, lower taxes, and more parent empowerment. They want educational, child welfare, and family law reform. They want safer streets and schools; they want higher standards in the media; they want a return to sounder moral and cultural values. In other words, they want family-responsive, child-friendly policy changes.

Until now they have largely remained a disenfranchised minority in passive retreat from the culture. But they are emerging as a force with which our government and professional elites will ultimately be forced to reckon. The New Familism is becoming political.

10

Toward a Family Policy:

Seven Pro-Family Proposals in Search of Political Courage

In a speech before the 1992 Republican convention, former Secretary of Education William Bennett urged his party to heed the wisdom of an ancient philosopher. "Plato understood," he said, "that, in the end, there is only one fundamental political issue: how we raise our children."[1]

I doubt many of the parents I talked to in researching this book have read Plato, but it has become obvious to me that the success of the next few political administrations may well rest upon the ability of government to respond to the needs of children and the concerns of families. I am not alone in thinking this. As we moved toward the 1996 elections, it even became evident that this was a perception many political candidates shared.

To be fair, Hillary Rodham Clinton, for one, has always been interested in children and their welfare. If her book, *It Takes a Village and Other Lessons Children Teach Us*, is essentially an apology for the highly bureaucratic "global village" that has replaced more intimate approaches to child-rearing in today's "impersonal and complicated world," at least she knows that how we as a society choose to raise our children is ultimately the most important, relevant, and resounding of all political questions. "Our challenge," she writes, "is to arrive at a consensus of values and a common vision of what we can do today, individually and collectively, to build strong families and communities." [2]

I began this book with an overview of the many challenges our society poses to parents in the rearing of their children. In the chapters following, I attempted to elucidate the parental critique of our culture, focusing on parents' answers to the challenge Mrs. Clinton so perceptively articulates. In doing so, I have tried to address parents' uppermost concerns, to refrain from taking up subjects that were not of vital interest to them, and to remain true to their vision of a society and culture more conducive to the work of parenthood. Up to now, I have not broached much the subject of family policy initiatives, because when I asked parents what government could do for families, the vast majority of them answered "Nothing." One African-American mother of three concisely summed up parental opinion: "If we look to government, we are looking to the wrong source for help."

But in this last chapter, I wish to go beyond the commission of the parents I spoke with and discuss exactly what government can and should do for families. Why? Maybe it is just a conceit—an outgrowth of my association with a family and social policy research organization. (You don't work in the field of family policy long before you start thinking that indeed government can do something for families—if government would only listen to *you*.) But if government can do so much *against* the interests of families (as parents consistently complain), why should it not have the same power to do something *for* them?

While parents' conservative voting patterns in the last three elections are some indication of the direction parents want to take in reforming family policy, that does not mean parents have become a loyal cheering section for libertarian ideologues. Rather, they are responding to the problems they face every day—issues that impress upon them their need for ever more self-reliance in an ever more hostile environment.

Not one parent I interviewed ever uttered the words "Democrat" or "Republican," or even "liberal" or "conservative." Parents are not political in the sense that partisan politicians would like to think. As I have indicated in Chapter 9, any extrapolation from voting participation statistics by age strongly suggests that most American parents do not even vote. But the ones who do vote can be characterized as values-conservative swing voters who are aligning themselves with the growing constituency of the American public that has become disillusioned with government.[3] Parents' preoccupation with the difficulties of raising children will eventually have profound political implications, but the electoral direction it will take is not certain, mainly because neither the

Republicans nor the Democrats have adequately spoken to family issues and concerns.

What could either party do to regain the trust of parents? Here are seven ideas that might save America for families, and families for America.

Tax Relief

While the proportionate income tax burden has remained relatively constant for single people and childless married couples since the 1950s, for a median-income married couple with two children it has swelled 150 percent.[4] As William Mattox of the Family Research Council observes, if today's "exemption shielded from taxation the same proportion of annual income . . . as it did in 1948, a median-income family today would be able to exempt approximately $8,000 per dependent child. Instead, it can shield only $2,150."[5] The average American family today pays more in taxes than for shelter, clothing, and food combined.

Here is an issue in which family advocates on both sides of the political fence have reached an unambiguous consensus. Liberal economist Sylvia Ann Hewlett and Conservative William Mattox have both observed that a couple can get a bigger tax break for breeding racehorses than for raising children, both of them echoing Patricia Schroeder of Colorado, former chairwoman of the House Select Committee on Children, Youth and Families, who has made this point on several occasions.[6]

With the notable exception of Clinton's recent proposed tax credit for families with children in college, Democrats tend to be opposed to all pro-family tax cuts (including the ones proposed in the rejected GOP tax-reform package of 1995, which aimed for a lowered marriage penalty and a heightened IRA deduction for married couples) on the tired old grounds that high taxes are the price of good government. But the Republicans have not been able to put forward any tax relief proposals meaningful enough to convince middle- and lower-income families that the party has a social conscience, and that whatever they might give up in government services will be made up in discretionary income. Nor did the fact that the 1995 GOP tax-reform package was tied to corporate tax relief do much to win the support of Democrats or the public trust. As I completed this manuscript in the summer of 1996, Republican presidential candidate Bob Dole unveiled an ambitious new tax-reform plan that promised to be even less beneficial to families than the 1995 version. It tied a measly $500 per child tax credit for families to a 15 percent across-the-board tax cut, a reduction by half of the capital gains tax, and a repeal of Social Security taxes on wealthier senior citizens. This "something for everyone" plan was bound to fail with the public, for it offered no more than a supply-side gamble on beating deficit spending, and the privileged classes stood to gain substantially more than did the average man or woman.

In the past few years several politicians have championed the flat tax as the new economic panacea. Flat tax schemes—in particular those of Dick Armey and Malcolm S. Forbes Jr.—may promise large exemptions for children, but have also been rightly criticized by analysts as "regressive," favorable to the wealthy, and ultimately even more burdensome to the middle class than the present graduated system of taxation.[7]

Are there no answers to the burdens our system imposes on middle-class families? Of course there are. Consider the Family Freedom for Families Plan, released in 1991 by the Family Research Council in conjunction with the Heritage Foundation. This plan called for a meaningful per child tax credit of $1,800 for preschool children, and $1,200 for school-age children—at the modest annual cost to the government of $65 billion, a little more than 10 percent of the current federal budget.[8] Naturally, such tax breaks for parents would have to be paid for. But paring government overhead, reforming Medicare, trimming defense spending (the 1996 Congress granted the Pentagon a full $11 billion more than it asked for in 1997), shifting some of the tax burden from parents to childless singles and childless marrieds, and phasing out Social Security benefits for wealthy senior citizens would probably do it.

Children are our most important investment in the future; those who create and raise them are providing our future social capital. Parents thus deserve to retain a greater portion of the fruits of their labors. If childless working people resent a larger tax burden, they should consider who will be working to pay their Social Security pensions and medical bills in the coming decades. As Allan C. Carlson, president of the Rockford Institute Center on the Family in America, has put it, "Persons without children are currently 'free riders' on the system, and so should be paying a much larger share of the overall tax bill. It is their social obligation to the nation."[9] If wealthy senior citizens don't like the idea of forgoing Social Security payments, they must consider that the system was created, like welfare, as a safety net and entitlement for those in need, not as an extra government perk for the privileged.

Thus, any family-friendly tax reform would include not only far higher income tax exemptions for dependent children—at least for middle- and lower-income families—but also significant reductions in payroll taxes for parents with minor children. It would retain earned-income tax credits (in the form of wage subsidies geared to family size) for low-income families, but would eliminate the marriage penalties of the current Earned Income Tax Credit.

Optimally, such tax reform would make significant changes to the Dependent Care Tax Credit, perhaps offering tax advantages to parents who care for their own children at home, or at least allowing all families with small children an equal tax credit for child care, whether parents pay for child care or provide it themselves. As it exists, the DCTC discourages parental child care by offering what amount to government subsidies to parents who have their children raised by proxy—that is, by sending them to day care or by hiring baby-sitters. As a Baltimore father says, "There are these government programs that allow the second parent to go to work, and they'll watch your kids for the extra incentives you get. But you get nothing for having kids and staying home to raise them yourself."

Our current tax system punishes one-income, two-parent families— especially tag-teamers—for hands-on, at-home child-rearing; at the same time, it is exploited by prosperous two-career families as a kind of tax shelter. Two working parents making a combined $100,000 a year can currently claim almost $2,000 in tax benefits for a child in day care, while a median-income family that renounces child care gets no tax benefit for what amounts either to double duty at work and at home or the financial sacrifice of forgoing paid labor.[10]

Given the sorry verdict on nonparental child-rearing in the early years, family-friendly tax reform must ensure child care credits for at-home parents, not only as an acknowledgment of the social benefits of engaged parenting, but as an impetus to more parental engagement. (In this context, it is encouraging that in 1996 Congress voted to increase the amount a nonworking spouse can contribute to an individual retirement account.) As William Mattox observes, the propensity of the tax system to treat children "as an under-funded client class of the welfare state rather than as unique individuals whose well-being is best served when they are raised in strong families" must end.[11]

Work Relief

For the average American family, work relief is just as important as tax relief. And no government administration, no matter how ostensibly pro-family, will pass muster with parents unless it is prepared to address an issue even more important than the parental cash deficit: the parental *time* deficit. This fact was brought home to me glaringly during a

National Public Radio panel discussion the day Ralph Reed and the Christian Coalition released their "Contract with the American Family" in the spring of 1995, in an effort to endorse the GOP-sponsored per-child tax credit and to push Congress on school prayer legislation. As a Massachusetts mother called in to point out, however, nowhere did the contract address work-family conflicts, or the perverse determination of our political leaders to ignore them. No set of legislative proposals that failed to address the economic and social obstacles that keep parents from staying at home to raise children, she claimed, could truly be called pro-family.

In Chapter 6 I discussed at length two kinds of work-family conflicts—those that devolve intrinsically from the structure of a market economy that discourages home-based work, and those that are super-imposed by government and corporate policies. Both can be alleviated, if we have the will. In our increasingly post-industrial economy, it becomes possible once again, through home-based and flex-time work policies, to easily combine work and family obligations. Part-time work, job sharing, home-centered employment, and "sequencing"—the practice of returning to a career after taking several years off to raise children—are viable options for organizing work lives, women's especially. Not only do they appeal to parents but, as we have seen, in corporate experiments they have passed the productivity test with flying colors.

What can government do to encourage these family-friendly work styles? Tax reforms could ease the current restrictions on tax deductions for home office expenses. Government might also require employers to institute preference-in-hiring policies for parents who are returning to work after a hiatus for child-rearing—the same sort of preference-in-hiring arrangement, indeed, given to veterans who have interrupted participation in the labor force to serve in the armed forces.

More generous family leave policies, most especially a Family Leave Law requiring our largest corporations to hold jobs for new mothers up to a year and offer them at least three months' leave with pay, are absolutely essential. (Most countries in Western Europe have enacted far more generous family leave laws than this.) It may increase productivity in the short term to deny working women such maternity benefits, but in the long term, the GNP is bound to suffer from a generation of children denied adequate mothering in the all-important first year of life.

Moreover, why should parents be required to "do it all" at once—that is, work and rear children at the same time—while most senior citizens have neither work nor child-rearing responsibilities? Earlier I mentioned a Family Research Council poll of 1993 which revealed that the majority of Americans "would trade early retirement tomorrow for family time today." Indeed, when asked to "choose between two different strategies for organizing work and family responsibilities over the life cycle," the majority noted they would rather "work fewer hours while raising children and postpone retirement until age 70" than "work more hours while raising children and be able to retire at age 60."[12] This poll has led many family advocates to ponder repealing the many inducements to early retirement, to consider raising the retirement age, to encourage retired persons to "twilight" or enter second careers by instituting preferential hiring policies and—especially among median and low income elderly people—by eliminating penalties to Social Security benefits for senior citizens who work. Raising the retirement age, incidentally, would have the advantage of lowering Medicare expenses, thus cutting federal entitlement outlays.

To sum up, instead of directing government monies toward increasing child care options for working parents, our government should actively engage itself in relieving parents of work pressures and encouraging solutions that maximize family time.

Media Responsibility

The issue of restoring standards of decency in the entertainment and broadcast industries is at the top of the list for parents—and crucial to working parents unable to supervise the after-school activities of older children. How can government help to reestablish media responsibility without drastically increasing its control over communications in general, or invoking censorship?

Several communities across the nation have begun, with the active support of parents, to issue what are called "Quality of Life" ordinances forbidding the display of offensive advertising and setting penalties for the use of obscene language and display in public places. The broadcasting, recording, and movie industries, however, operate beyond local jurisdiction.

Until deregulation of the airwaves in 1984, the FCC (Federal Communication Commission) did expect the broadcasting and print media to live up to some standards. In the 1970s, public pressure against increasing gratuitous sex and violence in television, along with mounting social-scientific evidence of the relationship between violence on television and aggressive behavior in children, prompted the FCC to declare that broadcasters must exert a "meaningful effort" to provide quality television programming for daytime afternoons and weekends. The regulations also limited advertising and forbade "host-selling"—the use of characters from children's programs in marketing products to viewers.

It should be noted that most broadcasters never adequately complied with the FCC's directive for educational programming, a situation that led the FCC in 1980 to issue a Notice of Proposed Rulemaking that would have obligated the television industry to produce a certain number of hours of informational children's programming each week. But with the ascension of the Reagan administration, the FCC relinquished all responsibility for quality television programming, deregulating the industry entirely. By 1984, even the directives limiting advertising and host-selling in children's programming had disappeared. By 1990, afternoon TV fare had become consistently inappropriate for children. As psychologists Lynette Friedrich Cofer and Robin Smith Jacobvitz pointed out in a 1991 article, "Television offers our children increasingly frightening and distorted views of a violent, hedonistic, sex-crazed world at a time when many parents are simply not at home.[13] In the past few years even the sacred "family hour" between 8:00 and 9:00 P.M. has been invaded by such "adult" subject matter.[14]

Since the mid-1980s even the quality of children's programming has declined precipitously. Public television—once the unassailable standard of educational programming—today offers what can at best be described as "edutainment," a form of children's programming (epitomized by *Sesame Street*) that invariably sacrifices weightier pedagogical content to entertainment aims.

A 1995 study conducted by the Florida Pre-school PTA revealed that only two out of every 168 broadcast hours on the four major networks were dedicated to educational programming, even after stepped-up public and FCC pressure since 1993.[15] And while TV watching declined precipitously among children ages two to eleven in the decade between 1984 and 1994—about five hours a week, from twenty-six to twenty-one hours a week—the quality of TV programs directed at children hardly improved. The *Christian Science Monitor* reported in June 1995 that children witness an average of at least twenty acts of violence per hour on children's programs, far more than adults see during prime time.[16]

There have been glimpses of light in this otherwise gloomy picture. One was the reinstitution in 1991 of regulations on commercial time during children's programming, prohibitions against host-selling and program-length commercials, and a resolution to ask broadcasters to enumerate their efforts at educational programming periodically. Finally, in the summer of 1996, the FCC and television broadcasters came to an agreement regarding the provision of at least three hours of children's educational programming per week. These measures were the fruit of years of parent activism, mainly on the part of a Massachusetts-based organization called Action for Children's Television.

In 1992, Congress sought to limit "indecent" material on radio and television (material that, according to FCC regulations, "depicts or describes in terms patently offensive as measured by contemporary community standards for the broadcast medium sexual or excretory activities or organs") to the late-night and early-morning hours. That law has faced a host of legal challenges, but was upheld in a Supreme Court decision of January 1996.[17] It remains to be seen what its parameters will eventually be, but it defines "indecency" so narrowly that it may ultimately not provide an adequate instrument for forcing afternoon and prime-time TV to improve its fare.

Finally, there was the famous V-chip legislation of 1996, which came with accompanying pressure on the broadcast industry to develop a rating system that could equip parents to block reception of shows they consider too violent or provocative for their children. Many parents I have talked to certainly appreciate and to some extent depend on film ratings in making decisions about which movies to allow their children to see. On the other hand, the introduction of ratings in the movie industry in the late 1960s made possible a decades-long descent into gratuitous vulgarity from which the film industry has only recently begun to emerge. The major studios are finally attending to what film critic Michael Medved had been trying to tell them all along: that family films bring in the bucks, and that a larger selection of G and PG fare would eventually make for an economically healthier industry.[18] (One Hollywood watchdog group, the Christian Film and Television Commission, claims that in 1994, 40 percent of the films produced by the larger studios could be considered appropriate for child viewing, up from 32 percent in 1993.[19]

If the television industry takes as long to accede to the milder tastes of the family audience as the movie industry did after ratings appeared, we are in trouble. Perhaps it won't take as long, if advertisers shy away from prime-time and afternoon programming labeled unfit for children.

But all in all, V-chips and ratings seem to be beside the point for parents. In the first place, parents are unlikely to be able to block undesirable programming from junior hackers left alone with the TV set afternoons and early evenings. In the second place, pressed for money and time, parents are more reliant on television than they ever have been, not only for entertainment but for information; V-chips and ratings won't satisfy their yearning for tasteful and informative programming—not only for their children but for themselves.

What, then, is to be done about television? Only tougher decency standards and other regulations designed to counteract the irresponsibility of the broadcast industry will. A certain number of hours must be set aside for serious, in-depth news reporting and high-quality cultural programming directed at family audiences. Certain practices—such as using news stories involving crime and violence as teasers for made-for-TV dramas—should be prohibited entirely. A certain amount of news programming time should be set aside for hard news. Finally, commercial time must be restricted not only for children's programming but for all daytime and prime-time programs that are targeted at a family audience.

As we have seen, the television industry is not the only entertainment medium in sore need of regulation. Standards of decency have veritably dissolved in music, in video games, in print media (including advertising), and on the Internet. In the recording and video game industries as in print media, ratings would clearly help, as would legally restricting sales of recordings, video games, and magazines bearing the equivalent of R and X ratings in the same way access to films bearing these ratings is restricted.

The Internet poses a more complicated picture. Curiously, when it passed the Communications Decency Act in February of 1996, Congress attempted to do for the Internet what it has refrained from doing for any other entertainment medium: to prohibit the output of "indecent" material altogether. Here, however, the First Amendment legal challenges to the act have so far been upheld in the courts. While on-line services have begun to offer information and software to parents that will enable them to keep their kids off inappropriate Web sites, the problem remains the same here as with television: how to keep technologically sophisticated kids from getting around the system. All in all, transmission of obscenity and junk is rampant on the Word Wide Web. Indeed, the overall quality of cyberspace offerings makes an Internet browse something akin to searching a trash can for valuables.

One way of making sure that the media as a whole does enough of what it should do, and less of what it is doing, may be to penalize broadcasters and production companies if more than, say, half of their output fails to meet PG standards of quality and decency, or if they consistently fail to adhere to quality-programming obligations. (It should be noted that the FCC already—at least theoretically—imposes fines on licensees who abuse current FCC prohibitions and regulations.) Penalties could take the form of an "obscenity tax" skimmed from companies' profits and used to support art, music, and sports programs in inner-city schools and juvenile rehabilitation facilities.

Education Reform

Millions of schoolchildren live in constant fear of attack by their peers on or near school grounds. The first business in any discussion of school reform is to make public schools safe.

A recent Supreme Court decision that challenged the Gun-Free School Zones Act of 1990 (a law that declared it a federal offense to carry a gun within a thousand feet of a public school) may have represented a blow to school safety, but solving the problem requires more than weapons bans or gun control. Clear disciplinary policies and curricular reform are the ultimate answers to violence in the schools. And curricular reform must be directed—to use former Secretary of Education William J. Bennett's phrase—toward "The Three C's: Content, Character, and Choice."

In March 1995, I appeared on the *Donahue* show to talk about my research on the failures of comprehensive sex education. When the subject turned to condom distribution, one of the other panel members referred to it as a "racist policy, since most schools engaged in this practice are in inner-city neighborhoods." A young black woman in the audience rose to defend this assertion. "They aren't putting the money in black schools for education," she declared. And "because the money isn't there, the attitude is, 'Give 'em a condom!' " This woman may have been wrong about the monetary resources allotted to urban schools, where, studies have shown, ample funding is often squandered by bloated bureaucracies, but her main point—that inner-city kids are getting condoms as substitutes for decent educations—was right on target. If we want our youth, particularly our poor inner-city youth, to sublimate their adolescent impulses, we have to give them something to sublimate with: literature, physics, calculus, and a decent arts education. Padding school days with "gut" courses in sex, drug, and death education, with human relations classes, sensitivity training, conflict mediation, and other failed exercises in social experimentation has not only proven to be a destructive influence on children; it robs them of what they need most: academic time and intellectual challenge.

Does that mean there should be no behavioral education in the schools? Of course not. But the number of social programs should be drastically reduced, and their moral tenor fundamentally changed. Schools must abandon invasive therapeutic techniques and bolster character development by setting unambiguous normative standards of behavior.

Reenfranchising parents in the educational process and reempowering them in educational policy-making will prove the most crucial steps in restoring public trust in public education. Any school reform that does not involve grassroots input and support from parents is bound to fail. The top-down reform strategy now being pursued by the Department of Education for its Goals 2000 project and its empty resolve to "promote" and "develop" parents' commitment to education will not win them over.[20] Parents *are* committed, but not to the kind of education that Washington promotes—not to education designed to dumb down curriculum, level children's accomplishments, and obscure their capacity for moral judgment. The business of "connecting families, schools and communities," which Secretary of Education Richard Riley repeatedly swore was among his first priorities between 1992 and 1996, will only work when Washington releases its monopoly on national educational policy-making, when it breaks the National Education Association's stranglehold on school reform attempts, and most of all when the entrenched educational bureaucracies at the national and state levels start listening to parents.

Meanwhile, American parents are hard at work on real reform. They have already begun the push to restructure educational options: forming charter schools, instigating and supporting school-choice legislation, and getting their legislative representatives to consider easing federal and state mandates that force unwieldy, expensive, and ineffective social programs on schools increasingly squeezed for academic time and resources.

Some of the sacred cows of educational experimentation in the past thirty years may soon disappear. For example, Congress is reconsidering its mandates for and funding of bilingual programs—this owing not the least to recent public outcry by Hispanic parents who claim their children have been forced into bilingual programs and denied the opportunity to develop English language proficiency.[21] California is one of several states that are reevaluating whole language reading and writing instruction and reintroducing phonics.[22]

At the March 1996 educational summit sponsored by the National Governors Association and IBM, there were signs that politicians, too, are beginning to rethink educational priorities. A tacit agreement was struck between the President and the governors to diminish the federal role in educational policy-making and to refocus state educational standards on academic rather than social aims. IBM CEO Louis V. Gerstner Jr. reminded the assembled politicians and educators that instruction in the basics, not technology, is the sine qua non of a functioning public school system. Send us people who can read and write, add and subtract, was his message, and we will teach them to use computers.[23]

In a number of states and cities, politicians and educrats are grudgingly beginning to accept parent-inspired school reforms. After the defeat of the educational-voucher initiative in 1994, California's Department of Education came out in support of an eleventh-hour plan for district-wide public school choice. As a result of a large-scale public "home rule" campaign for schools, Texas's Department of Education will be forced to accept a recently rewritten legislative bill that allows significant decentralization in school administration. In a number of cases, affluent communities in outlying urban areas have seceded or are considering seceding from urban governments whose bloated education budgets and slack educational services are targets of growing irritation. In Los Angeles, for example, the communities of Carson, Lomita, and Rancho Palos Verdes have all launched bids for independent incorporation on this basis.[24]

Parent-driven school reform and parent-responsive schools are not a wild dream; they are a possibility Americans are already painstakingly turning into reality. The question is: Will the federal government, the teachers' unions, and the entrenched educational bureaucracy relinquish power over educational policy to state and local control? Will state capitals, in setting higher academic goals for schools and ways of measuring progress toward those goals, solicit the input and involvement of local parents? Will the government and teachers unions, in short, return the schools to their clients, allowing parents to lead the way in revamping the public school system?

Child Welfare Reform

At present, a quarter of a million children whose birth parents have never abused or neglected them are trapped in foster care. Another quarter of a million abused or abandoned children who desperately want and need permanent families are shuttled from foster home to foster home, essentially warehoused by the foster care system for what they can draw in federal monies. About 700,000 families each year are put through wrenching and unnecessary child welfare investigations. Hundreds of thousands of parents each year are falsely or arbitrarily convicted of meaningless offenses and entered in state child abuse registries, their reputations ruined and their confidence in themselves as parents shattered. Thousands of innocent parents and children each year are subjected to quack psychological treatments and evaluations. Children are routinely strip-searched, homes invaded without legal warrant.

A first step in reforming the child-protective system so that it truly works to ensure children's well-being and to protect families would be to tighten everywhere legal definitions of child abuse and neglect. (The September 1996 reauthorization of the Mondale Act contains useful changes in language in this regard and can serve as a model for state legislative reform. The act goes so far as to restore liability for malicious child maltreatment reports, and to require states to establish citizen review panels to examine CPS agency procedures and activities; it further directs the Department of Health and Human Services to research the extent to which frivolous reports of child maltreatment have led to unnecessary child removal, or have endangered abused children. Still to be done: reducing Child Protective Services worker immunities to legal challenges, reviewing CPS therapeutic practices, restoring liability for bogus reporting, rejecting anonymous reports of child abuse and neglect, ending report solicitation in the broadcasting and print media, and conforming investigative and court procedures in child welfare cases to the due process standards of the criminal justice system. With respect to the foster care system, the CAPTA reauthorization allows states to terminate parental rights in cases in which a parent has been convicted of murder, voluntary manslaughter, or felony assault against one of his children. It also requires states to put into place procedures for quickly terminating parental rights in cases of abandonment. But Congress might consider enacting a federal law requiring CPS agencies to refer children for adoption within a year of legal termination of parental rights. Placing a time cap on federal foster care funds for adoptable children would also create an incentive to place children expeditiously into some of the more than 1 million families ready and willing to adopt. (Thankfully, President Clinton recently expressed an interest in moving kids from foster care to adoption, but as this manuscript goes to press he has not yet unveiled a concrete plan.) At any rate, the foregoing suggestions for reform would not only relieve decent families from the terrors of unwarranted government intrusion, but would most importantly focus child-protective resources and policies in ways most beneficial to the suffering children who need CPS most.

Family Law Reform

Parents are desperate for the kind of legal reform which will protect the family unit from the ravages of an increasingly rights-and litigation-oriented legal culture that shows little regard for the family's integrity. One of the chief evils of the family-hostile culture parents identify is divorce. Parents are convinced that broken homes too often mean broken children, broken communities, and broken futures. They would appreciate reform measures that would protect parents and children from the economic and emotional ravages of unilateral divorce and post-divorce custody litigation.

Critics of no-fault divorce have long lamented the fact that it is easier in our society to abandon a spouse of twenty years than it is to fire an employee of twenty weeks. Maggie Gallagher, author of *The Abolition of Marriage: How We Destroy Lasting Love*, sums up the peculiar legal status of marriages by asking in a recent *New York Times* opinion piece, "What would happen if courts treated business contracts as they now treat the marriage contract? What if our courts refused to enforce contracts and instead systematically favored the party that wished to withdraw, on the grounds that finding fault was messy, irrelevant and acrimonious?"[25]

Divorce reform has only just begun to get off the ground. The states of Washington and Michigan, unfortunately, have already rejected a proposal to end unilateral divorce on demand. But other states have yet to pass judgment on repealing no-fault legislation. David Blankenhorn notes that if they do, "these changes would eliminate the capriciousness of the current system and send a much healthier message to current and prospective couples. . . . When you say 'I do,' you are making a legally serious commitment. Society cares whether or not your marriage lasts."[26]

Adoption law is another area of family law where reform is imperative. Meaningful adoption law reform, however, has to emphasize family integrity and the inviolate nature of the day-to-day bonding process between children and parents and siblings.

In 1996 Congress took a positive step toward adoption law reform when it denied federal funding to adoption agencies that discriminate against interracial adoptions. It also passed a $5,000 adoption tax credit and a tax exemption on $5,000 of employee benefits for adoption expenses. (Adoption is an expensive process, costing the average family between $5,000 and $10,000.) These changes could constitute a huge step toward getting children out of foster care and into the between 1 and 2 million homes in America that are prepared to take them.[27]

In the summer of 1994, a convention of the National Commission on Uniform State Laws gave the go-ahead to a Uniform Adoption Act, aimed at conforming adoption legislation in all fifty states. Among the act's recommendations: Adoption cannot occur without a government-approved agency first evaluating a prospective home, and cannot be delayed for reasons of a child's race or ethnicity. Any agency or person arranging an adoption must provide the court with a complete social and medical history of the prospective parents. Most important, the act proposed to limit the time within which a birth parent may change his or her mind about giving up a child to eight days after placement. Adoptions after this "bright line" period would be irrevocable, and post-adoption birth parent searches would be limited to mutual consent registries. So far, the UAA is being passed around for consideration by state legislatures, who will eventually have the option of rejecting it altogether or tailoring it as they please. A show of public support on the UAA would go a long way toward helping to end cases like Baby Jessica's and Baby Richard's.

The most crucial item on the legal reform agenda of parents, however, is certainly the issue of increasing legal encroachments on parental authority over children's upbringing. Here again, help for parents may be emerging, in the form of the grassroots movement Of the People. This nonpartisan Virginia-based organization has since 1993 devoted itself to introducing a Parental Rights Amendment to the Constitution. It reads, "The right of parents to direct the upbringing and education of their children shall not be infringed." The organization's leaders believe that only by introducing a constitutional amendment can authority and responsibility for child-rearing—a basic and implicit right that was common sense at the time of the Founding Fathers—be "transferred from government back to families." The "real argument," Of the People spokesmen write,

> is between those who think parenting is an optional feature of society, replaceable by state institutions, and those who believe active parenting is the single biggest contributor to family health and therefore needs to be strongly encouraged by society. The parental rights debate boils down to this question: Who should decide what's in the best interests of children? The parents or the government?[28]

In February 1995, Of the People commissioned the Luntz research company to survey one thousand registered voters on the Parental Rights Amendment; 74 percent of them registered their support for the amendment as it reads, with no apparent distinction by party affiliation, gender, race, education, marital status, age, or geographic region. Yet, despite indications of broad public approval for the amendment, the amendment's supporters have had a rough time in state legislatures and at the polls. Child welfare advocates have claimed that child-abusing parents might be able to exploit it. The National Abortion and Reproductive Rights Action League has warned that it poses a threat to teenagers' "reproductive rights." The American Bar Association's Center on Children and the Law sees it as a threat to children's "having a voice in litigation."[29] Needless to say, teachers unions are against it because of its implications for public education: that parents will once again have a say in what is taught in the schools.

Greg Erken, Of the People's executive director, argues that such opposition exposes a deep-seated, elitist distrust of parents on the part of "entrenched special interests." He adds:

> While the Parental Rights Amendment provides a general right to raise one's child, this right is not absolute. The rights to free speech and religious freedom set forth in the Bill of Rights have their limits. So do parental rights. Critics who cite tragic cases of abuse as grounds for opposing the Parental Rights Amendment ignore the fact that a child's most important right is to have an actively involved, loving parent to protect that child's interests. . . . Parents are getting a mixed message: While leaders from the left and the right call for more parental responsibility, our laws continue to ignore parental rights.

One of the reasons many parents today fail to act responsibly, Erken notes, is that government and professional interventions in their child-rearing work has caused them a profound crisis of confidence. A Parental Rights Amendment, he believes, would "send a message . . . that at the same time the rights of parents must be honored, their responsibilities must be fulfilled." Moreover, Erken writes, "when their rights are respected, parents naturally will become more involved and more confident in exercising their responsibility."[30]

Ralph Benko, president of Of the People, hopes that the proposed amendment will provide a "banner" behind which disenfranchised parents can march. And although he is not sanguine about the amendment's hopes for passage in the immediate future, he compares it to the proposed Equal Rights Amendment, which, while it did not pass, "had an enormous impact on the way we view the position of women in society, by bringing to open, public debate many issues of discrimination that had never been addressed before."[31]

Of the People may be the best thing that has happened to parents in the past thirty years, with its clear mission, concise platform, and ability to provide an umbrella for the disparate issues that frustrate parents. Yet many legal thinkers, among them Milton Regan, Mary Ann Glendon, Walter Olson, and Joan G. Wexler, warn in so many words against the trap of "rights talk" in seeking to ameliorate contemporary defects of family law. They insist that if the law is ever to function properly in the interests of families and children, legal advocacy for families must be released from the trap of rights-mongering. Our legal image of family life must be metamorphosed from one depicting a battle among individuals to one depicting a commonality of purpose. Our family law statutes must be modified in ways that will once again obligate the courts to preserve and support the sacred and indispensable ties that bind parents to each other and to their children.

Unfortunately, the very existence of a movement that presses for "parental rights" may indeed aggravate the tendency of the courts to indulge in the kind of "rights-balancing" decisions that tear families apart and destabilize them as a child-rearing institution. The family is not just *any* social unit; it is an exceptional social unit of particular and indispensable social value in its child-rearing function, and our legal system must reaffirm that value.

Family-Based, Family-Supportive Community Revival

"Nobody sensible can sincerely believe anymore," responded National Parenting Association president Sylvia Hewlett, when asked about her recent work as an advocate for parent-driven, community responses to youth violence, "that professionals can take over family functions."[32]

> The most massive professional interventions, the armies of social workers and therapists we've sent into schools and neighborhoods . . . have achieved nothing more than a holding action on childhood distress. When we look at the rise in teenage crime alone, we are forced to admit we are not stemming failure. . . . We are just locking it up in jail cells.

What Hewlett describes as an emerging "rediscovery of parents" as essential players in children's well-being has been a hard-earned lesson for our nation. We pay its price daily in the senseless spilling of young blood in our schools and in our streets, and we will continue to pay it until every parent, educator, social worker, politician, and child-rearing expert finally acknowledges that engaged parenting is essential to the welfare and healthy development of children.

In Hewlett's view, there are no alternatives for alleviating the distress that has turned so many American neighborhoods into graveyards for children. Parents and professionals have to sit down together for the purpose of "distilling a blueprint of action" that maximizes family time, supports engaged and confident parenting, and tackles the chaos and disorder in schools and neighborhoods.

Hewlett's organization has a broad national agenda that addresses such disparate issues as gun control, reconnecting men with children in inner cities, and formulating family-friendly work policies such as parenting leave and flex-time. But real and lasting change, Hewlett believes, lies in creating community-based, community-sensitive organizations that appeal to local parents and provide them with a secure place at the policy-making table. In the three years since she founded the National Parenting Association, Hewlett has brought parents together with corporate management, educators, and social service professionals in two such programs—in St. Paul, Minnesota, and New York City—designed to tackle issues of national concern, such as youth violence and work-family conflicts, on the local level. She hopes they will serve as models for communities throughout the nation.

Hewlett is unusual among family advocates in that although she acknowledges the failures of bureaucratic child-rearing, she believes that the answer is not to draw battle lines between parents and professionals but to cultivate a dialogue between them. Hers is certainly the most hopeful vision that I know, and the efforts of her organization are perhaps the most interesting and ambitious of which I am aware.

But the National Parenting Association is still young, small, and focused, with a membership of fewer than twenty thousand. Many of its parent members are recruited with the help of the professional and corporate leadership. Thus, the marriage it has created between parents and "experts" is something of an arranged one, and still in its honeymoon. It remains to be seen whether the union will prove happy or fruitful. At this point, the child-rearing philosophies of most parents and professionals are far apart. Professionals are so well organized—and parents so overburdened and disillusioned with the culture child-rearing professionals have created—that both parties may quickly lose interest in dialogue.

On both sides, some bad faith is justified. In the past thirty years, professionals have watched as more and more parents have become self-obsessed, cursory in their dedication to maintaining close family ties and to the task of rearing and supporting their children. But well-meaning and devoted parents are still in the majority, and the glaring dichotomy between the public and private behaviors of child-rearing professionals does not escape them. They see teachers withdraw their own children from the public school systems. They see the media moguls and celebrities who glorify violence and sexual degradation retreat behind guarded fortresses to raise their families. They know that the judges who rip children from loving homes may go home at night to enjoy their own children. They understand that the politicians and pundits who extol the virtues of social service intervention, institutional child care, "affective" education, and working mothers are largely insulated from the destructive consequences of bureaucratic child-rearing.

I have mentioned my disappointment that few parents could think of anything government and policy-makers could do for families and children. Most do not even dream of participating in a dialogue with government and professionals on the future of our children. They implicitly define the primary issue facing families as Thomas Sowell does when he writes of school condom distribution policies:

> If someone came into your yard and ripped up your geraniums, replacing them with daffodils, you wouldn't debate the relative merits of geraniums and daffodils. You would tell them to get out of your yard. Once you start debating the relative merits of geraniums and daffodils, you have already given up the central issue: Whose yard is this? Similarly, the issue is not whether schools should teach sexual abstinence or hand out condoms. The issue is: Whose children are these?[33]

Whose children are these? Until that issue is settled, the hope for dialogue between parents and the professional elites who dominate government policy-making is a vain hope. Until that issue is settled, any compromise with the family-hostile culture may be a compromise of love, liberty, and the future of our nation's children.

Parents know this. To describe the New Familism, that counterculture of family life fast emerging in our nation, is to describe a culture of no-compromise, a culture whose primary message could be depicted by a "Keep Out!" sign. It is to describe a counterculture of retreat, of protest, and occasionally of open revolt. It is to describe the increasing phenomenon of parents raising children in what they clearly recognize as daily acts of political defiance and social and institutional subversion.

Like that African-American mother who declared, "I would rather be locked up for keeping my child on the straight and narrow than be locked up for not doing it," an ever-growing number of American parents realize that the enemies of children's well-being are well entrenched, and that parents have no choice but to take their positions, come what may.

Only a very few politicians and social policy thinkers appreciate the seriousness of this standoff between government and professional elites and the parents of our future citizenry. One of them is Senator Dan Coats of Indiana, whose Project for American Renewal consists of a series of proposed legislative acts (many of them discussed earlier in this chapter) geared toward empowering trusted, grassroots community institutions to tackle the great social challenges before us. Coats's proposals all involve creating government incentives for programs designed to strengthen and support families as the basis of civil society—especially where families are suffering most, in poor urban neighborhoods. Among them are financial incentives to promote traditional character education in the public schools; to allow churches to "adopt" needy families and nonviolent criminal offenders; to help poor families build financial assets and choose the schools where they send their children; to extend malpractice coverage to health professionals who provide free or low-cost medical services in poor communities; to combat teenage pregnancy with abstinence education; to provide shelter to young single mothers; to arrange for care of abused and neglected children by relatives, when possible; to improve neighborhood security via citizen watches and patrols; and to set aside some public housing for married couples. As I complete this book, four of the sixteen pieces of legislation in the Project for American Renewal have already become law: the Medical Volunteer Act, the Assets for Independence Act, the Adoption Assistance Act, and the Kinship Care Act.

The Project remains a mammoth agenda, its general direction aptly described by William Bennett, who observes, "As government has gotten bigger, it has taken over the work of, and had an enervating effect on the character-forming institutions of families, schools, churches and voluntary associations. And that, in turn, has (a) hurt the cause of self-government and (b) turned many citizens into part-time, de facto wards of a 'nanny state.' That includes, by the way, the middle and upper-middle class and not simply the underclass."[34]

We know that parents think the dismantling of the "nanny state" is long overdue. But if that dismantling does not come, or if it is tentative, parents will continue to become an ever angrier, more marginalized, more disaffected minority, seeking escape in any way possible from social and cultural institutions they no longer trust. Eventually they will deny those institutions their most precious resource—the next generation of civilized young men and women. If that dismantling is real and effective, however, parents can offer us more than we deserve, as a nation, to hope for—namely, redemption from the barbarism which presently engulfs us.

Notes

Introduction: The Family-Hating Culture

1. Statistics on juvenile crime and arrests are taken from U.S. Department of Justice statistics cited in Barbara Kantrowitz et al., "Teen Violence: Wild in the Streets," *Newsweek*, August 2, 1993, pp. 43, 45. A *Time* report of August 23, 1993, notes that "between 1986 and 1991, murders committed by teens ages 14 to 17 grew by 124%." (Nancy Gibbs, "Laying Down the Law," *Time*, August 23, 1993, p. 25.) On youth, weapons, and crime see also William J. Bennett, *The Index of Leading Cultural Indicators* (New York: Touchstone, 1994), pp. 29–33.

2. For the best rapid overview of teenage crime, pregnancy, and SAT scores, see Bennett, *The Index of Leading Cultural Indicators*, pp. 27–33, 72–77, and 82–85 respectively. On SAT verbal score declines among the brightest students, see Richard J. Herrnstein and Charles Murray, *The Bell Curve: Intelligence and Class Structure in American Life* (New York: Free Press, 1994), pp. 427–29. One interesting, albeit nonstatistical, study of increasing psychopathological behavior among children is Dr. Ken Magid and Carole A. McKelvey's 1987 book, *High Risk: Children Without a Conscience* (Golden, Colo.: M & M, 1987; New York: Bantam, 1989).

3. Several important longitudinal studies have traced the relationship between single parenthood and wayward child outcomes. Among them is a thirty-year study of five thousand British children, all born in March 1936, which noted that children raised in broken families were more vulnerable to delinquency. (See M. E. Wadsworth, *Roots of Delinquency* [New York: Barnes & Noble, 1979].) A Johns Hopkins University ten-year assessment of poor, inner-city black children conducted in the 1970s also found a connection between family structure, emotional problems, and delinquency. (See Sheppard Kellam et al. "Family Structure and the Mental Health of Children," *Archives of General Psychiatry*, Vol. 34, 1977, pp. 1012–22; and Margaret Ensminger et al., "School and Family Origins of Delinquency: Comparisons by Sex," in Katherine T. Van Dusen and Sarnoff A. Mednick, eds., *Prospective Studies of Crime and Delinquency*,

[Boston: Kluwer-Nijhoff, 1983].) The most telling study connection between family structure and childhood suffering and delinquency, however, came out in a comprehensive survey of sixty thousand children across the country conducted in 1988 by the U.S. Department of Health and Human Services. This study involved a look at children from varying family structures and economic environments. The findings were unambiguous. Except in very prosperous households, it seemed that children raised in single-parent homes were two times as likely to have emotional and behavioral problems. (See Deborah A. Dawson, "Family Structure and Children's Health; United States, 1988," *Vital and Health Statistics*, Series 10, No. 178, June 1991.) For a useful summary of all the above-mentioned research, see James Q. Wilson, "The Family Values Debate," *Commentary*, April 1993, pp. 24–31.

4. See Eleanor Clift, "The Murphy Brown Policy," *Newsweek*, June 1, 1992, p. 46; and Farai Chideya et al., "Endangered Family," *Newsweek*, August 30, 1993, p. 17, respectively.

5. I have talked to parents individually and in focus groups in the Baltimore, New York, New Jersey, and Cape Cod areas, in Texas, in northern California, and in many towns in Connecticut. My colleagues at the Institute for American Values, David Blankenhorn and Barbara Dafoe Whitehead, have enabled me to glean the fruits of their focus group interviews with parents in Ohio, New Jersey, and Mississippi. The mothers and fathers we have spoken to have in most cases been married and middle-income (typically, their annual household income lies between $25,000 and $60,000; they have at least one child between the ages of five and eighteen living at home; and they tend to proportionally reflect the ethnic and racial demographic profile of the area in which they live.

6. See Frank Furstenberg, "How Families Manage Risk and Opportunity in Dangerous Neighborhoods," American Sociological Association paper, 1991; and Farai Chideya and Malcolm Jones Jr., "Struck in Solitary, or, Still Life with Mom," *Newsweek*, August 30, 1993.

7. Some of the most powerful social critiques of the postwar period have recognized the phenomenon of the bureaucratization of child-rearing and the ensuing attenuation of family intimacy and parent-child bonds. Among these are Jules Henry's 1963 work, *Culture Against Man* (New York: Vintage) and two works of the 1970s by Christopher Lasch: *The Culture of Narcissism: American Life in an Age of Diminishing Expectations* (New York: Norton, 1978) and *Haven in a Heartless World: The Family Beseiged* (New York: Basic Books, 1977).

8. See Sylvia Ann Hewlett, *When the Bough Breaks: The Cost of Neglecting Our Children* (New York: HarperCollins, 1991); Arlie Hochschild (with Anne Machung), *The Second Shift* (New York: Avon, 1990); and Hillary Rodham Clinton, *It Takes a Village and Other Lessons Children Teach Us* (New York: Simon & Schuster, 1996).

PART I: CULTURE AGAINST THE FAMILY

Chapter 1: The Parent as Pariah

1. Susan Forward with Craig Buck, *Toxic Parents* (New York: Bantam, 1989).
2. Ibid., p. 97.
3. Claudette Wassil-Grimm, *How to Avoid Your Parents' Mistakes When You Raise Your Children* (New York: Simon & Schuster, 1990).

4. Laurie Ashner and Mitch Meyerson, *When Parents Love Too Much* (New York: Avon, 1990).

5. Patricia Love (with Jo Robinson), *The Emotional Incest Syndrome: What to Do When a Parent's Love Rules Your Life* (New York: Bantam, 1990).

6. Child fatality rates from parental abuse or neglect in 1991 were 2.15 per 100,000, up from 1.4 per 100,000 in 1985. Incidentally, these are rates compiled on 74.7 percent of the U.S. population under the age of eighteen. In comparison to child deaths of abuse or neglect, child homicide rates are far higher. For example, according to the National Center on Health Statistics, the rate of homicides of children under the age of one in 1988 was 8.2 per 100,000. See Deborah Daro, D.S.W., Director, and Karen McCurdy, M.A., Principal Analyst, *Current Trends in Child Abuse Reporting and Fatalities: The Results of the 1991 Annual Fifty-State Survey*, Working Paper No. 208 (The National Center on Child Abuse Prevention Research, April 1992).

7. Richard Wexler recounts the first two of these stories in his 1990 work, *Wounded Innocents: The Real Victims in the War Against Child Abuse* (Buffalo, NY: Prometheus Books, 1990), pp. 117 and 103–5, respectively. The third, of which I will speak at length in Chapter 3, was recounted in Elena Neuman, "Child Welfare or Family Trauma?," *Insight*, May 9, 1994, p. 6.

8. During the early part of this century, American research in child psychology concentrated heavily on longitudinal studies of physical and intellectual growth in childhood. Most of these studies ignored the impact of environmental factors in individual personality development.

9. Benjamin Spock, *Baby and Child Care*, reprint (London: Star Books, 1983), p. 441.

10. Rudolf Dreikurs, M.D., *The Challenge of Parenthood* (New York: Plume/Penguin, 1992), pp. 17–18. This work, which Dreikurs himself described as "a book on education based on the application of democratic principles," was actually written in Austria during the 1930s, in part as a political protest against the rising fascist movement. With the coming of fascism to Austria, he sought a first publisher in Holland. His ideas enjoyed enormous influence in this country in the 1950s, and Dreikurs himself considered the United States, with its democratic tradition, the most fruitful soil for his new theories of child-rearing.

11. Haim Ginott, *Between Parent and Child*, reprint (New York: Macmillan, 1965; New York: Avon, 1969); Haim Ginott, *Between Parent and Teenager* (New York: Macmillan, 1969).

12. Thomas Gordon, *P.E.T. Parent Effectiveness Training* (New York: Penguin, 1970).

13. Spock, *Baby and Child Care*, p. 12–18.

14. Dreikurs, *The Challenge of Parenthood*, Preface, p. V.

15. Ibid., pp. 94a, 94c.

16. Gordon, *P.E.T. Parent Effectiveness Training*, p. 263.

17. Ibid., p. 272.

18. Ginott, *Between Parent and Teenager*, p. 20.

19. Dr. James Dobson noted these in his apology for traditional parenting, *Dare to Discipline* (Wheaton, IL: Tyndale Publishers, 1970).

20. Lee Canter with Marlene Canter, *Assertive Discipline for Parents* (New York: Harper and Row, 1988), p. 4.

21. Dorothy Rich, *Megaskills: How Families Can Help Children Succeed in School and Beyond* (New York: Houghton Mifflin, 1988).

22. James Windell, *Discipline: A Sourcebook of Fifty Failsafe Techniques for Parents* (New York: Collier/Macmillan, 1991), p. 141.

23. Alice Miller, *For Your Own Good: Hidden Cruelty in Child-Rearing and the Roots of Violence*, tr. Hildegarde Hannum and Hunter Hannum (New York: Noonday Press, 1983); and *Thou Shalt Not Be Aware: Society's Betrayal of the Child* (New York: Meridian/Penguin, 1984).

24. Miller, *For Your Own Good*, p. 97.

25. Ibid., p. 106.

26. Ibid., p. 249.

27. Ibid., p. 106.

28. Ibid., p. 153.

29. Ibid., p. 168. For Miller's assessment of Hitler's father and the effect of their relationship on the boy's personality development, see pp. 147–80.

30. Ibid., p. 170.

31. Ibid., p. 188.

32. Ibid., p. 195.

33. Ibid., p. 187. Miller's accusations of widespread cruelty in German child-rearing is not to be trusted as empirically verifiable. Among Europeans, Germans seem to enjoy a reputation for indulgence—especially with small children, a fact that might explain Freud's fascination with the intense creativity and willfulness of early childhood.

34. Ibid., p. 146.

35. Ibid., pp. 204–5.

36. Ibid., p. 242.

37. Miller, *Thou Shalt Not Be Aware*, p. 307.

38. Quoted in Christopher Lasch, *Haven in a Heartless World: The Family Beseiged* (New York: Basic Books, 1977) p. 14.

39. For a summary of these famous experiments, undertaken by Lewin in conjunction with Ronald Lippett and Ralph White, see Alfred J. Marrow, *The Practical Theorist: The Life and Work of Kurt Lewin* (New York: Basic Books, 1969), pp. 123–28. Lewin was a seminal figure in the development of social and industrial psychology.

40. For a thorough discussion on the negative perspective of social reformers, academics, and professionals on traditional family life, especially what they considered the propensity of family life to undermine a democratic world view, see Lasch, *Haven in a Heartless World*.

41. Sidney E. Goldstein, "Aims and Objectives of the National Conference," *Marriage and Family Living* 8 (1946), pp. 57–58, quoted in Lasch, *Haven in a Heartless World*, p. 208. For a thorough discussion of the influence of the Frankfurt School's work on the family on American academia see Lasch, *Haven in a Heartless World*, pp. 85–93. Lasch's work is still the most comprehensive elucidation we have of the nearly universal hostility twentieth-century American academics and professionals have shown to family life.

42. Here again, see Lasch, *Haven in a Heartless World*, especially Chapters 6 and 7.

43. John Bradshaw, *Bradshaw on: The Family* (Deerfield Beach, FL: Health Communications, 1988), p. 19.

44. Ibid., p. 20.

45. J. Patrick Gannon, Ph.D., *Soul Survivors: A New Beginning for Adults Abused as Children* (New York: Prentice-Hall/Simon & Schuster, 1989), p. xiv.

46. Bradshaw, *Bradshaw on: The Family*, p. 100.

47. Gannon, *Soul Survivors*, p. 32.

48. Forward with Buck, *Toxic Parents*, p. 143.

49. See Michael P. Yapko, *Suggestions of Abuse* (New York: Simon & Schuster, 1994).

50. "Child Abuse and Teen Sexual Assault: What Your PTA Can Do" (Chicago: The National PTA, 1992), p. 2.

51. Anita Diamant, "Rethinking the Concept of the Dysfunctional Family," *Boston Globe*, September 7, 1992, p. 42.

52. Ibid., p. 43.

53. Eibhlin O'Solomon, "Suicide: Are Your Kids at Risk?," *Parent Guide*, December 1992, p. 18.

54. "Hotline and Shelter for Kids in Crisis," *Wilton Bulletin*, December 29, 1992, p. A1.

55. Neil Gilbert, "Teaching Children to Prevent Sexual Abuse," *The Public Interest*, Fall 1988, pp. 3–15. Gilbert investigated five commonly used sexual abuse prevention curricula and found that only one posited a difference between spanking and sexually assaultive behavior, or "bad touches." In one preschool sexual abuse prevention curriculum ("Red Flag/Green Flag") Gilbert notes that " 'yucky' kisses, tight hugs and spankings are put into the same 'Red Flag' category as incest, genital fondling and other forms of sexual abuse. At several points the curriculum guide reminds teachers to emphasize 'that it is how the person receiving the touch feels that makes it a Red Flag or Green Flag touch.' When children feel they have received a 'Red Flag' touch they are instructed to tell their parents, a police officer, or their teacher" (p. 9).

56. A number of parent surveys find that spanking is still a very widely practiced method of punishment. In a study encompassing 204 New York mothers—both well-to-do and poor—by Dr. Rebecca R. S. Socolar, clinical assistant professor of pediatrics at the University of North Carolina at Chapel Hill, almost three-quarters (73 percent) noted spanking to be appropriate punishment for toddlers between the ages of one to three, while less than 20 percent thought it appropriate for a child under the age of one. That particular study, reported in *Jet* magazine (See "Survey Says Some Mothers Still Believe That Spanking Is Good Discipline," January 30, 1995, p. 14), was slightly weighted by minority parents, but other more demographically balanced surveys also show the practice to be very common. A compilation of polls published in the *Boston Globe* on April 27, 1995, noted that 68 percent of Americans think spanking is "essential to child-rearing" and that two-thirds of parents of toddlers spank their children once a day. According to a 1994 Gallup/*USA Today* poll (reported on April 8, 1994, in *USA Today*), it appears that public attitudes are changing. In 1986, 84 percent of Americans would have agreed that " 'a good, hard spanking' is sometimes necessary to discipline a child," as compared with 67 percent in 1994. See "Poll: Discipline OK, Abuse Isn't," *USA Today*, April 8, 1994, p. 8A; "The Unsparing Rod," *Boston Globe*, April 27, 1995, p. A1.

57. David Elkind, *The Hurried Child*, rev. ed. (New York: Addison-Wesley, 1988), pp. xii–xiii.

58. See William A. Galston, Elaine Ciulla Kaymarck, and Elaine Ciulla, *Putting Children First: A Progressive Family Policy for the 1990s*. Progressive Policy Institute, Washington, D.C., September 27, 1990, pp. 14–15. The authors say that studies of juvenile crime in poor neighborhoods that have controlled for family configuration of juvenile criminals have effectively erased any substantial

connection between criminality and poverty, indicating that single-parent homes (and here, we are talking mainly of fatherless homes) are a major factor in wayward juvenile behavior.

Chapter 2: Child Welfare, Family Destruction

1. The details of the Wade case are here taken mainly from K. L. Billingsley's article "PC Kidnappers," *Heterodoxy,* January 1993, pp. 4–6. Billingsley himself took his account from a series of reports in the *San Diego Union* and from San Diego County grand jury investigative reports.
2. David Grogan and Lorenzo Benet, "A Time for Healing," *People,* October 5, 1992, p. 134.
3. This term was invented by Ray Helfer in an article entitled "The Litany of the Smoldering Neglect of Children," published in Helfer and Ruth Kempe, eds., *The Battered Child,* 4th ed. (Chicago: University of Chicago Press, 1984), p. 13.
4. K. L. Billingsley writes: "The [San Diego] grand jury . . . eventually subpoenaed . . . [the therapist's] notes, which contained many comments about how Alicia 'liked' her therapist. But Alicia's own testimony makes it clear that the child wanted only to go home. The grand jury was also alarmed that Goodfriend taught the child about masturbation 'without any parental input or apparent interest by the child.' " (Billingsley, "PC Kidnappers," p. 5.)
5. Ibid., p. 6.
6. Ibid.
7. John Merline, "Who's Abusing America's Kids? All Too Often, It's Those Trying to Protect Them," *Investor's Business Daily,* September 5, 1995, p. A2.
8. Nicole Gaouette, "A System as 'Neglected' as Kids It Serves: Child Advocates in New York and Elsewhere Turn to Courts to Overhaul Child-Welfare Agencies," *Christian Science Monitor,* February 21, 1996, p. 4.
9. David S. Liederman, letter to the editor, *Washington Post,* February 19, 1994.
10. Grogan and Benet, "A Time for Healing," p. 133.
11. The single exception to this silence seems to be John Merline's September 5, 1995, article in *Investor's Business Daily,* which cursorily mentioned "the Senate['s] . . . initial steps . . . to reform the child protection system." In July of 1995, the U.S. Senate amended the Child Abuse Prevention and Treatment Act of 1974, hoping by example to inspire state governments to implement some legal and administrative correctives to the child welfare system that might result in greater Child Protective Services accountability, both to families under investigation and to the public. One of the principal changes made to the act was a tightening of the definition of child abuse. Unfortunately this CAPTA reauthorization was rolled over into the welfare conference bill vetoed by President Clinton in January of 1996, but dropped from the welfare conference bill the President signed.
12. A typical example of the press's handling of this case is the December 11, 1995, cover story on the Elisa Izquierdo case in *Time,* "A Shameful Death," reported by Sharon E. Epperson and Elaine Rivera, pp. 32–36.
13. Ibid., p. 35.
14. The 1995 Senate Committee on Labor and Human Resources report on the reauthorization of CAPTA cites figures from the U.S. Advisory Board on Child Abuse and Neglect. These break down as follows: 141,700 children are seri-

ously injured as a result of abuse or neglect, 18,000 are severely disabled, and 2,000 are killed. (See Calendar No. 149; 104th Congress, 1st Session, Child Abuse Prevention and Treatment Act Amendments of 1995, July 20, 1995.) It is of some pertinence that these numbers regarding serious cases of abuse and neglect have remained constant for a decade in which child abuse and neglect reports have increased dramatically from 2 million to over 3 million. Using figures from the American Humane Association and the National Incidence and Prevalence of Child Abuse and Neglect Study, Richard Wexler, author of *Wounded Innocents: The Real Victims of the War Against Child Abuse* (Buffalo, NY: Prometheus Books, 1990), reports somewhere between 157,000 and 161,000 "serious" cases of child maltreatment in 1986—these included, according to AHA accounting, 21,000 cases of major physical abuse and 132,000 of sexual abuse (p. 88).

15. See Douglas Besharov, "The Child-Abuse Numbers Game," *Wall Street Journal,* August 4, 1988; and Douglas Besharov, "Gaining Control over Child Abuse Reports," *Public Welfare,* Spring 1990, pp. 34–41.

16. Merline, "Who's Abusing America's Kids?" p. A2 In *Wounded Innocents,* Richard Wexler has dozens of horror stories to tell in regard to frivolous indictments of parents for child abuse. Other investigative reporters, among them Seth Farber in a *National Review* piece of April 12, 1993, entitled "The Real Abuse: What Are the Child-Welfare Agencies Doing to Stop Child Abuse? The Reverse"; and Elena Neuman, in an *Insight* piece of May 9, 1994, entitled "Child Welfare or Family Trauma?," cite disturbing cases of unwarranted child abuse and neglect convictions. Parents unjustly convicted of abuse and neglect have also approached me personally to tell their stories, a few of which I relate in this chapter.

17. See Douglas Besharov, "Overreach of the Guardian State," *Wall Street Journal,* April 2, 1984. In twenty-nine out of fifty-five states and territories, workers can remove children from homes immediately if they fear children might be exposed to danger; in all but four of the rest they must only call the police to have them removed.

18. Douglas Besharov, *Recognizing Child Abuse: A Guide for the Concerned* (New York: Free Press, 1990), p. 29. The federal definition of child abuse and neglect was amended in the CAPTA reauthorization proposal of July 1995 to read "any recent act or failure to act on the part of a parent or caretaker which results in death, serious physical or emotional harm, sexual abuse or exploitation, or an act or failure to act which present an imminent risk of serious harm." It remains to be seen whether, should the reauthorization amendments go through, states—which are not required by the terms of CAPTA's reauthorization to adjust their legal definitions of child abuse and neglect to the new federal one—will adjust them accordingly.

19. Douglas Besharov, "How Child Abuse Programs Hurt Poor Children: The Misuse of Foster Care," *Clearinghouse Review,* July 1988, p. 219.

20. Besharov, *Recognizing Child Abuse,* p. 100.

21. Ibid., p. 67.

22. Ibid., p. 115.

23. Ibid., p. 87. The foregoing definition is quoted from "Child Sexual Abuse," Navy Family Advocacy Program Training, 1982, pp. 40–41, as a guideline for a legal definition of "sexual contact" in cases of reported abuse. Besharov notes that "to exclude normal parental touchings, child abuse statutes mandate reports only

when the touching is for the purpose of sexual arousal or gratification (of either the adult or the child)." Unfortunately, determining whether a child has been subjected to lewd or lascivious behavior on the part of an adult is very difficult, owing to the fact that acts of sexual abuse can be perpetrated without leaving physical evidence. Also, in the case of young children, leading questions or the premature imparting of information about sexual abuse may end up distorting a child's impression of an innocent act.

24. See National Coalition for Child Protection Reform, Issue Paper No. 5: "Child Abuse and Poverty."

25. Wexler, *Wounded Innocents*, p. 49.

26. Nancy E. Roman, "A Question of Judgment: Mom Appeals Neglect Ruling," *Washington Times*, August 4, 1993, pp. B1–B2. Interestingly, the social worker was actually investigating another harmless incident—reported to the child abuse hotline by a malicious neighbor—when she came upon this particular incident.

27. Besharov, *Recognizing Child Abuse*, p. 121. The exception here would be, of course, parents who have notified their local school district of their intention to home-school.

28. Wexler, *Wounded Innocents*, p. 126.

29. Ibid., p. 103.

30. This case was related to me by a Springfield, Virginia, mother.

31. Wexler, *Wounded Innocents*, p. 48.

32. In every focus group I held, at least two parents reported that they or close relatives had been investigated. The average size of a focus group is ten to twelve people. None of these people, who were recruited from general market research databases, were told any more about the subject of research except that it was about raising children.

33. On strip-searching as a common investigative practice of child welfare caseworkers, see Wexler, *Wounded Innocents*, pp. 109–13.

34. Neuman, "Child Welfare or Family Trauma?," p. 9.

35. Hannah B. Lapp, "Child Abuse: In the Name of Protecting Kids from Harm Social Workers Subject Them to Cruel and Unusual Punishment," *Reason*, February 1994, pp. 35–36.

36. See "Abuse in the Name of Protecting Children," a brochure of VOCAL.

37. Ibid., p. 3.

38. Neil Gilbert and Helen Noh Ahn, "Cultural Diversity and Sexual Abuse Prevention," *Social Service Review*, September 1992, p. 411.

39. Ibid., p. 413.

40. Ibid., p. 425. Ang Lee's poignant film *Pushing Hands*, features a family scene that is interesting in the context of this discussion. A Chinese grandfather teasingly grabs at the privates of his six-year-old grandson, saying he wants to have a look at the future of the family. The child is ambivalent about the gesture, but seems not to take it too seriously, while his Caucasian mother is horrified. It is but one of many cultural misunderstandings between father-in-law and daughter-in-law portrayed in this film.

41. Author interview with Shari Shapiro, November 22, 1993.

42. For a comprehensive description of the perils of the foster care system for children, see Wexler, *Wounded Innocents*, Chapters 7 and 8. Hannah Lapp's interviews with children of two families who were wrongly removed to foster care are also a crushing indictment of the system. They describe the desperation of

young people imprisoned in unsanitary shelters and mental hospitals and held incommunicado from loving parents for months at a time. (See Lapp, "Child Abuse.")

43. See Richard Lowry and Richard Samuelson, "How Many Battered Children?," *National Review,* April 12, 1993, p. 46.

44. Ibid.

45. Besharov, "How Child Abuse Programs Hurt Poor Children," pp. 222–23.

46. Memorandum of Points and Authorities in Support of Motion for Preliminary Injunction, *Hansen v. McMahon,* Superior Court, State of California, No. CA 000974, April 1986.

47. Association for Children of New Jersey, *Splintered Lives: A Report on Decision Making for Children in Foster Care,* June 1988, pp. ii, 15.

48. "Whatever Happened to the Boarder Babies?," City of New York Office of the Comptroller, Office of Policy Management, January 1989, pp. 11–12.

49. See Wexler, *Wounded Innocents,* pp. 50–53 and 119–21.

50. San Diego County Grand Jury Report, *Families in Crisis,* February 6, 1992, p. 4.

51. Besharov, "How Child Abuse Programs Hurt Poor Children," p. 221.

52. Quoted from National Coalition for Child Protection Reform, Issue Paper No. 9, "Foster Care: Misused and Overused."

53. Wexler, *Wounded Innocents.* In an Appendix entitled "Can You Live Up to Child Saver Standards?" Wexler presents a caseworker checklist. Some sample inquiries: "Mother plans at least one meal consisting of two courses/Mother plans meals with courses that go together/Bedtime for the child is set by the parents for about the same time every night/Child has been taught to swim or mother believes child should be taught to swim/Storm sashes or equivalent are present/Windows are caulked or sealed against drafts/Doors are weatherproofed/There are window screens in good repair in most windows/There are dirty dishes and utensils in rooms other than the kitchen/There are leaky faucets/Ears are usually clean/Planned overnight vacation trip has been taken by family/Child has been taken by parents to see a spectator sport/Child has been taken by parents to a carnival . . ." (pp. 303–8).

54. Ibid., pp. 44–46.

55. Besharov, "How Child Abuse Programs Hurt Poor Children," p. 222.

56. See National Coalition for Child Protection Reform, Issue Paper No. 5, "Child Abuse and Poverty."

57. Beshavrov, "How Child Abuse Programs Hurt Poor Children," p. 223.

58. On the relationship between multiple foster care placements and later sociopathy, see particularly Conna Craig, "What I Need Is a Mom: The Welfare State Denies Homes to Thousands of Foster Children," *Policy Review,* Summer 1995, No. 73, p. 46); Wexler, *Wounded Innocents,* pp. 174–75; and Michael Oreskes, "A System Overloaded: The Foster Care Crisis," *New York Times,* March 19, 1987.

59. Patricia Edmonds, "In Court, Troubled Tales, Painful Decisions," *USA Today,* April 8, 1994, p. 8A.

60. Farber, "The Real Abuse," p. 47.

61. Ibid., p. 44.

62. Billingsley, "PC Kidnappers," p. 5.

63. Wexler, *Wounded Innocents,* p. 219.

64. Billingsley, "PC Kidnappers," p. 5.

65. Wexler, *Wounded Innocents,* p. 209.

66. Craig, "What I Need Is a Mom," p. 42.
67. Foster care funds emanate from the Social Security Act, Title IVE; other child protective services are funded via title IVB. The former is unlimited, the latter is capped.
68. As I complete this book, New York City is considering revamping its foster care system by offering a flat rate rather than a daily fee to foster care agencies. One experimental project along this line undertaken in New York has yielded some promising results. See Kimberly J. McLarin, "Foster Care Agency's Plan Provides Model for New York," *New York Times*, November 20, 1995, pp. A1, B4.
69. Wexler, *Wounded Innocents*, p. 220.
70. Author interview with Conna Craig.
71. Craig, "What I Need Is a Mom," p. 41.
72. Ibid., p. 45.
73. Wexler, *Wounded Innocents*, p. 233.
74. Ibid., pp. 233–34
75. Besharov, "Overreach of the Guardian State."
76. Statistic taken from a National Committee to Prevent Child Abuse study reported in Patricia Edmonds, "A New Case Filed Every 10 Seconds," *USA Today*, April 8, 1994, p. 8A.
77. Richard Gelles, "Child Abuse as Psycho-pathology: A Sociological Critique and Reformulation," *American Journal of Orthopsychiatry*, Vol. 43, p. 611.
78. Craig, "What I Need Is a Mom," p. 46.
79. Rita Kramer, "In Foster Care, Children Come Last," *City Journal*, Autumn 1994. It should be noted here that Kramer's article is an attack on the child welfare system's renewed interest in "family preservation" policies, which, Kramer insists, inanely attempt to preserve the most seriously dysfunctional families.
80. See Richard J. Herrnstein and Charles Murray, *The Bell Curve: Intelligence and Class Structure in American Life* (New York: Free Press, 1994), pp. 211–13 and Chapter 22.
81. On child death statistics, see Deborah Daro, D.S.W., Director, and Karen Mc-Curdy, M.A., Principal Analyst, *Current Trends in Child Abuse Reporting and Fatalities: The Results of the 1991 Annual Fifty-State Survey*, Working Paper No. 208 (The National Center on Child Abuse Prevention Research, April 1992). The U.S. Department of Health and Human Services 1994 child maltreatment report (*Child Maltreatment 1994: Reports from the States to the National Center on Child Abuse and Neglect* [Washington, D.C.: U.S. Government Printing Office, 1996], shows child maltreatment fatalities slightly down, from 1,383 to 1,111.
82. David Blankenhorn, *Fatherless America* (New York: Basic Books, 1995), pp. 39–42.
83. See the National Coalition for Child Protective Reform, "Family Preservation: What It Is—And What It Isn't," Issue Paper No. 10; and "Family Preservation Under Attack," Issue Paper No. 11; and Wexler, *Wounded Innocents*, pp. 252–61.

Chapter 3: Undomesticated Law

1. Reported in Deeann Glamser, "Making Parents Pay the Price: Communities Seek to Stem Youth Crime," *USA Today*, February 21, 1995, p. 2A.

2. Brad Knickerbocker, "Oregon Drafts Parents in War on Teenage Crime," *Christian Science Monitor,* September 13, 1995, p. 1.

3. Glamser, "Making Parents Pay the Price," pp. 1A–2A.

4. Laurel Shaper Walters, "States to Parents: Pay for Your Children's Crimes," *Christian Science Monitor,* April 1, 1996, p. 3.

5. Knickerbocker, "Oregon Drafts Parents," p. 1. See also Peter Applebome, "Parents Face Consequences as Children's Misdeeds Rise," *New York Times,* April 10, 1996, pp. A1, B8.

6. Applebome, "Parents Face Consequences," p. A1.

7. Knickerbocker, "Oregon Drafts Parents," p. 18. In Silverton, Oregon, the parental responsibility law is credited with a 53 percent decrease in juvenile crime between September 1994 and September 1995.

8. Both quotations reported by Glamser, "Making Parents Pay the Price," p. 2A.

9. Reported in John Leo, "Punished for the Sins of the Children," *U.S. News & World Report,* June 12, 1995, p. 18.

10. Patrice K. Johnson, "Juvenile Justice: 'They Expect Us to Put the Fear of God in Their Child,'" *Stamford Advocate,* February 18, 1996, p. A10.

11. Laurel Shaper Walters, "Cops Enter Homes to Seize Kids' Guns," *Christian Science Monitor,* April 18, 1995, pp. 1, 18.

12. Johnson, "Juvenile Justice," p. A10.

13. Quoted in Rita Kramer, "Taking Off the Kid Gloves: How to Fix New York's Juvenile Justice System," *City Journal,* Spring 1994, p. 50.

14. See Patrice K. Johnson in her two-part story on the Stamford juvenile justice system: "Juvenile Justice"; and "Reaching for the Long Arm of Juvenile Justice," *The Advocate,* February 19, 1996, pp. A1, A7.

15. Kramer, "Taking Off the Kid Gloves," p. 50. Kramer's article on reforming the juvenile justice system is a comprehensive and coherent description of the failures of the system and what can be done about them. Kramer is not opposed to recent legislation that has allowed courts to prosecute violent juvenile criminals as adults, but she believes that stronger juvenile court decisions will help to deter the first- or second-time offender of lesser crimes from moving on to greater offenses. (See p. 53.)

16. Johnson, "Reaching for the Long Arm," pp. A1, A7.

17. Ibid., p. A7.

18. This story was reported by Elena Neuman in an article entitled "Child Welfare or Family Trauma?," *Insight,* May 9, 1994, pp. 6–12.

19. Mary Ann Mason, *From Father's Property to Children's Rights: The History of Child Custody in the United States* (New York: Columbia University Press, 1994), p. 58.

20. Ibid., p. 161.

21. Ibid., pp. 152–53.

22. Jan Hoffman, "Plan Is to Revamp New York's Family Courts," *New York Times,* October 14, 1994, p. B18. For a critique of repressed memory syndrome see Michael D. Yapko, Ph.D., *Suggestions of Abuse: True and False Memories of Childhood Sexual Trauma* (New York: Simon & Schuster, 1994).

23. I borrow the term "superparent" here from Mary Ann Mason. See *From Father's Property to Children's Rights,* particularly Chapter 3, "The State as Superparent."

24. Mason, *From Father's Property to Children's Rights,* p. 161.

25. Robert H. Mnookin, *Child, Family and State: Problems and Materials on Children and the Law* (New York: Little, Brown, 1978), p. 493.

26. Ibid., pp. 506–9.
27. Ibid., pp. 455–67.
28. Ibid., p. 464. The quotation is from the California Civil Code, Section 4600.
29. Ibid., p. 490.
30. Robert H. Mnookin, writing in 1978, observes, "Every state today has a statute allowing a court, typically a juvenile court, to assume jurisdiction over a neglected or abused child and to remove the child from parental custody under broad and vague standards reminiscent of those invoked by courts of equity in the nineteenth century. A complex social welfare bureaucracy, however, now is responsible for discovering children in need of protection and initiating appropriate judicial action. A case usually reaches juvenile court only after weaving its way through a process where numerous officials—including social workers, probation officers and court personnel—may have had contact with the family." (See *Child, Family, and State*, p. 470.)
31. Maggie Gallagher, *The Abolition of Marriage* (Washington, D.C.: Regnery, 1996), p. 22. For important critiques of contemporary American divorce law as it pertains to unilateral divorce, see also Mary Ann Glendon, *Divorce and Abortion in Western Society* (Cambridge: Harvard University Press, 1987).
32. For a succinct description of the transformation of divorce laws and their effect on custody arrangements, see Walter Olson, *The Litigation Explosion* (New York: Truman/Tally, 1991), pp. 131–38; and Robert H. Mnookin and Eleanor E. Maccoby, with Charlene Depner and H. Elizabeth Peters, *Dividing the Child: Social and Legal Dilemmas of Custody* (Cambridge: Harvard University Press, 1992).
33. *Representing Children: Standards for Attorneys and Guardians ad Litem in Custody or Visitation Proceedings*, published by the American Academy of Matrimonial Lawyers (Chicago, 1995), p. 1.
34. Author interview with James Altham, summer 1994.
35. Olson, *The Litigation Explosion*, p. 137.
36. Timothy J. Horgan, *Winning Your Divorce: A Man's Survival Guide* (New York: Dutton, 1994), p. 97.
37. These statistics are reported in Marilyn Gardner, "When Mom and Dad Battle to Visit Their Kids," *Christian Science Monitor*, April 4, 1995, p. 12.
38. Frank F. Furstenberg, Jr., and Andrew J. Cherlin, *Divided Families* (Cambridge, MA: Harvard University Press, 1991), pp. 42–44 and 73–74.
39. Ibid., pp. 113–14.
40. Mnookin and Maccoby, *Dividing the Child*, pp. 160, 289.
41. Ibid., pp. 284–85. See also Janet R. Johnston, Marsha Kline, and Jeanne Tschann, "Ongoing Post-Divorce Conflict: Effects on Children of Joint Custody and Frequent Access," *American Journal of Orthopsychiatry*, Vol. 59, October 1989, pp. 576–92.
42. See Furstenberg and Cherlin, *Divided Families*, p. 43. See also Terry Arendell, *Mothers and Divorce: Legal, Economic and Social Dilemmas* (Berkeley: University of California Press, 1986), pp. 18–20. While Furstenberg and Cherlin have combed the social science research in making this assertion, Arendell's skepticism regarding joint custody is based solely on anecdotal evidence. Arendell interviewed sixty divorced women with children in the early 1980s. Her often touching interviews with these women (only a few of whom had joint custody arrangements) form the basis of a searing indictment of the contemporary legal system in its handling of divorce. Of three respondents' feelings about their joint

legal custody arrangements, Arendell reports: "They were basically hostile to this arrangement, for it left their former husbands with considerable power over their lives and the lives of their children. Indeed, two of the three fathers in question did not even pay their child support, but they continued to harass their former spouses about child-rearing methods, ways of spending money, and social activities" (p. 19).

43. Olson, *The Litigation Explosion*, pp.132–33.
44. Arendell, *Mothers and Divorce*, p. 19.
45. Joan Wexler, "Rethinking the Modification of Child Custody Decrees," *Yale Law Journal*, Vol. 94, No. 4, March 1985, pp. 757–820.
46. This quotation from Beverly Pekala, in *Don't Settle for Less: A Woman's Guide to Getting a Fair Divorce and Custody Settlement* (New York: Doubleday, 1994), p. 204, is typical.
47. Olson, *The Litigation Explosion*, p. 97.
48. See Mason, *From Father's Property to Children's Rights*, pp. 168–69; and Joseph Goldstein, Anna Freud, and Albert Solnit, *Beyond the Best Interests of the Child* (New York: Free Press, 1979), p. 38.
49. The story of the Foretich-Morgan custody battle told here is based on Jonathan Groener's book, *Hilary's Trial* (New York: Simon & Schuster, 1991).
50. See Milton C. Regan Jr., "Post-Modern Family Law: Toward a New Model of Status," in David Popenoe, Jean Bethke Elshtain, and David Blankenhorn, *Promises to Keep: Decline and Renewal of Marriage in America* (Lanham, MD: Rowman and Littlefield, 1996), especially pp. 159–62. Regan writes of the older legal regime of "status" that it "expressed a substantive moral vision of what marriage and family life should be like," while the newer emphasis in family law on contract "sees family primarily as the domain of private ordering, an intimate setting in which people decide for themselves the terms of their relationships" (pp. 159–60).
51. Mary Ann Glendon, *The Transformation of Family Law* (Cambridge: Harvard University Press, 1989), pp. 102–3.
52. See Steve Largent, "Parents Know Best: A Congressman Testifies in Favor of His Parents'-Rights Bill," *World*, December 23/30, 1996, p. 24.
53. Glendon, *The Transformation of Family Law*, p. 100.
54. Linda Greenhouse, "Justices Allow Limits on Indecent Radio and TV Shows," *New York Times*, January 9, 1996.
55. Quoted from author's telephone interview with Beverly Peltzer, February 20, 1996.
56. For a detailed account of Gregory K.'s history, see Pat Wingert and Eloise Salholz, "Irreconcilable Differences," *Newsweek*, September 21, 1992, pp. 84–90.
57. For an excellent summary of the implications of the U.N. Convention on the Rights of the Child and the influence of American legal theorists on its provisions regarding child autonomy, see Bruce C. Hafen and Jonathan O. Hafen, "Abandoning Children to Their Rights," *First Things*, Vol. 55, August /September 1995, pp. 18–24.
58. Cathleen Cleaver, "Parental Rights: Whose Children Are They?," *Bangladesh Observer*, November 28, 1995.
59. Barbara Bennett Woodhouse, "Who Owns the Child? *Meyer* and *Pierce* and the Child as Property," 33 *William and Mary Law Review*, 995 (1992). For an excellent account of the history and expanding use of the doctrine *parens patriae*, see Mason, *From Father's Property to Children's Rights*. For a concise and excellent

summary of important legal decisions favoring the acknowledgment of fundamental parental rights, see Robert P. George and Jana V. T. Baldwin, "Constitutional Protection for Parental Rights: The *Meyer-Pierce* Legacy," published by
Of the People Foundation (June 1994).

60. Hafen and Hafen, "Abandoning Children to Their Rights," p. 18.

61. Dwight G. Duncan, *Religious Freedom in the 21st Century: Legal and Public Policy Issues* (The Rutherford Institute, 1996), p. 7. See *New Jersey v. T.L.O.*

62. Duncan, *Religious Freedom in the 21st Century*, p. 8.

63. "Christian Scientists Are Cleared of Manslaughter," *New York Times,* August 12,
1993, p. A16.

64. David N. Williams, "Christian Science and the Care of Children," in *Freedom
and Responsibility: Christian Science Healing for Children* (Boston: First
Church of Christ, Scientist, 1989), pp. 66–70. For other cases of Christian Scientists prosecuted for medical neglect, and reaction to them, see Williams, *Freedom and Responsibility* pp. 82–99. The fact that the courts' respect for
alternative religious healing practices is diminishing is nowhere better demonstrated than in the August 1996 decision of the Federal District Court in St.
Paul that Medicare and Medicaid reimbursements to Christian Science nursing
facilities violated the constitutional separation of church and state. See Gustav
Niebuhr, "U.S. Payment to a Church for Nursing Is Held Illegal," *New York
Times,* August 9, 1996.

65. Eugene D. Robin, M.D., column, *Press Enterprise* (Riverside, California), June
13, 1988, reprinted in Williams, *Freedom and Responsibility*, pp. 95–96.

66. Stephen L. Carter, *The Culture of Disbelief: How American Law and Politics
Trivialize Religious Devotion* (New York: Basic Books, 1993), pp. 214–15.

67. Quoted of Charles Loring Brace, founder of the New York Children's Aid Society, in Richard Wexler, *Wounded Innocents: The Real Victims in the War on Child
Abuse* (Buffalo, NY: Prometheus Books, 1990), p. 33.

68. Mason, *From Father's Property*, p. 154. Richard Wexler does not see the courts
any longer as racist, but claims that racism is a problem among social workers
who advise the courts, and is particularly rife in private foster care agencies. See
Wounded Innocents, especially pp. 221–25.

69. See Bronislaw Malinowski, *Sex and Repression in Savage Society* (Cleveland:
World Publishing Company, 1961), pp. 165, 192.

70. Rhonda Hillbery, "Adoptive Parents Fear That Recent Cases Erode Rights," *Los
Angeles Times,* August 11, 1993, p. A5.

71. For a good account of the story of Baby Richard, see Michele Ingrassia and John
McCormick, "Ordered to Surrender," *Newsweek,* February 6, 1995, pp. 44–45.
It should be noted that the U.S. Supreme Court upheld this ruling.

72. Tony Perry, "Adoption Battle Raises Painful Questions," *Los Angeles Times,* August 7, 1993, p. A1.

73. Maura Dolan, "Justices Rule for Adoptive Parents of San Diego Boy," *Los Angeles Times,* August 1, 1994, p. A3.

74. Quoted in Hillbery, "Adoptive Parents Fear That Recent Cases Erode Rights,"
p. 5.

75. Sidney Callahan, "Kinship Is Forever," *Commonweal,* November 18, 1994, p. 6.

76. Elizabeth Bartholet, *Family Bonds: Adoption and the Politics of Parenting*
(Boston: Houghton Mifflin, 1993), pp. 181–84.

77. Robby DeBoer, *Losing Jessica* (New York: Doubleday, 1994). It might be men-

tioned here that the DeBoers have, in my opinion, mistakenly identified the issue of contested adoptions as an issue of children's rights. They have even founded an Ann Arbor, Michigan, group named Jessica DeBoer Committee for the Rights of the Child. Rather, I think it is clear that the issue is one of parents' rights, specifically adoptive parents' rights.

78. Joseph Goldstein, Anna Freud, Albert Solit, and Sonja Goldstein, *In the Best Interest of the Child* (New York: Free Press, 1986), p. 123.
79. Glendon, *The Transformation of Family Law*, p. 297.
80. Ibid., p. 308.
81. Ibid., p. 297.

PART II: PARENTING, BUREAUCRATIC STYLE

Chapter 4: Schooling for Leveling

1. Quoted from "America's 'Moral Urgency' to Reconnect Children and Schools," *U.S. Department of Education Community Update*, No. 11, March 1994, p. 1; and "Secretary Riley Defines Education Challenges, Urges Americans to Come Together," *U.S. Department of Education Community Update*, No. 33, March 1996, pp. 1, 6. The survey referred to here was carefully orchestrated to favor public education. It involved soliciting the opinions of 2,400 Americans, only 439 of whom were parents with children in the public schools: 237 were public school teachers, 417 were education administrators, and 734 "decision makers in business, government, the media and other sectors." The American educational system's report card, however, was notably mediocre—71 percent of the respondents advocated higher standards for education, 92 percent insisting that "as a foundation for higher standards . . . teaching the basics is absolutely essential." Over half rated private education superior to public education, 61 percent saying that "private schools are more likely to provide order and discipline in the classroom" than public schools. See "Americans View the Basics as Central to High Standards," *U.S. Department of Education Community Update*, No. 30, November 1995.
2. Quotes are from Secretary Riley's "State of American Education Speech" of February 15, 1994. See "America's 'Moral Urgency' to Reconnect Children and Schools," pp. 1, 3.
3. Richard J. Herrnstein and Charles Murray, *The Bell Curve: Intelligence and Class Structure in American Life* (New York: Free Press, 1994), p. 420.
4. Charles J. Sykes, *Dumbing Down Our Kids: Why American Children Feel Good About Themselves but Can't Read, Write, or Add* (New York: St. Martin's 1995), p. 20.
5. Herrnstein and Murray, *The Bell Curve*, p. 420.
6. Ibid., p. 421.
7. Sykes, *Dumbing Down Our Kids*, p. 21.
8. Associated Press, "Decline Found in Reading Proficiency of High School Seniors," *New York Times*, April 28, 1995, p. A18.
9. Rita Kramer: *The Ed School Follies: The Miseducation of America's Teachers* (New York: Free Press, 1991), p. 75.
10. Ibid., p. 189.

11. Ibid., p. 184.

12. For a concise critical evaluation of this trend by a public school teacher, see Patrick Welsh, "Staying on Track: Can We Teach Honors and Hard Cases Together?," *Washington Post*, March 7, 1993. Because there is evidence that ability tracking is beneficial to both brighter and slower students (providing that standards for slower students do not sink too low), mixed-ability groupings are often justified by educators, not on the basis of scientific research, but on the basis of principle. See Sykes, *Dumbing Down Our Kids*, pp. 76–78.

13. The April 1994 report of the National Education Commission on Time and Learning, *Prisoners of Time*, stated, "Despite the obsession with time, little attention is paid to how it is used: in 42 states examined by the Commission, only 41 percent of secondary school time must be spent on core academic subjects. . . . In their final four years of secondary school, according to our estimates, French, German and Japanese students receive more than twice as much core academic instruction as American students" (pp. 1, 25).

14. Statistics taken from the "Monthly Letter to Friends of the Center for Education Reform," May 1995, pp. 1–2 .

15. Sykes, *Dumbing Down Our Kids*, p. 101.

16. Ibid., p. 107.

17. Rudolf Flesch, *Why Johnny Can't Read* (New York: Harper & Row, 1955).

18. Sykes, *Dumbing Down Our Kids*, p. 104.

19. Ibid., p. 106.

20. Ibid., p. 108.

21. Ibid., p. 102.

22. Ibid. NAEP assessment summarized on p. 20. The writing example is quoted on p. 98.

23. Richard Bernstein, *Dictatorship of Virtue: How the Battle Over Multiculturalism Is Reshaping Our Schools, Our Country, Our Lives* (New York: Vintage, 1995), p. 100.

24. Sykes, *Dumbing Down Our Kids*, p. 121.

25. Ibid., p. 118.

26. Ibid., p. 119.

27. Ibid., pp. 123–24.

28. Ibid., p. 116.

29. Gloria Goodale, "New-New Math Sparks Old Battle," *Christian Science Monitor*, June 17, 1996, p. 10.

30. Sykes, *Dumbing Down Our Kids*, p. 122.

31. Bernstein, *Dictatorship of Virtue*, p. 253.

32. Ibid., pp. 252–55.

33. This exercise, which my own child was also compelled to complete in third grade in 1993, is from the *Pitman Writing Skills Curriculum*, 1981. Entitled "Anger and Adventure," it is part fill in the blanks, part composition assignment, furnishing eight-year-olds with an explicit recipe to follow in preparing to leave home.

34. Lucy S. Dawidowicz, "How They Teach the Holocaust," *Commentary*, December, 1990, pp. 25–32. Dawidowicz writes that these "simulation games . . . have been known to produce unprecedented emotional tensions in the classroom, among some students arousing fear, panic, and over-identification with the victims and, among others, releasing sado-masochistic urges, violent responses, and over-identification with the murderers." (See p. 27.)

35. Thomas Sowell, *Inside American Education: The Decline, the Deception, the Dogmas* (New York: Free Press, 1993), p. 41.

36. These questions are from Sidney Simon et al.'s values clarification curriculum, cited in ibid., p. 45.

37. Quest, "Skills for Growing, Review Curriculum," Fourth Grade, Unit Four, p. 131.

38. Daniel Goleman, "Perils Seen in Warnings About Abuse," *New York Times*, November 21, 1989, quoted in Sykes, *Dumbing Down Our Kids*, p. 181; see also Neil Gilbert, "Teaching Children to Prevent Sexual Abuse," *The Public Interest*, Fall 1988, pp. 3–15.

39. Sykes, *Dumbing Down Our Kids*, p. 181.

40. Sowell, *Inside American Education*, p. 36.

41. Ibid., p. ix.

42. Debra Saunders, "Feelings . . . Nothing More Than Feelings," *Milwaukee Journal*, September 13, 1994.

43. Ruth Engs, S. Eugene Barnes, and Molly Wanta, *Health Games Students Play: Creative Strategies for Health Education* (Dubuque, IA: Kendall/Hunt, 1975), p. 2, quoted in Sowell, *Inside American Education*, p. 44.

44. Phyllis Schlafly, ed., *Child Abuse in the Classroom* (Westchester, IL: Crossway Books, 1988), p. 302.

45. Sowell, *Inside American Education*, p. 49.

46. The Here's Looking at You, 2000 second-grade teacher's manual reminds instructors that parents are bound to transmit "positive attitudes" toward drug use, and "involve" their children in it. How? When they request their kids "to bring a beer from the refrigerator."

47. Sowell, *Inside American Education*, p. 49.

48. Jayna Davis, "What Did You Learn in School Today?," KFOR-TV, Oklahoma City, June 6, 1993. These exercises seem to have been jettisoned in the 1992 rewriting of the Quest "Skills for Adolescence" workbook.

49. James Bovard, "DARE Scare: Turning Children into Informants?," *Washington Post Outlook*, January 30, 1994, p. C3.

50. Here's Looking at You, 2000, "The Prevention Connection Newsletter (Fourth Grade)," pp. 2–3.

51. This is the conclusion that both William K. Kilpatrick and Thomas Sowell came to in exhaustive reviews of life skills curricula in the early 1990s. See Kilpatrick's *Why Johnny Can't Tell Right from Wrong: Moral Illiteracy and the Case for Character Education* (New York: Simon & Schuster, 1992); and Sowell's *Inside American Education*.

52. Ruth Bell et al., *Changing Bodies, Changing Lives*, rev. ed. (New York: Random House, 1987), pp. 4, 3.

53. These quotes are from the *Skills for Adolescence Workshop Guidebook* (Granville, OH: Quest International, 1989), pp. 33, 43, 93, quoted in Kilpatrick, *Why Johnny Can't Tell Right from Wrong*, pp. 44, 37. The same kind of language however has been used in training for many other drug awareness curricula, including Project Charlie, Here's Looking at You, and Me-ology—all programs whose emphasis, like Quest's, has been largely on building "self-esteem."

54. Bell et al., *Changing Bodies, Changing Lives*, pp. 68, 6, 78, 57.

55. H. McGinley, *Caring, Deciding and Growing* (Lexington, MA: Ginn, 1983), p. 20, quoted in Kilpatrick, *Why Johnny Can't Tell Right from Wrong*, p. 39.

56. James P. Shaver and William Strong, *Facing Value Decisions: Rationale-Building*

for Teachers (New York: Teachers College Press/Columbia University, 1982), pp. 118–19, cited in Bryce J. Christensen, *Utopia Against the Family* (San Francisco: Ignatius Press, 1990), p. 90.

57. Sowell, *Inside American Education*, pp. 55–56.

58. Kilpatrick, *Why Johnny Can't Tell Right from Wrong*, p. 37.

59. See Sidney B. Simon et al., *Values Clarification* (New York: Hart, 1972), especially pp. 38–57. For an excellent critical appraisal of values clarification, see Kilpatrick, *Why Johnny Can't Tell Right from Wrong*, pp. 80–82.

60. This 1993 PALS curriculum lesson is quoted in Sykes, *Dumbing Down Our Kids*, p. 160.

61. At the center of this brewing movement in character education are two institutions: the San Antonio–based Character Education Institute (founded 1942) and the Jefferson Center for Character Education (founded 1963). Their programs reach about 100,000 classrooms each year. While they are an improvement on values clarification, their anti-authoritative emphasis on "personal responsibility" rather than on absolute values and morals seems a fragile basis for promoting good behavior. For a summary of this new trend in character education, see Angela Dale, "Johnny Be Good: Character Education Tries to Retake the American Classroom," *Report Card* (Los Angeles: Center for the Study of Popular Culture), May/June 1995, p. 8.

62. See Bovard, "DARE Scare."

63. This information is taken from a "Summary of Outcome Evaluations" of Here's Looking at You, 2000 provided me by the publishers of the program, the Comprehensive Health Education Foundation.

64. Fred Musante, "Schools Revise Drug Lessons," *New York Times*, December 11, 1994.

65. Kilpatrick, *Why Johnny Can't Tell Right from Wrong*, p. 45.

66. Summary of Evaluation Results for Lions-Quest's *Skills for Growing* (grades K–5) and Lions-Quest's *Skills for Adolescence* (grades 6–8), August 1995, p. 6.

67. B. K. Eakman, *Educating for the New World Order* (Portland, OR: Halcyon House, 1991). See especially Chapter 28.

68. Ibid., pp. 10–15.

69. Ibid., p. 45.

70. Ibid., pp. 15–18.

71. John Dewey, *Democracy and Education* (New York: Macmillan, 1922), p. 115.

72. Ibid., pp. 100–101.

73. Ibid., p. 89.

74. See Lawrence A. Cremin, *The Transformation of the School: Progressivism in American Education, 1876–1957* (New York: Knopf, 1961), p. 124.

75. Sykes, *Dumbing Down Our Kids*, p. 202.

76. See Cremin, *The Transformation of the School*, pp. 59–63.

77. D. K. Osborne, *Early Childhood Education in Historical Perspective* (Athens, GA: Education Association, 1980), p. 98.

78. Sykes, *Dumbing Down Our Kids*, pp. 206–7.

79. Diane Ravitch, *Schools We Deserve: Reflections on the Education Crises of Our Time* (New York: Basic Books, 1985), pp. 126–27.

80. Diane Ravitch, *The Troubled Crusade: American Education, 1945–1980* (New York: Basic Books, 1983), Chapter 2.

81. For two excellent overviews of the decline of local, parental control in education

policy, see Dwight Roper, "Parents as the Natural Enemy of the School System," *Phi Delta Kappan*, December 1977, pp. 239–42; and L. Harmon Zeigler, Harvey J. Tucker, and L. A. Wilson, "How School Control Was Wrested from the People," *Phi Delta Kappan*, March 1977, pp. 534–39.

82. Ravitch, *The Troubled Crusade*, pp. 52–54.

83. Quoted in Christensen, *Utopia Against the Family*, p. 88.

84. Sykes, *Dumbing Down Our Kids*, p. 215.

85. Arthur Bestor, *Educational Wastelands: The Retreat from Learning in our Public Schools*, 2nd ed. (Urbana, IL: University of Illinois Press, 1985), quoted in Sykes, *Dumbing Down Our Kids*, p. 216.

86. Sykes, *Dumbing Down Our Kids*, p. 197.

87. Ibid., p. 199.

88. Donald W. Oliver, "Educating Citizens for Responsible Individualism: 1960–1980," reprinted in *Democracy, Pluralism, and the Social Studies*, ed., James P. Shaver and Harold Berlack (New York: Houghton Mifflin, 1968), p. 101.

89. Carl Rogers and H. Jerome Freiberg, *Freedom to Learn* (Columbus, OH: Charles E. Merrill Publishing Co., 1969).

90. Kilpatrick, *Why Johnny Can't Tell Right from Wrong*, p. 36.

91. In her book *The Troubled Crusade*, Diane Ravitch describes in detail the educational reformation of the early 1970s, and the philosophy of the "open classroom" that informed it. (See Chapter 7.)

92. Sykes, *Dumbing Down Our Kids*, pp. 150, 140–42.

93. Bernstein, *The Dictatorship of Virtue*, pp. 263, 266. It may be interesting to note here that Brookline was the scene of an ugly confrontation between school administrators and parents who noticed a creeping political bias and a distinct lowering of academic standards in the high school curriculum. It was particularly ugly because high school administrators refused to let parents see curricular materials, forcing them to request these materials through the Freedom of Information Act. (See Chapter 8.)

94. Ibid., p. 265.

95. Sykes, *Dumbing Down Our Kids*, p. 138.

96. Ibid., p. 139. It should be mentioned that the impact of special interest groups on school curricula is not limited to political advocacy organizations, but includes also corporations and professional advocacy groups. The American Bar Association sponsors an interactive TV course for high school kids in matrimonial relations. Entitled "Partners: Developing Healthy Peer Relationships," this course in communication skills also teaches the rudiments of divorce law on the assumption of its sponsors that "It's very important to know how to get out of a marriage." See Ellen Joan Pollock, "Kids Get Education in Adult Relationships," *Wall Street Journal*, November 9, 1994, pp. B1, B13. The American Heart Association sponsors an interdisciplinary curriculum for third-graders on the subject of the heart. An inappropriately large part of that curriculum consists of song and dance activities built around anti-smoking appeals, and sensitivity exercises. Finally an increasing number of corporate-designed lesson plans and educational packages are entering the classroom. While some have educational value, others seem to add up to little more than busywork framed around product endorsements. See David Shenk, "The Pedagogy of Pasta Sauce: Pretending to Help Teachers, Campbell's Teaches Consumerism," *Harper's*, September 1995, pp. 52–53.

97. Kathleen J. Roth, "Second Thoughts About Interdisciplinary Studies," *American Educator,* Spring 1994, pp. 44–48.
98. Sykes, *Dumbing Down Our Kids,* p. 230.
99. Ibid., p. 231.
100. For an explanation of outcome-based education by its founder, William Spady, see "Organizing for Results: The Basis of Authentic Restructuring and Reform," *Educational Leadership,* Vol. 46, No. 2, 1988, pp. 4–8.
101. Davis, "What Did You Learn in School Today?"
102. Linda Conner Lambeck, "New Learning Plan: Curse or Cure?," *Connecticut Post,* November 14, 1993, pp. A1, A6.
103. On parent revolts against OBE, see especially Vincent Carrol, "In Littleton, Colo., Voters Expel Education Faddists," *Wall Street Journal,* November 18, 1993; also Bernard Holland "Mobilized Parents Can Make a Difference," *Fairfax Journal,* May 10, 1993; and George Judson, "Bid to Revise Education Is Fought in Connecticut," *New York Times,* January 9, 1994.
104. Sykes, *Dumbing Down Our Kids,* p. 244.
105. Michael de Coursy Hinds, "Where School Is More Than Just Showing Up," *New York Times,* July 21, 1993, p. B10.
106. Sykes, *Dumbing Down Our Kids,* p. 245.
107. The desired "outcomes" quoted above come from OBE proposals in the states of Kentucky, Pennsylvania, Connecticut and the Milwaukee public school system.
108. Alan Bunce, "Little Praise for This English Prose: National English Standards Draw Fire for Being Too Vague and Inconclusive," *Christian Science Monitor,* April 1, 1996, p. 13.
109. Sykes, *Dumbing Down Our Kids,* p. 245.
110. See *Connecticut's Common Core of Learning* (Hartford, CT: Connecticut State Board of Education, 1987), especially pp. 5–8.
111. Wilton Public Schools, "Student Rights and Responsibilities: Grades K–5, 1995–1996" (Wilton, CT: Office of the Superintendent of Schools), p. 1.
112. See Maurice Holt, "The Educational Consequences of W. Edwards Deming," *Phi Delta Kappan,* January 1993, pp. 382–88; and Mike Schmoker, "Transforming Schools Through Total Quality Education," *Phi Delta Kappan,* January 1993, pp. 389–95.
113. Marian Mathews, "Gifted Students Talk About Cooperative Learning," *Educational Leadership,* October 1992.
114. Quanwu Zhang, "An Intervention Model of Constructive Conflict Resolution and Cooperative Learning," *Journal of Social Issues,* Vol. 50, No. 1, 1994, pp. 99–116; see particularly pp. 101 and 112–13.
115. David W. Johnson, Roger T. Johnson, Edythe Johnson Holubec, *Circles of Learning: Cooperation in the Classroom* (Edina, MN: Interaction, 1986), pp. 75–76.
116. For a lucid description of conflict management theories in their application to pedagogy and the classroom, see David W. Johnson and Roger T. Johnson, "Constructive Conflict in the Schools," *Journal of Social Issues,* Vol. 50, No. 1, 1994, pp. 117–34.
117. Connie Leslie, Nina Biddle, Debra Rosenberg, and Joe Wayne, "Girls Will Be Girls," *Newsweek,* August 2, 1993, p. 44.
118. From "Juvenile Offenders and Victims: 1996 Update on Violence," Office of Juvenile Justice and Delinquency Prevention.

119. Laura Kann et al., "Youth Risk Behavior Surveillance System—United States, 1993," Centers for Disease Control Surveillance Summaries, *Morbidity and Mortality Weekly Report* 44, No. SS-1 (Washington, D.C.: U.S. Government Printing Office, March 24, 1995), p. 29.

120. Laurel Shaper Walters, "School Violence Enters Suburbs," *Christian Science Monitor,* April 19, 1993.

121. Karen S. Peterson, "Educational Report Card: Helping Teens Keep Risks at Bay," *USA Today,* August 7, 1995.

122. Tim Rodin and Neal Starkman, *Here's Looking at You, 2000* (Seattle: Comprehensive Health Education Foundation, 1986), Second Grade Curriculum, Lesson 13.

123. Sowell, *Inside American Education,* p. 37.

124. Barbara Kantrowitz et. al., "Teen Violence: Wild in the Streets," *Newsweek,* August 2, 1993, p. 40.

125. "Across the USA: News from Every State," *USA Today,* January 11, 1996, p. 9A.

126. Dan Cray, Scott Norvell, and Bonnie I. Rochman, "Home Sweet School," *Time,* October 31, 1994, p. 63.

Chapter 5: Sex Ed in the School of Hard Knocks

1. This brief list of classroom sexuality education activities for different ages is compiled from a number of sources, among them William K. Kilpatrick's comprehensive chapter on sex education in *Why Johnny Can't Tell Right from Wrong* (New York: Simon & Schuster, 1992), and Charles Sykes's chapter entitled "The Values Wasteland" in *Dumbing Down Our Kids* (New York: St. Martin's, 1995). Also included were journalistic accounts of AIDS and sex education in the New York City and New Jersey schools by Maxine Smith and Barbara Dafoe Whitehead, respectively: "The New Facts of Life: Are New York School Children Learning Everything They Need to Know About Sex in the Age of AIDS? And How Much Is That Exactly?," *New York Woman,* November 1991, pp. 80–87; and "The Failure of Sex Education," *Atlantic Monthly,* October 1994, pp. 55–80. Also consulted were the sex education texts by Ruth Bell et al., *Changing Bodies, Changing Lives* (New York: Random House, 1987), and Peggy Brick, *Teaching Safer Sex* (Center for Family Life Education, Planned Parenthood of Bergen County, 1989).

2. Brent Bozell II, "Hollywood Has Little Respect for Children's Rights," reprinted as "The Media Affects Teen Sexuality," in Karin L. Swisher, ed., *Teen Sexuality: Opposing Viewpoints* (San Diego: Greenhaven Press, 1994), p. 40.

3. These elements of the curriculum were described to me in an interview with Bobbie Whitney, director of AIDS/HIV Education for the New York City Department of Education, in an interview of May 1992.

4. For an excellent account of the parent insurrection in New York City see George Marlin, "Parents: 1, Elites: 0," *Crisis,* February 1993, pp. 15–20.

5. Many elements of parent objections to both the HIV/AIDS and "Children of the Rainbow" curricula were outlined for me in a March 17, 1993, telephone interview with Louise Phillips, president of Staten Island's Parents for Restoration of Values in Education, a grassroots parents organization.

6. Marlin, "Parents 1, Elites 0," p. 19.

7. In Los Angeles in particular, blacks and Hispanics, aided by the well-known Traditional Values Coalition, have exercised vigilance in the area of sex education. Due in large part to their influence, abstinence-based AIDS education has been written into California law, and the distribution of provocative literature in the schools by activist gay and lesbian organizations has been curtailed. For gay and lesbian propagandizing in public education, see Manley Witten, Project 10: "What Schools Teach Children About Gay Sex," *Valley Magazine,* August 1988.

8. Sykes, *Dumbing Down Our Kids,* p. 170.

9. In the introduction to the 1991 Sexual Information and Education Council "Guidelines for Comprehensive Sexuality Education, Kindergarten–12th Grade," the authors contend that "Over 9 in 10 parents want their children to have it." The question, of course, is, Have what? With what elements of comprehensive sexuality education are parents comfortable? A 1986 Harris poll indicated that 95 percent of parents wanted their children to receive some education in HIV/AIDS prevention; 77 percent thought children as young as twelve should learn about birth control. Slightly less than two-thirds believed sex education should include "information about homosexuality, abortion, sexual intercourse and premarital sex." All of this looks like a broad-based parent mandate for comprehensive sex education, but what it probably signifies is broad-based support for informational programs, not for the heavily ideological and sexually provocative programs that have infiltrated many school districts. Even the ostensible parent mandate in certain areas for condom distribution (a Rutgers University survey, for example, indicated that 61 percent of parents with schoolage children say they would permit their child to get condoms from the schools) should perhaps not be taken at face value. From my talks with parents, the majority of whom seem seriously ambivalent about condoms in schools, one can only surmise that the basis for this seeming support is in parents' fears about a rapacious adolescent sexual environment, and their increasing feelings of powerlessness to influence their children's sexual behavior. In a 1993 article for *The American Enterprise* entitled "Teen Sex: Risks and Realism," Douglas Besharov notes that in a 1985 Harris poll, "only 4 percent of parents nationwide believed they had a 'great deal of control over their teenagers' sexual activity,' 37 percent thought they had 'some control,' 40 percent said they had 'not too much control,' and 18 percent said they had 'no control at all.' "

10. Quoted in Greg D. Erken, "Question: Does the U.S. Need a Parental Rights Amendment?" *Insight,* May 12, 1995, p. 18. The occasion for this observation was a school board meeting on sex education jam-packed with parents.

11. See Maltech, "An Analysis of U.S. Sex Education Programs and Evaluation Methods." Commissioned by the U.S. Department of Health, Education and Welfare by the Carter administration, this study argued the need for "comprehensive programs" that focused on the "clarification of values," and would make American students "more tolerant of the sexual practices of others."

12. For a picture of the contempt with which educators and health professionals treated parental consternation with the new sexual mores being taught in the schools, see Mary Breasted's *Oh! Sex Education,* a 1970 study of one California community. For the larger picture of sex education in the 1970s and 1980s, see Rita Kramer, *In Defense of the Family* (New York: Basic Books, 1983), pp. 145–52.

13. Barbara Whitehead, "Perspectives on the New Familism," Institute for American Values working paper, No. 8, June 1991, pp. 1, 6.

14. Information on condom availability programs as of June 1996 came from Advocates for Youth (formerly the Center for Population Options) in Washington, D.C., which publishes a fact sheet entitled "School Condom Availability."

15. All preceding quotations are from the Sexual Information and Education Council, "Guidelines for Comprehensive Sexuality Education, Kindergarten–12th Grade," National Guidelines Task Force, 1991.

16. Suzanne Alexander, "New Grade-School Sexuality Classes Go Beyond Birds and Bees to Explicit Basics," *Wall Street Journal*, April 2, 1993, p. B7

17. Bell et al., *Changing Bodies, Changing Lives*, p. 115.

18. Described in Kilpatrick, *Why Johnny Can't Tell Right from Wrong*, p. 57.

19. Brick, *Teaching Safer Sex*, p. 75.

20. Barbara Dafoe Whitehead, "The Failure of Sex Education," *Atlantic Monthly*, October 1994, p. 66.

21. I personally attended a New York Independent Schools sexuality education training session in the spring of 1992.

22. "Teen Pregnancy and School Based Clinics and Comprehensive Sex Education: Report to the 1990 Washington State Legislature," published by the Consortium of Health and Education Professionals, January 1990, p. 15.

23. See Kilpatrick, *Why Johnny Can't Tell Right from Wrong*, pp. 66–67.

24. See William A. Fisher and Deborah M. Roffman, "Adolescence: A Risky Time," *Independent School: Sexuality Education in the Age of AIDS*, Spring 1992, pp. 25–32.

25. Ibid.

26. These statistics on the relationship between comprehensive sex education funding and pregnancy rates are taken from "Abstinence Based Sex Education in Historical Perspective," published by the National Association for Abstinence Education, 1991, pp. 2–5.

27. Stan E. Weed and Joseph A. Olsen, "Policy and Program Consideration for Teenage Pregnancy Prevention: A Summary for Policymakers," *Family Perspective*, Vol. 22, No. 3, 1989, pp. 235–52.

28. See Kilpatrick, *Why Johnny Can't Tell Right from Wrong*, p. 55. See also Ellen Flax, "Explosive Data Confirm Prediction: AIDS Is Spreading Among Teenagers," *Education Week*, October 1989, p. 12.

29. "Teen Pregnancy and School Based Clinics and Comprehensive Sex Education," p. 6.

30. M. Story, "A Longitudinal Study of Effects of a University Human Sexuality Course on Sexual Attitudes," *Journal of Sexual Research*, Vol. 15, No. 3, August 1979, pp. 184–204.

31. Hans H. Neumann, M.D. "Does Sex Education in Schools Help or Hurt?," *Medical Economics*, May 24, 1982, pp. 35–40.

32. A Lou Harris/Planned Parenthood poll found that kids who had gone through comprehensive sexuality programs stressing condom use were 53 percent more likely to initiate sexual intercourse. Lou Harris and Associates, "America's Teens Speak: Sex, Myths, and Birth Control: The Planned Parenthood Poll," 1986. A study by Humboldt State University Professor Jacqueline Kasun in the Humboldt County, California, school district, where a comprehensive sex education program was well established, found a teen pregnancy rate of ten times the national average. See Jacqueline R. Kasun, "Sex Education: The Hidden Agenda," *The World & I*, September 1989, p. 497. Similarly, a study done in Virginia linked comprehensive sex education with a 17 percent increase in pregnancy

rates. (See Josh McDowell, *The Myths of Sex Education* [San Bernardino, CA: Here's Life Publishers, 1990].)

33. Pamela Wilson, "Educating About Sexuality: Children Remember Tunes, Not Lyrics," *Independent School,* Spring 1992, pp. 8–9.

34. Unless otherwise noted, the report on Falmouth's comprehensive sex education and condom availability program is based on my observations in the Falmouth schools on two visits: on October 21–23, 1992, and January 11–12, 1993. At the time I interviewed the high school sex education instructors, the coordinator of the health curriculum, Helen Ladd, high school nurse Shirley Cullinane, and assistant superintendent of schools Peter L. Clark.

35. As I complete this manuscript, I read that in several areas of the country now, statuatory rape laws are being used to prosecute adult men who father the children of teenage girls. The reason is that research has shown that at least half of births to teenage girls are fathered by adult men. Also it appears that in some communities, girls are being prosecuted on the basis of old statutes that prohibit sexual intercourse between unmarried couples.

36. Facts on the condom availability controversy were gathered from talks with Falmouth parents—specifically in the context of a January 11 group discussion held at Falmouth High School with fourteen pro-condom parents, on a discussion with the leadership of Concerned Citizens, and on perusals of local newspapers, including the *Boston Globe* and the *Cape Cod Times.* I should note here that I am grateful for all the time and consideration the Falmouth parents on both sides of the issue lent me, as well as the openness and cooperation displayed by the high school faculty and school district administration.

37. I found these comments very interesting, because they confirmed what I had witnessed in attending two classes in January 1993 on sexual orientation. Many boys were openly hostile and mocking during discussion of homosexuality and homophobia.

38. This is confirmed in a memorandum of December 15, 1992, sent to the Falmouth School Committee by Assistant Superintendent Peter Clark.

39. Quotations from the survey come from a copy provided me by Concerned Citizens of Falmouth.

40. These two quotations gathered from a telephone interview with James Remillard in spring 1993 and his comments to the press. See Paul Anderson, "Falmouth Shreds Student Survey," *Cape Cod Times,* February 11, 1993.

41. Judith A. Reisman: "A Brief Review of Falmouth Schools' Drug and Alcohol Survey III," December 31, 1992, pp. 1, 5 (copy provided me by Concerned Citizens of Falmouth). Dr. Reisman was the first scholar to challenge the Kinsey Institute research on child sexuality, is an expert on child pornography, has been a consultant for the Department of Health and Human Services and the Department of Education, and has done in-service training for the FBI Academy and the Center for Missing and Exploited Children in Washington, D.C.

42. Reisman, "A Brief Review of Falmouth Schools' Drug and Alcohol Survey," p. 5.

43. Margaret Hough Russell, "New Health Survey Will Get Public Hearing; School Board Votes to Destroy '92 Results," *Falmouth Enterprise,* February 12, 1993.

44. In 1992, for example, there were forty-nine births to teenage mothers in the Falmouth-Mashpee area, the area of the school district's jurisdiction. Ninety-two percent of these teen mothers were single, their average age being the youngest ever—17.9 years. See "Toward a Better Future," published by Falmouth-Mashpee Teen Pregnancy Prevention Coalition, 1993, p. 4.

45. Information on STDs was received in a telephone call to the Massachusetts Department of Public Health in spring 1993.

46. Nineteen ninety-four pregnancy statistics taken from "Community Birth Fact Sheet: Barnstable/Dukes/Nantucket Counter, 1994," published by Bureau of Family and Community Health, Massachusetts Department of Public Health, table 21. STD statistics obtained in a telephone conversation in the spring of 1993 to the Massachusetts Department of Public Health.

47. Weed and Olsen, "Policy and Program Considerations for *Teenage Pregnancy Prevention*," pp. 240–41.

48. Centers for Disease Control statistics indicate that after having gone down, condom use is going up among sexually active teenagers. A study released in 1995 indicated that 52.8 percent of sexually active high school students in 1993 had used a condom during their last act of intercourse, up from 46.2 percent in 1991. See Jo Anna Natale, "The Hot New Word in Sex Ed," *American School Board Journal,* June 1995, p. 19.

49. Whitehead, "The Failure of Sex Education," p. 70.

50. Ibid., p. 80.

51. Jennifer Steinhauer, "Study Cites Adult Males for Most Teen-Age Births," *New York Times,* August 2, 1995, p. A10.

52. Leslie M. Kantor, "Scared Chaste? Fear-Based Educational Curricula," *SIECUS Report,* December 1992/January 1993, reprinted abridged as "Many Abstinence Based Programs Are Harmful," in Swisher, ed. *Teenage Sexuality,* pp. 158–66.

53. These encouraging reports about abstinence education cited in Kilpatrick, *Why Johnny Can't Tell Right from Wrong,* p. 73.

54. Jane Gross, "Sex Educators for Young See New Virtue in Chastity," *New York Times,* January 16, 1994.

55. Reported in Douglas J. Besharov, "Teen Sex: Risks and Realism," reprinted as "Improved Education Could Reduce Teen Pregnancy," in Swisher, ed., *Teenage Sexuality,* p.113.

56. "Learning to Play the Waiting Game," *Independent School,* Spring 1992, pp. 8–9.

57. Gross, "Sex Educators for Young See New Virtue in Chastity."

58. See "Saved for Marriage," *Washington Watch* (newsletter published by the Family Research Council), Vol. 6, No. 1, October 14, 1994, p. 1.

Chapter 6: The Workfare/Day Care Trap

1. The federal school lunch program was originally conceived as a national security initiative. During World War II, it was found that large numbers of men called up for military duty suffered nutritional deficiencies.

2. Elizabeth Gleick, "Welfare: To Be Leaner or Meaner? A Congressional Proposal to Eliminate Nutrition Programs Raises an Outcry," *Time,* March 6, 1995, p. 45.

3. Linda Feldman, "Welfare Debate: How Will Children Fare?" *Christian Science Monitor,* March 3, 1995, p. 1.

4. Ibid.

5. The Meridan story as recounted here is taken from my own research interviews, which resulted in a *Wall Street Journal* article of September 29, 1993, entitled "Breakfast at Tiffany's School." The breakfast program was estimated to bear a cost of between $16,000 and $19,000 per year, not including electricity, custo-

dial work, and other in-kind services that would be the responsibility of the town, even assuming the steady help of funding from above.

6. Cheryl Wetzstein, "Genital Exams at School Irk Parents," *Washington Times,* April 26, 1996, pp. A1, A5.
7. Cathleen Cleaver, "Whose Children Are They?," *Bangladesh Observer,* November 28, 1995.
8. Angela Dale, "Villages of the Damned," *Report Card* (Los Angeles: Center for the Study of Popular Culture), July-August, 1995, pp. 1, 12.
9. Ibid., p. 13.
10. M. Joycelyn Elders, "School-Based Clinics to the Rescue," *The School Administrator,* September 1992, pp. 16–21.
11. Jeanne Jehl and Michael Kirst, "Spinning a Family Support Web Among Agencies and Schools," *The School Administrator,* September 1992, pp. 8–15.
12. Charles Sykes, *Dumbing Down Our Kids* (New York: St. Martin's, 1995), p. 229.
13. Dale, "Villages of the Damned," p. 12.
14. Phyllis Schlafly, "Let Schools Take Over for Parents?," *Washington Times,* December 12, 1993.
15. Dale, "Villages of the Damned," p. 13.
16. Ibid., p. 14.
17. Margot Hornblower, "It Takes a School: A New Approach to Elementary Education Starts at Birth and Doesn't Stop When the Bell Rings," *Time,* June 3, 1996, p. 37.
18. Ibid.
19. "Project BEGIN, Bringing Early Growth (and Development) Into Neighborhoods," Centers for Disease Control, November 16, 1994.
20. Angela E. Couloumbis, "New Targets for Head Start: Children in Diapers," *Christian Science Monitor,* March 22, 1994, pp.1, 4.
21. Bryce Christensen, *Utopia Against the Family,* (San Francisco: Ignatius Press, 1990), pp. 71–73.
22. Ibid., pp. 74–75.
23. Ron Haskins, "Public School Aggression Among Children with Varying Day Care Experience," *Child Development,* Vol. 56, 1985, p. 700.
24. Peter Barglow et al., "Effects of Maternal Absence Due to Employment on the Quality of Infant-Mother Attachment in a Low Risk Sample," *Child Development,* Vol. 58, 1987, p. 952.
25. I use the term "bonding" here in the same way Magid does, in reference to the establishment over a period of several years of a close, emotionally engaged relationship between parent and child. Many psychologists would prefer to replace the term "bonding," when used in this sense, with "attachment," because of the popularity of a number of spurious psychological theories of bonding that centered on the importance of certain immediate steps following birth that were alleged to have far-reaching affects on personality development. See particularly William Damon, *Greater Expectations* (New York: Free Press, 1995), pp. 111–14.
26. Ken Magid and Carole A. McKelvey, *High Risk: Children Without a Conscience* (New York: Bantam, 1989), p. 130.
27. Ibid., p. 79.
28. Jay Belsky, "Infant Day Care and Socioemotional Development: The United States," *Journal of Child Psychology,* Vol. 29, 1988, p. 402.
29. Jerome Kagan, Richard Kearsley, and Philip Zelazo, *Infancy: Its Place in Human*

Development (Cambridge: Harvard University Press, 1978), p. 171, quoted in Christensen, *Utopia Against the Family*, p. 75.

30. Joseph J. Tobin, David Y. H. Wu, and Dana H. Davidson, *Preschool in Three Cultures: Japan, China and the United States* (New Haven: Yale University Press, 1989), pp. 147–48.

31. Couloumbis, "New Targets for Head Start," p. 1.

32. Richard J. Herrnstein and Charles Murray, *The Bell Curve: Intelligence and Class Structure in American Life* (New York: Free Press, 1994), p. 405.

33. See Douglas Besharov, "A New Start for Head Start," *American Enterprise Magazine*, March/April 1992, p. 54; and Herrnstein and Murray, *The Bell Curve*, p. 405. For the Cornell consortium's work, see I. Lazar and R. Darlington, "Lasting Effects of Early Education: A Report from the Consortium for Longitudinal Studies," *Monographs of the Society for Research in Child Development*, Vol. 47, 1982, Issues 2–3.

34. Douglas J. Besharov, "Welfare: An Albatross for Young Mothers," *Wall Street Journal*, February 28, 1996, p. A14.

35. Besharov, "A New Start for Head Start," p. 53.

36. Herrnstein and Murray, *The Bell Curve*, p. 523.

37. Ibid., p. 526.

38. Besharov, "A New Start for Head Start," p. 57.

39. A good summary of this research can be found in Brenda Hunter, Ph.D., "The Relationship Between a Woman's Attachment History and Her Work/Family Decisions," *Insight* (published by the Family Research Council), 1994.

40. Hillary Rodham Clinton, *It Takes a Village and Other Lessons Children Teach Us* (New York: Simon & Schuster, 1996), p. 78.

41. Author interview of Elizabeth Gill, May 1996.

42. Bryce Christensen quotes feminist psychologist Sandra Scarr in *Utopia Against the Family*, p. 77.

43. Mary Jo Bane and David Ellwood, *Welfare Realities: From Rhetoric to Reform* (Cambridge: Harvard University Press, 1994), pp. 48–53.

44. Quotation from the Family Support Act of 1988 cited in ibid., p. 1.

45. This was the conclusion of several surveys of workfare programs as reported in the Family Research Council's newsletter, *Washington Watch*, January 17, 1995, p. 3.

46. Ellen Willis, "Why I'm Not 'Pro-Family,' " *Glamour*, October 1994, p. 153.

47. David Blankenhorn, "Not Orphanages or Prisons, but Responsible Fathers," *Los Angeles Times*, December 19, 1994.

48. These figures are taken from Charles Murray, "What to Do About Welfare," *Commentary*, December 1994, pp. 29–30.

49. Wade F. Horn, Ph.D., "Fathers and Welfare Reform: Making Room for Daddy," *Fatherhood Today* (published by the National Fatherhood Initiative), Vol. 1, No. 4, Winter 1996, p. 3.

50. Horn, "Fathers and Welfare Reform," p. 3.

51. For more information on the Indianapolis Rebuilding Families Initiatives, which includes intensive family preservation efforts, peer-mentoring abstinence support for teenagers, linking unmarried teen parents and their families with churches, and many other good ideas, see "The Indianapolis Rebuilding Families Initatives," Spring/Summer 1996 (published by the Office of Mayor Stephen Goldsmith).

52. Bane and Ellwood, *Welfare Realities*, pp. 45, 150.
53. On the connection between fatherless homes and various social pathologies, including juvenile violence and teenage childbearing, see David Blankenhorn, *Fatherless America* (New York: Basic Books, 1995), Chapter 2. Many other well-known recent works discuss the apparent relationship between the disappearance of fathers in inner-city neighborhoods and the social pathologies of youth. It seems that family structure is an important predictor of successful child outcomes.
54. Irwin Garfinkel and Sara S. McLanahan, "Single Mothers and Their Children: A New American Dilemma" (Washington, D.C.: Urban Institute, 1986), pp. 30–31.
55. William A. Galston and Elaine Ciulla Kaymarck, "Putting Children First: A Progressive Family Policy for the 1990s" (Washington, D.C.: Progressive Policy Institute, September 1990), p. 14.
56. James Q. Wilson, "Culture, Incentives and the Underclass," in Henry J. Aaron, Thomas E. Mann, and Timothy Taylor, eds., *Values and Public Policy* (Washington, D.C.: Brookings Institution, 1994), pp. 70–71.
57. David Whitman, "A Reality Check on Welfare Reform: Detroit's Experience Shows It's Not So Simple," *U.S. News & World Report*, November 13, 1995.
58. Noted by author on May 29, 1996, at a meeting of the Council on American Families.
59. Similarly, the following advice is given by Gloria Norris and Jo Ann Miller on p. 261 of *The Working Mother's Complete Handbook* (New York: New American Library, 1984): "The best strategy a single mother can adopt is to establish a support system to replace the traditional two-parent family."
60. Arlie Hochschild with Anne Machung, *The Second Shift* (New York: Avon, 1990), p. 243.
61. John R. Seeley, R. Alexander Sim, and Elizabeth W. Loosley, *Crestwood Heights: A Study of the Culture of Suburban Life* (New York: Basic Books, 1956), p. 376.
62. Ibid., p. 284
63. Statistics taken from David R. Francis, "Who Works Hardest? Psst, Working Wives," *Christian Science Monitor*, March 24, 1995, p. 8.
64. "Mothers Speak Out on Child Care" (Merrifield, VA: Mothers at Home, 1989), p. 11.
65. Betty Friedan, *The Second Stage* (New York: Summit, 1981).
66. For a concise summary of this conflict, see Elizabeth Fox-Genovese, *"Feminism Is Not the Story of My Life": How Today's Feminist Elite Has Lost Touch with the Real Concerns of Women* (New York: Nan A. Talese/Doubleday, 1996), pp. 213–15. Schwartz outlined her views in *Breaking with Tradition: Women, Work and the New Facts of Life* (New York: Warner, 1992).
67. Fox-Genovese, *"Feminism Is Not the Story of My Life,"* p. 224.
68. Willis, "Why I'm Not 'Pro-Family,' " p. 152.
69. Author telephone interview with Heidi Brennan, April 1995.
70. Michele Ingrassia and Pat Wingert, "The New Providers," *Newsweek*, May 22, 1995, p. 38.
71. Hochschild with Machung, *The Second Shift*, p. 262.
72. Ibid., pp. 197–98.
73. Ibid., p. 262.
74. In conjunction with Louis Harris Associates, Julie Brines of the University of Washington did a 1995 survey of housework in two-income families. She found

that the biggest housework burden was on women who were housewives or whose earnings represented a minimal contribution to the household. In households where women's earnings were equal to men's, men contributed around ten hours to their wives' fifteen. But in marriages where wives contributed significantly more than husbands to income, women had proportionately more of the household burden once again. See Ingrassia and Wingert, "The New Providers," p. 37.

75. Sylvia Ann Hewlett, "Tough Choices, Great Rewards," *Parade*, July 16, 1994, p. 5.

76. William R. Mattox Jr., "The Parent Trap: So Many Bills, So Little Time," *Policy Review*, Winter 1991, p. 9.

77. Lester C. Thurow, "Companies Merge; Families Break Up," *New York Times*, September 3, 1995.

78. Blankenhorn, *Fatherless America*, p. 110.

79. Mattox, "The Parent Trap," p. 10.

80. Blankenhorn, *Fatherless America*, pp. 105–6.

81. Mattox, "The Parent Trap," p. 6.

82. William R. Mattox Jr., "The Family Friendly Corporation: Strengthening the Ties That Bind," *Family Policy* (a publication of the Family Research Council), November 1992.

83. Several research projects undertaken in the late 1980s and early 1990s showed that home-based work arrangements were not only family-friendly, because they offered parents more time with children and the luxury of organizing their work schedules around family lives, but also that they revealed significant bottom-line benefits. For a summary of these flex-place pilot programs and demonstration projects, see "Productivity Benefits of Home-Based Work," *In Focus* (a publication of the Family Research Council, 1992). See also Caroline Hull, "The Flexible Workplace," *Insight* (publication ISIS94C2WF of the Family Research Council, 1994).

84. The preceding information was taken from an information package sent to me by Work/Family Directions, the Boston-based consulting firm that is coordinator of the American Business Collaboration for Quality Dependent Care.

85. Sandra L. Burud, Pamela R. Aschbacher, and Jacquelyn McCroskey, *Employer Supported Child Care* (Dover, MA: Auburn House, 1984), quoted in Mattox, "The Family Friendly Corporation," p. 6.

86. *DuPont Corporate News*, October 30, 1995, pp.1, 4.

87. Marilyn Gardner, "Handling the Holiday Season's Time Crunch," *Christian Science Monitor*, December 4, 1995, p. 13.

88. David Ruben, "Clinton Scorecard: How's He Doing?," *Parenting*, August 1993, p. 66.

89. Marilyn Gardner, "U.S. Workers, Companies Give Family-Leave Law Good Grade: Study Finds Concerns of Cost, Burden Largely Unfounded," *Christian Science Monitor*, May 6, 1996, p. 15.

Chapter 7: Material Kids

1. Quotations from Jules Henry taken from *Culture Against Man* (New York: Vintage, 1963), p. 127.

2. Elizabeth Jensen, "It's 8 P.M. Your Kids Are Watching Sex on TV," *Wall Street Journal*, March 27, 1995, p. B6.

3. Statistics taken from Marilyn Gardner, "TV Values: Bart's Bad Influence," *Christian Science Monitor*, February 28, 1995, p. 4.

4. William Lutz, *Doublespeak: From "Revenue Enhancement" to "Terminal Living": How Government, Business, Advertisers, and Others Use Language to Deceive You* (New York: Harper Perennial, 1989), p. 73.

5. Gardner, "TV Values." These statistics are taken from a study done by Katharine Heintz-Knowles, of the University of Washington.

6. Jim Farber, "Music Reviews," *Seventeen*, December 1994, p. 76; and Cintra Scott, "News That Makes Your World Go 'Round: Brand New," *Seventeen*, December 1994, p. 50.

7. Barbara Kantrowitz et al., "Teen Violence: Wild in the Streets," *Newsweek*, August 2, 1993, p. 43.

8. David Gelman, "The Violence in Our Heads," *Newsweek*, August 2, 1993, p. 48.

9. See James Q. Wilson, "What to Do About Crime," *Commentary*, September 1994, pp. 25–34.

10. Gelman, "The Violence in Our Heads."

11. Michael Medved, *Hollywood vs. America: Popular Culture and the War on Traditional Values* (New York: HarperCollins/Zondervan, 1992), p. 199.

12. Deborah Prothrow-Stith, M.D. (with Michael Weissman), *Deadly Consequences* (New York: HarperCollins, 1991), particularly Chapter 3. The effects of media violence on viewer aggression are still a subject of controversy among social scientists, but several research studies indicate that steady viewing of violent images does have a measurable impact both on the disposition to commit violent acts, and on desensitization to violence. For a short summary of these, see Tipper Gore, *Raising PG Kids in an X-Rated Society* (New York: Bantam, 1988), pp. 50–53. See also Lynettte Friedrich-Cofer and Letha Huston, "Television Violence and Aggression: The Debate Continues," *Psychological Bulletin*, Vol. 100, 1986.

13. Snoop Doggy Dogg, "Ain't No Fun," *Doggystyle* (Death Row/Interscope Records, 1993).

14. William Bennett, Joe Lieberman, and C. DeLores Tucker, "Rap Rubbish: Shame Those Who Profit from Obnoxious Songs," *USA Today*, June 6, 1996.

15. N.W.A., "Findum, F—um & Flee," *Efil4zaggin* (Ruthless/Priority Records, 1991). This album, Michael Medved reports, "zoomed to the number-one position on the *Billboard* chart just two weeks after its release in June of 1991." Medved, *Hollywood vs. America*, p. 98.

16. Medved, *Hollywood vs. America*, p. 106.

17. Ibid., pp. 102–3.

18. Gore, *Raising PG Kids in an X-Rated Society*, p. 130.

19. Ibid., p. 63. The lyrics, from the song "Shoot to Thrill," come from an album entitled *Back in Black* recorded by the rock group AC/DC (Atlantic Records, 1980).

20. The quotation is from Tupac Shakur's 1996 CD *All Eyez on Me* (Death Row/Interscope Records) quoted in J. Whyatt Mondesire, "2Pac . . . When Will You Start Behaving Like a Real Black Man," *Philadelphia Sun*, February 23, 1996.

21. Green Day, "Longview," *Dookie* (Reprise Records, 1994).

22. Garbage, "Only Happy When It Rains," *Garbage* (Almo Records, 1995).

23. Bush, "Bomb," *Sixteen Stone* (Interscope Records, 1994).

24. Martha Bayles, *Hole in Our Soul: The Loss of Beauty and Meaning in American Popular Music* (New York: Free Press, 1994).

25. Donna Gaines, *Teenage Wasteland: Suburbia's Dead End Kids* (New York: Pantheon, 1991).

26. During the Christmas season of 1995, when C. DeLores Tucker led a protest against Tower Records' distribution of the album *Dogg Food* in Washington, D.C., Grace J. Berges, legal counsel for the parent company of the store, declared in defense of the material, "We're strong supporters of the right to free speech."

27. Bayles, *Hole in Our Soul*, pp. 258–59.

28. "Art and Young Americans, 1974–79: Results from the Second National Art Assessment" (Denver: National Assessment of Educational Progress, 1981), pp. 4, 5, 61.

29. Wynton Marsalis's 1995 PBS special on the elements of music, has I hope, in some way broadened American children's appreciation for the black American contribution to music.

30. Neil Postman, *The End of Education* (New York: Knopf, 1995), p. 162.

31. See Andrea Stone, "Jewish Teen Stands Against Utah Choir's Christian Tone," *USA Today*, November 2, 1995, p. 2A. It should be noted that in this particular case, it seems that the chorus director may indeed have pushed the line between responsible representation of religious music and proselytization; press reports on the case suggest that the pieces sung, although religious, were less than aesthetically rewarding. In 1995, the U.S. Department of Education issued guidelines on religious education and expression in public schools in order to avoid more such legal suits while protecting the fundamental right of students to religious expression. Unfortunately, since the publication of these guidelines, the number of cases revolving around "legally permissible" expressions of religion in public schools has increased 50 percent. The guidelines, incidentally, stress that public schools should teach the role of religion in history and literature, as well as expose children to the holy days of different religious faiths, but they may not endorse one particular religion over another. While students have the right to privately organize and engage in prayer, to wear religious clothing, and to express religious views in their individual schoolwork, the school may not require or sponsor prayer. Still a focus of contention is whether "non-sectarian, student-initiated, voluntary prayer" in a public setting (for example a graduation ceremony) is allowable. For a short summary of the guidelines, see Mark A. Kellner, "Guidelines Are Helpful, but Educators Uninformed," *Christianity Today*, March 4, 1996, p. 71.

32. Postman, *The End of Education*, pp. 151–52.

33. William Kilpatrick, *Why Johnny Can't Tell Right from Wrong* (New York: Simon & Schuster, 1992), pp. 213–14.

34. Ibid., pp. 214–22.

35. Nancy W. Yos, "Teach Me, a Catholic Cri de Coeur," *First Things*, April 1992, pp. 23–24. For a more recent reflection on the "doctrinal rootlessness" of Catholic religious education, see Jennifer Bradley, "My So-Called Faith: A Nice Catholic Girl Confesses, *New Republic*, January 9, 1995, pp. 18–19. Bradley laments that "throughout my adolescence, priests and Sunday school teachers were trying so hard to entertain us . . . that they neglected to educate us." See also Arthur Jones, "Tell Them Nose Rings Are Not Enough: The Faith We Teach," *National Catholic Reporter*, Vol. 42, September 3, 1993, p. 2. The letter, an argument against some of the false trappings of culture displayed among the young, tells the story of Tom and Maryanne Russell, La Jolla, California, parents

who believe community service is one avenue by which children can better learn the values of the Catholic Church.

36. *Youth Indicators, 1991: Trends in the Well Being of American Youth*, Office of Educational Research, U.S. Department of Education, p. 123.

37. Jeffrey Salkin, *Putting God on the Guest List: How to Reclaim the Spiritual Meaning of Your Child's Bar or Bat Mitzvah* (Woodstock, VT: Jewish Lights Publishing, 1992).

38. Irving Kristol, "Why Religion Is Good for the Jews," *Commentary*, August 1994, pp. 19–21.

39. Don Browning, "How the Family Became a Central Issue in America: 1990–1994," working paper for the upcoming volume *Religion and the American Family Debate* (New York: Institute for American Values, 1995), pp. 22–23.

40. Gilbert Meilaender, "The Christian View of the Family," in *Rebuilding the Nest*, David Blankenhorn, Steven Bayme, and Jean Bethke Elshtain, eds. (Milwaukee, WI: Family Service America, 1990), pp. 133–47.

41. These comments came in a telephone interview with Professor Don Browning in June 1996 on the subject of Christian theology and the symbol of the cross.

42. Two short works of the 1980s that were very influential in the new theology of love were Barbara Andolsen, "Agape in Feminist Ethics," *Journal of Religious Ethics*, Vol. 9, No. 1, Spring 1981, pp. 69–83; and Christine Doodorf, "Parenting, Mutual Love and Sacrifice," in Barbara Andolsen, ed., *Women's Consciousness, Women's Conscience* (New York: Winston Press, 1985), pp. 175–91.

43. Mary Daly, *Beyond God the Father: Towards a Philosophy of Women's Liberation* (Boston: Beacon Press, 1973), pp. 189–90.

44. Ibid., p. 198.

45. For Neil Postman's brilliant and amusing insight into the TV commercial as religious parable, see *The End of Education*, pp. 34–35.

46. Daly, *Beyond God the Father*, p. 69.

47. Dan Coats, excerpt from a speech before the Conference on Jewish and Christian Values, May 20, 1996.

48. Browning, "How the Family Became a Central Issue in America," p. 27.

49. Ibid., p. 28–29.

50. This conference took place May 20–21, 1996.

51. John Paul II, *Crossing the Threshold of Hope* (New York: Knopf, 1994), pp. 118, 123.

PART III: THE FAMILIST COUNTERCULTURE

Chapter 8: Alternative Schooling

1. 1996 Estimates of the Home School Legal Defense Association, provided by Christy Farris, of the National Center for Home Education, in a telephone interview, June 1996.

2. Nancy Gibbs, "Home Sweet School," *Time*, October 31, 1994, p. 62.

3. Author interview by telephone with Maureen Carey, May 1994.

4. Brian D. Ray, "Marching to the Beat of Their Own Drum" (Paeonian Springs, VA: Home School Legal Defense Association, 1992), p. 5.

5. Steve Stecklow, "Fed Up with Schools, More Parents Turn to Teaching at Home," *Wall Street Journal,* May 10, 1994, p. A1.

6. Ray, "Marching to the Beat of Their Own Drum," p. 5.

7. Ibid.

8. These comments were made in a telephone interview with Steve Stecklow, May 1994.

9. David Colfax and Micki Colfax, *Homeschooling for Excellence* (New York: Warner, 1988), pp. 33, 39.

10. David D. Williams, Larry Arnoldsen, Peter Reynolds, "Understanding Home Education: Case Studies of Home Schools," No. 5, Conference Paper for the Educational Research Association in New Orleans, April 1984.

11. Author telephone interview with Cheryl Ann Hughes, May 1994.

12. Grace Llewellyn, ed. *Real Lives: Eleven Teenagers Who Don't Go to School* (Eugene, OR: Lowry House, 1993), p. 88.

13. See "A Nationwide Study of Home Education: Home School Court Report, December 1990"; synopsis published by the Home School Legal Defense Association (Paeonian Springs, VA, 1990), pp. 5, 8.

14. Statistics on standardized achievement tests of home-schooled children are taken from "Marching to the Beat of Their Own Drum," pp. 6–9.

15. Benjamin Moore, "Home Schooling: An Idea Whose Time Has Returned," *Human Events,* Vol. 44, September 15, 1984, pp. 824–27.

16. David Guterson, *Family Matters: Why Home Schooling Makes Sense* (New York: Harcourt, Brace, Jovanovich, 1992), p. 16.

17. See James Coleman et al. *Equality of Educational Opportunity* (Washington, D.C.: U.S. Department of Health, Education and Welfare, 1966). In the past thirty years an enormous body of research on the characteristics of effective schools and the relationship of parent support to school effectiveness has emerged. Effective schools tend to serve larger numbers of families that are more prosperous and have obtained higher educational levels; however, other family-determined factors not so closely related to the socioeconomic level of the parent population characterize them: There are more two-parent families, more learning tools at home, homework is monitored by fathers as well as mothers, and parents encourage their kids. Family characteristics are, of course, one of many influences on educational success. School organization—an atmosphere of discipline, order, and high academic expectations—turns out to be every bit as important and can override negative family influences. For a good summary of family influences on student achievment, see John E. Chubb and Terry M. Moe, *Politics, Markets and America's Schools* (Washington, D.C.: Brookings Institution, 1990), particularly pp. 14–16 and 105–11. A new study by Temple University psychology professor Laurence Steinberg entitled *Beyond the Classroom: Why School Reform Has Failed and What Parents Need to Do* (New York: Simon & Schuster, 1996) warns that parents' "disconnect" from schools, their children, and their children's education renders young people increasingly susceptible to the negative influences of the peer culture, and is spelling school failure. The study goes overboard in assigning educators little blame for the failure of schools, but it does point (and rightly so) to the importance of parental involvement in the educational enterprise, and also to the dangers of a peer culture that denigrates academic achievement.

18. John Holt, *Teach Your Own* (New York: Delacorte, 1981), p. 4.

19. This Holt quote is from the jacket of *Teach Your Own*.

20. Bryce Christensen, *Utopia Against the Family* (San Francisco: Ignatius Press, 1990), p. 88.

21. J. David Colfax, "Beyond the Classroom," in Anne Pedersen and Peggy O'Mara, eds., *Schooling at Home: Parents, Kids and Learning* (Santa Fe, NM: John Muir Publications, 1990), p. 192.

22. Holt, *Teach Your Own*, p. 280. The details of the Perchemlides story along with quotations from Susan Perchemlides and the Amherst superintendent of schools come from an account in Chapter 7 of Stephen Arons, *Compelling Belief: The Culture of American Schooling* (New York: McGraw-Hill, 1983), pp. 78, 81, and 83.

23. Stephen Arons, *Compelling Belief: The Culture of American Schooling*, p. viii.

24. Brian Robertson, "Is Home Schooling in a Class of Its Own?," *Insight*, October 17, 1994, p. 6.

25. Guterson, *Family Matters*, p. 63.

26. On the dramatic rise in private school enrollment, see Steve Stecklow, "Born Again: Evangelical Schools Reinvent Themselves by Stressing Academics," *Wall Street Journal*, May 12, 1994, p. A1.

27. Dr. Steven Adamowski, senior fellow of the Hudson Institute, fears a downward spiral for the public schools, which, he says, seem in many areas of the country "unable to hold the middle-classes." Recently the *Christian Science Monitor* featured a cover story on the exodus of minorities in inner cities from the public schools, and the explosion among inner-city populations of church-based private education alternatives. According to Joan David Ratteray, president of the Washington-based Institute for Independent Education, there are at least four hundred black independent schools, at least half of which are Christian academies. The past five years have witnessed a dramatic growth in the number of African-American alternative schools, typified, according to the *Christian Science Monitor* report, by the case of Atlanta's Believer's Academy, which started out with nineteen preschool pupils in 1991 and by 1996 boasted a preschool to sixth-grade program of 250 students. What attracts African-Americans to alternative schooling? According to parents, the desire to have their children learn traditional Christian values and the greater possibilities for parental involvement in their children's education. See Elizabeth Levitan Spaid, "Blacks Eschew Public Schools for Classrooms with Scripture," *Christian Science Monitor*, August 21, 1996, p. 1.

28. Enrollment numbers are taken from National Association of Independent Schools Fact Sheets, August 1991 and November 1995, published by the NAIS Office of Public Information, Washington, D.C.

29. NAIS Statistics, 1995, Table 3, as sent to me by the NAIS Public Information Office, Washington, D.C.

30. NAIS statistics on boarding school enrollment in New York are taken from New York State Association of Independent Schools, Bulletin No. 153, November 1990. An overview of the boarding school problem was gleaned in telephone interviews with representatives of the NAIS Public Information Office in June 1996. See also Rick Tetzel, "Holden Caulfield, Where Are You?," *Fortune*, June 14, 1993, p. 12, and David V. Hicks, "The Strange Fate of the American Boarding School," *The American Scholar*, Vol. 65, Autumn 1996, pp. 523–36.

31. On declining enrollment in British boarding schools, see Wendy Sloane, "British Boarding Schools Fall on Hard Times," *Christian Science Monitor*, January 3,

1993, p. 12. According to Sloane, boarding in British private schools has declined 20 percent in the last five years alone. Eighty-five private British boarding schools shut down in 1994 alone, while seventy-three private day schools opened. Large numbers of the British elite, themselves products of boarding schools, send their kids to day schools. One exception to the decline in interest among parents in the boarding school is the American black community. An increasing number of inner-city black parents are sending their kids to all-black boarding schools. Why? To get them out of crime-ridden neighborhoods and into environments where they can enjoy structure, discipline, and a moral education. On the revival of interest in the boarding school in the black community see "Black Boarding Schools Are Popular Again," *Jet*, October 10, 1994, p. 22.

32. Statistics on charter schools taken from the *National Charter School Directory*, Third Edition, published by the Center for Educational Reform, Washington, D.C., Fall 1996. For a good description of how one small parent-formed private school got going, see Jim Robbins, "Teach Your Children Well," *Special Report*, September-October 1992, pp. 23–25, a firsthand account of a small group of parents in Helena, Montana, who, frustrated with their local school, created a small private, parent-run school that better reflected their pedagogical convictions. Robbins, writing in 1992, estimated the formation of such schools as private academies in the "dozens." Today, no doubt, they can be counted in the hundreds.

33. Stecklow, "Evangelical Schools Reinvent Themselves by Stressing Academics," p. A1.

34. Susan D. Rose, *Keeping Them Out of the Hands of Satan* (New York: Routledge, 1988), p. 13.

35. On phonics in the Christian schools, see especially Pauline B. Gough, "Room for Reason: Teaching Differences in Religious and Public Schools," *Phi Delta Kappan*, Vol. 75, May 1994, p. 658.

36. Rose, *Keeping Them Out of the Hands of Satan*, Chapter 1, "A Search for Coherence."

37. Ibid., p. 141; also see pp. 94–97 on parent-teacher relations.

38. Ibid., p. 148.

39. This, at least, is the impression given in an article about school participation in Boston's annual Gay Pride Parade by David Gelman et al., "Tune In, Come Out," *Newsweek*, November 8, 1993, p. 71.

40. All the information on Dalton's Emily Fischer-Landau project is taken from an investigative report by Michael Winerip, "A Disabilities Program That 'Got Out of Hand,'" *New York Times*, April 8, 1994, pp. A1, B6.

41. On these changes in the Catholic school landscape, See John J. Convey, *Catholic Schools Make a Difference: Twenty-five Years of Research* (National Catholic Educational Association, 1992), Chapter 3. Four thousand of the nation's thirteen thousand Catholic schools have disappeared since 1965.

42. The most important of many of these studies were James S. Coleman, Thomas Hoffer, and Sally Kilgore, *High School Achievement: Public, Catholic and Private Schools Compared* (New York: Basic Books, 1982); James S. Coleman et al., *Public and Private High Schools: The Impact of Communities* (New York: Basic Books, 1987); and A. S. Bryk, P. B. Holland, V. E. Lee, and R. A. Carriedo, *Effective Catholic Schools: An Exploration* (Washington, D.C.: National Catholic Educational Association, 1984).

43. Convey, *Catholic Schools Make a Difference*, p. 55.

44. Ibid., p. 191.

45. Ibid., p. 194.

46. Ibid., p. 48. As of 1989, the minority population of the Catholic elementary schools was 441,300. In the high schools (which demand considerably higher tuition) it was 134,600. A 1982 study of Catholic school inner-city families found that nearly half had incomes in 1978 under $10,000 (p. 193).

47. James Cibulka, Timothy O'Brien, and Donald Zewe, *Inner City Private Elementary Schools: A Study* (Milwaukee, WI: Marquette University Press, 1982), p. 13.

48. Convey, *Catholic Schools Make a Difference*, p. 148. Convey provides a summary of the state of research here.

49. A. M. Greeley, *Catholic High Schools and Minority Students* (New Brunswick, NJ: Transaction Books, 1982).

50. Cibulka et al., *Inner-City Private Elementary Schools.*

51. Anthony S. Bryk et al., *Effective Catholic Schools: An Exploration* (Washington, D.C.: National Catholic Educational Association, 1984).

52. Ibid., p. 65.

53. See Coleman et al., *Public and Private High Schools;* and P. L. Benson et al., *Catholic High Schools: Their Impact on Low-Income Students* (Washington, D.C.: National Catholic Educational Association, 1986).

54. Oliver's comment is taken from an interview with the author in the fall of 1991.

55. Dr. Steven Adamowski, senior fellow at the Hudson Institute, asserted in a telephone interview of June 1996 that more new schools in the years between 1993 and 1996 were formed as charter schools than independent or private schools. For a good report on the charter schools movement, see Claudia Wallis, "A Class of Their Own: Bucking Bureaucracy, Brashly Independent Public Schools Have Much to Teach About Saving Education," *Time,* October 31, 1994, pp. 53–61.

56. This number is taken from the *National Charter School Directory,* p. 71.

57. Seymour Fliegel and James MacGuire, *Miracle in East Harlem* (New York: Times Books, 1993), p. 5.

58. Wallis, "A Class of Their Own," p. 54.

59. Ibid., p. 53.

60. "Learning Zones: Breaking Up Educational Gridlock," *City Journal,* Spring 1994, pp. 67–68.

61. Ibid., p. 71.

62. Kay S. Hymowitz, "Up the Up Staircase: At Manhattan's Wildcat Academy, the City's Most Troubled Youngsters Have a Chance to Succeed," *City Journal,* Spring 1994, p. 32.

63. Ibid., p. 39.

Chapter 9: The New Familism

1. Statistics taken from Census Bureau report, Child Care Arrangement, Fall 1991, "Who's Minding the Kids?" Reported in "Trends in Fathering: Father Count," published by the National Center for Fathering.

2. Peter Baylies, "Exclusive At Home Dad Survey Results," *At Home Dad,* No. 10, p. 1.

3. Marilyn Gardner, "At Home Dads Give Their New Career High Marks," *Christian Science Monitor,* May 30, 1996, p. 12.

4. Darcie Sanders and Martha M. Bullen, *Staying Home: From Full-Time Professional to Full-Time Parent* (New York: Little, Brown, 1992).

5. It should be mentioned that according to surveys, almost two-thirds of at-home dads report feelings of isolation as opposed to less than 40 percent of at-home moms. See Gardner, "At Home Dads."

6. "Trends in Fathering: Father Count."

7. For an overview of the emerging trend toward more mothering at home, see Karen S. Peterson, "In Balancing Act, Scale Tips Toward Family," *USA Today,* January 25, 1995, p. 1A.

8. Elena Neuman, "More Moms Are Homeward Bound," *Insight,* January 10, 1994, p. 17.

9. Gardner, "At Home Dads."

10. Author interview with Debbie Sawicki of FEMALE, June 1996.

11. Neuman, "More Moms Are Homeward Bound."

12. Ibid., p. 18.

13. See "9 Out of 10 Dual Earner Couples Believe Mother at Home Better Than Day Care," *In Focus* (publication IF93L2PL of the Family Research Council, 1993) and "Trends in Fathering: Father Count."

14. "Most Workers Would Trade Early Retirement Tomorrow for Family Time Today," *In Focus* (publication IF93MIPL of the Family Research Council, 1993).

15. Barbara Dafoe Whitehead, "The New Familism: Crossing the Cultural Divide," Institute for American Values, Working Paper No. 8, pp. 3–5.

16. Rosalind C. Barnett and Caryl Rivers, *He Works/She Works: How Two-Income Families Are Happier, Healthier, and Better Off* (New York: HarperCollins, 1996), pp. 217–19.

17. At least this is the way it was explained to me in 1994 talks with Heidi Brennan of Mothers at Home.

18. Author telephone interview with Debbie Sawicki, June 1996.

19. Neuman, "More Moms Are Homeward Bound," p. 16.

20. Maggie Gallagher, *Enemies of Eros: How the Sexual Revolution Is Killing Family, Marriage and Sex and What We Can Do About It* (Chicago: Bonus Books, 1989), p. 55.

21. Dorothy Dinnerstein, *The Mermaid and the Minotaur* (New York: Harper and Row, 1976), p. 19, quoted in ibid., p. 56.

22. Bernice Kanner, "Advertisers Take Aim at Women at Home," *New York Times,* January 2, 1995, p. 42.

23. Mary Eberstadt, "Putting Children Last," *Commentary,* May 1995, pp. 45–50.

24. Sanders and Bullen, *Staying Home,* p. 215–16.

25. Linda Duxbury, Christopher Higgens, and Catherine Lee, "Work-Family Conflict," *Transition,* Vol. 23, No. 2, 1993, cited in David Blankenhorn, *Fatherless America,* (New York: Basic Books, 1995), p. 110.

26. Dorian Friedman, "Working Women: Findings from a Sweeping New Study," *U.S. News & World Report,* May 22, 1995, p. 55.

27. Caroline Hull, "The Flexible Workplace," *Insight* (publication IS94C2WF of the Family Research Council, 1994), p. 1.

28. These statistics were provided in a telephone interview on June 26, 1996, by Joanne H. Pratt of Joanne H. Pratt & Associates, a consulting and research firm specializing in home-based businesses and telecommuting. Pratt has done research on home-based work for the Bureau of Transportation Statistics and has

designed home-based work questions for the Bureau of the Census's Survey of Income and Program Participation.

29. Ibid.
30. Ellen Galinsky, Carollee Howes, Susan Kontos, and Marybeth Shinn, *The Study of Children in Family Child Care and Relative Care: Highlights of Findings* (New York: Families and Work Institute, 1994), pp. 7–8.
31. Ibid., p. 84.
32. Louis Uchitelle, "Lacking Child Care, Parents Take Their Children to Work," *New York Times*, December 23, 1994, pp. A1, D2.
33. Marilyn Gardner, "When Offices Double as Nurseries: California Firms Encourage Mothers to Bring Their Babies to the Workplace," *Christian Science Monitor*, April 7, 1994, p. 13.
34. A 1993 Family Research Council poll found that when asked whether they would rather have "plenty of time to spend with your family and friends" or "plenty of money to meet the needs and wants of you and your family," 61 percent of Americans chose the first.
35. Marilyn Gardner, "Many '90s Families Seek Quality and Quantity Time: Working Parents Find 'Hanging Out' with Their Children More Satisfying for All Than Tightly Programmed Activities," *Christian Science Monitor*, April 21, 1995, p. 13.
36. Abraham T. McLaughlin, "Family Dinners Provide Food for Thought as Well," *Christian Science Monitor*, March 14, 1996, pp. 1, 10.
37. A *Time* poll of 1990 revealed that 63 percent of young people ages eighteen to twenty-nine wanted to spend more time with their children than their own parents had spent with them.
38. The list of such studies is long, and encompasses the fields of anthropology, sociobiology, pediatrics, and psychology. For a good overview, see David Popenoe, "Modern Marriage: Revising the Cultural Script," in David Popenoe, Jean Bethke Elshtain, and David Blankenhorn, *Promises to Keep: Decline and Renewal of Marriage in America* (Lanham, MD: Rowman and Littlefield, 1996), Chapter 11, pp. 260–61. Some important studies include Alice Rossi, ed., *Gender and the Life Course* (New York: Aldine de Gruyter, 1985); Diana Baumrind, "Are Androgynous Individuals More Effective Persons and Parents?" *Child Development*, Vol. 53, 1982, pp. 44–75; M. W. Yogman, "Development of the Father-Infant Relationship," in *Theory and Research in Behavioral Pediatrics*, Vol. 1, H. E. Fitzgerald, B. M. Lester, and M. W. Yogman, eds. (New York: Plenum Press, 1982), pp. 221–80; and J. L. Roopnarine and N. S. Mounts, "Mother-Child and Father-Child Play," *Early Child Development Care* 20, Vol. 20, 1985, pp. 157–69.
39. Here again, there is much important literature, which Popenoe summarizes concisely in his article "Modern Marriage: Revising the Cultural Script," pp. 258–59. Most of this research from the fields of anthropology and evolutionary biology emphasizes, in Popenoe's words, that "males universally are the more sexually driven and promiscuous," and that long-lasting paternal investment must be "culturally fostered."
40. Gary Bauer, *Our Journey Home: What Parents Are Doing to Preserve Family Values* (Dallas: Word Publishing, 1992), p. 82.
41. Blankenhorn's remark was made to me in a conversation on September 7, 1993, in which we discussed the pandering of social services to children by the schools.

42. See "Young and Old Battle for Resources," *Great Decisions* (Foreign Policy Association, 1993), p. 87.

43. See Robert D. Putnam, "The Strange Disappearance of Civic America," *The American Prospect,* Winter 1996, p. 35.

44. Sanders and Bullen, *Staying Home,* pp. 218–19, 221–22.

45. "Young and Old Battle for Resources," p. 87.

46. The substance of Elshtain's argument is taken from Jean Bethke Elshtain, "What Makes Democracy Possible?," *Family Affairs,* Spring 1996, Vol. 7, No. 1–2 (New York: Institute for American Values), pp. 1–5.

47. Robert Wuthnow, quoted in Elshtain, "What Makes Democracy Possible?," p. 2.

48. Charlene Haar, "PTA: It's Not 'Parents Taking Action,'" *Organization Trends,* November 1994, p. 4.

49. Ibid., p. 3.

50. Ibid., p. 5.

51. Ibid., pp. 8, 2.

52. Ibid., p. 1.

53. Ibid., p. 2.

54. Anonymous letter to the *Wilton Bulletin,* March 1, 1995.

55. Laurel Shaper Walters, "Search for Relevance Puts National PTA to the Test," *Christian Science Monitor,* June 3, 1996, p. 13.

56. "Homework for Parents," *Christian Science Monitor,* September 12, 1994, p. 18.

57. "School Choice Update," prepared by Jara Burnett, public issues vice president, League of Women Voters of Connecticut, January 1996.

58. For the growth of the Christian right and their impact on politics see Michael Vlahos, "The New Wave," *National Review,* September 26, 1994, pp. 38–46 and Richard L. Berke, "Christian Right Defies Categories: Survey Discloses Diversity of Politics and Doctrine," *New York Times,* July 22, 1994, pp. A1, A16.

59. Barbara Bennett Woodhouse of the University of Pennsylvania, quoted in Greg Erken, "Does the U.S. Need a Parental-Rights Amendment?," *Insight,* May 15, 1995, p. 20.

60. Ben J. Wattenberg, *Values Matter Most: How Republicans or Democrats or a Third Party Can Win and Renew the American Way of Life* (New York: Free Press, 1995).

61. John Fund, "The Media Revolution," *Imprimis,* Vol. 23, No. 12, December 1994, pp. 1, 3.

62. Sanders and Bullen, *Staying Home,* p. 149.

63. David Warnick, assistant to the president of the National Center for Fathering, an organization dedicated to both father education and research on trends in fathering, believes that at-home-dads support organizations have not become involved in family advocacy because they are latecomers to the scene.

64. Marilyn Gardner, "R-Rated Ads Drive Parents to Protest," *Christian Science Monitor,* March 23, 1995, pp. 1, 13.

65. Author interview with Hewlett, May 1995.

66. "Summary of Key Findings," *Polling Families,* Family Research Council, LH92KI.

67. Ibid.

68. William R. Mattox Jr., "Putting Children First Key to Consensus on Family Issues," *Perspective* (publication PV93L7PL of the Family Research Council, 1993).

69. "Most Americans Value 'Traditional Values' More Than Tolerance," *In Focus* (publication IF93L4PL of the Family Research Council, 1993).
70. From "Top 10 Findings from FRC's 1993 Family Issues Survey" (Washington, D.C.: Family Research Council, 1993).
71. William R. Mattox Jr., "Is Change Beneficial? Baby-Boomer Parents Have Their Doubts," *Miami Herald,* January 24, 1993, p. 5M.
72. Ibid. On the 1996 elections and the values politics of American parents, see in particular Jonathan Alter, "Thinking of Family Values," *Newsweek,* January 6, 1997. Alter calls the phenomenon of baby boomer values conservatism a "non-ideological" centrism that turns on "family, faith and work" (p. 32).
73. Diane Rado, "Chiles Vetoes Spanking Bill," *St. Petersburg Times,* May 28, 1994, pp. 1A, 16A. See also Mark Silva, "Senate Backs Parents' Rights to Spank Child," *Miami Herald,* April 27, 1995, and Associated Press, "2 Bills Allowed to Become Law," *Miami Herald,* June 5, 1996, p. 5B.
74. For the alignment of forces on both sides of the Parental Rights Amendment, see Al Knight, "Huge Forces Collide on Parents' Rights," *Denver Post,* June 12, 1996, p. 11B.

Chapter 10: Toward a Family Policy: Seven Pro-Family Proposals in Search of Political Courage

1. Ben J. Wattenberg, *Values Matter Most: How Republicans or Democrats or a Third Party Can Win and Renew the American Way of Life* (New York: Free Press, 1995), p. 63.
2. Hillary Rodham Clinton, *It Takes a Village and Other Lessons Children Teach Us* (New York: Simon & Schuster, 1996), p. 14. Mrs. Clinton writes, "We cannot move forward by looking to the past for easy solutions. Even if a golden age had existed, we could not simply graft it onto today's busier, more impersonal and complicated world."
3. For an interesting look at the American public and their frustration with the political status quo, and the unresponsiveness of politicians and government to the needs and concerns of ordinary Americans, see Haynes Johnson, *Divided We Fall: Gambling with History in the Nineties* (New York: Norton, 1995).
4. Robert Rector, "The Family Tax Freedom Plan," Backgrounder (Washington, D.C.: Heritage Foundation, May 1991).
5. William R. Mattox, "Tax Fairness for Families," *Family Policy* (Washington, D.C.: Family Research Council, Vol. 4, No. 2), p. 2. By 1993, the income tax dependent exemption, had it kept pace with American's per capita personal income, would have been worth more than $9,000. See "Honey, They Shrunk the Kids' Tax Exemption," *In Focus* (publication IF94D1FE of the Family Research Council, 1994).
6. See Sylvia Ann Hewlett, "Tough Choices, Great Rewards," *Parade,* July 16, 1994, p. 5; and Mattox, "Tax Fairness for Families," p. 1.
7. For a good critique on Forbes's proposal, see John B. Judis, "The Reactionary," *New Republic,* March 25, 1996, pp. 20–23.
8. Rector, "The Family Tax Freedom Plan."
9. Allan Carlson, "Taxation and the Family: Philosophical and Historical Considerations," *Insight* (publication IS94B8FE of the Family Research Council, 1994).

10. Mattox, "Tax Fairness for Families," p. 3.

11. William R. Mattox, "The Parent Trap: So Many Bills, So Little Time," *Policy Review,* Winter 1991, p. 6.

12. "Most Workers Would Trade Early Retirement Tomorrow for Family Time Today," *In Focus* (publication IF93MIPL of the Family Research Council, 1993).

13. Lynette Friedrich Cofer and Robin Smith Jacobvitz, "The Loss of Moral Turf: Mass Media and Family Values," *Rebuilding the Nest* (Milwaukee, WI: Family Service America, 1990), p. 194.

14. For a concise history of the decline of standards in the broadcasting industry, see Cofer and Jacobvitz, "The Loss of Moral Turf," pp. 179–204; and Elizabeth Jensen, "It's 8 P.M. Your Kids Are Watching Sex on TV," *Wall Street Journal,* March 27, 1995, p. B6.

15. "April's Town Meeting Emphasizes Family's Role in Learning Readiness," U.S. Department of Education *Community Update,* No. 24, May 1995.

16. Alan Bunce, "Old Foes Rekindle Battle Over Children's Television," *Christian Science Monitor,* June 6, 1995, p. 10.

17. Linda Greenhouse, "Justices Allow Limits on Indecent Radio and TV Shows," *New York Times,* January 9, 1996, p. 25.

18. See Michael Medved, *Hollywood vs. America: Popular Culture and the War on Traditional Values* (New York: HarperCollins/Zondervan, 1992), pp. 286–90. Medved still maintains that "the bottom line in Hollywood is prestige, not money," and that for some perverse reason, Hollywood's producers and directors think they haven't made a serious film unless it contains some element—either language or visuals—bound to shock and disgust the audience.

19. Gloria Goodale, "Movies' Liberal Dose of Conservatism: Studios Churn Out Highest Portion Ever of Family Movies," *Christian Science Monitor,* June 5, 1995, p. 18.

20. "Family Involvement Partnership Completes Strategic Plan."

21. The literature on the failure of bilingual education is plentiful. But for a concise description of the typical problems of bilingual education, the bureaucratic entrenchment of bilingual programs, the coercing of children into bilingual programs against their will and against the will of their parents, and the parental frustrations associated with bilingual education, see Linda Chavez, *Out of the Barrio: Toward a New Politics of Hispanic Assimilation* (New York: Basic Books, 1991); and Rosalie Pedalino Porter, *Forked Tongue: The Politics of Bilingual Education* (New York: Basic Books, 1990).

22. "California Leads Revival of Teaching by Phonics," *New York Times,* May 22, 1996, p. B8.

23. For a concise summary of the 1996 Education Summit, see Denis P. Doyle, "A Personal Report from the Education Summit: What Does It Mean for Education Reform?" The Heritage Lectures, No. 564.

24. Jonathan P. Decker, "Splintering Cities: Taxes, Lack of Services Fuel Secession Drives," *Christian Science Monitor,* May 5, 1995, p. 3.

25. Maggie Gallagher, "Why Make Divorce Easy?" *New York Times,* February 20, 1996.

26. David Blankenhorn, "Government Has a Stake in Preserving Marriage," *Daily Local News* (West Chester, PA), March 18, 1996.

27. Mary Beth Seader Stiles, former vice president for policy and practice at the

National Council for Adoption, estimates this to be the number of American families who at present want to adopt.

28. "The Parental Rights Amendment: Guiding Public Policy" (Arlington, VA: Of the People, 1994), p. 1.

29. Kelly Owen, "Parents Group Seek Law for More Say at Children's Schools," *Los Angeles Times,* February 7, 1994.

30. Greg Erken, "Symposium: Does the U.S. Need a Parental Rights Amendment?," *Insight,* May 15, 1995.

31. Author interview with Ralph Benko, October 14, 1994.

32. Author interview with Sylvia Ann Hewlett, May 1995.

33. Thomas Sowell, quoted in "Quotable," *Voice of the People* (newsletter of the organization Of the People, Washington, D.C.), Vol. 1, No. 2, March 1995, p. 5.

34. William J. Bennett, Introduction to Dan Coats, *The Project for American Renewal* (Washington, D.C., 1996).

Index